"THE PROPER STUDY OF MANKIND IS MAN"

These words of the poet Alexander Pope might have served as the credo for David Hume when, at the age of twenty-three, he began one of the milestone works of Western thought, *A Treatise of Human Nature*.

His method was to seek to understand the world by discovering by what means man could acquire knowledge of that world. His field of study was not ideas but the way ideas were formed. His achievement was to shatter forever any unthinking acceptance of a relationship between internal and external reality, between accepted ideas and provable truth.

All this he did in a style memorably described in noted scholar Robert Paul Wolff's brilliant Introduction to this volume: *"When the eye slips most smoothly over Hume's words, then the mind must be wariest. Hume the man was a quick and agile intelligence imprisoned in a lumpish body; his philosophy, by contrast, is a juggernaut of powerful arguments masquerading behind light words and amusing examples. To read him is a pleasure, but to understand him is a challenge."*

Other MENTOR Books of Special Interest

The Essential David Hume

Edited with an Introduction by
ROBERT PAUL WOLFF

A MENTOR BOOK

Published by
THE NEW AMERICAN LIBRARY,
New York and Toronto
The New English Library Limited, London

Library of Congress Catalog Card Number: 69-14290

MENTOR TRADEMARK REG. U.S. PAT. OFF. AND FOREIGN COUNTRIES
REGISTERED TRADEMARK—MARCA REGISTRADA
HECHO EN CHICAGO, U.S.A.

MENTOR BOOKS are published *in the United States* by
The New American Library, Inc.,
1301 Avenue of the Americas, New York, New York 10019,
in Canada by The New American Library of Canada Limited,
295 King Street East, Toronto 2, Ontario,
in the United Kingdom by The New English Library Limited,
Barnard's Inn, Holborn, London, E.C. 1, England

FIRST PRINTING, JANUARY, 1969

PRINTED IN THE UNITED STATES OF AMERICA

CONTENTS

The Essential
David Hume

Introduction

1.

Philosophy, Callicles argues in the *Gorgias*, is a fitting amusement for clever youths, but scarcely a dignified pursuit for mature men. Philosophy, Socrates replies in the *Phaedo*, is in reality a preparation for death, and hence more natural to those near the end of life than to those who have barely begun their journey. If we consider the great philosophers, we find some, like Berkeley, whose finest works were written when they were barely out of their teens, and others, like Kant and Locke, who would not be remembered for what they wrote before they were fifty. To his contemporaries, David Hume must have appeared to incline somewhat to the latter course, for though he made a certain reputation with the philosophical and literary essays which he published in his late thirties and early forties, his most successful work by far was *A History of England* in six volumes, completed after his fiftieth birthday. To us, however, with the advantage of two hundred years of reflective hindsight, it is clear that Hume belongs in the class of philosophical prodigies, for his lasting place in the history of Western philosophy is secured by the brilliance and power of a single work, the *Treatise of Human Nature*, conceived before his twentieth birthday and written between his twenty-third and twenty-sixth years. Despite Hume's later repudiation of the anonymously published *Treatise*, it remains the most complete and revealing exposition of philosophical themes central to his thought. When we come to consider his doctrines in some detail, we shall discover that Hume, with rare foresight, laid down in the very first words of his first book the fundamental premises which were to guide his philosophical writing for the remainder of his life.

Hume was born in Edinburgh in 1711, the son of Joseph

Hume, a member of the Scottish gentry. At the age of twelve, he went to Edinburgh University (the customary age in his day) and spent the next three years studying the usual Greek, Latin, and what we would today call Physics, Moral Philosophy, and Theology. Almost alone among the great philosophers, Hume seems not to have had any special aptitude for mathematics and science, and his own philosophical writings, despite their enormous impact in the fields of theory of knowledge and philosophy of science, exhibit no more detailed grasp of the new science of his day than might be expected from any intelligent and educated man. Two years after leaving the university (our knowledge of this part of his life is regrettably thin), he suffered some form of nervous disorder which persisted for five years, which is to say until he was twenty-three. It must certainly be the case that he devoted some of this time to the study of philosophy, for when, in the summer of 1734, he went to France to rest and recuperate, he managed to write the entire *Treatise of Human Nature* in just three years. The length of that work and the luxurious richness of its arguments, speculations, examples, and asides suggest that bits and fragments of it had been germinating in his mind for some time.

Volumes One (*Of the Understanding*) and Two (*Of the Passions*) were published as a single book in 1739, and Volume Three (*Of Morals*) in 1740. Hume's name is not to be found in either part of the work, but it was not unusual for such books to appear anonymously in the 18th century, and in later years it was well known that Hume was the author.

The first two books of the *Treatise* came off the presses in January of 1739. In the November and December issues of a journal entitled *A History of the Works of the Learned* we find an anonymous review of Book One, the first notice to be taken of the momentous work. The review is in most ways calculated to dissuade the young author from ever again venturing into print on matters philosophical. Two quotations will suffice to convey the tone of the piece:

[A] man who has never had the Pleasure of reading Mr. Locke's incomparable Essay, will peruse our author with much less Disgust, than those can who have been used to the irresistible Reasoning and wonderful Perspicuity of that admirable Writer.

I have afore hinted the mighty Value of this Discovery (i.e., "that all our Ideas are copied from our Impressions"), the Honour of which is intirely due to our Author, but it cannot be too often inculcated. I verily think, if it were closely perused, it would lead us to several inestimable *Desiderata*, such as the *perpetual Motion*, the *grand Elixir*, a *Dissolvent of the Stone*, etc.

The entire review proceeds in this manner. Its saving feature is the reasonably accurate, though completely unsympathetic, summary it gives of the principal doctrines of Book One of the *Treatise*. Had the reviewer bethought himself to sign his tirade, he would thereby have earned himself a footnote in the history of philosophy. Still, we can sympathize with the unhappy reviewer, handed the task of reading, digesting, and commenting upon one of the great philosophical treatises, all within the brief space of ten months after its publication. But this must have been small comfort to the author, who wrote late in his life that "my love of literary fame [was] my ruling passion."

Hume had rather more success with some light essays on various topics, published in 1741 and 1742. A variety of employments as tutor and private secretary enabled him to accumulate by 1748 a competence adequate to support him modestly but independently, and the middle years of his life, from 1748 to 1762, were spent in the writing of the several works by which his literary reputation was secured and his fame in England and France established. In 1748, a revised, shortened, and rather more popular version of Book One of the *Treatise* appeared under the title *Enquiry Concerning the Human Understanding*. The third Book of the *Treatise* was rewritten as an *Enquiry Concerning the Principles of Morals* and was published in 1751. A number of other essays and occasional papers were gathered together into several volumes, among which we find a *Natural History of Religion*. The six volumes of the *History of England* came out during the eight years between 1754 and 1762. They had an immediate success, and did more to build Hume's name than any other work he published. Reading it today, we may be put off by the anecdotal and excessively narrative character of the *History*, but it is well to remember that Hume's contribution to historiography antedates Gibbon's *Decline and Fall* by a quarter of a century and thus qualifies as the first major piece of historical writing in the English language.

It was during the 1750's that Hume produced his most brilliant literary effort, the *Dialogues Concerning Natural Religion*. Their agnostic, not to say atheistical, tone alarmed Hume's friends, who already had reason to be dismayed at the harm which Hume's unconventional views had done to his career. Under the influence of their entreaties, Hume with-held the *Dialogues* during the remainder of his life, and they were not to see the light of day until 1779, when his nephew and literary executor had them published. Happily for the history of philosophy, this was just in time for their argu-ments to influence Immanuel Kant, through the intermedia-tion of the Anglophile Hamaan. In the Dialectic of the *Cri-tique of Pure Reason* (1781), and many years later in the portions of the *Critique of Judgment* devoted to theology, we can hear the echoes of Hume's delicate and witty refutations of religious doctrines, very much as though an "ayre" of Pur-cell had found its way into a symphony by Beethoven.

Of Hume the man much can be said, though little that helps us in understanding his philosophy. There has probably never been a man whose physical appearance so entirely con-tradicted his qualities of mind and spirit. His quick, supple, darting mind was encased in a great clumsy bear of a body, and the windows of his rapier intelligence were two pig-eyes sunk in a fat, pudding face. He was apparently mild of man-ner and affable in company, and a number of reports attest to his popularity with young ladies at social gatherings. His phil-osophical writings are so far superior to anything else pro-duced in English during his lifetime that we can only think of him as a solitary genius whose philosophical isolation was aptly reflected in the implausibility of his face and figure.

2.

Socrates may have thought philosophy a preparation for death, but most philosophers have seemed intent upon putting it to death. There is hardly a great philosopher in the West-ern tradition who does not promise, as the finest fruit of his own labors, a new method of philosophizing which will quickly settle all outstanding disputes and bring the wran-gling of philosophers to a close. Hume, with the enthusiasm of youth, announces in the Introduction to the *Treatise* that he has discovered a way of setting philosophy on a firm foundation, so that it will no more exhibit the inconsequen-tial contentiousness which has caused it to sink so low in the estimation of the general public.

At first appearance, Hume's "new method" comes to no more than the cliché that one must examine man before one studies the world in which he lives. As Pope had put it some five years earlier with rather more elegance, "Know then thy-self, presume not God to scan;/ the proper study of Mankind is Man." So Hume writes: "It is evident that all the sciences have a relation, greater or less, to human nature . . . [so that it] is impossible to tell what changes and improvements we might make in these sciences were we thoroughly acquainted with the extent and force of human understanding and could explain the nature of the ideas we employ and of the operations we perform in our reasonings."

Upon closer examination, however, we discover that Hume is not principally interested in "human nature," if by such an interest we understand a curiosity about the universal traits of character and propensities of behavior which today are the province of anthropology and sociology. To be sure, Hume shares with his contemporaries a taste for collating reports of cultural variation and seeking the underlying constancies which they exhibit; in the *Dialogue* included in this volume, we find him rather fancifully engaged in this pastime. Nevertheless, "human nature" is assigned a very different meaning in the *Treatise*. Hume seeks to ground all science—which is to say, all claims to any knowledge whatsoever—not on a set of generalizations about human behavior but on a theory of the operations and limits of human cognitive faculties. In brief, Hume proposes to base human knowledge on a theory of the human capacity for knowledge. He thus sets himself squarely in a philosophical tradition which began with the great 17th-century French philosopher Descartes and reached its highest point in the philosophy of the late 18th-century German, Immanuel Kant. The keynote of that tradition was the thoroughgoing subordination of all branches of philosophy—metaphysics, ethics, aesthetics, even theology—to a single one, the theory of knowledge. Before we can appreciate Hume's philosophical endeavors, we must understand the rationale behind this radical reduction of philosophy to the theory of knowledge.

All of our real or purported knowledge, whether of the natural world, of the standards of right conduct, of the criteria of beauty, or of the existence and attributes of a divine creator, is expressed in propositions. Judgments are assertions of propositions by some conscious thinking being or other, as when I judge *that* sugar dissolves in water or you judge *that* $2 + 2 = 4$. Sometimes, of course, the propositions asserted are false: I may claim that the sun is ten million miles from the earth or that five is twice two. Hence, if we wish to talk about judgments in general without for the moment concerning ourselves with their truth, we will perhaps do better to speak of them as *knowledge-claims*. This bit of jargon has the virtue of suggesting simultaneously three things about judgments: that they are acts, that they assert some proposition as true, and that they may be wrong.

For our purposes, the most important fact about judgments is that they are always acts of assertion *by* someone (or by some mind—we shall leave aside the intriguing question whether any beings besides human beings have minds). Usually, of course, this fact is obscured by the absence of any first-personal announcement at the beginning of the judgment, such as "I think this" or "I believe that," but as Kant rather ponderously pointed out, the "I think" can always be attached to any judgment. No matter how impersonal the subject matter of a judgment, no matter how self-effacing its author, every judgment is a claim to knowledge *by* some person whose act of assertion the judgment is. (Needless to say, not everything we utter is in the form of judgments; questions, commands, expressions of emotion, and many other more complex speech acts require different analyses. Contemporary English and American philosophers have devoted considerable attention to the nonjudgmental uses of language and in some cases have even sought to base on them refutations of the theories advanced by Descartes, Hume, Kant, and other members of the tradition we are discussing.)

Now, it may be that the judging subject, the "I" in whose consciousness the judgment is asserted, possesses no particular characteristics *as judging subject*. Perhaps, as Aristotle thought, the knowing mind is perfectly neutral with regard to what it can know, adjusting itself and its thought processes to the objects which present themselves. In that case, it will be of little use to reflect on the nature of the mind before turning to a consideration of the universe. But suppose that the mind has certain innate constraints on its cognitive capacities. Suppose even that the activity of asserting a judgment has a structure which somehow limits or circumscribes the sort of propositions which can be asserted. Then a preliminary study of the act of judgment and of the cognitive apparatus which performs that act will be fruitful indeed, for it may reveal a boundary beyond which the human mind, in the very nature of its being, cannot venture. In much the same way, a biologist can tell from an examination of the magnifying power of his microscope that certain organisms are simply too small to be seen by it. What is more, a general reflection on the nature of light will indicate the absolute limits on any magnifying apparatus at all. We simply cannot build a microscope powerful enough to enable us to see a single electron, because the light which we shine on the electron would push it out of the way.

When Hume proposes to examine "human nature" in order

14

to lay the foundations for all knowledge, he has in mind this sort of dissection of the cognitive faculties themselves. He intends to embark on a theoretical analysis of the very possibility and limits of knowledge in general, an enterprise which Kant was later to label "transcendental philosophy," and which today goes under the title Epistemology.

Thus far, we are merely retracing a path laid out by Descartes in France and John Locke in England. But Hume conceives himself to have made two major advances, one methodological and the other substantive. In place of the conceptual analysis and pure reasoning by which previous philosophers had sought to lay bare the structure of man's cognitive powers, he proposes to rely upon observation and "experiment," which is to say the collection and comparison of examples drawn from everyday experience. This experimental method, which Hume thinks himself to have derived from the great physicist Newton, will serve as a court to which disputing theories may appeal for the resolution of their differences. At this point, it will very likely occur to the alert student that it is somewhat peculiar to appeal to *experience* and *empirical knowledge* in order to resolve disagreements about what can and cannot be *known*. Until we know what we can know, how can we be sure that the knowledge we appeal to is legitimate? The objection is valid, and in the body of the *Treatise* we find Hume engaged more often in conceptual analysis of the sort he intended to supersede than in empirical description of cognitive experience. Nevertheless, Hume set great store by his experimental method and thought that it distinguished his philosophy from that which preceded him.

The substantive discovery on which Hume hoped to base his theories was the principle of the association of ideas. Hume saw in the workings of the mind a tendency of certain ideas to become associated together through the effect of experience, so that the occurrence of one in our thoughts would tend to remind us of the other. This "gentle force," as he described it, seemed to him in the universality of its operations to play in our minds a role as great as that which Newton had attributed to gravity in the behavior of physical bodies. Particularly in Book One of the *Treatise,* Hume makes much of the association of ideas, putting it forward as an explanation of memory, belief, causal inference, our ideas of material objects, and even as a clue to the nature of the self itself.

The notion of erecting a system of human nature analogous to Newton's system of physical nature and of basing it on a force of association analogous to Newton's force of gravitation was one which would naturally appeal to the young and enthusiastic Hume. But he was too honest a philosopher to cling to an initial plan when the force of his arguments led in new and different directions. As the *Treatise* unfolds, the simple theory of association, like the method of experiment, recedes into the background, so that when Hume came to recast the materials of the *Treatise* in the two *Enquiries*, little was heard of the "gentle force." Instead, there emerges bit by bit in the *Treatise* a complex and highly original account of the powers, habits, dispositions, and capacities of the mind. Though Hume himself never drew together the many fragments of this account into a coherent theory, we might label it his theory of mental activity, for it traces our several beliefs and knowledge-claims to the innate, universal activities of the human mind.* In the remainder of these brief introductory remarks I shall try to sketch the outlines of Hume's theory and suggest some of the ways in which it is reflected in the works collected in this volume.

3.

The key to Hume's critical analysis of our claims to knowledge is the simple observation that as all knowledge-claims are expressed in judgments, so all judgments are formed by combining ideas. In evaluating any knowledge-claim, therefore, we may confine ourselves to two questions: First, do the words in which the judgment is couched correspond to any actual ideas in our mind? and second, have the ideas in the judgment been combined in a manner which can be justified by evidence or argument? If the terms of the judgment do not refer to genuine ideas, or if the ideas are combined in a manner for which no adequate ground can be adduced, then we may reject the knowledge-claim out of hand as illegitimate. For example, if a friend tells me that he possesses a desk in the shape of a four-sided triangle, I need not go to his rooms to confirm the claim. I know immediately that it *must* be false, for "four-sided triangle" is a phrase to which no genuine idea can correspond. Somewhat analogously, if a mystic claims that he can *see* radio waves, I will be inclined to reject the claim out of hand, for I have learned that the human visual apparatus is incapable of responding to electromagnetic radiation of radio-wave frequency. In the first

---

* I have attempted a partial systematization of this theory in a paper entitled "Hume's Theory of Mental Activity," in *Philosophical Review* for July, 1960. The essay has recently been reprinted in more accessible form in *Hume: Modern Studies in Philosophy*, ed. by Vere Chappell, Anchor Books (1966).

case by a logical analysis of the supposed concepts contained in the judgment, in the second case by appeal to the limits of the human sensory capacities, I am able to evaluate a knowledge-claim independently of an appeal to the facts of the particular case.

In the opening pages of the *Treatise*, Hume announces as an absolutely universal principle that all our ideas are copies either of the impressions which come to us through our senses or of the impressions which arise naturally within us (like the feelings of love and fear) in response to sense-experience. No genuine argument is advanced for this dictum (which derives in part from Locke). Hume merely asks us to reflect upon the facts and see whether he is right. Once we accept it, however, we find ourselves forced to acknowledge the remarkable skeptical conclusions which Hume draws from it. For example, if every idea is a copy of a precedent impression, then there can be no abstract ideas—ideas of general classes of things like the idea of man, the idea of silver, or the idea of democracy. The reason is that impressions are specific and determinate, whereas abstract ideas are general and indeterminate. As Bishop Berkeley had pointed out, no one can form a mental image (or impression) of man-in-general. Any impression I form must necessarily be of some height, color, shape, and appearance or other, and hence must be the impression of a particular man. But if there can be no abstract ideas, then all the knowledge-claims couched in abstract ideas must either be translatable into judgments referring to particulars or else be rejected as illegitimate! Similarly, Hume argues, I have no sense-impression of the causal force or efficacy by which one event brings another into being. Hence, I cannot have a legitimate idea of causation, and so my causal judgments must be unsound, one and all. Again and again, Hume invokes the copy-theory of ideas to destroy all the classes of knowledge-claims which earlier philosophers had sought to justify. In Part One of the first Book of the *Treatise*, abstract ideas succumb to this principle. In Part Two, our "ideas" of space and time are exploded. In Part Three, causal inference, the very foundation of natural science, is subjected to Hume's skeptical critique. And in Part Four, even our ideas of material objects and of the self are shown to be illegitimate confusions. By the end of Book One, Hume has apparently undermined the entire sweep of knowledge-claims on which our scientific and everyday knowledge of the world around us is based.

But here we encounter a problem, as Hume well realizes. It is an undeniable fact that all men believe in the existence of physical objects and in causal interactions among them.

All men use terms which seem to refer to abstract notions. Each of us supposes himself to be a real and continuing person or self, and all save the maddest among us assume that the world is populated by other similar persons with conscious experiences much like our own. Hume himself gives eloquent voice to this universal propensity in a famous passage: "Most fortunately it happens, that since reason is incapable of dispelling these clouds [of skepticism], Nature herself suffices to that purpose. . . . I dine, I play a game of backgammon, I converse, and am merry with my friends; and, when, after three or four hours' amusement, I would return to these speculations, they appear so cold, and strained, and ridiculous, that I cannot find in my heart to enter into them any further. . . . I find myself absolutely and necessarily determined to live, and talk, and act like other people in the common affairs of life."

If, as Hume says, we are unable to *believe* or to *act upon* the skeptical conclusions which our philosophical critique of knowledge-claims leads us to, then as philosophers we ought to give some explanation of that fact. After all, when the logician shows us that a certain form of argument is fallacious, we do not find it impossible to correct our thinking so as to avoid committing the error again. We have given up readily enough the beguiling but false theories that the earth is at the center of the solar system and that the physical characteristics acquired by the father are inherited by the son. If we can learn from the logician and the scientist, why can we not learn from the philosopher?

It is in order to answer these questions that Hume advances his original and constructive theory of the innate capacities of the mind. By a system of propensities and dispositions to group its impressions and ideas together and intensify or weaken the force of their effect, the mind naturally and unavoidably gives rise to *beliefs* which it can neither justify nor deny. In the words of the British scholar of the history of philosophy, Norman Kemp Smith, Hume offers us a theory of "natural belief" which explains the fact that we all accept as true a variety of knowledge-claims which logic and evidence cannot certify.

Thus, Hume's treatment of each philosophical problem proceeds in two stages. First he examines some knowledge-claim from the point of view of its cognitive legitimacy. By appeal to the theory of impressions and ideas, he shows that the claim is illegitimate. This is the skeptical side of his analysis, for which he is principally known. Then, Hume turns around and asks what mental mechanism it is that generates within us a belief in the unfounded claim. Sometimes, he must even explain why we falsely but incorrigibly believe that our words refer to genuine ideas, when the simplest analysis shows that they cannot possibly do so. By appeal to a theory of habits and dispositions, fleshed out by the doctrine of association, Hume offers his explanation. He concludes with the observation that our belief is based upon natural and universal sentiments rather than being rational and grounded in valid argument. His counsel, if we can call it that, is to recognize the fragility of our reasoning powers and to continue acting and believing as we have in the past, without the comfort of rational support but equally without the power to cease.

An example will make the nature of the procedure clearer. In Part Three of Book One, Hume examines the causal inferences by which we seek to explain and predict the flow of events in the world around us. Every causal judgment, Hume notes, asserts a connection between some event, C, and some other event, E. The first event, or cause, is said by the judgment to produce or generate the second event, or effect. The heart of the judgment is this assertion of causal efficacy or, as Hume puts it, necessity of connection. Only by this assertion is a genuine causal judgment distinguished from the mere observation that event C preceded event E. Our idea of necessary connection, therefore, must be explained and justified if we are to show that causal judgments are legitimate.

Now Hume begins his skeptical attack. Every idea is a copy of a preceding impression. What impression then can be the original of this idea of necessary connection? Surely we do not observe the connection between a particular cause and its event, as though they were literally held together like two parts of a puzzle by a hook. If that were so, then we should know the causes of things by looking at them, just as we now can tell an object's color by a single glance. But if there is no sense-impression in a single instance of the causal connection from which we may derive our idea of necessity, then there will be nothing either in any repetition of instances. We are left with the conclusion that our idea of necessary connection has no legitimate foundation in sense-experience, and hence that our attributions of causal efficacy to various events are entirely without merit. To put the matter simply, we never have any right to say that one thing causes another!

But no one will be satisfied to leave the matter there, for however illegitimate the idea of causal necessity may be, there is no denying that we all possess and use it. Where then does the idea come from, if not from experience? Here Hume turns to the second half of his inquiry. Having settled (he believes) the epistemological question of conceptual legitimacy, he must now give a psychological explanation for the persistence of belief.

Briefly (the detailed theory can be found in the selections from *Treatise,* I, III, in this volume), Hume argues that the experience of repeated conjunctions of events like C with events like E produces in us a certain habit of mind. We become conditioned to associate C with E, so that when we are presented with C alone, our mind immediately forms an idea of E and thrusts that idea forward with such vivacity that it is taken by the mind as veridical and is believed. In short, our experience of the conjunction of C and E habituates us to associate them in the future. This forceful expectation is the feeling from which we derive the idea of necessary connection. The impression is of course internal to the mind, but by a sort of pathetic fallacy the mind projects the feeling into the events, C and E, themselves, and attributes to them the connection which in fact only exists between the ideas of C and E in the mind. Needless to say, this projection *is* a fallacy, albeit one which the mind inevitably and unavoidably commits. There is no perceived connection between events, however vividly we may imagine one.

If we could assume that our minds would only link in thought those events which will actually be paired in experience—if, that is to say, a sort of harmony existed between the operations of the mind and the operations of nature—then we could rely on our habits of association to give us legitimate information about nature. Unfortunately, there is no reason whatever to suppose that God or fate has so nicely arranged matters, and so we must be content with the observation that we are unable to give up our belief in the illegitimate causal judgments we persist in asserting.

In morals as in science Hume offers psychological explanations of our modes of judgment rather than justifications of them. He traces our judgments of value and disvalue, of good and evil, to sentiments of approval and disapproval which are evoked in us by certain innate propensities. These propensities are no more susceptible of ultimate justification than the propensities of association by which our empirical beliefs are explained. Just as it is perfectly conceivable that we might have been constructed differently so as not to associate together events which have been frequently conjoined in past experience, so we might have been without the sentiments of approval and disapproval, in which case we would entirely lack the ideas of good and bad. The same is true of our aesthetic judgments, which rest upon sentiments of taste for which no deeper rationale can ever be offered.

In the matter of religion, Hume takes a somewhat different

tack. Quite obviously, he does not think that our religious beliefs are inevitable, as are our causal and moral beliefs. Hence, he seems not to despair of permanently eradicating religious belief from the repertory of human error. Considerable debate has occurred over the correct interpretation of the posthumously published *Dialogues Concerning Natural Religion*, but I confess myself totally persuaded that they are unrelentingly atheistical in implication. If one attends to the arguments and ignores for a bit the rhetorical flourishes, it becomes apparent that Hume considers every argument in favor of the existence of God to be fraudulent, and what is more, he offers no psychological theory which would suggest that religious belief is an inevitable element in the human makeup. In this estimate of the case, Hume seems to be correct, for though few persons today can get through many hours without making a causal judgment or a moral evaluation, large numbers of people seem quite able to live their entire lives outside a religious framework, either formal or informal.

4.

Hume's philosophy has never lacked for commentators. In his own day, he was the object of virulent attacks from defenders of "common sense," such as James Beattie, who wrote a highly popular *Essay on the Nature and Immutability of the Truth,* directed against Hume and other skeptics. Since that time, he has been defended (by Kant, for example, who thought Hume far superior to his critics, though still in the end wrong) and, what is more important, studied, so that it is possible to say today that he is the most influential philosopher ever to write in the English language. Although interest in his writings has never totally died for any period of time, there has in the past generation been a considerable outpouring of books and articles on Hume's philosophy, prompted in part by a renewed awareness of the debt which contemporary American and English philosophers owe to him. A number of recent scholarly papers are collected in an anthology edited by Professor Vere Chappell, entitled *Hume: Modern Studies in Philosophy,* 1966, published by Anchor Books. Chappell's volume has a useful bibliography of recent writings in English on Hume. Among the books which will repay study are Charles Hendel's *Studies in the Philosophy of David Hume,* new ed., Indianapolis, Ind., 1963; E. C. Mossner's great biography *The Life of David Hume,* London, 1954; J. A. Passmore, *Hume's Intentions,* Cambridge, 1952; H. H. Price, *Hume's Theory of the External World,* Oxford, 1940; and most valuable of all, Norman Kemp Smith, *The Philosophy of David Hume,* London, 1941.

One final word of warning. Hume is one of the most elegant stylists ever to write about serious philosophical problems. The ease with which his paragraphs flow and the felicity with which even the most subtle logical points are made may fool the reader into supposing that nothing of great weight could possibly be contained in such insubstantial prose. Nothing could be farther from the truth! When the eye slips most smoothly over Hume's words, then the mind must be wariest. Hume the man was a quick and agile intelligence imprisoned in a lumpish body; his philosophy, by contrast, is a juggernaut of powerful arguments masquerading behind light phrases and amusing examples. To read him is a pleasure, but to understand him is a challenge.

—ROBERT WOLFF

A Treatise of

Human Nature

INTRODUCTION

Nothing is more usual and more natural for those who pretend to discover anything new to the world in philosophy and the sciences than to insinuate the praises of their own systems by decrying all those which have been advanced before them. And indeed, were they content with lamenting that ignorance, which we still lie under in the most important questions than can come before the tribunal of human reason, there are few, who have an acquaintance with the sciences, that would not readily agree with them. It is easy for one of judgment and learning to perceive the weak foundation even of those systems which have obtained the greatest credit and have carried their pretensions highest to accurate and profound reasoning. Principles taken upon trust, consequences lamely deduced from them, want of coherence in the parts and of evidence in the whole, these are everywhere, to be met with the systems of the most eminent philosophers and seem to have drawn disgrace upon philosophy itself.

Nor is there required such profound knowledge to discover the present imperfect condition of the sciences, but even the rabble without doors may judge from the noise and clamor which they hear that all goes not well within. There is nothing which is not the subject of debate and in which men of learning are not of contrary opinions. The most trivial question escapes not our controversy, and in the most momentous we are not able to give any certain decision. Disputes are multiplied, as if everything was uncertain, and these disputes are managed with the greatest warmth, as if everything was certain. Amidst all this bustle, it is not reason which carries the prize, but eloquence; and no man needs ever despair of gaining proselytes to the most extravagant hypothesis who has art enough to represent it in any favorable colors. The victory is not gained by the men at arms, who manage the pike and the sword, but by the trumpeters, drummers, and musicians of the army.

From hence in my opinion arises that common prejudice

against metaphysical reasonings of all kinds, even amongst those who profess themselves scholars and have a just value for every other part of literature. By metaphysical reasonings they do not understand those on any particular branch of science but every kind of argument which is any way abstruse and requires some attention to be comprehended. We have so often lost our labor in such researches that we commonly reject them without hesitation and resolve, if we must forever be a prey to errors and delusions, that they shall at least be natural and entertaining. And indeed, nothing but the most determined skepticism, along with a great degree of indolence, can justify this aversion to metaphysics. For if truth be at all within the reach of human capacity, it is certain it must lie very deep and abstruse; and to hope we shall arrive at it without pains, while the greatest geniuses have failed with the utmost pains, must certainly be esteemed sufficiently vain and presumptuous. I pretend to no such advantage in the philosophy I am going to unfold and would esteem it a strong presumption against it were it so very easy and obvious.

It is evident that all the sciences have a relation, greater or less, to human nature and that, however wide any of them may seem to run from it, they still return back by one passage or another. Even *Mathematics, Natural Philosophy*, and *Natural Religion* are in some measure dependent on the science of Man, since they lie under the cognizance of men and are judged of by their powers and faculties. It is impossible to tell what changes and improvements we might make in these sciences were we thoroughly acquainted with the extent and force of human understanding and could explain the nature of the ideas we employ and of the operations we perform in our reasonings. And these improvements are the more to be hoped for in natural religion, as it is not content with instructing us in the nature of superior powers but carries its views further, to their disposition towards us and our duties towards them; and consequently, we ourselves are not only the beings that reason but also one of the objects concerning which we reason.

If therefore the sciences of Mathematics, Natural Philosophy, and Natural Religion have such a dependence on the knowledge of man, what may be expected in the other sciences, whose connection with human nature is more close and intimate? The sole end of logic is to explain the principles and operations of our reasoning faculty, and the nature of our ideas; morals and criticism regard our tastes and sentiments; and politics consider men as united in society and dependent on each other. In these four sciences of *Logic, Morals, Criticism*, and *Politics* is comprehended almost everything which it can anyway import us to be acquainted with or which can tend either to the improvement or ornament of the human mind.

Here then is the only expedient from which we can hope for success in our philosophical researches, to leave the tedious lingering method which we have hitherto followed and instead of taking now and then a castle or village on the frontier, to march up directly to the capital or center of these sciences, to human nature itself, which being once masters of, we may everywhere else hope for an easy victory. From this station we may extend our conquests over all those sciences which more intimately concern human life and may afterwards proceed at leisure to discover more fully those which are the objects of pure curiosity. There is no question of importance whose decision is not comprised in the science of man; and there is none which can be decided with any certainty before we become acquainted with that science. In pretending, therefore, to explain the principles of human nature, we in effect propose a complete system of the sciences, built on a foundation almost entirely new, and the only one upon which they can stand with any security.

And as the science of man is the only solid foundation for the other sciences, so the only solid foundation we can give to this science itself must be laid on experience and observation. It is no astonishing reflection to consider that the application of experimental philosophy to moral subjects should come after that to natural, at the distance of above a whole century, since we find, in fact, that there was about the same interval betwixt the origins of these sciences and that, reckoning from Thales to Socrates, the space of time is nearly equal to that betwixt my Lord Bacon and some late philosophers * in England who have begun to put the science of man on a new footing and have engaged the attention and excited the curiosity of the public. So true it is, that however other nations may rival us in poetry, and excel us in some other agreeable arts, the improvements in reason and philosophy can only be owing to a land of toleration and of liberty.

Nor ought we to think that this latter improvement in the science of man will do less honor to our native country than the former in natural philosophy, but ought rather to esteem it a greater glory, upon account of the greater importance of that science, as well as the necessity it lay under of such a reformation. For to me it seems evident that the essence of the mind being equally unknown to us with that of external

* Mr. Locke, my Lord Shaftesbury, Dr. Mandeville, Mr. Hutchinson, Dr. Butler, etc.

bodies, it must be equally impossible to form any notion of its powers and qualities otherwise than from careful and exact experiments and the observation of those particular effects which result from its different circumstances and situations. And though we must endeavor to render all our principles as universal as possible by tracing up our experiments to the utmost and explaining all effects from the simplest and fewest causes, it is still certain we cannot go beyond experience; and any hypothesis that pretends to discover the ultimate original qualities of human nature ought at first to be rejected as presumptuous and chimerical.

I do not think a philosopher who would apply himself so earnestly to the explaining the ultimate principles of the soul would show himself a great master in that very science of human nature which he pretends to explain or very knowing in what is naturally satisfactory to the mind of man. For nothing is more certain than that despair has almost the same effect upon us with enjoyment and that we are no sooner acquainted with the impossibility of satisfying any desire than the desire itself vanishes. When we see that we have arrived at the utmost extent of human reason, we sit down contented, though we be perfectly satisfied in the main of our ignorance and perceive that we can give no reason for our most general and most refined principles, beside our experience of their reality—which is the reason of the mere vulgar and what it required no study at first to have discovered for the most particular and most extraordinary phenomenon. And as this impossiblity of making any further progress is enough to satisfy the reader, so the writer may derive a more delicate satisfaction from the free confession of his ignorance and from his prudence in avoiding that error into which so many have fallen of imposing their conjectures and hypotheses on the world for the most certain principles. When this mutual contentment and satisfaction can be obtained betwixt the master and scholar, I know not what more we can require of our philosophy.

But if this impossibility of explaining ultimate principles should be esteemed a defect in the science of man, I will venture to affirm that it is a defect common to it with all the sciences and all the arts in which we can employ ourselves, whether they be such as are cultivated in the schools of the philosophers or practiced in the shops of the meanest artisans. None of them can go beyond experience or establish any principles which are not founded on that authority. Moral philosophy has, indeed, this peculiar disadvantage, which is not found in natural, that in collecting its experiments, it cannot make them purposely, with premeditation, and after such a manner as to satisfy itself concerning every particular difficulty which may arise. When I am at a loss to know the effects of one body upon another in any situation, I need only put them in that situation and observe what results from it. But should I endeavor to clear up after the same manner any doubt in moral philosophy, by placing myself in the same case with that which I consider, it is evident this reflection and premeditation would so disturb the operation of my natural principles as must render it impossible to form any just conclusion from the phenomenon. We must therefore glean up our experiments in this science from a cautious observation of human life and take them as they appear in the common course of the world, by men's behavior in company, in affairs, and in their pleasures. Where experiments of this kind are judiciously collected and compared, we may hope to establish on them a science which will not be inferior in certainty, and will be much superior in utility, to any other of human comprehension.

Part I

OF IDEAS, THEIR ORIGIN, COMPOSITION CONNECTION, ABSTRACTION, ETC.

Section I

OF THE ORIGIN OF OUR IDEAS

All the perceptions of the human mind resolve themselves into two distinct kinds, which I shall call *impressions* and *ideas*. The difference betwixt these consists in the degrees of force and liveliness, with which they strike upon the mind, and make their way into our thought or consciousness. Those perceptions which enter with most force and violence we may name *impressions;* and under this name I comprehend all our sensations, passions, and emotions, as they make their first appearance in the soul. By *ideas* I mean the faint images of these in thinking and reasoning, such as, for instance, are all the perceptions excited by the present discourse, excepting only those which arise from the sight and touch, and excepting the immediate pleasure or uneasiness it may occasion. I believe it will not be very necessary to employ many words in explaining this distinction. Everyone of himself will readily perceive the difference betwixt feeling and thinking. The common degrees of these are easily distinguished, though it is not impossible but in particular instances they may very nearly approach to each other. Thus, in sleep, in a fever, in madness, or in any very violent emotions of soul, our ideas may approach to our impressions—as on the other hand it sometimes happens that our impressions are so faint and low that we cannot distinguish them from our ideas. But notwithstanding this near resemblance in a few instances, they are in general so very different that no one can make a scruple to rank them under distinct heads and assign to each a peculiar name to mark the difference.*

There is another division of our perceptions which it will be convenient to observe and which extends itself both to our impressions and ideas. This division is into *simple* and *complex*. Simple perceptions, or impressions and ideas, are such as admit of no distinction nor separation. The complex are the contrary to these and may be distinguished into parts. Though a particular color, taste, and smell are qualities all united together in this apple, it is easy to perceive they are not the same but are at least distinguishable from each other.

Having by these divisions given an order and arrangement to our objects, we may now apply ourselves to consider with the more accuracy their qualities and relations. The first circumstance that strikes my eye is the great resemblance betwixt our impressions and ideas in every other particular, except their degree of force and vivacity. The one seems to be, in a manner, the reflection of the other, so that all the perceptions of the mind are double and appear both as impressions and ideas. When I shut my eyes and think of my chamber, the ideas I form are exact representations of the impressions I felt, nor is there any circumstances of the one which is not to be found in the other. In running over my other perceptions, I find still the same resemblance and representation. Ideas and impressions appear always to correspond to each other. This circumstance seems to me remarkable and engages my attention for a moment.

Upon a more accurate survey, I find I have been carried away too far by the first appearance and that I must make use of the distinction of perceptions into *simple* and *complex* to limit this general decision, *that all our ideas and impressions are resembling*. I observe that many of our complex ideas never had impressions that corresponded to them and that many of our complex impressions never are exactly copied in ideas. I can imagine to myself such a city as the New Jerusalem, whose pavement is gold and walls are rubies, though I never saw any such. I have seen Paris; but shall I affirm I can form such an idea of that city as will perfectly

* I here make use of these terms, *impression* and *idea*, in a sense different from what is usual, and I hope this liberty will be allowed me. Perhaps I rather restore the word idea to its original sense, from which Mr. Locke had perverted it, in making it stand for all our perceptions. By the term of impression I would not be understood to express the manner in which our lively perceptions are produced in the soul, but merely the perceptions themselves, for which there is no particular name, either in the English or any other language that I know of.

represent all its streets and houses in their real and just proportions?

I perceive, therefore, that though there is, in general, a great resemblance betwixt our *complex* impressions and ideas, yet the rule is not universally true that they are exact copies of each other. We may next consider how the case stands with our *simple* perceptions. After the most accurate examination of which I am capable, I venture to affirm that the rule here holds without any exception and that every simple idea has a simple impression which resembles it and every simple impression a correspondent idea. That idea of red, which we form in the dark, and that impression which strikes our eyes in sunshine differ only in degree, not in nature. That the case is the same with all our simple impressions and ideas it is impossible to prove by a particular enumeration of them. Everyone may satisfy himself in this point by running over as many as he pleases. But if anyone should deny this universal resemblance, I know no way of convincing him but by desiring him to show a simple impression that has not a correspondent idea or a simple idea that has not a correspondent impression. If he does not answer this challenge, as it is certain he cannot, we may, from his silence and our own observation, establish our conclusion.

Thus, we find that all simple ideas and impressions resemble each other; and as the complex are formed from them, we may affirm in general that these two species of perception are exactly correspondent. Having discovered this relation, which requires no further examination, I am curious to find some other of their qualities. Let us consider how they stand with regard to their existence and which of the impressions and ideas are causes and which effects.

The full examination of this question is the subject of the present treatise; and therefore we shall here content ourselves with establishing one general proposition: *That all our simple ideas in their first appearance are derived from simple impressions, which are correspondent to them, and which they exactly represent.*

In seeking for phenomena to prove this proposition, I find only those of two kinds; but in each kind the phenomena are obvious, numerous, and conclusive. I first make myself certain, by a new review of what I have already asserted, that every simple impression is attended with a correspondent idea and every simple idea with a correspondent impression. From this constant conjunction of resembling perceptions I immediately conclude that there is a great connection betwixt our correspondent impressions and ideas and that the existence of the one has a considerable influence upon that of the other. Such a constant conjunction, in such an infinite number of instances, can never arise from chance, but clearly proves a dependence of the impressions on the ideas or of the ideas on the impressions. That I may know on which side this dependence lies, I consider the order of their *first appearance* and find by constant experience that the simple impressions always take the precedence of their correspondent ideas but never appear in the contrary order. To give a child an idea of scarlet or orange, of sweet or bitter, I present the objects, or in other words, convey to him these impressions, but proceed not so absurdly as to endeavor to produce the impressions by exciting the ideas. Our ideas, upon their appearance, produce not their correspondent impressions, nor do we perceive any color or feel any sensation merely upon thinking of them. On the other hand, we find that any impression either of the mind or body is constantly followed by an idea which resembles it and is only different in the degrees of force and liveliness. The constant conjunction of our resembling perceptions is a convincing proof that the one are the causes of the other; and this priority of the impressions is an equal proof that our impressions are the causes of our ideas, not our ideas of our impressions.

To confirm this, I consider another plain and convincing phenomenon, which is that wherever by any accident the faculties which give rise to any impression are obstructed in their operations, as when one is born blind or deaf, not only the impressions are lost but also their correspondent ideas, so that there never appear in the mind the least trace of either of them. Nor is this only true where the organs of sensation are entirely destroyed, but likewise where they have never been put in action to produce a particular impression. We cannot form to ourselves a just idea of the taste of a pineapple without having actually tasted it.

There is, however, one contradictory phenomenon which may prove that it is not absolutely impossible for ideas to go before their correspondent impressions. I believe it will readily be allowed that the several distinct ideas of colors, which enter by the eyes, or those of sounds, which are conveyed by the hearing, are really different from each other, though at the same time resembling. Now if this be true of different colors, it must be no less so of the different shades of the same color that each of them produces a distinct idea, independent of the rest. For if this should be denied, it is possible, by the continual gradation of shades, to run a color insensibly into what is most remote from it; and if you will not allow any of the means to be different, you cannot without absurdity deny the extremes to be the same. Suppose, therefore, a person to have enjoyed his sight for thirty years and to have become perfectly well acquainted with colors of all kinds, excepting one particular shade of blue, for instance, which it never has been his fortune to meet with. Let all the different shades of that color, except that single one, be placed before him, descending gradually from the deepest to the lightest; it is plain that he will perceive a blank where that shade is wanting and will be sensible that there is a greater distance in that place betwixt the contiguous colors than in any other. Now I ask whether it is possible for him, from his own imagination, to supply this deficiency and raise up to himself the idea of that particular shade, though it had never been conveyed to him by his senses? I believe there are few but will be of opinion that he can; and this may serve as a proof that the simple ideas are not always derived from the correspondent impressions, though the instance is so particular and singular that it is scarce worth our observing and does not merit that for it alone we should alter our general maxim.

But besides this exception, it may not be amiss to remark, on this head, that the principle of the priority of impressions to ideas must be understood with another limitation, viz. that as our ideas are images of our impressions, so we can form secondary ideas which are images of the primary, as appears from this very reasoning concerning them. This is not, properly speaking, an exception to the rule so much as an explanation of it. Ideas produce the images of themselves in new ideas; but as the first ideas are supposed to be derived from impressions, it still remains true that all our simple ideas proceed either mediately or immediately from their correspondent impressions.

This, then, is the first principle I establish in the science of human nature; nor ought we to despise it because of the simplicity of its appearance. For it is remarkable that the present question concerning the precedency of our impressions or ideas is the same with what has made so much noise in other terms, when it has been disputed whether there be any *innate ideas* or whether all ideas be derived from sensation and reflection. We may observe that in order to prove the ideas of extension and color not to be innate, philosophers do nothing but show that they are conveyed by our senses. To prove the ideas of passion and desire not to be innate, they observe that we have a preceding experience of these emotions in ourselves. Now if we carefully examine these arguments, we shall find that they prove nothing but the ideas are preceded by other more lively perceptions from which they are derived and which they represent. I hope this clear stating of the question will remove all disputes concerning it and will render this principle of more use in our reasonings than it seems hitherto have been.

Section II

DIVISION OF THE SUBJECT

Since it appears that our simple impressions are prior to their correspondent ideas and that the exceptions are very rare, method seems to require we should examine our impressions before we consider our ideas. Impressions may be divided into two kinds, those of *sensation* and those of *reflection*. The first kind arises in the soul originally, from unknown causes. The second is derived in a great measure from our ideas, and that in the following order. An impression first strikes upon the senses and makes us perceive heat or cold, thirst or hunger, pleasure or pain, of some kind or other. Of this impression there is a copy taken by the mind which remains after the impression ceases; and this we call an idea. This idea of pleasure or pain, when it returns upon the soul, produces the new impressions of desire and aversion, hope and fear, which may properly be called impressions of reflection because derived from it. These again are copied by the memory and imagination and become ideas, which, perhaps, in their turn give rise to other impressions and ideas, so that the impressions of reflection are not only antecedent to their correspondent ideas but posterior to those of sensation, and derived from them. The examination of our sensations belongs more to anatomists and natural philosophers than to moral and therefore shall not at present be entered upon. And as the impressions of reflection, viz. passions, desires, and emotions, which principally deserve our attention, arise mostly from ideas, it will be necessary to reverse that method which at first sight seems most natural and in order to explain the nature and principles of the human mind, give a particular account of ideas before we proceed to impressions. For this reason, I have here chosen to begin with ideas.

Section III

OF THE IDEAS OF THE MEMORY
AND IMAGINATION

We find by experience that when any impression has been present with the mind, it again makes its appearance there as an idea; and this it may do after two different ways: either when, in its new appearance, it retains a considerable degree of its first vivacity and is somewhat intermediate betwixt an impression and an idea; or when it entirely loses that vivacity and is a perfect idea. The faculty by which we repeat our impressions in the first manner is called the *memory* and the other the *imagination*. It is evident at first sight that the ideas of the memory are much more lively and strong than those of the imagination and that the former faculty paints its objects in more distinct colors than any which are employed by the latter. When we remember any past event, the idea of it flows in upon the mind in a forcible manner; whereas in the imagination the perception is faint and languid and cannot without difficulty be preserved by the mind steady and uniform for any considerable time. Here, then, is a sensible difference betwixt one species of ideas and another. But of this more fully hereafter.

There is another difference betwixt these two kinds of ideas which is no less evident, namely that though neither the ideas of the memory nor imagination, neither the lively nor faint ideas, can make their appearance in the mind unless their correspondent impressions have gone before to prepare the way for them, yet the imagination is not restrained to the same order and form with the original impressions, while the memory is in a manner tied down in that respect, without any power of variation.

It is evident that the memory preserves the original form in which its objects were presented and that wherever we depart from it in recollecting anything, it proceeds from some defect or imperfection in that faculty. An historian may, perhaps, for the more convenient carrying on of his narration relate an event before another to which it was in fact posterior; but then he takes notice of this disorder, if he be exact, and by that means replaces the idea in its due position. It is the same case in our recollection of those places and persons with which we were formerly acquainted. The chief exercise of the memory is not to preserve the simple ideas but their order and position. In short, this principle is supported by such a number of common and vulgar phenomena that we may spare ourselves the trouble of insisting on it any further.

The same evidence follows us in our second principle, *of the liberty of the imagination to transpose and change its ideas*. The fables we meet with in poems and romances put this entirely out of question. Nature there is totally confounded and nothing mentioned but winged horses, fiery dragons, and monstrous giants. Nor will this liberty of the fancy appear strange, when we consider that all our ideas are copied from our impressions and that there are not any two impressions which are perfectly inseparable. Not to mention that this is an evident consequence of the division of ideas into simple and complex. Wherever the imagination perceives a difference among ideas, it can easily produce a separation.

Section IV

OF THE CONNECTION OR ASSOCIATION OF IDEAS

As all simple ideas may be separated by the imagination, and may be united again in what form it pleases, nothing would be more unaccountable than the operations of that faculty were it not guided by some universal principles which render it, in some measure, uniform with itself in all times and places. Were ideas entirely loose and unconnected, chance alone would join them; and it is impossible the same simple ideas should fall regularly into complex ones (as they commonly do) without some bond of union among them, some associating quality, by which one idea naturally introduces another. This uniting principle among ideas is not to be considered as an inseparable connection, for that has been already excluded from the imagination; nor yet are we to conclude that without it the mind cannot join two ideas, for nothing is more free than that faculty; but we are only to regard it as a gentle force which commonly prevails and is the cause why, among other things, languages so nearly correspond to each other—Nature, in a manner, pointing out to everyone those simple ideas which are most proper to be united into a complex one. The qualities from which this association arises, and by which the mind is after this manner conveyed from one idea to another, are three, viz. *resemblance, contiguity* in time or place, and *cause* and *effect*.

I believe it will not be very necessary to prove that these qualities produce an association among ideas and upon the appearance of one idea naturally introduce another. It is plain that in the course of our thinking, and in the constant revolution of our ideas, our imagination runs easily from one idea to any other that *resembles* it and that this quality alone is to the fancy a sufficient bond and association. It is likewise evident that as the senses, in changing their objects, are necessitated to change them regularly and take them as they lie *contiguous* to each other, the imagination must by long custom acquire the same method of thinking and run along the parts of space and time in conceiving its objects. As to the connection that is made by the relation of *cause* and *effect,* we shall have occasion afterwards to examine it to the bottom and therefore shall not at present insist upon it. It is sufficient to observe that there is no relation which produces a stronger connection in the fancy and makes one idea more readily recall another than the relation of cause and effect betwixt their objects.

That we may understand the full extent of these relations, we must consider that two objects are connected together in the imagination not only when the one is immediately resembling, contiguous to, or the cause of the other, but also when there is interposed betwixt them a third object which bears to both of them any of these relations. This may be carried on to a great length; though at the same time we may observe that each remove considerably weakens the relation. Cousins in the fourth degree are connected by *causation,* if I may be allowed to use that term, but not so closely as brothers, much less as child and parent. In general, we may observe that all the relations of blood depend upon cause and effect and are esteemed near or remote according to the number of connecting causes interposed betwixt the persons.

Of the three relations above mentioned, this of causation is the most extensive. Two objects may be considered as placed in this relation as well when one is the cause of any of the actions or motions of the other as when the former is the cause of the existence of the latter. For as that action or motion is nothing but the object itself, considered in a certain light, and as the object continues the same in all its different situations, it is easy to imagine how such an influence of objects upon one another may connect them in the imagination.

We may carry this further and remark not only that two objects are connected by the relation of cause and effect when the one produces a motion or any action in the other, but also when it has a power of producing it. And this we may observe to be the source of all the relations of interest and duty by which men influence each other in society and are placed in the ties of government and subordination. A master is such a one as by his situation, arising either from force or agreement, has a power of directing in certain particulars the actions of another, whom we call servant. A judge is one who in all disputed cases can fix by his opinion the possession or property of anything betwixt any members of the society. When a person is possessed of any power, there is no more required to convert it into action but the exertion of the will; and *that* in every case is considered as possible, and in many as probable, especially in the case of authority, where the obedience of the subject is a pleasure and advantage to the superior.

These are, therefore, the principles of union or cohesion among our simple ideas, and in the imagination supply the place of that inseparable connection by which they are united in our memory. Here is a kind of *attraction* which in the mental world will be found to have as extraordinary effects as in the natural and to show itself in as many and as various forms. Its effects are everywhere conspicuous; but as to its causes, they are mostly unknown and must be resolved into *original* qualities of human nature, which I pretend not to explain. Nothing is more requisite for a true philosopher than to restrain the intemperate desire of searching into causes, and having established any doctrine upon a sufficient number of experiments, rest contented with that when he sees a further examination would lead him into obscure and uncertain speculations. In that case, his inquiry would be much better employed in examining the effects than the causes of his principle.

Amongst the effects of this union or association of ideas, there are none more remarkable than those complex ideas which are the common subjects of our thoughts and reasoning and generally arise from some principle of union among our simple ideas. These complex ideas may be divided into *relations, modes,* and *substances.* We shall briefly examine

39

each of these in order and shall subjoin some considerations concerning our *general* and *particular ideas* before we leave the present subject, which may be considered as the elements of this philosophy.

Section V

OF RELATIONS

The word *relation* is commonly used in two senses considerably different from each other. Either for that quality by which two ideas are connected together in the imagination, and the one naturally introduces the other, after the manner above explained; or for that particular circumstance in which, even upon the arbitrary union of two ideas in the fancy, we may think proper to compare them. In common language, the former is always the sense in which we use the word relation; and it is only in philosophy that we extend it to mean any particular subject of comparison, without a connecting principle. Thus, distance will be allowed by philosophers to be a true relation, because we acquire an idea of it by the comparing of objects; but in a common way we say *that nothing can be more distant than such or such things from each other, nothing can have less relation,* as if distance and relation were incompatible.

It may, perhaps, be esteemed an endless task to enumerate all those qualities which make objects admit of comparison and by which the ideas of *philosophical* relation are produced. But if we diligently consider them, we shall find that without difficulty they may be comprised under seven general heads, which may be considered as the sources of all philosophical relation.

1. The first is *resemblance,* and this is a relation without which no philosophical relation can exist, since no objects will admit of comparison but what have some degree of resemblance. But though resemblance be necessary to all philosophical relation, it does not follow that it always produces a connection or association of ideas. When a quality becomes very general, and is common to a great many individuals, it leads not the mind directly to any one of them, but, by presenting

at once too great a choice, does thereby prevent the imagination from fixing on any single object.

2. *Identity* may be esteemed a second species of relation. This relation I here consider as applied in its strictest sense to constant and unchangeable objects, without examining the nature and foundation of personal identity, which shall find its place afterwards. Of all relations, the most universal is that of identity, being common to every being whose existence has any duration.

3. After identity, the most universal and comprehensive relations are those of *space* and *time,* which are the sources of an infinite number of comparisons, such as *distant, contiguous, above. below, before, after,* etc.

4. All those objects which admit of *quantity* or *number* may be compared in that particular, which is another very fertile source of relation.

5. When any two objects possess the same *quality* in common, the *degrees* in which they possess it form a fifth species of relation. Thus, of two objects which are both heavy, the one may be either of greater or less weight than the other. Two colors that are of the same kind may yet be of different shades, and in that respect admit of comparison.

6. The relation of *contrariety* may at first sight be regarded as an exception to the rule *that no relation of any kind can subsist without some degree of resemblance.* But let us consider that no two ideas are in themselves contrary, except those of existence and nonexistence, which are plainly resembling. as implying both of them an idea of the object, though the latter excludes the object from all times and places in which it is supposed not to exist.

7. All other objects, such as fire and water, heat and cold, are only found to be contrary from experience and from the contrariety of their *causes* or *effects;* which relation of cause and effect is a seventh philosophical relation, as well as a natural one. The resemblance implied in this relation shall be explained afterwards.

It might naturally be expected that I should join *difference* to the other relations, but that I consider rather as a negation of relation than as anything real or positive. Difference is of two kinds, as opposed either to identity or resemblance. The first is called a difference of *number,* the other of *kind.*

Section VI

OF MODES AND SUBSTANCES

I would fain ask those philosophers who found so much of their reasonings on the distinction of substance and accident, and imagine we have clear ideas of each, whether the idea of *substance* be derived from the impressions of sensation or reflection? If it be conveyed to us by our senses, I ask, which of them, and after what manner? If it be perceived by the eyes, it must be a color; if by the ears, a sound; if by the palate, a taste; and so of the other senses. But I believe none will assert that substance is either a color, a sound, or a taste. The idea of substance must, therefore, be derived from an impression of reflection, if it really exist. But the impressions of reflection resolve themselves into our passions and emotions, none of which can possibly represent a substance. We have therefore no idea of substance, distinct from that of a collection of particular qualities, nor have we any other meaning when we either talk or reason concerning it.

The idea of a substance as well as that of a mode is nothing but a collection of simple ideas that are united by the imagination and have a particular name assigned them, by which we are able to recall, either to ourselves or others, that collection. But the difference betwixt these ideas consists in this, that the particular qualities which form a substance are commonly referred to an unknown *something,* in which they are supposed to inhere, or granting this fiction should not take place, are at least supposed to be closely and inseparably connected by the relations of contiguity and causation. The effect of this is that whatever new simple quality we discover to have the same connection with the rest, we immediately comprehend it among them, even though it did not enter into the first conception of the substance. Thus, our idea of gold may at first be a yellow color, weight, malleableness, fusibility; but upon the discovery of its dissolubility in *aqua regia,* we join that to the other qualities and suppose it to belong to the substance as much as if its idea had from the beginning made a part of a compound one. The principle of union, being regarded as the chief part of the complex idea, gives entrance to whatever quality afterwards occurs, and is equally comprehended by it, as are the others which first presented themselves.

That this cannot take place in modes is evident from considering their nature. The simple ideas of which modes are formed either represent qualities which are not united by contiguity and causation but are dispersed in different subjects; or if they be all united together, the uniting principle is not regarded as the foundation of the complex idea. The idea of a dance is an instance of the first kind of modes, that of beauty of the second. The reason is obvious why such complex ideas cannot receive any new idea without changing the name, which distinguishes the mode.

Section VII

OF ABSTRACT IDEAS

A very material question has been started concerning *abstract* or *general* ideas, *whether they be general or particular in the mind's conception of them.* A great philosopher * has disputed the received opinion in this particular and has asserted that all general ideas are nothing but particular ones annexed to a certain term, which gives them a more extensive signification and makes them recall upon occasion other individuals which are similar to them. As I look upon this to be one of the greatest and most valuable discoveries that has been made of late years in the republic of letters, I shall here endeavor to confirm it by some arguments which I hope will put it beyond all doubt and controversy.

It is evident that in forming most of our general ideas, if not all of them, we abstract from every particular degree of quantity and quality, and that an object ceases not to be of any particular species on account of every small alteration in its extension, duration, and other properties. It may, therefore, be thought that here is a plain dilemma that decides concerning the nature of those abstract ideas, which have afforded so much speculation to philosophers. The abstract idea of a man represents men of all sizes and all qualities,

---

* Dr. Berkeley.

which it is concluded it cannot do, but either by representing at once all possible sizes and all possible qualities or by representing no particular one at all. Now, it having been esteemed absurd to defend the former proposition as implying an infinite capacity in the mind, it has been commonly inferred in favor of the latter; and our abstract ideas have been supposed to represent no particular degree either of quantity or quality. But that this inference is erroneous, I shall endeavor to make appear, *first*, by proving that it is utterly impossible to conceive any quantity or quality without forming a precise notion of its degrees; and, *secondly*, by showing that though the capacity of the mind be not infinite, yet we can at once form a notion of all possible degrees of quantity and quality in such a manner, at least, as, however imperfect, may serve all the purposes of reflection and conversation.

To begin with the first proposition, *that the mind cannot form any notion of quantity or quality without forming a precise notion of degrees of each*, we may prove this by the three following arguments. First, we have observed that whatever objects are different are distinguishable, and that whatever objects are distinguishable are separable by the thought and imagination. And we may here add that these propositions are equally true in the *inverse*, and that whatever objects are separable are also distinguishable, and that whatever objects are distinguishable are also different. For how is it possible we can separate what is not distinguishable or distinguish what is not different? In order therefore to know whether abstraction implies a separation, we need only consider it in this view and examine whether all the circumstances which we abstract from in our general ideas be such as are distinguishable and different from those which we retain as essential parts of them. But it is evident at first sight that the precise length of a line is not different nor distinguishable from the line itself, nor the precise degree of any quality from the quality. These ideas therefore admit no more of separation than they do of distinction and difference. They are consequently conjoined with each other in the conception; and the general idea of a line, notwithstanding all our abstractions and refinements, has in its appearance in the mind a precise degree of quantity and quality, however it may be made to represent others which have different degrees of both.

Secondly, it is confessed that no object can appear to the senses, or, in other words, that no impression can become present to the mind without being determined in its degrees both of quantity and quality. The confusion, in which impressions are sometimes involved, proceeds only from their faint-

44

ness and unsteadiness, not from any capacity in the mind to receive any impression which in its real existence has no particular degree nor proportion. That is a contradiction in terms and even implies the flattest of all contradictions, viz. that it is possible for the same thing both to be and not to be.

Now, since all ideas are derived from impressions, and are nothing but copies and representations of them, whatever is true of the one must be acknowledged concerning the other. Impressions and ideas differ only in their strength and vivacity. The foregoing conclusion is not founded on any particular degree of vivacity. It cannot, therefore, be affected by any variation in that particular. An idea is a weaker impression; and as a strong impression must necessarily have a determinate quantity and quality, the case must be the same with its copy or representative.

Thirdly, it is a principle generally received in philosophy that everything in nature is individual and that it is utterly absurd to suppose a triangle really existent which has no precise proportion of sides and angles. If this, therefore, be absurd in *fact and reality*, it must also be absurd *in idea*, since nothing of which we can form a clear and distinct idea is absurd and impossible. But to form the idea of an object, and to form an idea simply, is the same thing, the reference of the idea to an object being an extraneous denomination of which in itself it bears no mark or character. Now, as it is impossible to form an idea of an object that is possessed of quantity and quality and yet is possessed of no precise degree of either, it follows that there is an equal impossibility of forming an idea that is not limited and confined in both these particulars. Abstract ideas are therefore in themselves individual, however they may become general in their representation. The image in the mind is only that of a particular object, though the application of it in our reasoning be the same as if it were universal.

This application of ideas beyond their nature proceeds from our collecting all their possible degrees of quantity and quality in such an imperfect manner as may serve the purposes of life, which is the second proposition I proposed to explain. When we have found a resemblance * among sev-

* It is evident that even different simple ideas may have a similarity or resemblance to each other; nor is it necessary that the point or circumstance of resemblance should be distinct or separable from that in which they differ. *Blue* and *green* are different simple ideas but are more resembling than *blue* and *scarlet*, though their perfect simplicity excludes all possibility of separation or distinction. It is the same case with particular sounds, and tastes, and smells. These admit of infinite resemblances upon the general appearance and comparison, without having any common circumstance the same. And of this we may be

eral objects that often occur to us, we apply the same name to all of them, whatever differences we may observe in the degrees of their quantity and quality, and whatever other differences may appear among them. After we have acquired a custom of this kind, the hearing of that name revives the idea of one of these objects and makes the imagination conceive it with all its particular circumstances and proportions. But as the same word is supposed to have been frequently applied to other individuals that are different in many respects from that idea which is immediately present to the mind, the word, not being able to revive the idea of all these individuals, only touches the soul, if I may be allowed so to speak, and revives that custom which we have acquired by surveying them. They are not really and in fact present to the mind, but only in power; nor do we draw them all out distinctly in the imagination, but keep ourselves in a readiness to survey any of them, as we may be prompted by a present design or necessity. The word raises up an individual idea, along with a certain custom, and that custom produces any other individual one for which we may have occasion. But as the production of all the ideas to which the name may be applied is in most cases impossible, we abridge that work by a more partial consideration and find but few inconveniences to arise in our reasoning from that abridgment.

For this is one of the most extraordinary circumstances in the present affair, that after the mind has produced an individual idea upon which we reason, the attendant custom, revived by the general or abstract term, readily suggests any other individual, if by chance we form any reasoning that agrees not with it. Thus, should we mention the word triangle and form the idea of a particular equilateral one to correspond to it, and should we afterwards assert *that the three angles of a triangle are equal to each other,* the other individuals of a scalenum and isosceles, which we overlooked at first, immediately crowd in upon us and make us perceive the falsehood of this proposition, though it be true with relation to that idea which we had formed. If the mind suggests not always these ideas upon occasion, it proceeds from some imperfection in its faculties, and such a one as is often the source of false reasoning and sophistry. But this is principally the case with those ideas which are abstruse and com-

certain, even from the very abstract terms *simple idea.* They comprehend all simple ideas under them. These resemble each other in their simplicity. And yet, from their very nature, which excludes all composition, this circumstance in which they resemble is not distinguishable or separable from the rest. It is the same case with all the degrees in any quality. They are all resembling, and yet the quality in any individual is not distinct from the degree.

pounded. On other occasions, the custom is more entire, and it is seldom we run into such errors.

Nay, so entire is the custom that the very same idea be annexed to several different words and may be employed in different reasonings without any danger of mistake. Thus, the idea of an equilateral triangle of an inch perpendicular may serve us in talking of a figure, of a rectilineal figure, of a regular figure, of a triangle, and of an equilateral triangle. All these terms, therefore, are in this case attended with the same idea; but as they are wont to be applied in a greater or lesser compass, they excite their particular habits and thereby keep the mind in a readiness to observe that no conclusion be formed contrary to any ideas which are usually comprised under them.

Before those habits have become entirely perfect, perhaps the mind may not be content with forming the idea of only one individual, but may run over several, in order to make itself comprehend its own meaning and the compass of that collection which it intends to express by the general term. That we may fix the meaning of the word figure, we may revolve in our minds the ideas of circles, squares, parallelograms, triangles of different sizes and proportions, and may not rest on one image or idea. However this may be, it is certain *that* we form the idea of individuals whenever we use any general term; *that* we seldom or never can exhaust these individuals; and *that* those which remain are only represented by means of that habit by which we recall them whenever any present occasion requires it. This, then, is the nature of our abstract ideas and general terms; and it is after this manner we account for the foregoing paradox, *that some ideas are particular in their nature, but general in their representation*. A particular idea becomes general by being annexed to a general term, that is, to a term which, from a customary conjunction, has a relation to many other particular ideas and readily recalls them in the imagination.

The only difficulty that can remain on this subject must be with regard to that custom which so readily recalls every particular idea for which we may have occasion and one particular idea may serve us in reasoning concerning other ideas, however different from it in several circumstances.

Fourthly, as the individuals are collected together and placed under a general term with a view to that resemblance which they bear to each other, this relation must facilitate their entrance in the imagination and make them be suggested more readily upon occasion. And indeed, if we consider the common progress of the thought, either in reflection or conversation, we shall find great reason to be satisfied in

47

this particular. Nothing is more admirable than the readiness with which the imagination suggests its ideas and presents them at the very instant in which they become necessary or useful. The fancy runs from one end of the universe to the other in collecting those ideas which belong to any subject. One would think the whole intellectual world of ideas was at once subjected to our view and that we did nothing but pick out such as were most proper for our purpose. There may not, however, be any present, beside those very ideas that are thus collected by a kind of magical faculty in the soul, which, though it be always most perfect in the greatest geniuses, and is properly what we call a genius, is, however, inexplicable by the utmost efforts of human understanding.

Perhaps these four reflections may help to remove all difficulties to the hypothesis I have proposed concerning abstract ideas, so contrary to that which has hitherto prevailed in philosophy. But to tell the truth, I place my chief confidence in what I have already proved concerning the impossibility of general ideas, according to the common method of explaining them. We must certainly seek some new system on this head, and there plainly is none beside what I have proposed. If ideas be particular in their nature, and at the same time finite in their number, it is only by custom they can become general in their representation and contain an infinite number of other ideas under them.

Before I leave this subject, I shall employ the same principles to explain that *distinction of reason*, which is so much talked of and is so little understood in the schools. Of this kind is the distinction betwixt figure and the body figured, motion and the body moved. The difficulty of explaining this distinction arises from the principle above explained, *that all ideas which are different are separable*. For it follows from thence that if the figure be different from the body, their ideas must be separable as well as distinguishable; if they be not different, their ideas can neither be separable nor distinguishable. What then is meant by a distinction of reason, since it implies neither a difference nor separation?

To remove this difficulty, we must have recourse to the foregoing explication of abstract ideas. It is certain that the mind would never have dreamed of distinguishing a figure from the body figured as being in reality neither distinguishable, nor different, nor separable, did it not observe that even in this simplicity there might be contained many different resemblances and relations. Thus, when a globe of white marble is presented, we receive only the impression of a white color disposed in a certain form, nor are we able to separate and distinguish the color from the form. But observing after-

48

wards a globe of black marble and a cube of white and comparing them with our former object, we find two separate resemblances in what formerly seemed, and really is, perfectly inseparable. After a little more practice of this kind, we begin to distinguish the figure from the color by a *distinction of reason;* that is, we consider the figure and color together, since they are, in effect, the same and undistinguishable, but still view them in different aspects, according to the resemblances of which they are susceptible. When we would consider only the figure of the globe of white marble, we form in reality an idea both of the figure and color, but tacitly carry our eye to its resemblance with the globe of black marble; and in the same manner, when we would consider its color only, we turn our view to its resemblance with the cube of white marble. By this means, we accompany our ideas with a kind of reflection of which custom renders us, in a great measure, insensible. A person who desires us to consider the figure of a globe of white marble without thinking on its color desires an impossibility; but his meaning is that we should consider the color and figure together, but still keep in our eye the resemblance to the globe of black marble, or that to any other globe of whatever color or substance.

Part II

OF OUR IDEAS OF SPACE AND TIME

Section VI

OF THE IDEAS OF EXISTENCE, AND OF EXTERNAL EXISTENCE

It may not be amiss, before we leave this subject, to explain the ideas of *existence* and of *external existence*, which have their difficulties as well as the ideas of space and time. By this means, we shall be the better prepared for the examination of knowledge and probability when we understand perfectly all those particular ideas which may enter into our reasoning.

There is no impression nor idea of any kind of which we have any consciousness or memory that is not conceived as existent; and it is evident that, from this consciousness, the most perfect idea and assurance of *being* is derived. From hence we may form a dilemma, the most clear and conclusive that can be imagined, viz. that since we never remember any idea or impression without attributing existence to it, the idea of existence must either be derived from a distinct impression, conjoined with every perception or object of our thought, or must be the very same with the idea of the perception or object.

As this dilemma is an evident consequence of the principle that every idea arises from a similar impression, so our decision betwixt the propositions of the dilemma is no more doubtful. So far from there being any distinct impression attending every impression and every idea, that I do not think there are any two distinct impressions which are inseparably conjoined. Though certain sensations may at one time be united, we quickly find they admit of a separation and may be presented apart. And thus, though every impression and idea we remember be considered as existent, the idea of existence is not derived from any particular impression.

The idea of existence, then, is the very same with the idea of what we conceive to be existent. To reflect on anything simply and to reflect on it as existent are nothing different from each other. That idea, when conjoined with the idea of any object, makes no addition to it. Whatever we conceive, we conceive to be existent. Any idea we please to form is the idea of a being; and the idea of a being is any idea we please to form.

Whoever opposes this must necessarily point out that distinct impression from which the idea of entity is derived and must prove that this impression is inseparable from every perception we believe to be existent. This we may without hesitation conclude to be impossible.

Our foregoing reasoning concerning the *distinction* of ideas without any real *difference* will not here serve us in any stead. That kind of distinction is founded on the different resemblances which the same simple idea may have to several different ideas. But no object can be presented resembling some object with respect to its existence and different from others in the same particular, since every object that is presented must necessarily be existent.

A like reasoning will account for the idea of *external existence*. We may observe that it is universally allowed by philosophers, and is besides pretty obvious of itself, that nothing is ever really present with the mind but its perceptions or impressions and ideas, and that external objects become known to us only by those perceptions they occasion. To hate, to love, to think, to feel, to see; all this is nothing but to perceive.

Now, since nothing is ever present to the mind but perceptions, and since all ideas are derived from something antecedently present to the mind, it follows that it is impossible for us so much as to conceive or form an idea of anything specifically different from ideas and impressions. Let us fix our attention out of ourselves as much as possible; let us chase our imagination to the heavens or to the utmost limits of the universe; we never really advance a step beyond ourselves nor can conceive any kind of existence but those perceptions which have appeared in that narrow compass. This is the universe of the imagination, nor have we any idea but what is there produced.

The furthest we can go toward a conception of external objects, when supposed *specifically* different from our perceptions, is to form a relative idea of them without pretending to comprehend the related objects. Generally speaking, we do not suppose them specifically different but only attribute to them different relations, connections, and durations. But of this more fully hereafter.

Part III

OF KNOWLEDGE AND PROBABILITY

Section I

OF KNOWLEDGE

There are several different kinds of philosophical relation, viz. *resemblance, identity, relations of time and place, proportion in quantity or number, degrees in any quality, contrariety, and causation.* These relations may be divided into two classes: into such as depend entirely on the ideas, which we compare together, and such as may be changed without any change in the ideas. It is from the idea of a triangle that we discover the relation of equality which its three angles bear to two right ones; and this relation is invariable as long as our idea remains the same. On the contrary, the relations of *contiguity,* and *distance* betwixt two objects may be changed merely by an alteration of their place, without any change on the objects themselves or on their ideas; and the place depends on a hundred different accidents, which cannot be foreseen by the mind. It is the same case with *identity* and *causation.* Two objects, though perfectly resembling each other, and even appearing in the same place at different times, may be numerically different; and as the power by which one object produces another is never discoverable merely from their idea, it is evident *cause* and *effect* are relations of which we receive information from experience and not from any abstract reasoning or reflection. There is no single phenomenon, even the most simple, which can be accounted for from the qualities of the objects as they appear to us or which we could foresee without the help of our memory and experience.

It appears therefore that of these seven philosophical relations, there remain only four which, depending solely upon ideas, can be the objects of knowledge and certainty. These four are *resemblance, contrariety, degrees in quality, and proportions in quantity or number.* Three of these relations are discoverable at first sight and fall more properly under the province of intuition than demonstration. When any objects *resemble* each other, the resemblance will at first strike the eye, or rather the mind, and seldom requires a second examination. The case is the same with *contrariety* and with the *degree* of any *quality.* No one can once doubt but existence and nonexistence destroy each other and are perfectly incompatible and contrary. And thought it be impossible to judge exactly of the degrees of any quality, such as color, taste, heat, cold, when the difference betwixt them is very small, yet it is easy to decide that any of them is superior or inferior to another when their difference is considerable. And this decision we always pronounce at first sight, without any inquiry or reasoning.

We might proceed, after the same manner, in fixing the *proportions* of *quantity* or *number* and might at one view observe a superiority or inferiority betwixt any numbers, or figures, especially where the difference is very great and remarkable. As to equality or any exact proportion, we can only guess at it from a single consideration, except in very short numbers or very limited portions of extension, which are comprehended in an instant and where we perceive an impossibilty of falling into any considerable error. In all other cases, we must settle the proportions with some liberty or proceed in a more *artificial* manner.

I have already observed that geometry, or the *art* by which we fix the proportions of figures, though it much excels both in universality and exactness the loose judgments of the senses and imagination, yet never attains a perfect precision and exactness. Its first principles are still drawn from the general appearance of the objects; and that appearance can never afford us any security when we examine the prodigious minuteness of which nature is susceptible. Our ideas seem to give a perfect assurance that no two right lines can have a common segment: but if we consider these ideas, we shall find that they always suppose a sensible inclination of the two lines, and that where the angle they form is extremely small, we have no standard of a right line so precise as to assure us of the truth of this proposition. It is the same case with most of the primary decisions of the mathematicians.

There remain therefore algebra and arithmetic as the only sciences in which we can carry on a chain of reasoning to any degree of intricacy and yet preserve a perfect exactness and certainty. We are possessed of a precise standard by which we can judge of the equality and proportion of numbers; and according as they correspond or not to that standard, we determine their relations without any possibility of error. When two numbers are so combined as that the one has always a unit answering to every unit of the other, we pronounce them equal; and it is for want of such a standard of equality in extension that geometry can scarce be esteemed a perfect and infallible science.

But here it may not be amiss to obviate a difficulty which may arise from my asserting that though geometry falls short of that perfect precision and certainty which are peculiar to arithmetic and algebra, yet it excels the imperfect judgments of our senses and imagination. The reason why I impute any defect to geometry is because its original and fundamental principles are derived merely from appearances; and it may perhaps be imagined that this defect must always attend it and keep it from ever reaching a great exactness in the comparison of objects or ideas than what our eye or imagination alone is able to attain. I own that this defect so far attends it as to keep it from ever aspiring to a full certainty; but since these fundamental principles depend on the easiest and least deceitful appearances, they bestow on their consequences a degree of exactness of which these consequences are singly incapable. It is impossible for the eye to determine the angles of a chiliagon to be equal to 1996 right angles or make any conjecture that approaches this proportion; but when it determines that right lines cannot concur, that we cannot draw more than one right line between two given points, its mistakes can never be of any consequence. And this is the nature and use of geometry, to run us up to such appearances as, by reason of their simplicity, cannot lead us into any considerable error.

I shall here take occasion to propose a second observation concerning our demonstrative reasonings which is suggested by the same object of the mathematics. It is usual with mathematicians to pretend that those ideas which are their objects are of so refined and spiritual a nature that they fall not under the conception of the fancy, but must be comprehended by a pure and intellectual view, of which the superior faculties of the soul are alone capable. The same notion runs through most parts of philosophy and is principally made use of to explain our abstract ideas and to show how we can form an idea of a triangle, for instance, which shall neither be an isosceles nor scalenum, nor be confined to any particular length and proportion of sides. It is easy to see why philosophers are so fond of this notion of some spiritual and refined perceptions. since by that means they cover many of their absurdities and may refuse to submit to the decisions of clear ideas by appealing to such as are obscure and uncertain. But to destroy this artifice, we need but reflect on that principle so oft insisted on. *that all our ideas are copied from our impressions* For from thence we may immediately conclude that since all impressions are clear and precise, the ideas which are copied from them must be of the same nature and can never, but from our fault, contain anything so dark and intricate. An idea is by its very nature weaker and fainter than an impression, but being in every other respect the same, cannot imply any very great mystery. If its weakness render it obscure, it is our business to remedy that defect as much as possible by keeping the idea steady and precise; and till we have done so, it is in vain to pretend to reasoning and philosophy.

Section II

OF PROBABILITY, AND OF THE IDEA
OF CAUSE AND EFFECT

This is all I think necessary to observe concerning those four relations which are the foundation of science; but as to the other three. which depend not upon the idea and may be absent or present even while *that* remains the same, it will be proper to explain them more particularly. These three relations are *identity, the situations in time and place, and causation.*

All kinds of reasoning consist in nothing but a *comparison* and a discovery of those relations, either constant or inconstant, where two or more objects bear to each other. This comparison we may make either when both the objects are present to the senses. or when neither of them is present, or when only one When both the objects are present to the senses along with the relation, we call *this* perception rather than reasoning; nor is there in this case any exercise of the thought or any action, properly speaking, but a mere passive admission of the impressions through the organs of sensation. According to this way of thinking, we ought not to receive as reasoning any of the observations we may make concerning *identity* and the *relations* of *time* and *place*, since in none of them the mind can go beyond what is immediately present to the senses either to discover the real existence or the relations of objects. It is only *causation* which produces such a connection as to give us assurance from the existence or action of one object that it was followed or preceded by any other existence or action; nor can the other two relations ever be made use of in reasoning, except so far as they either affect or are affected by it. There is nothing in any objects to persuade us that they are either always *remote* or always *contiguous;* and when from experience and observation we discover that their relation in this particular is invariable, we always conclude there is some secret *cause* which separates or unites them. The same reasoning extends to *identity.* We readily suppose an object may continue individually the same, though several times absent from and present to the senses, and ascribe to it an identity, notwithstanding the interruption of the perception, whenever we conclude that if we had kept our eye or hand constantly upon it, it would have conveyed an invariable and uninterrupted perception. But this conclusion beyond the impression of our senses can be founded only on the connection of *cause and effect;* nor can we otherwise have any security that the object is not changed upon us, however much the new object may resemble that which was formerly present to the senses. Whenever we discover such a perfect resemblance, we consider whether it be common in that species of objects, whether possibly or probably any cause could operate in producing the change and resemblance: and according as we determine concerning these causes and effects, we form our judgment concerning the identity of the object.

Here, then, it appears that of those three relations which depend not upon the mere ideas, the only one that can be traced beyond our senses and informs us of existences and objects which we do not see or feel is *causation*. This relation therefore we shall endeavor to explain fully before we leave the subject of the understanding.

To begin regularly, we must consider the idea of *causation* and see from what origin it is derived. It is impossible to reason justly without understanding perfectly the idea concerning which we reason; and it is impossible perfectly to understand any idea without tracing it up to its origin and examining that primary impression from which it arises. The examination of the impression bestows a clearness on the idea; and the examination of the idea bestows a like clearness on all our reasoning.

Let us therefore cast our eye on any two objects which we call cause and effect and turn them on all sides, in order to find that impression which produces an idea of such prodigious consequence. At first sight, I perceive that I must not search for it in any of the particular *qualities* of the objects, since, whichever of these qualities I pitch on, I find some object that is not possessed of it and yet falls under the denomination of cause or effect. And indeed, there is nothing existent, either externally or internally, which is not to be considered either as a cause or an effect, though it is plain there is no one quality which universally belongs to all beings and gives them a title to that denomination.

The idea then of causation must be derived from some *relation* among objects; and that relation we must now endeavor to discover. I find in the first place that whatever objects are considered as causes or effects are *contiguous*, and that nothing can operate in a time or place, which is ever so little removed from those of its existence. Though distant objects may sometimes seem productive of each other, they are commonly found upon examination to be linked by a chain of causes which are contiguous among themselves and to the distant objects; and when in any particular instance we cannot discover this connection, we still presume it to exist. We may therefore consider the relation of *contiguity* as essential to that of causation, at least may suppose it such, according to the general opinion, till we can find a more proper occasion to clear up this matter by examining what objects are or are not susceptible of juxtaposition and conjunction.

The second relation I shall observe as essential to causes and effects is not so universally acknowledged but is liable to some controversy. It is that of *priority* of time in the cause before the effect. Some pretend that it is not absolutely necessary a cause should precede its effect, but that any object or action, in the very first moment of its existence, may exert its productive quality and give rise to another object or action perfectly contemporary with itself. But beside that experience in most instances seems to contradict this opinion, we may establish the relation of priority by a kind of inference or reasoning. It is an established maxim, both in natural and moral philosophy, that an object which exists for any time in its full perfection without producing another is not its sole cause but is assisted by some other principle which pushes it from its state of inactivity and makes it exert that energy, of which it was secretly possessed. Now, if any cause may be perfectly contemporary with its effect, it is certain, according to this maxim, that they must all of them be so, since any one of them which retards its operation for a single moment exerts not itself at that very individual time in which it might have operated and therefore is no proper cause. The consequence of this would be no less than the destruction of that succession of causes which we observe in the world and indeed the utter annihilation of time. For if one cause were contemporary with its effect, and this effect was *its* effect, and so on, it is plain there would be no such thing as succession, and all objects must be coexistent.

If this argument appear satisfactory, it is well. If not, I beg the reader to allow me the same liberty which I have used in the preceding case of supposing it such. For he shall find that the affair is of no great importance.

Having thus discovered or supposed the two relations of *contiguity* and *succession* to be essential to causes and effects, I find I am stopped short and can proceed no further in considering any single instance of cause and effect. Motion in one body is regarded upon impulse as cause of motion in another. When we consider these objects with the utmost attention, we find only that the one body approaches the other and that the motion of it precedes that of the other, but without any sensible interval. It is in vain to rack ourselves with *further* thought and reflection upon this subject. We can go no *further* in considering this particular instance.

Should anyone leave this instance and pretend to define a cause by saying it is something productive of another, it is evident he would say nothing. For what does he mean by *production?* Can he give any definition of it that will not be the same with that of causation? If he can, I desire it may be produced. If he cannot, he here runs in a circle and gives a synonymous term instead of a definition.

Shall we then rest contented with these two relations of contiguity and succession as affording a complete idea of causation? By no means. An object may be contiguous and prior to another without being considered as its cause. There is a *necessary connection* to be taken into consideration, and that relation is of much greater importance than any of the other two above mentioned.

Here again I turn the object on all sides in order to discover the nature of this necessary connection and find the impression, or impressions, from which its idea may be derived. When I cast my eye on the *known qualities* of objects, I immediately discover that the relation of cause and effect depends not in the least on *them*. When I consider their *relations,* I can find none but those of contiguity and succession,

59

which I have already regarded as imperfect and unsatisfactory. Shall the despair of success make me assert that I am here possessed of an idea which is not preceded by any similar impression? This would be too strong a proof of levity and inconstancy, since the contrary principle has been already so firmly established as to admit of no further doubt, at least till we have more fully examined the present difficulty.

We must therefore proceed like those who, being in search of anything that lies concealed from them, and not finding it in the place they expected, beat about all the neighboring fields without any certain view or design in hopes their good fortune will at last guide them to what they search for. It is necessary for us to leave the direct survey of this question concerning the nature of that *necessary connection* which enters into our idea of cause and effect and endeavor to find some other questions, the examination of which will perhaps afford a hint that may serve to clear up the present difficulty. Of these questions, there occur two, which I shall proceed to examine, viz.

First, for what reason we pronounce it *necessary* that everything whose existence has a beginning should also have a cause?

Secondly, why we conclude that such particular causes must *necessarily* have such particular effects; and what is the nature of that *inference* we draw from the one to the other and of the *belief* we repose in it?

I shall only observe before I proceed any further that though the ideas of cause and effect be derived from the impressions of reflection as well as from those of sensation, yet for brevity's sake, I commonly mention only the latter as the origin of these ideas, though I desire that whatever I say of them may also extend to the former. Passions are connected with their objects and with one another no less than external bodies are connected together. The same relation then of cause and effect which belongs to one must be common to all of them.

Section VIII

WHY A CAUSE IS ALWAYS
NECESSARY

To begin with the first question concerning the necessity of a cause: It is a general maxim in philosophy that *whatever begins to exist must have a cause of existence*. This is commonly taken for granted in all reasonings without any proof given or demanded. It is supposed to be founded on intuition and to be one of those maxims which, though they may be denied with the lips, it is impossible for men in their hearts really to doubt of. But if we examine this maxim by the idea of knowledge above explained, we shall discover in it no mark of any such intuitive certainty, but on the contrary shall find that it is of a nature quite foreign to that species of conviction.

All certainty arises from the comparison of ideas and from the discovery of such relations as are unalterable so long as the ideas continue the same. These relations are *resemblance, proportions in quantity and number, degrees of any quality, and contrariety,* none of which are implied in this proposition, *Whatever has a beginning has also a cause of existence.* That proposition therefore is not intuitively certain. At least, anyone who would assert it to be intuitively certain must deny these to be the only infallible relations and must find some other relation of that kind to be implied in it, which it will then be time enough to examine.

But here is an argument which proves at once that the foregoing proposition is neither intuitively nor demonstrably certain. We can never demonstrate the necessity of a cause to every new existence or new modification of existence without showing at the same time the impossibility there is that anything can ever begin to exist without some productive principle; and where the latter proposition cannot be proved, we must despair of ever being able to prove the former. Now, that the latter proposition is utterly incapable of a demonstrative proof we may satisfy ourselves by considering that as all distinct ideas are separable from each other, and as the ideas of cause and effect are evidently distinct, it will be easy for us to conceive any object to be nonexistent this moment and existent the next without conjoining to it the distinct idea of a cause or productive principle. The separation therefore of the idea of a cause from that of a beginning of existence is plainly possible for the imagination; and consequently, the actual separation of these objects is so far possible that it implies no contradiction nor absurdity and is therefore incapable of being refuted by any reasoning from mere ideas, without which it is impossible to demonstrate the necessity of a cause.

Accordingly, we shall find upon examination that every demonstration which has been produced for the necessity of a cause is fallacious and sophistical. All the points of time and place, say some philosophers,* in which we can suppose any object to begin to exist are in themselves equal; and unless there be some cause which is peculiar to one time and to one place, and which by that means determines and fixes the existence, it must remain in eternal suspense; and the object can never begin to be for want of something to fix its beginning. But I ask, is there any more difficulty in supposing the time and place to be fixed without a cause than to suppose the existence to be determined in that manner? The first question that occurs on this subject is always *whether* the object shall exist or not; the next, *when* and *where* it shall begin to exist. If the removal of a cause be intuitively absurd in the one case, it must be so in the other; and if that absurdity be not clear without a proof in the one case, it will equally require one in the other. The absurdity then of the one supposition can never be a proof of that of the other, since they are both upon the same footing and must stand or fall by the same reasoning.

The second argument† which I find used on this head labors under an equal difficulty. Everything, it is said, must have a cause; for if anything wanted a cause, *it* would produce *itself*, that is, exist before it existed, which is impossible. But this reasoning is plainly unconclusive, because it supposes that, in our denial of a cause, we still grant what we expressly deny, viz. that there must be a cause, which therefore is taken to be the object itself; and *that*, no doubt, is an evident contradiction. But to say that anything is produced, or, to express myself more properly, comes into existence without a cause is not to affirm that it is itself its own cause, but, on the contrary, in excluding all external causes, excludes *a fortiori*

* Mr. Hobbs.
† Dr. Clarke and others.

the thing itself which is created. An object that exists absolutely without any cause certainly is not its own cause; and when you assert that the one follows from the other, you suppose the very point in question and take it for granted that it is utterly impossible anything can ever begin to exist without a cause, but that, under the exclusion of one productive principle, we must still have recourse to another.

It is exactly the same case with the third argument,* which has been employed to demonstrate the necessity of a cause. Whatever is produced without any cause is produced by *nothing*, or, in other words, has nothing for its cause. But nothing can never be a cause, no more than it can be something or equal to two right angles. By the same intuition that we perceive nothing not to be equal to two right angles or not to be something, we perceive that it can never be a cause, and consequently must perceive that every object has a real cause of its existence.

I believe it will not be necessary to employ many words in showing the weakness of this argument, after what I have said of the foregoing. They are all of them founded on the same fallacy and are derived from the same turn of thought. It is sufficient only to observe that when we exclude all causes we really do exclude them, and neither suppose nothing nor the object itself to be the cause of the existence, and consequently can draw no argument from the absurdity of these suppositions to prove the absurdity of that exclusion. If everything must have a cause, it follows that, upon the exclusion of other causes, we must accept of the object itself or of nothing as causes. But it is the very point in question whether everything must have a cause or not; and therefore, according to all just reasoning, it ought never to be taken for granted.

They are still more frivolous who say that every effect must have a cause because it is implied in the very idea of effect. Every effect necessarily presupposes a cause; effect being a relative term of which cause is the correlative. But this does not prove that every being must be preceded by a cause; no more than it follows, because every husband must have a wife that therefore every man must be married. The true state of the question is, whether every object which begins to exist must owe its existence to a cause; and this I assert neither to be intuitively nor demonstratively certain and hope to have proved it sufficiently by the foregoing arguments.

Since it is not from knowledge or any scientific reasoning

* Mr. Locke.

that we derive the opinion of the necessity of a cause to every new production, that opinion must necessarily arise from observation and experience. The next question, then, should naturally be, *how experience gives rise to such a principle?* But as I find it will be more convenient to sink this question in the following, *why we conclude that such particular causes must necessarily have such particular effects, and why we form an inference from one to another?* we shall make that the subject of our future inquiry. It will, perhaps, be found in the end that the same answer will serve for both questions.

Section IV

OF THE COMPONENT PARTS OF OUR REASONINGS CONCERNING CAUSE AND EFFECT

Though the mind in its reasonings from causes or effects carries its view beyond those objects which it sees or remembers, it must never lose sight of them entirely nor reason merely upon its own ideas without some mixture of impressions, or at least of ideas of the memory, which are equivalent to impressions. When we infer effects from causes, we must establish the existence of these causes, which we have only two ways of doing, either by an immediate perception of our memory or senses or by an inference from other causes, which causes again we must ascertain in the same manner, either by a present impression or by an inference from *their* causes, and so on, till we arrive at some object which we see or remember. It is impossible for us to carry on our inferences *ad infinitum;* and the only thing that can stop them is an impression of the memory or senses, beyond which there is no room for doubt or inquiry.

To give an instance of this, we may choose any point of history and consider for what reason we either believe or reject it. Thus, we believe that Cæsar was killed in the senate house on the ides of March, and that because this fact is established on the unanimous testimony of historians, who agree to assign this precise time and place to that event. Here are certain characters and letters present either to our memory or senses, which characters we likewise remember to have been used as the signs of certain ideas; and these ideas were either in the minds of such as were immediately present at that action and received the ideas directly from its existence or they were derived from the testimony of others, and that again from another testimony, by a visible gradation, till we arrive at those who were eyewitnesses and spectators of the event. It is obvious all this chain of argument or connection of causes and effects is at first founded on those characters or letters which are seen or remembered, and that without the authority either of the memory or senses, our whole reasoning would be chimerical and without foundation. Every link of the chain would in that case hang upon another; but there would not be anything fixed to one end of it capable of sustaining the whole; and consequently, there would be no belief nor evidence. And this actually is the case with all *hypothetical* arguments or reasonings upon a supposition, there being in them neither any present impression nor belief of a real existence.

I need not observe that it is no just objection to the present doctrine that we can reason upon our past conclusions or principles without having recourse to those impressions from which they first arose. For even supposing these impressions should be entirely effaced from the memory, the conviction they produced may still remain; and it is equally true that all reasonings concerning causes and effects are originally derived from some impression in the same manner as the assurance of a demonstration proceeds always from a comparison of ideas, though it may continue after the comparison is forgot.

Section V

OF THE IMPRESSIONS OF THE SENSES AND MEMORY

In this kind of reasoning, then, from causation, we employ materials which are of a mixed and heterogeneous nature and which, however connected, are yet essentially different from each other. All our arguments concerning causes and effects consist both of an impression of the memory or senses and of the idea of that existence which produces the object of the impression or is produced by it. Here therefore we have three things to explain, viz. *first,* the original impression, *secondly,* the transition to the idea of the connected cause or effect, *thirdly,* the nature and qualities of that idea.

As to those *impressions* which arise from the *senses,* their ultimate cause is, in my opinion, perfectly inexplicable by human reason, and it will always be impossible to decide with certainty whether they arise immediately from the object, or are produced by the creative power of the mind, or are derived from the Author of our being. Nor is such a question any way material to our present purpose. We may draw inferences from the coherence of our perceptions whether they be true or false, whether they represent nature justly or be mere illusions of the senses.

When we search for the characteristic which distinguishes the *memory* from the imagination, we must immediately perceive that it cannot lie in the simple ideas it presents to us, since both these faculties borrow their simple ideas from the impressions and can never go beyond these original perceptions. These faculties are as little distinguished from each other by the arrangement of their complex ideas. For, though it be a peculiar property of the memory to preserve the original order and position of its ideas, while the imagination transposes and changes them as it pleases, yet this difference is not sufficient to distinguish them in their operation or make us know the one from the other, it being impossible to recall the past impressions in order to compare them with our present ideas and see whether their arrangement be exactly similar. Since therefore the memory is known neither by the order of its *complex* ideas nor the nature of its *simple* ones, it follows that the difference betwixt it and the imagination lies in its superior force and vivacity. A man may indulge his fancy in feigning any past scene of adventures; nor would there be any possibility of distinguishing this from a remembrance of a like kind were not the ideas of the imagination fainter and more obscure.

[It frequently happens that when two men have been engaged in any scene of action, the one shall remember it much better than the other and shall have all the difficulty in the world to make his companion recollect it. He runs over several circumstances in vain, mentions the time, the place, the company, what was said, what was done on all sides, till at last he hits on some lucky circumstance that revives the whole and gives his friend a perfect memory of everything. Here the person that forgets receives at first all the ideas from the discourse of the other, with the same circumstances of time and place, though he considers them as mere fictions of the imagination. But as soon as the circumstance is mentioned that touches the memory, the very same ideas now appear in a new light and have, in a manner, a different feeling from what they had before. Without any other alteration beside that of the feeling, they become immediately ideas of the memory and are assented to.

Since therefore the imagination can represent all the same objects that the memory can offer to us, and since those faculties are only distinguished by the different *feeling* of the ideas they present, it may be proper to consider what is the nature of that feeling. And here I believe everyone will readily agree with me that the ideas of the memory are more *strong* and *lively* than those of the fancy.]

A painter who intended to represent a passion or emotion of any kind would endeavor to get a sight of a person actuated by a like emotion in order to enliven his ideas and give them a force and vivacity superior to what is found in those which are mere fictions of the imagination. The more recent this memory is, the clearer is the idea; and when, after a long interval, he would return to the contemplation of his object, he always finds its idea to be much decayed, if not wholly obliterated. We are frequently in doubt concerning the ideas of the memory, as they become very weak and feeble, and are at a loss to determine whether any image proceeds from the fancy or the memory when it is not drawn in such lively colors as distinguish that latter faculty. I think I remember such an event, says one, but am not sure. A long tract of time has almost worn it out of my memory and leaves me uncertain whether or not it be the pure offspring of my fancy.

And as an idea of the memory, by losing its force and vivacity, may degenerate to such a degree as to be taken for an idea of the imagination, so on the other hand an idea of the imagination may acquire such a force and vivacity as to pass for an idea of the memory and counterfeit its effects on the belief and judgment. This is noted in the case of liars, who by the frequent repetition of their lies come at last to believe and remember them as realities, custom and habit having, in this case, as in many others, the same influence on the mind as nature and infixing the idea with equal force and vigor.

Thus, it appears that the *belief* or *assent* which always attends the memory and senses is nothing but the vivacity of those perceptions they present, and that this alone distinguishes them from the imagination. To believe is in this case to feel an immediate impression of the senses or a repetition of that impression in the memory. It is merely the force and liveliness of the perception which constitutes the first act of the judgment and lays the foundation of that reasoning, which we build upon it, when we trace the relation of cause and effect.

Section VI

OF THE INFERENCE FROM THE IMPRESSION TO THE IDEA

It is easy to observe that in tracing this relation, the inference we draw from cause to effect is not derived merely from a survey of these particular objects and from such a penetration into their essences as may discover the dependence of the one upon the other. There is no object which implies the existence of any other, if we consider these objects in themselves and never look beyond the ideas which we form of them. Such an inference would amount to knowledge and would imply the absolute contradiction and impossibility of conceiving anything different. But as all distinct ideas are separable, it is evident there can be no impossibility of that kind. When we pass from a present impression to the idea of any object, we might possibly have separated the idea from the impression and have substituted any other idea in its room.

It is therefore by *experience* only that we can infer the existence of one object from that of another. The nature of experience is this. We remember to have had frequent instances of the existence of one species of objects and also remember that the individuals of another species of objects have always attended them and have existed in a regular order of contiguity and succession with regard to them. Thus, we remember to have seen that species of object we call *flame* and to have felt that species of sensation we call *heat*. We likewise call to mind their constant conjunction in all past instances. Without any further ceremony, we call the one *cause* and the other *effect* and infer the existence of the one from that of the other. In all those instances from which we learn the conjunction of particular causes and effects, both the causes and effects have been perceived by the senses and are remembered; but in all cases wherein we reason concerning them, there is only one perceived or remembered, and the other is supplied in conformity to our past experience.

Thus, in advancing, we have insensibly discovered a new relation betwixt cause and effect when we least expected it and were entirely employed upon another subject. This relation is their *constant conjunction.* Contiguity and succession are not sufficient to make us pronounce any two objects to be cause and effect, unless we perceive that these two relations are preserved in several instances. We may now see the advantage of quitting the direct survey of this relation in order to discover the nature of that *necessary connection* which makes so essential a part of it. There are hopes that by this means we may at last arrive at our proposed end; though to tell the truth, this new-discovered relation of a constant conjunction seems to advance us but very little in our way. For it implies no more than this, that like objects have always been placed in like relations of contiguity and succession; and it seems evident, at least at first sight, that by this means we can never discover any new idea and can only multiply, but not enlarge, the objects of our mind. It may be thought that what we learn not from one object we can never learn from a hundred which are all of the same kind and are perfectly resembling in every circumstance. As our senses show us in one instance two bodies, or motions, or qualities, in certain relations of succession and contiguity, so our memory presents us only with a multitude of instances wherein we always find like bodies, motions, or qualities in like relations. From the mere repetition of any past impression, even to infinity, there never will arise any new original idea, such as that of a necessary connection; and the number of impressions has in this case no more effect than if we confined ourselves to one only. But though this reasoning seems just and obvious, yet, as it would be folly to despair too soon, we shall continue the thread of our discourse; and having found that after the discovery of the constant conjunction of any objects we always draw an inference from one object to another, we shall now examine the nature of that inference and of the transition from the impression to the idea. Perhaps it will appear in the end that the necessary connection depends on the inference, instead of the inference's depending on the necessary connection.

Since it appears that the transition from an impression present to the memory or senses to the idea of an object which we call cause or effect, is founded on past *experience* and on our remembrance of their *constant conjunction,* the next question is whether experience produces the idea by means of the understanding or imagination, whether we are determined by reason to make the transition or by a certain association and relation of perceptions. If reason determined us, it would proceed upon that principle *that instances, of which we have had no experience, must resemble those of which we have had experience, and that the course of nature continues always uniformly the same.* In order, therefore, to clear up this matter, let us consider all the arguments upon which such a proposition may be supposed to be founded; and as these must be derived either from *knowledge* or *probability,* let us cast our eye on each of these degrees of evidence and see whether they afford any just conclusion of this nature.

Our foregoing method of reasoning will easily convince us that there can be no *demonstrative* arguments to prove *that those instances of which we have had no experience resemble those of which we have had experience.* We can at least conceive a change in the course of nature, which sufficiently proves that such a change is not absolutely impossible. To form a clear idea of anything is an undeniable argument for its possibility and is alone a refutation of any pretended demonstration against it.

Probability, as it discovers not the relations of ideas, considered as such, but only those of objects, must, in some respects, be founded on the impressions of our memory and senses and in some respects on our ideas. Were there no mixture of any impression in our probable reasonings, the conclusion would be entirely chimerical; and were there no mixture of ideas, the action of the mind, in observing the relation, would, properly speaking, be sensation, not reasoning. It is, therefore, necessary that in all probable reasonings there be something present to the mind, either seen or remembered, and that from this we infer something connected with it which is not seen nor remembered.

The only connection or relation of objects which can lead us beyond the immediate impressions of our memory and senses is that of cause and effect; and that because it is the only one on which we can found a just inference from one object to another. The idea of cause and effect is derived from *experience,* which informs us that such particular objects, in all past instances, have been constantly conjoined with each other; and as an object similar to one of these is supposed to be immediately present in its impression, we thence presume on the existence of one similar to its usual attendant. According to this account of things, which is, I think, in every point unquestionable, probability is founded

70

on the presumption of a resemblance betwixt those objects of which we have had experience and those of which we have had none; and, therefore, it is impossible this presumption can arise from probability. The same principle cannot be both the cause and effect of another; and this is, perhaps, the only proposition concerning that relation which is either intuitively or demonstratively certain.

Should anyone think to elude this argument and, without determining whether our reasoning on this subject be derived from demonstration or probability, pretend that all conclusions from causes and effects are built on solid reasoning, I can only desire that this reasoning may be produced in order to be exposed to our examination. It may perhaps be said that after experience of the constant conjunction of certain objects, we reason in the following manner. Such an object is always found to produce another. It is impossible it could have this effect if it was not endowed with a power of production. The power necessarily implies the effect; and therefore there is just foundation for drawing a conclusion from the existence of one object to those of its usual attendant. The past production implies a power; the power implies a new production; and the new production is what we infer from the power and the past production.

It were easy for me to show the weakness of this reasoning, were I willing to make use of those observations I have already made, that the idea of *production* is the same with that of *causation* and that no existence certainly and demonstratively implies a power in any other object, or were it proper to anticipate what I shall have occasion to remark afterwards concerning the idea we form of *power* and *efficacy*. But as such a method of proceeding may seem either to weaken my system, by resting one part of it on another, or to breed a confusion in my reasoning, I shall endeavor to maintain my present assertion without any such assistance.

It shall therefore be allowed for a moment that the production of one object by another in any one instance implies a power, and that this power is connected with its effect. But it having been already proved that the power lies not in the sensible qualities of the cause, and there being nothing but the sensible qualities present to us, I ask, why in other instances you presume that the same power still exists, merely upon the appearance of these qualities? Your appeal to past experience decides nothing in the present case, and at the utmost can only prove that the very object which produced any other was at that very instant endowed with such a power, but can never prove that the same power must continue in the same object or collection of sensible qualities, much less that a like power is always conjoined with like sensible qualities. Should it be said that we have experience, that the same power continues united with the same object, and that like objects are endowed with like powers, I would renew my question, *why from this experience we form any conclusion beyond those past instances, of which we have had experience?* If you answer this question in the same manner as the preceding, your answer gives still occasion to a new question of the same kind, even *in infinitum,* which clearly proves that the foregoing reasoning had no just foundation.

Thus, not only your reason fails us in the discovery of the *ultimate connection* of causes and effects, but even after experience has informed us of their *constant conjunction,* it is impossible for us to satisfy ourselves by our reason why we should extend that experience beyond those particular instances which have fallen under our observation. We suppose, but are never able to prove, that there must be a resemblance betwixt those objects of which we have had experience and those which lie beyond the reach of our discovery.

We have already taken notice of certain relations which make us pass from one object to another, even though there be no reason to determine us to that transition; and this we may establish for a general rule, that wherever the mind constantly and uniformly makes a transition without any reason, it is influenced by these relations. Now, this is exactly the present case. Reason can never show us the connection of one object with another, though aided by experience and the observation of their constant conjunction in all past instances. When the mind therefore passes from the idea or impression of one object to the idea or belief of another, it is not determined by reason but by certain principles which associate together the ideas of these objects and unite them in the imagination. Had ideas no more union in the fancy than objects seem to have to the understanding, we could never draw any inference from causes to effects nor repose belief in any matter of fact. The inference therefore depends solely on the union of ideas.

The principles of union among ideas I have reduced to three general ones and have asserted that the idea or impression of any object naturally introduces the idea of any other object that is resembling, contiguous to, or connected with it. These principles I allow to be neither the *infallible* nor the *sole* causes of a union among ideas. They are not the infallible causes. For one may fix his attention during some time on any one object without looking further. They are not the sole causes. For the thought has evidently a very irregular motion in running along its objects and may leap from the heavens to the earth, from one end of the creation to the other, without any certain method or order. But though I allow this weakness in these three relations, and this irregularity in the imagination, yet I assert that the only *general* principles which associate ideas are resemblance, contiguity, and causation.

There is indeed a principle of union among ideas which at first sight may be esteemed different from any of these but will be found at the bottom to depend on the same origin. When every individual of any species of objects is found by experience to be constantly united with an individual of another species, the appearance of any new individual of either species naturally conveys the thought to its usual attendant. Thus, because such a particular idea is commonly annexed to such a particular word, nothing is required but the hearing of that word to produce the correspondent idea; and it will scarce be possible for the mind, by its utmost efforts, to prevent that transition. In this case it is not absolutely necessary that upon hearing such a particular sound, we should reflect on any past experience and consider what idea has been usually connected with the sound. The imagination of itself supplies the place of this reflection and is so accustomed to pass from the word to the idea that it interposes not a moment's delay betwixt the hearing of the one and the conception of the other.

But though I acknowledge this to be a true principle of association among ideas, I assert it to be the very same with that betwixt the ideas of cause and effect and to be an essential part in all our reasonings from that relation. We have no other notion of cause and effect but that of certain objects which have been *always conjoined* together and which in all past instances have been found inseparable. We cannot penetrate into the reason of the conjunction. We only observe the thing itself and always find that from the constant conjunction the objects require a union in the imagination. When the impression of one becomes present to us, we immediately form an idea of its usual attendant; and consequently, we may establish this as one part of the definition of an opinion or belief, that it is *an idea related to or associated with a present impression.*

Thus, though causation be a *philosophical* relation, as implying contiguity, succession, and constant conjunction, yet it is only so far as it is a *natural* relation and produces a union among our ideas that we are able to reason upon it or draw any inference from it.

Section VII

OF THE NATURE OF THE IDEA
OR BELIEF

The idea of an object is an essential part of the belief of it, but not the whole. We conceive many things which we do not believe. In order, then, to discover more fully the nature of belief, or the qualities of those ideas we assent to, let us weigh the following considerations.

It is evident that all reasonings from causes or effects terminate in conclusions concerning matter of fact, that is, concerning the existence of objects or of their qualities. It is also evident that the idea of existence is nothing different from the idea of any object, and that when after the simple conception of anything we would conceive it as existent, we in reality make no addition to or alteration on our first idea. Thus, when we affirm that God is existent, we simply form the idea of such a Being as he is represented to us; nor is the existence which we attribute to him conceived by a particular idea which we join to the idea of his other qualities and can again separate and distinguish from them. But I go further; and, not content with asserting that the conception of the existence of any object is no addition to the simple conception of it, I likewise maintain that the belief of the existence joins no new ideas to those which compose the idea of the object. When I think of God, when I think of him as existent, and when I believe him to be existent, my idea of him neither increases nor diminishes. But as it is certain there is a great difference betwixt the simple conception of the existence of an object and the belief of it, and as this difference lies not in the parts or composition of the idea which we conceive, it follows that it must lie in the *manner* in which we conceive it.

Suppose a person present with me who advances propositions, to which I do not assent, *that Cæsar died in his bed, that silver is more fusible than lead, or mercury heavier than gold,* it is evident, that, notwithstanding my incredulity, I clearly understand his meaning and form all the same ideas

74

which he forms. My imagination is endowed with the same powers as his; nor is it possible for him to conceive any idea which I cannot conceive or conjoin any which I cannot conjoin. I therefore ask, wherein consists the difference betwixt believing and disbelieving any proposition? The answer is easy with regard to propositions that are proved by intuition or demonstration. In that case, the person who assents not only conceives the idea according to the proposition, but is necessarily determined to conceive them in that particular manner, either immediately or by the interposition of other ideas. Whatever is absurd is unintelligible; nor is it possible for the imagination to conceive anything contrary to a demonstration. But as, in reasoning from causation and concerning matters of fact, this absolute necessity cannot take place, and the imagination is free to conceive both sides of the question, I still ask, *wherein consists the difference betwixt incredulity and belief?* since in both cases the conception of the idea is equally possible and requisite.

It will not be a satisfactory answer to say that a person who does not assent to a proposition you advance, after having conceived the object in the same manner with you, immediately conceives it in a different manner and has different ideas of it. This answer is unsatisfactory, not because it contains any falsehood, but because it discovers not all the truth. It is confessed that in all cases wherein we dissent from any person, we conceive both sides of the question; but as we can believe only one, it evidently follows that the belief must make some difference betwixt that conception to which we assent and that from which we dissent. We may mingle, and unite, and separate, and confound, and vary our ideas in a hundred different ways; but until there appears some principle which fixes one of these different situations, we have in reality no opinion; and this principle, as it plainly makes no addition to our precedent ideas, can only change the *manner* of our conceiving them.

All the perceptions of the mind are of two kinds, viz. impressions and ideas, which differ from each other only in their different degrees of force and vivacity. Our ideas are copied from our impressions and represent them in all their parts. When you would any way vary the idea of a particular object, you can only increase or diminish its force and vivacity. If you make any other change on it, it represents a different object or impression. The case is the same as in colors. A particular shade of any color may acquire a new degree of liveliness or brightness without any other variation. But when you produce any other variation, it is no longer the same shade or color; so that as belief does nothing but vary

75

the manner in which we conceive any object, it can only bestow on our ideas an additional force and vivacity. An opinion, therefore, or belief may be most accurately defined *a lively idea related to or associated with a present impression.**

Here are the heads of those arguments which lead us to this conclusion. When we infer the existence of an object from that of others, some object must always be present either to the memory or senses in order to be the foundation of our reasoning, since the mind cannot run up with its inferences *in infinitum*. Reason can never satisfy us that the existence of any one object does ever imply that of another; so that when we pass from the impression of one to the idea or belief of another, we are not determined by reason but by custom or a principle of association. But belief is somewhat more than a simple idea. It is a particular manner of forming an idea; and as the same idea can only be varied by a variation of its degrees of forces and vivacity, it follows upon the whole that belief is a lively idea produced by a relation to a present impression, according to the foregoing definition.

* We may here take occasion to observe a very remarkable error which, being frequently inculcated in the schools, has become a kind of established maxim and is universally received by all logicians. This error consists in the vulgar division of the acts of the understanding into *conception, judgment,* and *reasoning* and in the definitions we give of them. Conception is defined to be the simple survey of one or more ideas; judgment to be the separating or uniting of different ideas; reasoning to be the separating or uniting of different ideas by the interposition of others which show the relation they bear to each other. But these distinctions and definitions are faulty in very considerable articles. For, *first*, it is far from being true that in every judgment which we form, we unite two different ideas, since in that proposition, *God is,* or indeed any other which regards existence, the idea of existence is no distinct idea which we unite with that of the object and which is capable of forming a compound idea by the union. *Secondly,* as we can thus form a proposition which contains only one idea, so we may exert our reason without employing more than two ideas and without having recourse to a third to serve as a medium betwixt them. We infer a cause immediately from its effect; and this inference is not only a true species of reasoning, but the strongest of all others, and more convincing than when we interpose another idea to connect the two extremes. What we may in general affirm concerning these three acts of the understanding is that taking them in a proper light, they all resolve themselves into the first and are nothing but particular ways of conceiving our objects. Whether we consider a single object or several; whether we dwell on these objects or run from them to others; and in whatever form or order we survey them—the act of the mind exceeds not a simple conception; and the only remarkable difference which occurs on this occasion is when we join belief to the conception and are persuaded of the truth of what we conceive. This act of the mind has never yet been explained by any philosopher; and therefore I am at liberty to propose my hypothesis concerning it, which is that it is only a strong and steady conception of any idea and such as approaches in some measure to an immediate impression.

This operation of the mind, which forms the belief of any matter of fact, seems hitherto to have been one of the greatest mysteries of philosophy, though no one has so much as suspected that there was any difficulty in explaining it. For my part, I must own that I find a considerable difficulty in the case, and that even when I think I understand the subject perfectly, I am at a loss for terms to express my meaning. I conclude, by an induction which seems to me very evident, that an opinion or belief is nothing but an idea that is different from a fiction not in the nature or the order of its parts but in the *manner* of its being conceived. But when I would explain this *manner,* I scarce find any word that fully answers the case but am obliged to have recourse to everyone's feeling in order to give him a perfect notion of this operation of the mind. An idea assented to *feels* different from a fictitious idea that the fancy alone presents to us; and this different feeling I endeavor to explain by calling it a superior *force,* or *vivacity,* or *solidity,* or *firmness,* or *steadiness.* This variety of terms, which may seem so unphilosophical, is intended only to express that act of the mind which renders realities more present to us than fictions, causes them to weigh more in the thought, and gives them a superior influence on the passions and imagination. Provided we agree about the thing, it is needless to dispute about the terms. The imagination has the command over all its ideas and can join, and mix, and vary them in all the ways possible. It may conceive objects with all the circumstances of place and time. It may set them, in a manner, before our eyes in their true colors just as they might have existed. But as it is impossible that that faculty can ever of itself reach belief, it is evident that belief consists not in the nature and order of our ideas but in the manner of their conception and in their feeling to the mind. I confess that it is impossible to explain perfectly this feeling or manner of conception. We may make use of words that express something near it. But its true and proper name is *belief,* which is a term that everyone sufficiently understands in common life. And in philosophy, we can go no further than assert that it is something *felt* by the mind which distinguishes the ideas of the judgment from the fictions of the imagination. It gives them more force and influence, makes them appear of greater importance, infixes them in the mind, and renders them the governing principles of all our actions.

This definition will also be found to be entirely conformable to everyone's feeling and experience. Nothing is more evident, than that those ideas to which we assent are more strong, firm, and vivid than the loose reveries of a castle-

77

builder. If one person sits down to read a book as a romance and another as a true history, they plainly receive the same ideas, and in the same order; nor does the incredulity of the one and the belief of the other hinder them from putting the very same sense upon their author. His words produce the same ideas in both, though his testimony has not the same influence on them. The latter has a more lively conception of all the incidents. He enters deeper into the concerns of the persons; represents to himself their actions, and characters, and friendships, and enmities; he even goes so far as to form a notion of their features, and air, and person. While the former, who gives no credit to the testimony of the author, has a more faint and languid conception of all these particulars, and, except on account of the style and ingenuity of the composition, can receive little entertainment from it.

Section VIII

OF THE CAUSES OF BELIEF

Having thus explained the nature of belief and shown that it consists in a lively idea related to a present impression, let us now proceed to examine from what principles it is derived and what bestows the vivacity on the idea.

I would willingly establish it as a general maxim in the science of human nature *that when any impression becomes present to us, it not only transports the mind to such ideas as are related to it, but likewise communicates to them a share of its force and vivacity*. All the operations of the mind depend, in a great measure, on its disposition when it performs them; and according as the spirits are more or less elevated, and the attention more or less fixed, the action will always have more or less vigor and vivacity. When, therefore, any object is presented which elevates and enlivens the thought, every action to which the mind applies itself will be more strong and vivid as long as that disposition continues. Now, it is evident the continuance of the disposition depends entirely on the objects about which the mind is employed, and that any new object naturally gives a new direction to the spirits and changes the disposition; as on the contrary, when the mind fixes constantly on the same object, or passes easily and insensibly along related objects, the disposition has a much longer duration. Hence, it happens that when the mind is once enlivened by a present impression, it proceeds to form a more lively idea of the related objects by a natural transition of the disposition from the one to the other. The change of the objects is so easy that the mind is scarce sensible of it but applies itself to the conception of the related idea with all the force and vivacity it acquired from the present impression.

If, in considering the nature of relation and that facility of transition which is essential to it, we can satisfy ourselves concerning the reality of this phenomenon, it is well; but I must confess I place my chief confidence in experience to prove so material a principle. We may therefore observe, as the first experiment to our present purpose, that upon the appearance of the picture of an absent friend, our idea of him is evidently enlivened by the *resemblance*, and that every passion which that idea occasions, whether of joy or sorrow, acquires new force and vigor. In producing this effect, there concur both a relation and a present impression. Where the picture bears him no resemblance, or at least was not intended for him, it never so much as conveys our thought to him; and where it is absent as well as the person, though the mind may pass from the thought of the one to that of the other, it feels its idea to be rather weakened than enlivened by that transition. We take a pleasure in viewing the picture of a friend when it is set before us; but when it is removed, rather choose to consider him directly than by reflection in an image, which is equally distant and obscure.

The ceremonies of the Roman Catholic religion may be considered as experiments of the same nature. The devotees of that strange superstition usually plead in excuse of the mummeries with which they are upbraided that they feel the good effect of those external motions, and postures, and actions in enlivening their devotion and quickening their fervor, which otherwise would decay away if directed entirely to distant and immaterial objects. We shadow out the objects of our faith, they say, in sensible types and images and render them more present to us by the immediate presence of these types than it is possible for us to do merely by an intellectual view and contemplation. Sensible objects have always a greater influence on the fancy than any other; and this influence they readily convey to those ideas to which they are related and which they resemble. I shall only infer from these practices, and this reasoning, that the effect of resemblance in enlivening the idea is very common; and as in every case a resemblance and a present impression must concur, we are abundantly supplied with experiments to prove the reality of the foregoing principle.

We may add force to these experiments by others of a different kind in considering the effects of *contiguity* as well as of *resemblance*. It is certain that distance diminishes the force of every idea, and that upon our approach to any object, though it does not discover itself to our senses, it operates upon the mind with an influence that imitates an immediate impression. The thinking on any object readily transports the mind to what is contiguous; but it is only the actual presence of an object that transports it with a superior vivacity. When I am a few miles from home, whatever relates to it touches me more nearly than when I am two hundred leagues distant, though even at that distance the reflecting on anything in the neighborhood of my friends and family naturally produces an idea of them. But as in this latter case both the objects of the mind are ideas, notwithstanding there is an easy transition betwixt them, that transition alone is not able to give a superior vivacity to any of the ideas for want of some immediate impression.

No one can doubt but causation has the same influence as the other two relations of resemblance and contiguity. Superstitious people are fond of the relics of saints and holy men for the same reason that they seek after types and images in order to enliven their devotion and give them a more intimate and strong conception of those exemplary lives which they desire to imitate. Now, it is evident one of the best relics a devotee could procure would be the handiwork of a saint; and if his clothes and furniture are ever to be considered in this light, it is because they were once at his disposal and were moved and affected by him, in which respect they are to be considered as imperfect effects and as connected with him by a shorter chain of consequences than any of those from which we learn the reality of his existence. This phenomenon clearly proves that a present impression with a relation of causation may enliven any idea and consequently produce belief or assent, according to the precedent definition of it.

But why need we seek for other arguments to prove that a present impression with a relation or transition of the fancy may enliven any idea, when this very instance of our reasonings from cause and effect will alone suffice to that purpose? It is certain we must have an idea of every matter of fact which we believe. It is certain that this idea arises only from a relation to a present impression. It is certain that the belief superadds nothing to the idea but only changes our manner of conceiving it and renders it more strong and lively. The present conclusion concerning the influence of relation is the immediate consequence of all these steps; and every step appears to be sure and infallible. There enters nothing into this operation of the mind but a present impression, a lively idea, and a relation of association in the fancy betwixt the impression and the idea, so that there can be no suspicion of mistake.

In order to put this whole affair in a fuller light, let us consider it as a question in natural philosophy which we must determine by experience and observation. I suppose there is an object presented, from which I draw a certain conclusion and form to myself ideas which I am said to believe or assent to. Here it is evident that however that object, which is present to my senses, and that other, whose existence I infer by reasoning, may be thought to influence each other by their particular powers or qualities, yet as the phenomenon of belief, which we at present examine, is merely internal, these powers and qualities, being entirely unknown, can have no hand in producing it. It is the present impression which is to be considered as the true and real cause of the idea and of the belief which attends it. We must therefore endeavor to discover by experiments the particular qualities by which it is enabled to produce so extraordinary an effect.

First, then, I observe that the present impression has not this effect by its own proper power and efficacy, and, when considered alone as a single perception, limited to the present moment. I find that an impression, from which, on its first appearance, I can draw no conclusion, may afterwards become the foundation of belief when I have had experience of its usual consequences. We must in every case have observed the same impression in past instances and have found it to be constantly conjoined with some other impression. This is confirmed by such a multitude of experiments that it admits not of the smallest doubt.

From a second observation, I conclude that the belief which attends the present impression, and is produced by a number of past impressions and conjunctions, that this belief, I say, arises immediately, without any new operation of the reason or imagination. Of this I can be certain, because I never am conscious of any such operation and find nothing in the subject on which it can be founded. Now, as we call everything *custom* which proceeds from a past repetition, without any new reasoning or conclusion, we may establish it as a certain truth that all the belief, which follows upon any present impression, is derived solely from that origin. When we are accustomed to see two impressions conjoined together, the appearance or idea of the one immediately carries us to the idea of the other.

81

Being fully satisfied on this head, I make a third set of experiments, in order to know whether anything be requisite, beside the customary transition, towards the production of this phenomenon of belief. I therefore change the first impression into an idea and observe that though the customary transition to the correlative idea still remains, yet there is in reality no belief nor persuasion. A present impression, then, is absolutely requisite to this whole operation; and when after this I compare an impression with an idea and find that their only difference consists in their different degrees of force and vivacity, I conclude upon the whole that belief is a more vivid and intense conception of an idea, proceeding from its relation to a present impression.

Thus, all probable reasoning is nothing but a species of sensation. It is not solely in poetry and music we must follow our taste and sentiment, but likewise in philosophy. When I am convinced of any principle, it is only an idea which strikes more strongly upon me. When I give the preference to one set of arguments above another, I do nothing but decide from my feeling concerning the superiority of their influence. Objects have no discoverable connection together; nor is it from any other principle but custom operating upon the imagination that we can draw any inference from the appearance of one of the existence of another.

It will here be worth our observation that the past experience on which all our judgments concerning cause and effect depend may operate on our mind in such an insensible manner as never to be taken notice of and may even in some measure be unknown to us. A person who stops short in his journey upon meeting a river in his way foresees the consequences of his proceeding forward; and his knowledge of these consequences is conveyed to him by past experience, which informs him of such certain conjunctions of causes and effects. But can we think that on this occasion he reflects on any past experience and calls to remembrance instances that he has seen or heard of in order to discover the effects of water on animal bodies? No, surely; this is not the method in which he proceeds in his reasoning. The idea of sinking is so closely connected with that of water, and the idea of suffocating with that of sinking, that the mind makes the transition without the assistance of the memory. The custom operates before we have time for reflection. The objects seem so inseparable that we interpose not a moment's delay in passing from the one or the other. But as this transition proceeds from experience, and not from any primary connection betwixt the ideas, we must necessarily acknowledge that experience may produce a belief and a judgment of causes and effects by a separate operation and without being once thought of. This removes all pretext, if there yet remains any, for asserting that the mind is convinced by reasoning of that principle *that instances of which we have no experience must necessarily resemble those of which we have.* For we here find that the understanding or imagination can draw inference from past experience without reflecting on it, much more without forming any principle concerning it or reasoning upon that principle.

In general, we may observe that in all the most established and uniform conjunctions of causes and effects, such as those of gravity, impulse, solidity, etc., the mind never carries its view expressly to consider any past experience, though in other associations of objects, which are more rare and unusual, it may assist the custom and transition of ideas by this reflection. Nay, we find in some cases that the reflection produces the belief without the custom, or, more properly speaking, that the reflection produces the custom in an *oblique* and *artificial* manner. I explain myself. It is certain that not only in philosophy but even in common life we may attain the knowledge of a particular cause merely by one experiment, provided it be made with judgment, and after a careful removal of all foreign and superfluous circumstances. Now, as after one experiment of this kind the mind, upon the appearance either of the cause or the effect, can draw an inference concerning the existence of its correlative, and as a habit can never be acquired merely by one instance, it may be thought that belief cannot in this case be esteemed the effect of custom. But this difficulty will vanish if we consider that though we are here supposed to have had only one experiment of a particular effect, yet we have many millions to convince us of this principle, *that like objects, placed in like circumstances, will always produce like effects;* and as this principle has established itself by a sufficient custom, it bestows an evidence and firmness on any opinion to which it can be applied. The connection of the ideas is not habitual after one experiment; but this connection is comprehended under another principle that is habitual, which brings us back to our hypothesis. In all cases, we transfer our experience to instances of which we have no experience, either *expressly* or *tacitly,* either *directly* or *indirectly.*

I must not conclude this subject without observing that it is very difficult to talk of the operations of the mind with perfect propriety and exactness, because common language has seldom made any very nice distinctions among them, but has generally called by the same term all such as nearly resemble each other. And as this is a source almost inevitable of obscurity and confusion in the author, so it may frequently give rise to doubts and objections in the reader which otherwise he would never have dreamed of. Thus, my general position, that an opinion or belief is *nothing but a strong and lively idea derived from a present impression related to it,* may be liable to the following objection by reason of a little ambiguity in those words *strong* and *lively*. It may be said that not only an impression may give rise to reasoning but that an idea may also have the same influence, especially upon my principle, *that all our ideas are derived from correspondent impressions.* For, suppose I form at present an idea, of which I have forgot the correspondent impression, I am able to conclude from this idea that such an impression did once exist; and as this conclusion is attended with belief, it may be asked, from whence are the qualities of force and vivacity derived which constitute this belief? And to this I answer very readily, *from the present idea.* For as this idea is not here considered as the representation of any absent object but as a real perception in the mind, of which we are intimately conscious, it must be able to bestow, on whatever is related to it, the same quality, call it *firmness,* or *solidity,* or *force,* or *vivacity,* with which the mind reflects upon it and is assured of its present existence. The idea here supplies the place of an impression and is entirely the same, so far as regards our present purpose.

Upon the same principles we need not be surprised to hear of the remembrance of an idea, that is, of the idea of an idea, and of its force and vivacity superior to the loose conceptions of the imagination. In thinking of our past thoughts, we not only delineate out the objects of which we were thinking but also conceive the action of the mind in the meditation, that certain *je-ne-scai-quoi,* of which it is impossible to give any definition or description, but which everyone sufficiently understands. When the memory offers an idea of this, and represents it as past, it is easily conceived how that idea may have more vigor and firmness than when we think of a past thought of which we have no remembrance.

After this, anyone will understand how we may form the idea of an impression and of an idea, and how we may believe the existence of an impression and of an idea.

Section XIV

OF THE IDEA OF NECESSARY CONNECTION

Having thus explained the manner *in which we reason beyond our immediate impressions and conclude that such particular causes must have such particular effects,* we must now return upon our footsteps to examine that question which first occurred to us and which we dropped in our way, viz. *what is our idea of necessity when we say that two objects are necessarily connected together?* Upon this head I repeat what I have often had occasion to observe, that as we have no idea that is not derived from an impression, we must find some impression that gives rise to this idea of necessity, if we assert we have really such an idea. In order to do this, I consider in what objects necessity is commonly supposed to lie; and finding that it is always ascribed to causes and effects, I turn my eye to two objects supposed to be placed in that relation and examine them in all the situations of which they are susceptible. I immediately perceive that they are *contiguous* in time and place and that the object we call cause *precedes* the other we call effect. In no one instance can I go any further, nor is it possible for me to discover any third relation betwixt these objects. I therefore enlarge my view to comprehend several instances where I find like objects always existing in like relations of contiguity and succession. At first sight, this seems to serve but little to my purpose. The reflection on several instances only repeats the same objects and therefore can never give rise to a new idea. But upon further inquiry, I find that the repetition is not in every particular the same but produces a new impression and by that means the idea which I at present examine. For after a frequent repetition, I find that upon the appearance of one of the objects the mind is *determined* by custom to consider its usual attendant, and to consider it in a stronger light upon account of its relation to the first object. It is this impression, then, or *determination,* which affords me the idea of necessity.

85

I doubt not but these consequences will at first sight be received without difficulty as being evident deductions from principles which we have already established and which we have often employed in our reasonings. This evidence, both in the first principles and in the deductions, may seduce us unwarily into the conclusion and make us imagine it contains nothing extraordinary nor worthy of our curiosity. But though such an inadvertence may facilitate the reception of this reasoning, it will make it be the more easily forgot; for which reason I think it proper to give warning that I have just now examined one of the most sublime questions in philosophy, viz. *that concerning the power and efficacy of causes* where all the sciences seem so much interested. Such a warning will naturally rouse up the attention of the reader and make him desire a more full account of my doctrine as well as of the arguments on which it is founded. This request is so reasonable that I cannot refuse complying with it, especially as I am hopeful that these principles, the more they are examined, will acquire the more force and evidence.

There is no question which, on account of its importance, as well as difficulty, has caused more disputes both among ancient and modern philosophers than this concerning the efficacy of causes, or that quality which makes them be followed by their effects. But before they entered upon these disputes, methinks it would not have been improper to have examined what idea we have of that efficacy which is the subject of the controversy. This is what I find principally wanting in their reasonings and what I shall here endeavor to supply.

I begin with observing that the terms of *efficacy, agency, power, force, energy, necessity, connection,* and *productive quality* are all nearly synonymous; and therefore it is an absurdity to employ any of them in defining the rest. By this observation we reject at once all the vulgar definitions which philosophers have given of power and efficacy and, instead of searching for the ideas in these definitions, must look for it in the impressions from which it is originally derived. If it be a compound idea, it must arise from compound impressions. If simple, from simple impressions.

I believe the most general and most popular explication of this matter is to say * that finding from experience that there are several new productions in matter, such as the motions and variations of body, and concluding that there must somewhere be a power capable of producing them, we arrive at

* See Mr. Locke: chapter of Power. (*Essay Concerning the Human Understanding. Ed.*)

last by this reasoning at the idea of power and efficacy. But to be convinced that this explication is more popular than philosophical, we need but reflect on two very obvious principles. *First,* that reason alone can never give rise to any original idea; and, *secondly,* that reason, as distinguished from experience, can never make us conclude that a cause or productive quality is absolutely requisite to every beginning of existence. Both these considerations have been sufficiently explained and therefore shall not at present be any further insisted on.

I shall only infer from them that since reason can never give rise to the idea of efficacy, that idea must be derived from experience, and from some particular instances of this efficacy which make their passage into the mind by the common channels of sensation or reflection. Ideas always represent their objects or impressions; and vice versa, there are some objects necessary to give rise to every idea. If we pretend, therefore, to have any just idea of this efficacy, we must produce some instance wherein the efficacy is plainly discoverable to the mind and its operations obvious to our consciousness or sensation. By the refusal of this, we acknowledge that the idea is impossible and imaginary, since the principle of innate ideas, which alone can save us from this dilemma, has been already refuted and is now almost universally rejected in the learned world. Our present business, then, must be to find some natural production where the operation and efficacy of a cause can be clearly conceived and comprehended by the mind, without any danger of obscurity or mistake.

In this research, we meet with very little encouragement from that prodigious diversity which is found in the opinions of those philosophers who have pretended to explain the secret force and energy of causes.* There are some who maintain that bodies operate by their substantial form; others, by their accidents or qualities; several, by their matter and form; some, by their form and accidents; others, by certain virtues and faculties distinct from all this. All these sentiments, again, are mixed and varied in a thousand different ways and form a strong presumption that none of them have any solidity or evidence and that the supposition of an efficacy in any of the known qualities of matter is entirely without foundation. This presumption must increase upon us when we consider that these principles of substantial forms, and accidents, and faculties are not in reality any of the known properties of bodies but are perfectly unintelligible and inexplicable. For

---

* See Father Malebranche, Book VI, *Part* II, Chap. 3, and the illustrations upon it. (*Recherche de la Verité.*)

it is evident philosophers would never have had recourse to such obscure and uncertain principles had they met with any satisfaction in such as are clear and intelligible, especially in such an affair as this, which must be an object of the simplest understanding, if not of the senses. Upon the whole, we may conclude that it is impossible, in any one instance, to show the principle in which the force and agency of a cause is placed, and that the most refined and most vulgar understandings are equally at a loss in this particular. If anyone think proper to refute this assertion, he need not put himself to the trouble of inventing any long reasonings but may at once show us an instance of a cause where we discover the power or operating principle. This defiance we are obliged frequently to make use of, as being almost the only means of proving a negative in philosophy.

The small success which has been met with in all the attempts to fix this power has at last obliged philosophers to conclude that the ultimate force and efficacy of nature is perfectly unknown to us and that it is in vain we search for it in all the known qualities of matter. In this opinion they are almost unanimous; and it is only in the inference they draw from it that they discover any difference in their sentiments. For some of them, as the Cartesians in particular, having established it as a principle that we are perfectly acquainted with the essence of matter, have very naturally inferred that it is endowed with no efficacy and that it is impossible for it of itself to communicate motion or produce any of those effects which we ascribe to it. As the essence of matter consists in extension, and as extension implies not actual motion but only mobility, they conclude that the energy which produces the motion cannot lie in the extension.

This conclusion leads them into another, which they regard as perfectly unavoidable. Matter, say they, is in itself entirely unactive and deprived of any power by which it may produce, or continue, or communicate motion; but since these effects are evident to our senses, and since the power that produces them must be placed somewhere, it must lie in the Deity, or that Divine Being who contains in his nature all excellency and perfection. It is the Deity, therefore, who is the prime mover of the universe and who not only first created matter and gave it its original impulse, but likewise, by a continued exertion of omnipotence, supports its existence and successively bestows on it all those motions, and configurations, and qualities with which it is endowed.

This opinion is certainly very curious and well worth our attention; but it will appear superfluous to examine it in this place, if we reflect a moment on our present purpose in taking notice of it. We have established it as a principle that as all ideas are derived from impressions, or some precedent *perceptions,* it is impossible we can have any idea of power and efficacy, unless some instances can be produced wherein this power *is perceived* to exert itself. Now, as these instances can never be discovered in body, the Cartesians, proceeding upon their principle of innate ideas, have had recourse to a Supreme Spirit or Deity, whom they consider as the only active being in the universe and as the immediate cause of every alteration in matter. But the principle of innate ideas being allowed to be false, it follows that the supposition of a Deity can serve us in no stead in accounting for that idea of agency which we search for in vain in all the objects which are presented to our senses or which we are internally conscious of in our own minds. For if every idea be derived from an impression, the idea of a Deity proceeds from the same origin; and if no impression, either of sensation or reflection, implies any force or efficacy, it is equally impossible to discover or even imagine any such active principle in the Deity. Since these philosophers, therefore, have concluded that matter cannot be endowed with any efficacious principle because it is impossible to discover in it such a principle, the same course of reasoning should determine them to exclude it from the Supreme Being. Or if they esteem that opinion absurd and impious, as it really is, I shall tell them how they may avoid it; and that is, by concluding from the very first that they have no adequate idea of power or efficacy in any object, since neither in body nor spirit, neither in superior nor inferior natures are they able to discover one single instance of it.

The same conclusion is unavoidable upon the hypothesis of those who maintain the efficacy of second causes and attribute a derivative, but a real power and energy to matter. For as they confess that this energy lies not in any of the known qualities of matter, the difficulty still remains concerning the origin of its idea. If we have really an idea of power, we may attribute power to an unknown quality; but as it is impossible that that idea can be derived from such a quality, and as there is nothing in known qualities which can produce it, it follows that we deceive ourselves when we imagine we are possessed of any idea of this kind after the manner we commonly understand it. All ideas are derived from and represent power or efficacy. We never therefore have any idea of impressions. We never have any impression that contains any power.

[Some have asserted that we feel an energy or power in our own mind, and that having in this manner acquired the idea

89

of power, we transfer that quality to matter, where we are not able immediately to discover it. The motions of our body, and the thoughts and sentiments of our mind, (say they), obey the will; nor do we seek any further to acquire a just notion of force or power. But to convince us how fallacious this reasoning is, we need only consider that the will being here considered as a cause has no more a discoverable connection with its effects than any material cause has with its proper effect. So far from perceiving the connection betwixt an act of volition and a motion of the body, it is allowed that no effect is more inexplicable from the powers and essence of thought and matter. Nor is the empire of the will over our mind more intelligible. The effect is there distinguishable and separable from the cause and could not be foreseen without the experience of their constant conjunction. We have command over our mind to a certain degree, but beyond *that* lose all empire over it; and it is evidently impossible to fix any precise bounds to our authority where we consult not experience. In short, the actions of the mind are, in this respect, the same with those of matter. We perceive only their constant conjunction; nor can we ever reason beyond it. No internal impression has an apparent energy more than external objects have. Since, therefore, matter is confessed by philosophers to operate by an unknown force, we should in vain hope to attain an idea of force by consulting our own minds.*]

It has been established as a certain principle that general or abstract ideas are nothing but individual ones taken in a certain light, and that, in reflecting on any object, it is as impossible to exclude from our thought all particular degrees of quantity and quality as from the real nature of things. If we be possessed, therefore, of any idea of power in general, we must also be able to conceive some particular species of it; and as power cannot subsist alone, but is always regarded as an attribute of some being or existence, we must be able to place this power in some particular being and conceive that being as endowed with a real force and energy by which such a particular effect necessarily results from its operation. We must distinctly and particularly conceive the connection betwixt the cause and effect and be able to pronounce, from a

---

* The same imperfection attends our ideas of the Deity; but this can have no effect either on religion or morals. The order of the universe proves an omnipotent mind; that is, a mind whose will is *constantly attended* with the obedience of every creature and being. Nothing more is requisite to give a foundation to all the articles of religion; nor is it necessary we should form a distinct idea of the force and energy of the Supreme Being.

simple view of the one, that it must be followed or preceded by the other. This is the true manner of conceiving a particular power in a particular body; and a general idea being impossible without an individual, where the latter is impossible, it is certain the former can never exist. Now, nothing is more evident than that the human mind cannot form such an idea of two objects as to conceive any connection betwixt them or comprehend distinctly that power or efficacy by which they are united. Such a connection would amount to a demonstration and would imply the absolute impossibility for the one object not to follow or to be conceived not to follow upon the other, which kind of connection has already been rejected in all cases. If anyone is of a contrary opinion and thinks he has attained a notion of power in any particular object, I desire he may point out to me that object. But till I meet with such a one, which I despair of, I cannot forbear concluding that since we can never distinctly conceive how any particular power can possibly reside in any particular object, we deceive ourselves in imagining we can form any such general idea.

Thus, upon the whole, we may infer that when we talk of any being, whether of a superior or inferior nature, as endowed with a power or force proportioned to any effect; when we speak of a necessary connection betwixt objects and suppose that this connection depends upon an efficacy or energy with which any of these objects are endowed—in all the expressions, *so applied*, we have really no distinct meaning and make use only of common words, without any clear and determinate ideas. But as it is more probable that these expressions do here lose their true meaning by being *wrong applied* than that they never have any meaning, it will be proper to bestow another consideration on this subject to see if possibly we can discover the nature and origin of those ideas we annex to them.

Suppose two objects to be presented to us, of which the one is the cause and the other the effect, it is plain that from the simple consideration of one or both these objects, we never shall perceive the tie by which they are united or be able certainly to pronounce that there is a connection betwixt them. It is not, therefore, from any one instance, that we arrive at the idea of cause and effect, of a necessary connection of power, of force, of energy, and of efficacy. Did we never see any but particular conjunctions of objects, entirely different from each other, we should never be able to form any such ideas.

But, again, suppose we observe several instances in which the same objects are always conjoined together, we immediately conceive a connection betwixt them and begin to draw

91

an inference from one to another. This multiplicity of resembling instances, therefore, constitutes the very essence of power or connection and is the source from which the idea of it arises. In order, then, to understand the idea of power, we must consider that multiplicity; nor do I ask more to give a solution of that difficulty which has so long perplexed us. For thus I reason. The repetition of perfectly similar instances can never *alone* give rise to an original idea, different from what is to be found in any particular instance as has been observed and as evidently follows from our fundamental principle *that all ideas are copied from impressions*. Since therefore the idea of power is a new original idea, not to be found in any one instance, and which yet arises from the repetition of several instances, it follows that the repetition *alone* has not that effect but must either *discover* or *produce* something new which is the source of that idea. Did the repetition neither discover nor produce anything new, our ideas might be multiplied by it but would not be enlarged above what they are upon the observation of one single instance. Every enlargement, therefore (such as the idea of power or connection), which arises from the multiplicity of similar instances is copied from some effects of the multiplicity and will be perfectly understood by understanding these effects. Wherever we find anything new to be discovered or produced by the repetition, there we must place the power and must never look for it in any other object.

But it is evident, in the first place, that the repetition of like objects in like relations of succession and contiguity, *discovers* nothing new in any one of them, since we can draw no inference from it nor make it a subject either of our demonstrative or probable reasonings, as has been already proved. Nay, suppose we could draw an inference, it would be of no consequence in the present case, since no kind of reasoning can give rise to a new idea, such as this of power is; but wherever we reason, we must antecedently be possessed of clear ideas which may be the objects of our reasoning. The conception always precedes the understanding; and where the one is obscure, the other is uncertain; where the one fails, the other must fail also.

Secondly, it is certain that this repetition of similar objects in similar situations *produces* nothing new, either in these objects or in any external body. For it will readily be allowed that the several instances we have of the conjunction of resembling causes and effects are in themselves entirely independent, and that the communication of motion, which I see result at present from the shock of two billiard balls, is totally distinct from that which I saw result from such an impulse a twelvemonth ago. These impulses have no influence on each other. They are entirely divided by time and place; and the one might have existed and communicated motion, though the other never had been in being.

There is, then, nothing new, either discovered or produced, in any objects by their constant conjunction and by the uninterrupted resemblance of their relations of succession and contiguity. But it is from this resemblance that the ideas of necessity, of power, and of efficacy are derived. These ideas, therefore, represent not anything that does or can belong to the objects which are constantly conjoined. This is an argument which, in every view we can examine it, will be found perfectly unanswerable. Similar instances are still the first source of our idea of power or necessity, at the same time that they have no influence by their similarity, either on each other or on any external object. We must, therefore, turn ourselves to some other quarter to seek the origin of that idea.

Though the several resembling instances which give rise to the idea of power have no influence on each other and can never produce any new quality *in the object* which can be the model of that idea, yet the *observation* of this resemblance produces a new impression *in the mind*, which is its real model. For after we have observed the resemblance in a sufficient number of instances, we immediately feel a determination of the mind to pass from one object to its usual attendant and to conceive it in a stronger light upon account of that relation. This determination is the only effect of the resemblance and therefore must be the same with power or efficacy, whose idea is derived from the resemblance. The several instances of resembling conjunctions lead us into the notion of power and necessity. These instances are in themselves totally distinct from each other and have no union but in the mind, which observes them and collects their ideas. Necessity then is the effect of this observation and is nothing but an internal impression of the mind or a determination to carry our thoughts from one object to another. Without considering it in this view, we can never arrive at the most distant notion of it or be able to attribute it either to external or internal objects, to spirit or body, to causes or effects.

The necessary connection betwixt causes and effects is the foundation of our inference from one to the other. The foundation of our inference is the transition arising from the accustomed union. These are, therefore, the same.

The idea of necessity arises from some impression. There is no impression conveyed by our senses which can give rise to that idea. It must, therefore, be derived from some internal impression or impression of reflection. There is no internal impression which has any relation to the present business but that propensity, which custom produces, to pass from an object to the idea of its usual attendant. This, therefore, is the essence of necessity. Upon the whole, necessity is something that exists in the mind, not in objects; nor is it possible for us ever to form the most distant idea of it considered as a quality in bodies. Either we have no idea of necessity, or necessity is nothing but that determination of the thought to pass from causes to effects, and from effects to causes, according to their experienced union.

Thus, as the necessity which makes two times two equal to four, or three angles of a triangle equal to two right ones, lies only in the act of the understanding by which we consider and compare these ideas, in like manner the necessity of power, which unites causes and effects, lies in the determination of the mind to pass from the one to the other. The efficacy or energy of causes is neither placed in the causes themselves, nor in the Deity, nor in the concurrence of these two principles, but belongs entirely to the soul, which considers the union of two or more objects in all past instances. It is here that the real power of causes is placed, along with their connection and necessity.

I am sensible that of all the paradoxes which I have had, or shall hereafter have occasion to advance in the course of this Treatise, the present one is the most violent, and that it is merely by dint of solid proof and reasoning I can ever hope it will have admission and overcome the inveterate prejudices of mankind. Before we are reconciled to this doctrine, how often must we repeat to ourselves *that* the simple view of any two objects or actions, however related, can never give us any idea of power or of a connection betwixt them; *that* this idea arises from the repetition of their union; *that* the repetition neither discovers nor causes anything in the objects, but has an influence only on the mind by that customary transition it produces; *that* this customary transition is therefore the same with the power and necessity, which are consequently qualities of power and necessity, which are consequently qualities of perceptions, not of objects, and are internally felt by the soul, and not perceived externally in bodies? There is commonly an astonishment attending everything extraordinary; and this astonishment changes immediately into the highest degree of esteem or contempt, according as we approve or disapprove of the subject. I am much afraid that though the foregoing reasoning appears to me the shortest and most decisive imaginable, yet, with the generality of readers, the bias of the mind will prevail and give them a prejudice against the present doctrine.

This contrary bias is easily accounted for. It is a common observation that the mind has a great propensity to spread itself on external objects and to conjoin with them any internal impressions which they occasion and which always make their appearance at the same time that these objects discover themselves to the senses. Thus, as certain sounds and smells are always found to attend certain visible objects, we naturally imagine a conjunction, even in place, betwixt the objects and qualities, though the qualities be of such a nature as to admit of no such conjunction and really exist nowhere. But of this more fully hereafter. Meanwhile, it is sufficient to observe that the same propensity is the reason why we suppose necessity and power to lie in the objects we consider, not in our mind that considers them, notwithstanding it is not possible for us to form the most distant idea of that quality when it is not taken for the determination of the mind, to pass from the idea of an object to that of its usual attendant.

But though this be the only reasonable account we can give of necessity, the contrary notion is so riveted in the mind from the principles above mentioned that I doubt not but my sentiments will be treated by many as extravagant and ridiculous. What! the efficacy of causes lie in the determination of the mind! As if causes did not operate entirely independent of the mind and would not continue their operation, even though there was no mind existent to contemplate them or reason concerning them. Thought may well depend on causes for its operation, but not causes on thought. This is to reverse the order of nature and make that secondary which is really primary. To every operation there is a power proportioned; and this power must be placed on the body that operates. If we remove the power from one cause, we must ascribe it to another; but to remove it from all causes and bestow it on a being that is noways related to the cause or effect but by perceiving them is a gross absurdity and contrary to the most certain principles of human reason.

I can only reply to all these arguments that the case is here much the same as if a blind man should pretend to find a great many absurdities in the supposition that the color of scarlet is not the same with the sound of a trumpet, nor light the same with solidity. If we have really no idea of a power or efficacy in any object, or of any real connection betwixt causes and effects, it will be to little purpose to prove that an efficacy is necessary in all operations. We do not understand our own meaning in talking so but ignorantly confound ideas which are entirely distinct from each other. I am, indeed,

95

ready to allow that there may be several qualities, both in material and immaterial objects, with which we are utterly unacquainted; and if we please to call these *power* or *efficacy*, it will be of little consequence to the world. But when, instead of meaning these unknown qualities, we make the terms of power and efficacy signify something of which we have a clear idea, and which is incompatible with those objects to which we apply it, obscurity and error begin then to take place, and we are led astray by a false philosophy. This is the case when we transfer the determination of the thought to external objects and suppose any real intelligible connection betwixt them—that being a quality which can only belong to the mind that considers them.

As to what may be said, that the operations of nature are independent of our thought and reasoning, I allow it and accordingly have observed that objects bear to each other the relations of contiguity and succession; that like objects may be observed, in several instances, to have like relations; and that all this is independent of, and antecedent to, the operations of the understanding. But if we go any further and ascribe a power or necessary connection to these objects, this is what we can never observe in them, but must draw the idea of it from what we feel internally in contemplating them. And this I carry so far that I am ready to convert my present reasoning into an instance of it, by subtlety which it will not be difficult to comprehend.

When any object is presented to us, it immediately conveys to the mind a lively idea of that object which is usually found to attend it; and this determination of the mind forms the necessary connection of these objects. But when we change the point of view from the objects to the perceptions, in that case the impression is to be considered as the cause and the lively idea as the effect; and their necessary connection is that new determination which we feel to pass from the idea of the one to that of the other. The uniting principle among our internal perceptions is as unintelligible as that among external objects and is not known to us any other way than by experience. Now, the nature and effects of experience have been already sufficiently examined and explained. It never gives us any insight into the internal structure or operating principle of objects but only accustoms the mind to pass from one to another.

It is now time to collect all the different parts of this reasoning and, by joining them together, form an exact definition of the relation of cause and effect, which makes the subject of the present inquiry. This order would not have been excusable, of first examining our inference from the relation before we had explained the relation itself, had it been possible to proceed in a different method. But as the nature of the relation depends so much on that of the inference, we have been obliged to advance in this seemingly preposterous manner and make use of terms before we were able exactly to define them or fix their meaning. We shall now correct this fault by giving a precise definition of cause and effect.

There may two definitions be given of this relation, which are only different by their presenting a different view of the same object and making us consider it either as a *philosophical* or as a *natural* relation, either as a comparison of two ideas or as an association betwixt them. We may define a *cause* to be "An object precedent and contiguous to another and where all the objects resembling the former are placed in like relations of precedency and contiguity to those objects that resemble the latter." If this definition be esteemed defective, because drawn from objects foreign to the cause, we may substitute this other definition in its place, viz. "A *cause* is an object precedent and contiguous to another and so united with it that the idea of the one determines the mind to form the idea of the other and the impression of the one to form a more lively idea of the other." Should this definition also be rejected for the same reason, I know no other remedy than that the persons who express this delicacy should substitute a juster definition in its place. But, for my part, I must own my incapacity for such an undertaking. When I examine with the utmost accuracy those objects which are commonly denominated causes and effects, I find, in considering a single instance, that the one object is precedent and contiguous to the other; and in enlarging my view to consider several instances, I find only that like objects are constantly placed in like relations of succession and contiguity. Again, when I consider the influence of this constant conjunction, I perceive that such a relation can never be an object of reasoning and can never operate upon the mind but by means of custom, which determines the imagination to make a transition from the idea of one object to that of its usual attendant and from the impression of one to a more lively idea of the other. However extraordinary these sentiments may appear, I think it fruitless to trouble myself with any further inquiry or reasoning upon the subject, but shall repose myself on them as on established maxims.

It will only be proper, before we leave this subject, to draw some corollaries from it, by which we may remove several prejudices and popular errors that have very much prevailed in philosophy. First, we may learn from the foregoing doctrine that all causes are of the same kind, and that in particular there is no foundation for that distinction which we sometimes make betwixt efficient causes and causes *sine qua non*, or betwixt efficient causes and formal, and material, and exemplary, and final causes. For as our idea of efficiency is derived from the constant conjunction of two objects, wherever this is observed, the cause is efficient; and where it is not, there can never be a cause of any kind. For the same reason, we must reject the distinction betwixt *cause* and *occasion*, when supposed to signify anything essentially different from each other. If constant conjunction be implied in what we call occasion, it is a real cause; if not, it is no relation at all and cannot give rise to any argument or reasoning.

Secondly, the same course of reasoning will make us conclude that there is but one kind of *necessity*, as there is but one kind of cause, and that the common distinction betwixt *moral* and *physical* necessity is without any foundation in nature. This clearly appears from the precedent explication of necessity. It is the constant conjunction of objects along with the determination of the mind which constitutes a physical necessity; and the removal of these is the same thing with *chance*. As objects must either be conjoined or not, and as the mind must either be determined or not to pass from one object to another, it is impossible to admit of any medium betwixt chance and an absolute necessity. In weakening this conjunction and determination you do not change the nature of the necessity, since even in the operation of bodies these have different degrees of constancy and force, without producing a different species of that relation.

The distinction which we often make betwixt *power* and the *exercise* of it is equally without foundation.

Thirdly, we may now be able fully to overcome all that repugnance, which it is so natural for us to entertain against the foregoing reasoning, by which we endeavored to prove that the necessity of a cause to every beginning of existence is not founded on any arguments, either demonstrative or intuitive. Such an opinion will not appear strange after the foregoing definitions. If we define a cause to be *an object precedent and contiguous to another and where all the objects resembling the former are placed in a like relation of priority and contiguity to those objects that resemble the latter,* we may easily conceive that there is no absolute nor metaphysical necessity that every beginning of existence should be attended with such an object. If we define a cause to be *an object precedent and contiguous to another and so united with it in the imagination, that the idea of the one determines the mind to form the idea of the other and the impression of the one to form a more lively idea of the other,* we shall make still less difficulty of assenting to this opinion. Such an influence on the mind is in itself perfectly extraordinary and incomprehensible; nor can we be certain of its reality but from experience and observation.

I shall add as a fourth corollary that we can never have reason to believe that any object exists of which we cannot form an idea. For as all our reasonings concerning existence are derived from causation, and as all our reasonings concerning causation are derived from the experienced conjunction of objects, not from any reasoning or reflection, the same experience must give us a notion of these objects and must remove all mystery from our conclusions. This is so evident that it would scarce have merited our attention were it not to obviate certain objections of this kind which might arise against the following reasonings concerning *matter* and *substance*. I need not observe that a full knowledge of the object is not requisite, but only of those qualities of it which we believe to exist.

Part IV

OF THE SKEPTICAL AND OTHER SYSTEMS OF PHILOSOPHY

Section I

OF SKEPTICISM WITH REGARD TO REASON

In all demonstrative sciences, the rules are certain and infallible; but when we apply them, our fallible and uncertain faculties are very apt to depart from them and fall into error. We must, therefore, in every reasoning form a new judgment as a check or control on our first judgment or belief and must enlarge our view to comprehend a kind of history of all the instances wherein our understanding has deceived us, compared with those wherein its testimony was just and true. Our reason must be considered as a kind of cause, of which truth is the natural effect; but such a one as, by the irruption of other causes, and by the inconstancy of our mental powers, may frequently be prevented. By this means, all knowledge degenerates into probability; and this probability is greater or less, according to our experience of the veracity or deceitfulness of our understanding and according to the simplicity or intricacy of the question.

There is no algebraist nor mathematician so expert in his science as to place entire confidence in any truth immediately upon his discovery of it or regard it as anything but a mere probability. Every time he runs over his proofs, his confidence increases; but still more by the approbation of his friends; and is raised to its utmost perfection by the universal assent and applauses of the learned world. Now, it is evident that this gradual increase of assurance is nothing but the addition of new probabilities and is derived from the constant union of causes and effects, according to past experience and observation.

In accounts of any length or importance, merchants seldom trust to the infallible certainty of numbers for their security but, by the artificial structure of the accounts, produce a probability beyond what is derived from the skill and experience of the accountant. For that is plainly of itself some degree of probability, though uncertain and variable, according to the degrees of his experience and length of the account. Now, as none will maintain that our assurance in a long numeration exceeds probability, I may safely affirm that there scarce is any proposition concerning numbers of which we can have a fuller security. For it is easily possible, by gradually diminishing the numbers, to reduce the longest series of addition to the most simple question which can be formed, to an addition of two single numbers; and upon this supposition, we shall find it impracticable to show the precise limits of knowledge and of probability or discover that particular number at which the one ends and the other begins. But knowledge and probability are of such contrary and disagreeing natures that they cannot well run insensibly into each other, and that because they will not divide but must be either entirely present or entirely absent. Besides, if any single addition were certain, every one would be so, and consequently the whole or total sum, unless the whole can be different from all its parts. I had almost said that this was certain; but I reflect that it must reduce *itself*, as well as every other reasoning, and from knowledge degenerate into probability.

Since, therefore, all knowledge resolves itself into probability and becomes at last of the same nature with that evidence which we employ in common life, we must now examine this latter species of reasoning and see on what foundation it stands.

In every judgment which we can form concerning probability, as well as concerning knowledge, we ought always to correct the first judgment, derived from the nature of the object, by another judgment, derived from the nature of the understanding. It is certain a man of solid sense and long experience ought to have, and usually has, a greater assurance in his opinions than one that is foolish and ignorant, and that our sentiments have different degrees of authority, even with ourselves, in proportion to the degrees of our reason and experience. In the man of the best sense and longest experience, this authority is never entire, since even such a one must be conscious of many errors in the past and must still dread the like for the future. Here then arises a new species of probability to correct and regulate the first and fix its just standard and proportion. As demonstration is subject to the control of probability, so is probability liable to a new correction by a reflex act of the mind, wherein the nature of our understanding and our reasoning from the first probability become our objects.

Having thus found in every probability, beside the original uncertainty inherent in the subject, a new uncertainty, derived from the weakness of that faculty which judges, and having adjusted these two together, we are obliged by our reason to add a new doubt, derived from the possibility of error in the estimation we make of the truth and fidelity of our faculties. This is a doubt which immediately occurs to us and of which, if we would closely pursue our reason, we cannot avoid giving a decision. But this decision, though it should be favorable to our preceding judgment, being founded only on probability, must weaken still further our first evidence and must itself be weakened by a fourth doubt of the same kind, and so on *in infinitum*, till at last there remain nothing of the original probability, however great we may suppose it to have been, and however small the diminution by every new uncertainty. No finite object can subsist under a decrease repeated *in infinitum;* and even the vastest quantity which can enter into human imagination must in this manner be reduced to nothing. Let our first belief be never so strong, it must infallibly perish by passing through so many new examinations, of which each diminishes somewhat of its force and vigor. When I reflect on the natural fallibility of my judgment, I have less confidence in my opinions than when I only consider the objects concerning which I reason; and when I proceed still further to turn the scrutiny against every successive estimation I make of my faculties, all the rules of logic require a continual diminution and at last a total extinction of belief and evidence.

Should it here be asked me whether I sincerely assent to this argument, which I seem to take such pains to inculcate, and whether I be really one of those skeptics who hold that all is uncertain and that our judgment is not in *any* thing possessed of *any* measures of truth and falsehood, I should reply that this question is entirely superfluous and that neither I, nor any other person, was ever sincerely and constantly of that opinion. Nature, by an absolute and uncontrollable necessity, has determined us to judge as well as to breathe and feel; nor can we anymore forbear viewing certain objects in a stronger and fuller light, upon account of their customary connection with a present impression, than we can hinder ourselves from thinking as long as we are awake or seeing the surrounding bodies when we turn our eyes toward them in broad sunshine. Whoever has taken the pains to refute the cavils of this *total* skepticism has really disputed without an antagonist and endeavored by arguments to establish a faculty which nature has antecedently implanted in the mind and rendered unavoidable.

My intention, then, in displaying so carefully the arguments of that fantastic sect is only to make the reader sensible of the truth of my hypothesis, *that all our reasonings concerning causes and effects are derived from nothing but custom, and that belief is more properly an act of the sensitive than of the cogitative part of our natures.* I have here proved that the very same principles which make us form a decision upon any subject and correct that decision by the consideration of our genius and capacity and of the situation of our mind when we examined that subject, I say, I have proved that these same principles, when carried further and applied to every new reflex judgment, must, by continually diminishing the original evidence, at last reduce it to nothing and utterly subvert all belief and opinion. If belief, therefore, were a simple act of the thought, without any peculiar manner of conception, or the addition of a force and vivacity, it must infallibly destroy itself and in every case terminate in a total suspense of judgment. But as experience will sufficiently convince anyone who thinks it worth while to try that though he can find no error in the foregoing arguments, yet he still continues to believe, and think, and reason as usual, he may safely conclude that his reasoning and belief is some sensation or peculiar manner of conception which it is impossible for mere ideas and reflections to destroy.

But here, perhaps, it may be demanded, how it happens, even upon my hypothesis, that these arguments above explained produce not a total suspense of judgment, and after what manner the mind ever retains a degree of assurance in any subject? For as these new probabilities, which by their repetition perpetually diminish the original evidence, are founded on the very same principles, whether of thought or sensation, as the primary judgment, it may seem unavoidable that in either case they must equally subvert it and by the opposition, either of contrary thoughts or sensations, reduce the mind to a total uncertainty. I suppose there is some question proposed to me, and that after revolving over the impressions of my memory and senses, and carrying my thoughts from them to such objects as are commonly conjoined with them, I feel a stronger and more forcible conception on the one side than on the other. This strong conception forms my first decision. I suppose that afterwards I examine my judgment itself, and observing from experience that it is sometimes just and sometimes erroneous, I consider it as regulated by contrary principles or causes, of which some lead to truth and some to error: and in balancing these contrary causes, I diminish by a new probability the assurance of my first decision. This new probability is liable to the same diminution as the foregoing, and so on, *in infinitum*. It is therefore demanded, *how it happens that even after all, we retain a degree of belief which is sufficient for our purpose, either in philosophy or common life?*

I answer that after the first and second decision, as the action of the mind becomes forced and unnatural, and the ideas faint and obscure, though the principles of judgment and the balancing of opposite causes be the same as at the very beginning, yet their influence on the imagination, and the vigor they add to or diminish from the thought, is by no means equal. Where the mind reaches not its objects with easiness and facility, the same principles have not the same effect as in a more natural conception of the ideas: nor does the imagination feel a sensation which holds any proportion with that which arises from its common judgments and opinions. The attention is on the stretch: the posture of the mind is uneasy; and the spirits being diverted from their natural course are not governed in their movements by the same laws, at least not to the same degree, as when they flow in their usual channel.

If we desire similar instances, it will not be very difficult to find them. The present subject of metaphysics will supply us abundantly. The same argument, which would have been esteemed convincing in a reasoning concerning history or politics, has little or no influence in these abstruser subjects, even though it be perfectly comprehended, and that because there is required a study and an effort of thought in order to its being comprehended; and this effort of thought disturbs the operation of our sentiments, on which the belief depends. The case is the same in other subjects. The straining of the imagination always hinders the regular flowing of the passions and sentiments. A tragic poet that would represent his heroes as very ingenious and witty in their misfortunes would never touch the passions. As the emotions of the soul prevent any subtle reasoning and reflection, so these latter actions of the mind are equally prejudicial to the former. The mind, as well as the body, seems to be endowed with a certain precise degree of force and activity which it never employs in one action, but at the expense of all the rest. This is more evidently true where the actions are of quite different natures, since in that case the force of the mind is not only diverted but even the disposition changed, so as to render us incapable of a sudden transition from one action to the other, and still more of performing both at once. No wonder, then, the conviction which arises from a subtle reasoning diminishes in proportion to the efforts which the imagination makes to enter into the reasoning and to conceive it in all its parts. Belief, being a lively conception, can never be entire where it is not founded on something natural and easy.

This I take to be the true state of the question and cannot approve of that expeditious way which some take with the skeptics to reject at once all their arguments without inquiry or examination. If the skeptical reasonings be strong, say they, it is a proof that reason may have some force and authority; if weak, they can never be sufficient to invalidate all the conclusions of our understanding. This argument is not just, because the skeptical reasonings, were it possible for them to exist, and were they not destroyed by their subtlety, would be successively both strong and weak, according to the successive dispositions of the mind. Reason first appears in possession of the throne, prescribing laws and imposing maxims with an absolute sway and authority. Her enemy, therefore, is obliged to take shelter under her protection, and by making use of rational arguments to prove the fallaciousness and imbecility of reason, produces, in a manner, a patent under her hand and seal. This patent has at first an authority, proportioned to the present and immediate authority of reason, from which it is derived. But as it is supposed to be contradictory to reason, it gradually diminishes the force of that governing power and its own at the same time, till at last they both vanish away into nothing by a regular and just diminution. The skeptical and dogmatical reasons are of the same kind, though contrary in their operation and tendency, so that where the latter is strong, it has an enemy of equal force in the former to encounter; and as their forces were at first equal, they still continue so, as long as either of them subsists; nor does one of them lose any force in the contest without taking as much from its antagonist. It is happy, therefore, that nature breaks the force of all skeptical arguments in time and keeps them from having any considerable influence on the understanding. Were we to trust entirely to their self-destruction, that can never take place until they have first subverted all conviction and have totally destroyed human reason.

Section II

OF SKEPTICISM WITH REGARD
TO THE SENSES

Thus, the skeptic still continues to reason and believe, even though he asserts that he cannot defend his reason by reason; and by the same rule, he must assent to the principle concerning the existence of body, though he cannot pretend, by any arguments of philosophy, to maintain its veracity. Nature has not left this to his choice and has doubtless esteemed it an affair of too great importance to be trusted to our uncertain reasonings and speculations. We may well ask, *what causes induce us to believe in the existence of body?* but it is in vain to ask, *whether there be body or not?* That is a point which we must take for granted in all our reasonings.

The subject, then, of our present inquiry is concerning the *causes* which induce us to believe in the existence of body; and my reasonings on this head I shall begin with a distinction which at first sight may seem superfluous but which will contribute very much to the perfect understanding of what follows. We ought to examine apart those two questions which are commonly confounded together, viz. why we attribute a *continued* existence to objects, even when they are not present to the senses, and why we suppose them to have an existence *distinct* from the mind and perception? Under this last head, I comprehend their situation as well as relations, their *external* position as well as the *independence* of their existence and operation. These two questions concerning the continued and distinct existence of body are intimately connected together. For if the objects of our senses continue to exist, even when they are not perceived, their existence is of course independent of and distinct from the perception; and vice versa, if their existence be independent of the perception and distinct from it, they must continue to exist, even though they be not perceived. But though the decision of the one question decides the other, yet that we may the more easily discover the principles of human nature, from whence the decision arises, we shall carry along with us this distinction and shall consider whether it be the *senses, reason,* or the *imagination* that produces the opinion of a *continued* or of a *distinct* existence. These are the only questions that are intelligible on the present subject. For as to the notion of external existence when taken for something specifically different from our perceptions, we have already shown its absurdity.

To begin with the *senses,* it is evident these faculties are incapable of giving rise to the notion of the *continued* existence of their objects after they no longer appear to the senses. For that is a contradiction in terms and supposes that the senses continue to operate even after they have ceased all manner of operation. These faculties, therefore, if they have any influence in the present case, must produce the opinion of a distinct, not of a continued existence, and in order to that, must present their impressions either as images and representations or as these very distinct and external existences.

That our senses offer not their impressions as the images of something *distinct,* or *independent,* and *external* is evident, because they convey to us nothing but a single perception and never give us the least intimation of anything beyond. A single perception can never produce the idea of a double existence but by some inference either of the reason or imagination. When the mind looks further than what immediately appears to it, its conclusions can never be put to the account of the senses; and it certainly looks further when from a single perception it infers a double existence and supposes the relations of resemblance and causation betwixt them.

If our senses, therefore, suggest any idea of distinct existences, they must convey the impressions as those very existences by a kind of fallacy and illusion. Upon this head we may observe that all sensations are felt by the mind such as they really are and that when we doubt whether they present themselves as distinct objects or as mere impressions, the difficulty is not concerning their nature but concerning their relations and situation. Now, if the senses presented our impressions as external to and independent of ourselves, both the objects and ourselves must be obvious to our senses, otherwise they could not be compared by these faculties. The difficulty, then, is, how far we are *ourselves* the objects of our senses.

It is certain there is no question in philosophy more abstruse than that concerning identity and the nature of the uniting principle which constitutes a person. So far from being able by our senses merely to determine this question, we must have recourse to the most profound metaphysics to give a satisfactory answer to it; and in common life, it is evident these ideas of self and person are never very fixed nor determinate. It is absurd therefore to imagine the senses can ever distinguish betwixt ourselves and external objects.

Add to this that every impression, external and internal, passions, affections, sensations, pains, and pleasures are originally on the same footing, and that whatever other differences we may observe among them, they appear, all of them, in their true colors, as impressions or perceptions. And indeed, if we consider the matter aright, it is scarce possible it should be otherwise; nor is it conceivable that our senses should be more capable of deceiving us in the situation and relations than in the nature of our impressions. For since all actions and sensations of the mind are known to us by consciousness, they must necessarily appear in every particular what they are and be what they appear. Everything that enters the mind, being in *reality* as the perception, it is impossible anything should to *feeling* appear different. This were to suppose that even where we are most intimately conscious we might be mistaken.

But not to lose time in examining whether it is possible for our senses to deceive us and represent our perceptions as distinct from ourselves, that is, as *external* to and *independent* of us, let us consider whether they really do so and whether this error proceeds from an immediate sensation or from some other causes.

To begin with the question concerning *external* existence, it may perhaps be said that setting aside the metaphysical question of the identity of a thinking substance, our own body evidently belongs to us; and as several impressions appear exterior to the body, we suppose them also exterior to ourselves. The paper on which I write at present is beyond my hand. The table is beyond the paper. The walls of the chamber beyond the table. And in casting my eye toward the window, I perceive a great extent of fields and buildings beyond my chamber. From all this it may be inferred that no other faculty is required, beside the senses, to convince us of the external existence of body. But to prevent this inference, we need only weigh the three following considerations. *First,* that, properly speaking, it is *not* our body we perceive when we regard our limbs and members but certain impressions which enter by the senses, so that the ascribing a real and corporeal existence to these impressions, or to their objects, is an act of the mind as difficult to explain as that which we examine at present. *Secondly,* sounds, and tastes, and smells, though commonly regarded by the mind as continued independent qualities, appear not to have any existence in extension and consequently cannot appear to the senses as situated externally to the body. The reason why we ascribe a place to them shall be considered afterwards. *Thirdly,* even our sight informs us not of distances or outness (so to speak) immediately and without a certain reasoning and experience, as is acknowledged by the most rational philosophers.

As to the *independency* of our perceptions on ourselves, this can never be an object of the senses; but any opinion we form concerning it must be derived from experience and observation; and we shall see afterwards that our conclusions from experience are far from being favorable to the doctrine of the independency of our perceptions. Meanwhile, we may observe that when we talk of real distinct existences, we have commonly more in our eye their independency than external situation in place and think an object has a sufficient reality when its being is uninterrupted and independent of the incessant revolutions which we are conscious of in ourselves.

Thus, to resume what I have said concerning the senses, they give us no notion of continued existence, because they cannot operate beyond the extent in which they really operate. They as little produce the opinion of a distinct existence, because they neither can offer it to the mind as represented nor as original. To offer it as represented, they must present both an object and an image. To make it appear as original, they must convey a falsehood; and this falsehood must lie in the relations and situation; in order to which, they must be able to compare the object with ourselves; and even in that case they do not, nor is it possible they should deceive us. We may therefore conclude with certainty that the opinion of a continued and of a distinct existence never arises from the senses.

To confirm this, we may observe that there are three different kinds of impressions conveyed by the senses. The first are those of the figure, bulk, motion, and solidity of bodies. The second, those of colors, tastes, smells, sounds, heat, and cold. The third are the pains and pleasures that arise from the application of objects to our bodies, as by the cutting of our flesh with steel and such like. Both philosophers and the vulgar suppose the first of these to have a distinct continued existence. The vulgar only regard the second as on the same footing. Both philosophers and the vulgar, again, esteem the third to be merely perceptions and consequently interrupted and dependent beings.

Now, it is evident that whatever may be our philosophical opinion, color, sounds, heat, and cold, as far as appears to the senses exist after the same manner with motion and solidity, and that the difference we make betwixt them, in this respect, arises not from the mere perception. So strong is the prejudice for the distinct continued existence of the former qualities that when the contrary opinion is advanced by modern philosophers, people imagine they can almost refute it from their feeling and experience and that their very senses contradict this philosophy. It is also evident that colors, sounds, etc., are originally on the same footing with the pain that arises from steel and pleasure that proceeds from a fire, and that the difference betwixt them is founded neither on perception nor reason but on the imagination. For as they are confessed to be, both of them, nothing but perceptions arising from the particular configurations and motions of the parts of body, wherein possibly can their difference consist? Upon the whole, then, we may conclude that as far as the senses are judges, all perceptions are the same in the manner of their existence.

We may also observe, in this instance of sounds and colors, that we can contribute a distinct continued existence to objects without ever consulting *reason* or weighing our opinions by any philosophical principles. And, indeed, whatever convincing arguments philosophers may fancy they can produce to establish the belief of objects independent of the mind, it is obvious these arguments are known but to very few and that it is not by them that children, peasants, and the greatest part of mankind are induced to attribute objects to some impressions and deny them to others. Accordingly, we find that all the conclusions which the vulgar form on this head are directly contrary to those which are confirmed by philosophy. For philosophy informs us that everything which appears to the mind is nothing but a perception and is interrupted and dependent on the mind; whereas the vulgar confound perceptions and objects and attribute a distinct continued existence to the very things they feel or see. This sentiment, then, as it is entirely unreasonable, must proceed from some other faculty than the understanding. To which we may add that as long as we take our perceptions and objects to be the same, we can never infer the existence of the one from that of the other nor form any argument from the relation of cause and effect, which is the only one that can assure us of matter of fact. Even after we distinguish our perceptions from our objects, it will appear presently that we are still incapable of reasoning from the existence of one to that of the other; so that, upon the whole, our reason neither does, nor is it possible it ever should, upon any supposition, give us an assurance of the continued and distinct existence of body. That opinion must be entirely owing to the *imagination* which must now be the subject of our inquiry.

Since all impressions are internal and perishing existences, and appear as such, the notion of their distinct and continued existence must arise from a concurrence of some of their qualities with the qualities of the imagination; and since this notion does not extend to all of them, it must arise from certain qualities peculiar to some impressions. It will, therefore, be easy for us to discover these qualities by a comparison of the impressions to which we attribute a distinct and continued existence with those which we regard as internal and perishing.

We may observe, then, that it is neither upon account of the involuntariness of certain impressions, as is commonly supposed, nor of their superior force and violence that we attribute to them a reality and continued existence which we refuse to others that are voluntary or feeble. For it is evident our pains and pleasures, our passions and affections, which we never suppose to have any existence beyond our perception, operate with greater violence, and are equally involuntary, as the impressions of figure and extension, color and sound, which we suppose to be permanent beings. The heat of a fire, when moderate, is supposed to exist in the fire; but the pain which it causes upon a near approach is not taken to have any being except in the perception.

These vulgar opinions, then, being rejected, we must search for some other hypothesis by which we may discover those peculiar qualities in our impressions which makes us attribute to them a distinct and continued existence.

After a little examination, we shall find that all those objects to which we attribute a continued existence have a peculiar *constancy* which distinguishes them from the impressions whose existence depends upon our perception. Those mountains, and houses, and trees which lie at present under my eye have always appeared to me in the same order; and when I lose sight of them by shutting my eyes or turning my head, I soon after find them return upon me without the least alteration. My bed and table, my books and papers, present themselves in the same uniform manner and change not upon account of any interruption in my seeing or perceiving them. This is the case with all the impressions whose objects are supposed to have an external existence and is the case with no other impressions, whether gentle or violent, voluntary or involuntary.

This constancy, however, is not so perfect as not to admit of very considerable exceptions. Bodies often change their position and qualities, and, after a little absence or interruption, may become hardly knowable. But here it is observable that even in these changes they preserve a *coherence* and have a regular dependence on each other, which is the foun-

111

dation of a kind of reasoning from causation and produces the opinion of their continued existence. When I return to my chamber after an hour's absence, I find not my fire in the same situation in which I left it; but then I am accustomed, in other instances, to see a like alteration produced in a like time, whether I am present or absent, near or remote. This coherence, therefore, in their changes is one of the characteristics of external objects, as well as their constancy.

Having found that the opinion of the continued existence of body depends on the *coherence* and *constancy* of certain impressions, I now proceed to examine after what manner these qualities give rise to so extraordinary an opinion. To begin with the coherence, we may observe that though those internal impressions which we regard as fleeting and perishing have also a certain coherence or regularity in their appearances, yet it is of somewhat a different nature from that which we discover in our bodies. Our passions are found by experience to have a mutual connection with and dependence on each other; but on no occasion is it necessary to suppose that they have existed and operated, when they were not perceived, in order to preserve the same dependence and connection of which we have had experience. The case is not the same with relation to external objects. Those require a continued existence or otherwise lose, in a great measure, the regularity of their operation. I am here seated in my chamber, with my face to the fire; and all the objects that strike my senses are contained in a few yards around me. My memory, indeed, informs me of the existence of many objects; but, then, this information extends not beyond their past existence, nor do either my senses or memory give any testimony to the continuance of their being. When, therefore, I am thus seated and revolve over these thoughts, I hear on a sudden a noise as of a door turning upon its hinges and a little after see a porter who advances towards me. This gives occasion to many new reflections and reasonings. First, I never have observed that this noise could proceed from anything but the motion of a door and therefore conclude that the present phenomenon is a contradiction to all past experience, unless the door, which I remember on the other side of the chamber, be still in being. Again, I have always found that a human body was possessed of a quality which I call gravity and which hinders it from mounting in the air, as this porter must have done to arrive at my chamber, unless the stairs I remember be not annihilated by my absence. But this is not all. I receive a letter which, upon opening it, I perceive by the handwriting and subscription to have come from a friend, who says he is two hundred leagues distant. It is evident I can never account for this phenomenon, conformable to my experience in other instances, without spreading out in my mind the whole sea and continent between us and supposing the effects and continued existence of posts and ferries, according to my memory and observation. To consider these phenomena of the porter and letter in a certain light, they are contradictions to common experience and may be regarded as objections to those maxims which we form concerning the connections of causes and effects. I am accustomed to hear such a sound and see such an object in motion at the same time. I have not received, in this particular instance, both these perceptions. These observations are contrary, unless I suppose that the door still remains and that it was opened without my perceiving it; and this supposition, which was at first entirely arbitrary and hypothetical, acquires a force and evidence by its being the only one upon which I can reconcile these contradictions. There is scarce a moment of my life wherein there is not a similar instance presented to me, and I have not occasion to suppose the continued existence of objects, in order to connect their past and present appearances, and give them such a union with each other, as I have found, by experience, to be suitable to their particular natures and circumstances. Here, then, I am naturally led to regard the world as something real and durable and as preserving its existence, even when it is no longer present to my perception.

But, though this conclusion, from the coherence of appearances, may seem to be of the same nature with our reasonings concerning causes and effects, as being derived from custom and regulated by past experience, we shall find upon examination that they are at the bottom considerably different from each other, and that this inference arises from the understanding and from custom in an indirect and oblique manner. For it will readily be allowed that since nothing is ever really present to the mind besides its own perceptions, it is not only impossible that any habit should ever be acquired otherwise than by the regular succession of these perceptions, but also that any habit should ever exceed that degree of regularity. Any degree, therefore, of regularity in our perceptions can never be a foundation for us to infer a greater degree of regularity in some objects which are not perceived, since this supposes a contradiction, viz. a habit acquired by what was never present to the mind. But it is evident that whenever we infer the continued existence of the objects of sense from their coherence and the frequency of their union, it is in order to bestow on the objects a greater regularity than what is observed in our mere perceptions. We remark a connection betwixt two kinds of objects in their past appear-

113

ance to the senses but are not able to observe this connection to be perfectly constant, since the turning about of our head, or the shutting of our eyes, is able to break it. What, then, do we suppose in this case but that these objects still continue their usual connection, notwithstanding their apparent interruption, and that the irregular appearances are joined by something of which we are insensible? But as all reasoning concerning matters of fact arises only from custom, and custom can only be the effect of repeated perceptions, the extending of custom and reasoning beyond the perceptions can never be the direct and natural effect of the constant repetition and connection, but must arise from the cooperation of some other principles.

I have already observed, in examining the foundation of mathematics, that the imagination, when set into any train of thinking, is apt to continue even when its object fails it and, like a galley put in motion by the oars, carries on its course without any new impulse. This I have assigned for the reason why, after considering several loose standards of equality and correcting them by each other, we proceed to imagine so correct and exact a standard of that relation as is not liable to the least error or variation. The same principle makes us easily entertain this opinion of the continued existence of body. Objects have a certain coherence even as they appear to our senses; but this coherence is much greater and more uniform if we suppose the objects to have a continued existence; and as the mind is once in the train of observing a uniformity among objects, it naturally continues till it renders the uniformity as complete as possible. The simple supposition of their continued existence suffices for this purpose and gives us a notion of a much greater regularity among objects than what they have when we look no further than our senses.

But whatever force we may ascribe to this principle, I am afraid it is too weak to support alone so vast an edifice as is that of the continued existence of all external bodies, and that we must join the *constancy* of their appearance to the *coherence* in order to give a satisfactory account of that opinion. As the explication of this will lead me into a considerable compass of very profound reasoning, I think it proper, in order to avoid confusion, to give a short sketch or abridgment of my system and afterwards draw out all its parts in their full compass. This inference from the constancy of our perceptions, like the precedent from their coherence, gives rise to the opinion of the *continued* existence of body, which is prior to that of its *distinct* existence and produces that latter principle.

When we have been accustomed to observe a constancy in

certain impressions and have found that the perception of the sun or ocean, for instance, returns upon us, after an absence or annihilation, with like parts and in a like order as at its first appearance, we are not apt to regard these interrupted perceptions as different (which they really are) but on the contrary consider them as individually the same, upon account of their resemblance. But as this interruption of their existence is contrary to their perfect identity and makes us regard the first impression as annihilated and the second as newly created, we find ourselves somewhat at a loss and are involved in a kind of contradiction. In order to free ourselves from this difficulty, we disguise, as much as possible, the interruption, or rather remove it entirely, by supposing that these interrupted perceptions are connected by a real existence of which we are insensible. This supposition, or idea of continued existence, acquires a force and vivacity from the memory of these broken impressions and from that propensity which they give us to suppose them the same; and according to the precedent reasoning, the very essence of belief consists in the force and vivacity of the conceptions.

In order to justify this system, there are four things requisite. *First,* to explain the *principium individuationis,* or principle of identity. *Secondly,* give a reason why the resemblance of our broken and interrupted perceptions induces us to attribute an identity to them. *Thirdly,* account for that propensity, which this illusion gives, to unite these broken appearances by a continued existence. *Fourthly,* and lastly, explain that force and vivacity of conception which arises from the propensity.

First as to the principle of individuation, we may observe that the view of any one object is not sufficient to convey the idea of identity. For in that proposition, *an object is the same with itself,* if the idea expressed by the word *object* were noways distinguished from that meant by *itself,* we really should mean nothing, nor would the proposition contain a predicate and a subject, which, however, are implied in this affirmation. One single object conveys the idea of unity, not that of identity.

On the other hand, a multiplicity of objects can never convey this idea, however resembling they may be supposed. The mind always pronounces the one not to be the other and considers them as forming two, three, or any determinate number of objects, whose existences are entirely distinct and independent.

Since, then, both number and unity are incompatible with the relation of identity, it must lie in something that is neither of them. But to tell the truth, at first sight this seems utterly impossible. Betwixt unity and number there can be no me-

115

dium, no more than betwixt existence and nonexistence. After one object is supposed to exist, we must either suppose another also to exist, in which case we have the idea of number; or we must suppose it not to exist, in which case the first object remains at unity.

To remove this difficulty, let us have recourse to the idea of time or duration. I have already observed that time, in a strict sense, implies succession, and that when we apply its idea to any unchangeable object, it is only by a fiction of the imagination by which the unchangeable object is supposed to participate of the changes of the coexisting objects, and in particular of that of our perceptions. This fiction of the imagination almost universally takes place; and it is by means of it that a single object, placed before us and surveyed for any time without our discovering in it any interruption or variation, is able to give us a notion of identity. For when we consider any two points of this time, we may place them in different lights: we may either survey them at the very same instant, in which case they give us the idea of number, both by themselves and by the object, which must be multiplied in order to be conceived at once as existent in these two different points of time; or, on the other hand, we may trace the succession of time by a like succession of ideas and conceiving first one moment, along with the object then existent, imagine afterwards a change in the time without any *variation* or *interruption* in the object, in which case it gives the idea of unity. Here, then, is an idea which is a medium betwixt unity and number, or, more properly speaking, is either of them, according to the view in which we take it; and this idea we call that of identity. We cannot, in any propriety of speech, say that an object existent at one time is the same with itself existent at another, unless we mean that the object existent one time is the same with itself existent at another. By this means, we make a difference betwixt the idea meant by the word *object* and that meant by *itself,* without going the length of number, and at the same time without restraining ourselves to a strict and absolute unity.

Thus, the principle of individuation is nothing but the *invariableness* and *uninterruptedness* of any object through a supposed variation of time, by which the mind can trace it in the different periods of its existence, without any break of the view, and without being obliged to form the idea of multiplicity or number.

I now proceed to explain the *second* part of my system and show why the constancy of our perceptions makes us ascribe to them a perfect numerical identity, though there be very long intervals betwixt their appearance and they have only one of the essential qualities of identity, viz. *invariableness*. That I may avoid all ambiguity and confusion on this head, I shall observe that I here account for the opinions and belief of the vulgar with regard to the existence of body and therefore must entirely conform myself to their manner of thinking and of expressing themselves. Now, we have already observed that however philosophers may distinguish betwixt the objects and perceptions of the senses, which they suppose coexistent and resembling, yet this is a distinction which is not comprehended by the generality of mankind, who, as they perceive only one being, can never assent to the opinion of a double existence and representation. Those very sensations which enter by the eye or ear are with them the true objects, nor can they readily conceive that this pen or paper, which is immediately perceived, represent another which is different from, but resembling it. In order, therefore, to accommodate myself to their notions, I shall at first suppose that there is only a single existence, which I shall call indifferently *object* or *perception,* according as it shall seem best to suit my purpose, understanding by both of them what any common man means by a hat, or shoe, or stone, or any other impression conveyed to him by his senses. I shall be sure to give warning when I return to a more philosophical way of speaking and thinking.

To enter therefore upon the question concerning the source of the error and deception with regard to identity when we attribute it to our resembling perceptions, notwithstanding their interruption, I must here recall an observation which I have already proved and explained. Nothing is more apt to make us mistake one idea for another than any relation betwixt them which associates them together in the imagination and makes it pass with facility from one to the other. Of all relations, that of resemblance is in this respect the most efficacious, and that because it not only causes an association of ideas but also of dispositions and makes us conceive the one idea by an act or operation of the mind similar to that by which we conceive the other. This circumstance I have observed to be of great moment; and we may establish it for a general rule that whatever ideas place the mind in the same disposition or in similar ones are very apt to be confounded. The mind readily passes from one to the other and perceives not the change without a strict attention, of which, generally speaking, it is wholly incapable.

In order to apply this general maxim, we must first examine the disposition of the mind in viewing any object which preserves a perfect identity and then find some other object that is confounded with it by causing a similar disposition.

117

When we fix our thought on any object and suppose it to continue the same for some time, it is evident we suppose the change to lie only in the time and never exert ourselves to produce any new image or idea of the object. The faculties of the mind repose themselves in a manner and take no more exercise than what is necessary to continue that idea of which we were formerly possessed and which subsists without variation or interruption. The passage from one moment to another is scarce felt and distinguishes not itself by a different perception or idea, which may require a different direction of the spirits, in order to its conception.

Now, what other objects, besides identical ones, are capable of placing the mind in the same disposition when it considers them and of causing the same uninterrupted passage of the imagination from one idea to another? This question is of the last importance. For if we can find any such objects, we may certainly conclude, from the foregoing principle, that they are very naturally confounded with identical ones and are taken for them in most of our reasonings. But though this question be very important, it is not very difficult nor doubtful. For I immediately reply that a succession of related objects places the mind in this disposition and is considered with the same smooth and uninterrupted progress of the imagination as attends the view of the same invariable object. The very nature and essence of relation is to connect our ideas with each other and, upon the appearance of one, to facilitate the transition to its correlative. The passage betwixt related ideas is therefore so smooth and easy that it produces little alteration of the mind and seems like the continuation of the same action; and as the continuation of the same action is an effect of the continued view of the same object, it is for this reason we attribute sameness to every succession of related objects. The thought slides along the succession with equal facility, as if it considered only one object, and therefore confounds the succession with the identity.

We shall afterward see many instances of this tendency of relation to make us ascribe an *identity* to *different* objects but shall here confine ourselves to the present subject. We find by experience that there is such a *constancy* in almost all the impressions of the senses that their interruption produces no alteration on them and hinders them not from returning the same in appearance and in situation as at their first existence. I survey the furniture of my chamber; I shut my eyes and afterwards open them and find the new perceptions to resemble perfectly those which formerly struck my senses. This resemblance is observed in a thousand instances and naturally connects together our ideas of these interrupted perceptions

118

by the strongest relation and conveys the mind with an easy transition from one to another. An easy transition or passage of the imagination, along the ideas of these different and interrupted perceptions, is almost the same disposition of mind with that in which we consider one constant and uninterrupted perception. It is therefore very natural for us to mistake the one for the other.*

The persons who entertain this opinion concerning the identity of our resembling perceptions are in general all the unthinking and unphilosophical part of mankind (that is, all of us at one time or other) and consequently such as suppose their perceptions to be their only objects and never think of a double existence internal and external, representing and represented. The very image which is present to the senses is with us the real body; and it is to these interrupted images we ascribe a perfect identity. But as the interruption of the appearance seems contrary to the identity and naturally leads us to regard these resembling perceptions as different from each other, we here find ourselves at a loss how to reconcile such opposite opinions. The smooth passage of the imagination along the ideas of the resembling perceptions makes us ascribe to them a perfect identity. The interrupted manner of their appearance makes us consider them as so many resembling but still distinct beings which appear after certain intervals. The perplexity arising from this contradiction produces a propensity to unite these broken appearances by the fiction of a continued existence, which is the *third* part of that hypothesis I proposed to explain.

Nothing is more certain from experience than that any contradiction either to the sentiments or passions gives a sensible uneasiness, whether it proceeds from without or from within, from the opposition of external objects or from the combat of internal principles. On the contrary, whatever strikes in with the natural propensities and either externally forwards their satisfaction, or internally concurs with their movements, is sure to give a sensible pleasure. Now, there

* This reasoning, it must be confessed, is somewhat abstruse and difficult to be comprehended; but it is remarkable that this very difficulty may be converted into a proof of the reasoning. We may observe that there are two relations, and both of them resemblances, which contribute to our mistaking the succession of our interrupted perceptions for an identical object. The first is the resemblance of the perceptions; the second is the resemblance which the act of the mind, in surveying a succession of resembling objects, bears to that in surveying an identical object. Now, these resemblances we are apt to confound with each other; and it is natural we should, according to this very reasoning. But let us keep them distinct, and we shall find no difficulty in conceiving the precedent argument.

being here an opposition betwixt the notion of the identity of resembling perceptions and the interruption of their appearance, the mind must be uneasy in that situation and will naturally seek relief from the uneasiness. Since the uneasiness arises from the opposition of two contrary principles, it must look for relief by sacrificing the one to the other. But as the smooth passage of our thought along our resembling perceptions makes us ascribe to them an identity, we can never, without reluctance, yield up that opinion. We must therefore turn to the other side and suppose that our perceptions are no longer interrupted but preserve a continued as well as an invariable existence and are by that means entirely the same. But here the interruptions in the appearance of these perceptions are so long and frequent that it is impossible to overlook them; and as the *appearance* of a perception in the mind and its *existence* seem at first sight entirely the same, it may be doubted whether we can ever assent to so palpable a contradiction and suppose a perception to exist without being present to the mind. In order to clear up this matter and learn how the interruption in the appearance of a perception implies not necessarily an interruption in its existence, it will be proper to touch upon some principles which we shall have occasion to explain more fully afterwards.

We may begin with observing that the difficulty in the present case is not concerning the matter of fact or whether the mind forms such a conclusion concerning the continued existence of its perceptions, but only concerning the manner in which the conclusion is formed and principles from which it is derived. It is certain that almost all mankind, and even philosophers themselves, for the greatest part of their lives take their perceptions to be their only objects and suppose that the very being which is intimately present to the mind is the real body or material existence. It is also certain that this very perception or object is supposed to have a continued uninterrupted being, and neither to be annihilated by our absence nor to be brought into existence by our presence. When we are absent from it, we say it still exists but that we do not feel, we do not see it. When we are present, we say we feel or see it. Here, then, may arise two questions; *first,* how we can satisfy ourselves in supposing a perception to be absent from the mind without being annihilated; *secondly,* after what manner we conceive an object to become present to the mind without some new creation of a perception or image, and what we mean by this *seeing,* and *feeling,* and *perceiving.*

As to the first question, we may observe that what we call a *mind* is nothing but a heap or collection of different perceptions united together by certain relations and supposed, though falsely, to be endowed with a perfect simplicity and identity. Now, as every perception is distinguishable from another and may be considered as separately existent, it evidently follows that there is no absurdity in separating any particular perception from the mind, that is, in breaking off all its relations with that connected mass of perceptions which constitute a thinking being.

The same reasoning affords us an answer to the second question. If the name of *perception* renders not this separation from a mind absurd and contradictory, the name of *object,* standing for the same thing, can never render their conjunction impossible. External objects are seen and felt and become present to the mind, that is, they acquire such a relation to a connected heap of perceptions as to influence them very considerably in augmenting their number by present reflections and passions and in storing the memory with ideas. The same continued and uninterrupted being may, therefore, be sometimes present to the mind and sometimes absent from it without any real or essential change in the being itself. An interrupted appearance to the senses implies not necessarily an interruption in the existence. The supposition of the continued existence of sensible objects or perceptions involves no contradiction. We may easily indulge our inclination to that supposition. When the exact resemblance of our perceptions makes us ascribe to them an identity, we may remove the seeming interruption by feigning a continued being which may fill those intervals and preserve a perfect and entire identity to our perceptions.

But as we here not only *feign* but *believe* this continued existence, the question is, *from whence arises such a belief?* and this question leads us to the *fourth* member of this system. It has been proved already that belief, in general, consists in nothing but the vivacity of an idea, and that an idea may acquire this vivacity by its relation to some present impression. Impressions are naturally the most vivid perceptions of the mind; and this quality is in part conveyed by the relation to every connected idea. The relation causes a smooth passage from the impression to the idea and even gives a propensity to that passage. The mind falls so easily from the one perception to the other that it scarce perceives the change but retains in the second a considerable share of the vivacity of the first. It is excited by the lively impression, and this vivacity is conveyed to the related idea, without any great diminution in the passage, by reason of the smooth transition and the propensity of the imagination.

But suppose that this propensity arises from some other principle besides that of relation; it is evident it must still have

121

the same effect and convey the vivacity from the impression to the idea. Now, this is exactly the present case. Our memory presents us with a vast number of instances of perceptions perfectly resembling each other that return at different distances of time, after considerable interruptions. This resemblance gives us a propensity to consider these interrupted perceptions as the same and also a propensity to connect them by a continued existence, in order to justify this identity and avoid the contradiction in which the interrupted appearance of these perceptions seems necessarily to involve us. Here, then, we have a propensity to feign the continued existence of all sensible objects; and as this propensity arises from some lively impressions of the memory, it bestows a vivacity on that fiction, or, in other words, makes us believe the continued existence of body. If sometimes we ascribe a continued existence to objects which are perfectly new to us and of whose constancy and coherence we have no experience, it is because the manner in which they present themselves to our senses resembles that of constant and coherent objects; and this resemblance is a source of reasoning and analogy and leads us to attribute the same qualities to the similar objects.

I believe an intelligent reader will find less difficulty to assent to this system than to comprehend it fully and distinctly and will allow, after a little reflection, that every part carries its own proof along with it. It is indeed evident that as the vulgar *suppose* their perceptions to be their only objects, and at the same time *believe* the continued existence of matter, we must account for the origin of the belief upon that supposition. Now, upon that supposition, it is a false opinion that any of our objects, or perceptions, are identically the same after an interruption; and consequently, the opinion of their identity can never arise from reason but must arise from the imagination. The imagination is seduced into such an opinion only by means of the resemblance of certain perceptions, since we find they are only our resembling perceptions, which we have a propensity to suppose the same. This propensity to bestow an identity on our resembling perceptions produces the fiction of a continued existence, since that fiction, as well as the identity, is really false, as is acknowledged by all philosophers, and has no other effect than to remedy the interruption of our perceptions, which is the only circumstance that is contrary to their identity. In the last place, this propensity causes belief by means of the present impressions of the memory, since, without the remembrance of former sensations, it is plain we never should have any belief of the continued existence of body. Thus, in examining all these parts, we find that each of them is supported by the strongest

122

proofs and that all of them together form a consistent system which is perfectly convincing. A strong propensity or inclination alone, without any present impression, will sometimes cause a belief or opinion. How much more when aided by that circumstance!

But though we are led after this manner, by the natural propensity of the imagination, to ascribe a continued existence to those sensible objects or perceptions which we find to resemble each other in their interrupted appearance, yet a very little reflection and philosophy is sufficient to make us perceive the fallacy of that opinion. I have already observed that there is an intimate connection betwixt those two principles, of a *continued* and of a *distinct* or *independent* existence, and that we no sooner establish the one than the other follows as a necessary consequence. It is the opinion of a continued existence which first takes place and without much study or reflection draws the other along with it, wherever the mind follows its first and most natural tendency. But when we compare experiments and reason a little upon them, we quickly perceive that the doctrine of the independent existence of our sensible perceptions is contrary to the plainest experience. This leads us backward upon our footsteps to perceive our error in attributing a continued existence to our perceptions and is the origin of many very curious opinions which we shall here endeavor to account for.

It will first be proper to observe a few of those experiments which convince us that our perceptions are not possessed of any independent existence. When we press one eye with a finger, we immediately perceive all the objects to become double and one half of them to be removed from their common and natural position. But as we do not attribute a continued existence to both these perceptions, and as they are both of the same nature, we clearly perceive that all our perceptions are dependent on our organs and the disposition of our nerves and animal spirits. This opinion is confirmed by the seeming increase and diminution of objects according to their distance; by the apparent alterations in their figure; by the changes in their color and other qualities; from our sickness and distempers; and by an infinite number of other experiments of the same kind—from all which we learn that our sensible perceptions are not possessed of any distinct or independent existence.

The natural consequence of this reasoning should be that our perceptions have no more a continued than an independent existence; and, indeed, philosophers have so far run into this opinion that they change their system and distinguish (as we shall do for the future) betwixt perceptions and objects, of which the former are supposed to be interrupted and perishing and different at every different return, the latter to be uninterrupted and to preserve a continued existence and identity. But however philosophical this new system may be esteemed, I assert that it is only a palliative remedy and that it contains all the difficulties of the vulgar system, with some others that are peculiar to itself. There are no principles either of the understanding or fancy which lead us directly to embrace this opinion of the double existence of perceptions and objects, nor can we arrive at it but by passing through the common hypothesis of the identity and continuance of our interrupted perceptions. Were we not first persuaded that our perceptions are our only objects and continue to exist even when they no longer make their appearance to the senses, we should never be led to think that our perceptions and objects are different and that our objects alone preserve a continued existence. "The latter hypothesis has no primary recommendation either to reason or the imagination, but acquires all its influence on the imagination from the former." This proposition contains two parts which we shall endeavor to prove as distinctly and clearly as such abstruse subjects will permit.

As to the first part of the proposition, *that this philosophical hypothesis has no primary recommendation, either to reason or the imagination,* we may soon satisfy ourselves with regard to *reason* by the following reflections. The only existences of which we are certain are perceptions, which, being immediately present to us by consciousness, command our strongest assent and are the first foundations of all our conclusions. The only conclusion we can draw from the existence of one thing to that of another is by means of the relation of cause and effect, which shows that there is a connection betwixt them and that the existence of one is dependent on that of the other. The idea of this relation is derived from past experience, by which we find that two beings are constantly conjoined together and are always present at once to the mind. But as no beings are ever present to the mind but perceptions, it follows that we may observe a conjunction or a relation of cause and effect between different perceptions, but can never observe it between perceptions and objects. It is impossible, therefore, that from the existence of any of the qualities of the former we can ever form any conclusion concerning the existence of the latter or ever satisfy our reason in this particular.

It is no less certain that this philosophical system has no primary recommendation to the *imagination* and that that faculty would never, of itself, and by its original tendency, have fallen upon such a principle. I confess it will be somewhat difficult to prove this to the full satisfaction of the reader, because it implies a negative which in many cases will not admit of any positive proof. If anyone would take the pains to examine this question and would invent a system to account for the direct origin of this opinion from the imagination, we should be able, by the examination of that system, to pronounce a certain judgment in the present subject. Let it be taken for granted that our perceptions are broken and interrupted and, however like, are still different from each other; and let anyone, upon this supposition, show why the fancy, directly and immediately, proceeds to the belief of another existence, resembling these perceptions in their nature but yet continued, and uninterrupted, and identical; and after he has done this to my satisfaction, I promise to renounce my present opinion. Meanwhile, I cannot forbear concluding, from the very abstractedness and difficulty of the first supposition, that it is an improper subject for the fancy to work upon. Whoever would explain the origin of the *common* opinion concerning the continued and distinct existence of body must take the mind in its *common* situation, and must proceed upon the supposition that our perceptions are our only objects and continue to exist even when they are not perceived. Though this opinion be false, it is the most natural of any and has alone any primary recommendation to the fancy.

As to the second part of the proposition, *that the philosophical system acquires all its influence on the imagination from the vulgar one*, we may observe that this is a natural and unavoidable consequence of the foregoing conclusion, *that it has no primary recommendation to reason or the imagination*. For as the philosophical system is found by experience to take hold of many minds, and, in particular, of all those who reflect ever so little on this subject, it must derive all its authority from the vulgar system, since it has no original authority of its own. The manner in which these two systems, though directly contrary, are connected together may be explained as follows.

The imagination naturally runs on in this train of thinking. Our perceptions are our only objects; resembling perceptions are the same, however broken or uninterrupted in their appearance; this appearing interruption is contrary to the identity; the interruption consequently extends not beyond the appearance, and the perception or object really continues to exist, even when absent from us; our sensible perceptions have, therefore, a continued and uninterrupted existence. But as a little reflection destroys this conclusion, that our perceptions have a continued existence, by showing that they have a dependent one, it would naturally be expected that we must altogether reject the opinion that there is such a thing in nature as a continued existence which is preserved even when it no longer appears to the senses. The case, however, is otherwise. Philosophers are so far from rejecting the opinion of a continued existence upon rejecting that of the independence and continuance of our sensible perceptions that though all sects agree in the latter sentiment, the former, which is in a manner its necessary consequence, has been peculiar to a few extravagant skeptics, who, after all, maintained that opinion in words only and were never able to bring themselves sincerely to believe it.

There is a great difference betwixt such opinions as we form after a calm and profound reflection and such as we embrace by a kind of instinct or natural impulse on account of their suitableness and conformity to the mind. If these opinions become contrary, it is not difficult to foresee which of them will have the advantage. As long as our attention is bent upon the subject, the philosophical and studied principle may prevail; but the moment we relax our thoughts, nature will display herself and draw us back to our former opinion. Nay, she has sometimes such an influence that she can stop our progress, even in the midst of our most profound reflections, and keep us from running on with all the consequences of any philosophical opinion. Thus, though we clearly perceive the dependence and interruption of our perceptions, we stop short in our career and never upon that account reject the notion of an independent and continued existence. That opinion has taken such deep root in the imagination that it is impossible ever to eradicate it, nor will any strained metaphysical conviction of the dependence of our perceptions be sufficient for that purpose.

But though our natural and obvious principles here prevail above our studied reflections, it is certain there must be some struggle and opposition in this case; at least so long as these reflections retain any force or vivacity. In order to set ourselves at ease in this particular, we contrive a new hypothesis which seems to comprehend both these principles of reason and imagination. This hypothesis is the philosophical one of the double existence of perceptions and objects which pleases our reason in allowing that our dependent perceptions are interrupted and different, and at the same time is agreeable to the imagination in attributing a continued existence to something else, which we call *objects*. This philosophical system, therefore, is the monstrous offspring of two principles which are contrary to each other, which are both at once embraced by the mind, and which are unable mutually to destroy each

126

other. The imagination tells us that our resembling perceptions have a continued and uninterrupted existence and are not annihilated by their absence. Reflection tells us that even our resembling perceptions are interrupted in their existence and different from each other. The contradiction betwixt these opinions we elude by a new fiction, which is conformable to the hypothesis both of reflection and fancy, by ascribing these contrary qualities to different existences, the *interruption* to perceptions, and the *continuance* to objects. Nature is obstinate and will not quit the field, however strongly attacked by reason; and at the same time, reason is so clear in the point that there is no possibility of disguising her. Not being able to reconcile these two enemies, we endeavor to set ourselves at ease as much as possible by successively granting to each whatever it demands and by feigning a double existence where each may find something that has all the conditions it desires. Were we fully convinced that our resembling perceptions are continued, and identical, and independent, we should never run into this opinion of a double existence, since we should find satisfaction in our first supposition and would not look beyond. Again, were we fully convinced that our perceptions are dependent, and interrupted, and different, we should be as little inclined to embrace the opinion of a double existence, since in that case we should clearly perceive the error of our first supposition of a continued existence and would never regard it any further. It is therefore from the intermediate situation of the mind that this opinion arises and from such an adherence to these two contrary principles as makes us seek some pretext to justify our receiving both, which happily at last is found in the system of a double existence.

Another advantage of this philosophical system is its similarity to the vulgar one, by which means we can humor our reason for a moment when it becomes troublesome and solicitous, and yet upon its least negligence or inattention can easily return to our vulgar and natural notions. Accordingly, we find that philosophers neglect not this advantage, but immediately upon leaving their closets, mingle with the rest of mankind in those exploded opinions that our perceptions are our only objects and continue identically and uninterruptedly the same in all their interrupted appearances.

There are other particulars of this system, wherein we may remark its dependence on the fancy in a very conspicuous manner. Of these, I shall observe the two following. *First*, we suppose external objects to resemble internal perceptions. I have already shown that the relation of cause and effect can never afford us any just conclusion from the existence or qualities of our perceptions to the existence of external continued objects; and I shall further add that even though they could afford such a conclusion, we should never have any reason to infer that our objects resemble our perceptions. That opinion, therefore, is derived from nothing but the quality of the fancy above explained, *that it borrows all its ideas from some precedent perception.* We never can conceive anything but perceptions and therefore must make everything resemble them.

Secondly, as we suppose our objects in general to resemble our perceptions, so we take it for granted that every particular object resembles that perception which it causes. The relation of cause and effect determines us to join the other of resemblance; and the ideas of these existences being already united together in the fancy by the former relation, we naturally add the latter to complete the union. We have a strong propensity to complete every union by joining new relations to those which we have before observed betwixt any ideas, as we shall have occasion to observe presently.

Having thus given an account of all the systems, both popular and philosophical, with regard to external existences, I cannot forbear giving vent to a certain sentiment which arises upon reviewing those systems. I began this subject with premising that we ought to have an implicit faith in our senses and that this would be the conclusion I should draw from the whole of my reasoning. But to be ingenuous, I feel myself *at present* of a quite contrary sentiment and am more inclined to repose no faith at all in my senses, or rather imagination, than to place in it such an implicit confidence. I cannot conceive how such trivial qualities of the fancy, conducted by such false suppositions, can ever lead to any solid and rational system. They are the coherence and constancy of our perceptions, which produce the opinion of their continued existence, though these qualities of perceptions have no perceivable connection with such an existence. The constancy of our perceptions has the most considerable effect and yet is attended with the greatest difficulties. It is a gross illusion to suppose that our resembling perceptions are numerically the same; and it is this illusion which leads us into the opinion that these perceptions are uninterrupted and are still existent, even when they are not present to the senses. This is the case with our popular system. And as to our philosophical one, it is liable to the same difficulties and is over and above loaded with this absurdity, that it at once denies and establishes the vulgar supposition. Philosophers deny our resembling perceptions to be identically the same and uninterrupted, and yet have so great a propensity to believe them such that they ar-

128

bitrarily invent a new set of perceptions to which they attribute these qualities. I say, a new set of perceptions; for we may well suppose in general, but it is impossible for us distinctly to conceive, objects to be in their nature anything but exactly the same with perceptions. What then can we look for from this confusion of groundless and extraordinary opinions but error and falsehood? And how can we justify to ourselves any belief we repose in them?

This skeptical doubt, both with respect to reason and the senses, is a malady which can never be radically cured but must return upon us every moment, however we may chase it away and sometimes may seem entirely free from it. It is impossible, upon any system, to defend either our understanding or senses; and we but expose them further when we endeavor to justify them in that manner. As the skeptical doubt arises naturally from a profound and intense reflection on those subjects, it always increases the further we carry our reflections, whether in opposition or conformity to it. Carelessness and inattention alone can afford us any remedy. For this reason I rely entirely upon them and take it for granted, whatever may be the reader's opinion at this present moment, that an hour hence he will be persuaded there is both an external and internal world; and, going upon that supposition, I intend to examine some general systems, both ancient and modern, which have been proposed of both before I proceed to a more particular inquiry concerning our impressions. This will not, perhaps, in the end, be found foreign to our present purpose.

Section VI

OF PERSONAL IDENTITY

There are some philosophers who imagine we are every moment intimately conscious of what we call our *self;* that we feel its existence and its continuance in existence and are certain, beyond the evidence of a demonstration, both of its perfect identity and simplicity. The strongest sensation, the most violent passion, say they, instead of distracting us from this view, only fix it the more intensely and make us consider their influence on *self* either by their pain or pleasure. To attempt a further proof of this were to weaken its evidence, since no proof can be derived from any fact of which we are so intimately conscious, nor is there anything of which we can be certain if we doubt of this.

Unluckily, all these positive assertions are contrary to that very experience which is pleaded for them, nor have we any idea of *self*, after the manner it is here explained. For from what impression could this idea be derived? This question it is impossible to answer without a manifest contradiction and absurdity; and yet it is a question which must necessarily be answered, if we would have the idea of self pass for clear and intelligible. It must be some one impression that gives rise to every real idea. But self or person is not any one impression, but that to which our several impressions and ideas are supposed to have a reference. If any impression gives rise to the idea of self, that impression must continue invariably the same through the whole course of our lives, since self is supposed to exist after that manner. But there is no impression constant and invariable. Pain and pleasure, grief and joy, passions and sensations succeed each other and never all exist at the same time. It cannot therefore be from any of these impressions, or from any other, that the idea of self is derived, and consequently there is no such idea.

But further, what must become of all our particular perceptions upon this hypothesis? All these are different, and distinguishable, and separable from each other, and may be separately considered, and may exist separately, and have no need of anything to support their existence. After what manner therefore do they belong to self, and how are they connected with it? For my part, when I enter most intimately into what I call *myself*, I always stumble on some particular perception or other, of heat or cold, light or shade, love or hatred, pain or pleasure. I never can catch *myself* at any time without a perception and never can observe anything but the perception. When my perceptions are removed for any time, as by sound sleep, so long am I insensible of *myself* and may truly be said not to exist. And were all my perceptions removed by death, and could I neither think, nor feel, nor see, nor love, nor hate, after the dissolution of my body, I should be entirely annihilated, nor do I conceive what is further requisite to make me a perfect nonentity. If anyone upon serious and unprejudiced reflection thinks he has a different notion of *himself*, I must confess I can reason no longer with him. All I can allow him is that he may be in the right as well as I and that we are essentially different in this particular. He may, perhaps, perceive something simple and contin-

130

ued which he calls *himself*, though I am certain there is no such principle in me.

By setting aside some metaphysicians of this kind, I may venture to affirm of the rest of mankind that they are nothing but a bundle or collection of different perceptions which succeed each other with an inconceivable rapidity and are in a perpetual flux and movement. Our eyes cannot turn in their sockets without varying our perceptions. Our thought is still more variable than our sight; and all our other senses and faculties contribute to this change; nor is there any single power of the soul which remains unalterably the same perhaps for one moment. The mind is a kind of theater where several perceptions successively make their appearance, pass, repass, glide away, and mingle in an infinite variety of postures and situations. There is properly no *simplicity* in it at one time nor *identity* in different, whatever natural propensity we may have to imagine that simplicity and identity. The comparison of the theater must not mislead us. They are the successive perceptions only that constitute the mind nor have we the most distant notion of the place where these scenes are represented or of the materials of which it is composed.

What then gives us so great a propensity to ascribe an identity to these successive perceptions and to suppose ourselves possessed of an invariable and uninterrupted existence through the whole course of our lives? In order to answer this question, we must distinguish betwixt personal identity as it regards our thought or imagination and as it regards our passions or the concern we take in ourselves. The first is our present subject; and to explain it perfectly we must take the matter pretty deep and account for that identity which we attribute to plants and animals, there being a great analogy betwixt it and the identity of a self or person.

We have a distinct idea of an object that remains invariable and uninterrupted through a supposed variation of time; and this idea we call that of *identity* or *sameness*. We have also a distinct idea of several different objects existing in succession and connected together by a close relation; and this to an accurate view affords as perfect a notion of *diversity* as if there was no manner of relation among the objects. But though these two ideas of identity and a succession of related objects be in themselves perfectly distinct, and even contrary, yet it is certain that, in our common way of thinking, they are generally confounded with each other. That action of the imagination by which we consider the uninterrupted and invariable object and that by which we reflect on the succession of related objects are almost the same to the feeling; nor is there much more effort of thought required in the latter case than in the former. The relation facilitates the transition of the mind from one object to another and renders its passage as smooth as if it contemplated one continued object. This resemblance is the cause of the confusion and mistake and makes us substitute the notion of identity instead of that of related objects. However at one instant we may consider the related succession as variable or interrupted, we are sure the next to ascribe to it a perfect identity and regard it as invariable and uninterrupted. Our propensity to this mistake is so great from the resemblance above mentioned that we fall into it before we are aware; and though we incessantly correct ourselves by reflection and return to a more accurate method of thinking, yet we cannot long sustain our philosophy or take off this bias from the imagination. Our last resource is to yield to it and boldly assert that these different related objects are in effect the same, however interrupted and variable. In order to justify to ourselves this absurdity, we often feign some new and unintelligible principle that connects the objects together and prevents their interruption or variation. Thus, we feign the continued existence of the perceptions of our senses to remove the interruption and run into the notion of a *soul*, and *self*, and *substance* to disguise the variation. But, we may further observe, that where we do not give rise to such a fiction, our propensity to confound identity with relation is so great that we are apt to imagine something unknown and mysterious * connecting the parts beside their relation; and this I take to be the case with regard to the identity we ascribe to plants and vegetables. And even when this does not take place, we still feel a propensity to confound these ideas, though we are not able fully to satisfy ourselves in that particular nor find anything invariable and uninterrupted to justify our notion of identity.

Thus, the controversy concerning identity is not merely a dispute of words. For when we attribute identity, in an improper sense, to variable or interrupted objects, our mistake is not confined to the expression but is commonly attended with a fiction, either of something invariable and uninterrupted, or of something mysterious and inexplicable, or at least with a propensity to such fictions. What will suffice to prove this hypothesis to the satisfaction of every fair inquirer is to show, from daily experience and observation, that the objects which are variable or interrupted, and yet are sup-

---

* If the reader is desirous to see how a great genius may be influenced by these seemingly trivial principles of the imagination, as well as the mere vulgar, let him read my Lord Shaftesbury's reasonings concerning the uniting principle of the universe and the identity of plants and animals. See his *Moralists* or *Philosophical Rhapsody*.

posed to continue the same, are such only as consist of a succession of parts, connected together by resemblance, contiguity, or causation. For as such a succession answers evidently to our notion of diversity, it can only be by mistake we ascribe to it an identity; and as the relation of parts which leads us into this mistake is really nothing but a quality which produces an association of ideas and an easy transition of the imagination from one to another, it can only be from the resemblance which this act of mind bears to that by which we contemplate one continued object that the error arises. Our chief business, then, must be to prove that all objects to which we ascribe identity without observing their invariableness and uninterruptedness are such as consist of a succession of related objects.

In order to this, suppose any mass of matter, of which the parts are contiguous and connected, to be placed before us; it is plain we must attribute a perfect identity to this mass, provided all the parts continue uninterruptedly and invariably the same, whatever motion or change of place we may observe either in the whole or in any of the parts. But supposing some very *small* or *inconsiderable* part to be added to the mass or subtracted from it, though this absolutely destroys the identity of the whole, strictly speaking; yet as we seldom think so accurately, we scruple not to pronounce a mass of matter the same where we find so trivial an alteration. The passage of the thought from the object before the change to the object after it is so smooth and easy that we scarce perceive the transition and are apt to imagine that it is nothing but a continued survey of the same object.

There is a very remarkable circumstance that attends this experiment, which is that though the change of any considerable part in a mass of matter destroys the identity of the whole, yet we must measure the greatness of the part not absolutely, but by its *proportion* to the whole. The addition or diminution of a mountain would not be sufficient to produce a diversity in a planet, though the change of a very few inches would be able to destroy the identity of some bodies. It will be impossible to account for this but by reflecting that objects operate upon the mind, and break or interrupt the continuity of its actions, not according to their real greatness but according to their proportion to each other, and therefore, since this interruption makes an object cease to appear the same, it must be the uninterrupted progress of the thought which constitutes the imperfect identity.

This may be confirmed by another phenomenon. A change in any considerable part of a body destroys its identity; but it is remarkable that where the change is produced *gradually*

133

and *insensibly,* we are less apt to ascribe to it the same effect. The reason can plainly be no other than that the mind, in following the successive changes of the body, feels an easy passage from the surveying its condition in one moment to the viewing of it in another, and in no particular time perceives any interruption in its actions. From which continued perception it ascribes a continued existence and identity to the object.

But whatever precaution we may use in introducing the changes gradually and making them proportionable to the whole, it is certain that where the changes are at last observed to become considerable, we make a scruple of ascribing identity to such different objects. There is, however, another artifice by which we may induce the imagination to advance a step further, and that is by producing a reference of the parts to each other and a combination to some *common end* or purpose. A ship of which a considerable part has been changed by frequent reparations is still considered as the same, nor does the difference of the materials hinder us from ascribing an identity to it. The common end in which the parts conspire is the same under all their variations and affords an easy transition of the imagination from one situation of the body to another.

But this is still more remarkable when we add a *sympathy* of parts to their *common end* and suppose that they bear to each other the reciprocal relation of cause and effect in all their actions and operations. This is the case with all animals and vegetables, where not only the several parts have a reference to some general purpose, but also a mutual dependence on, and connection with, each other. The effect of so strong a relation is that though everyone must allow that in a very few years both vegetables and animals endure a *total* change, yet we still attribute identity to them, while their form, size, and substance are entirely altered. An oak that grows from a small plant to a large tree is still the same oak, though there be not one particle of matter or figure of its parts the same. An infant becomes a man and is sometimes fat, sometimes lean, without any change in his identity.

We may also consider the two following phenomena, which are remarkable in their kind. The first is that though we commonly be able to distinguish pretty exactly betwixt numerical and specific identity, yet it sometimes happens that we confound them and in our thinking and reasoning employ the one for the other. Thus, a man who hears a noise that is frequently interrupted and renewed says it is still the same noise, though it is evident the sounds have only a specific identity of resemblance and there is nothing numerically the

134

same but the cause which produced them. In like manner, it may be said, without breach of the propriety of language, that such a church which was formerly of brick fell to ruin and that the parish rebuilt the same church of freestone and according to modern architecture. Here neither the form nor materials are the same, nor is there anything common to the two objects but their relation to the inhabitants of the parish; and yet this alone is sufficient to make us denominate them the same. But we must observe that in these cases the first object is in a manner annihilated before the second comes into existence, by which means we are never presented, in any one point of time, with the idea of difference and multiplicity, and for that reason are less scrupulous in calling them the same name.

Secondly, we may remark that though in a succession of related objects it be in a manner requisite that the change of parts be not sudden nor entire in order to preserve the identity, yet where the objects are in their nature changeable and inconstant, we admit of a more sudden transition than would otherwise be consistent with that relation. Thus, as the nature of a river consists in the motion and change of parts, though in less than four-and-twenty hours these be totally altered, this hinders not the river from continuing the same during several ages. What is natural and essential to anything is, in a manner, expected; and what is expected makes less impression and appears of less moment than what is unusual and extraordinary. A considerable change of the former kind seems really less to the imagination than the most trivial alteration of the latter .and, by breaking less the continuity of the thought, has less influence in destroying the identity.

We now proceed to explain the nature of *personal identity*, which has become so great a question in philosophy, especially of late years in England, where all the abstruser sciences are studied with a peculiar ardor and application. And here it is evident the same method of reasoning must be continued which has so successfully explained the identity of plants, and animals, and ships, and houses, and of all compounded and changeable productions either of art or nature. The identity which we ascribe to the mind of man is only a fictitious one and of a like kind with that which we ascribe to vegetable and animal bodies. It cannot therefore have a different origin but must proceed from a like operation of the imagination upon like objects.

But lest this argument should not convince the reader, though in my opinion perfectly decisive, let him weigh the following reasoning, which is still closer and more immediate. It is evident that the identity which we attribute to the human mind, however perfect we may imagine it to be, is not able to run the several different perceptions into one and make them lose their characters of distinction and difference which are essential to them. It is still true that every distinct perception which enters into the composition of the mind is a distinct existence, and is different, and distinguishable, and separable from every other perception, either contemporary or successive. But as, notwithstanding this distinction and separability, we suppose the whole train of perceptions to be united by identity, a question naturally arises concerning this relation of identity, whether it be something that really binds our several perceptions together or only associates their ideas in the imagination, that is, in other words, whether in pronouncing concerning the identity of a person we observe some real bond among his perceptions or only feel one among the ideas we form of them. This question we might easily decide if we would recollect what has been already proved at large, that the understanding never observes any real connection among objects and that even the union of cause and effect, when strictly examined, resolves itself into a customary association of ideas. For from thence it evidently follows that identity is nothing really belonging to these different perceptions and uniting them together but is merely a quality which we attribute to them, because of the union of their ideas in the imagination when we reflect upon them. Now, the only qualities which can give ideas a union in the imagination are these three relations above mentioned. These are the uniting principles in the ideal world, and without them every distinct object is separable by the mind, and may be separately considered, and appears to have anymore connection with any other object than if disjoined by the greatest difference and remoteness. It is therefore on some of these three relations of resemblance, contiguity, and causation that identity depends; and as the very essence of these relations consists in their producing an easy transition of ideas, it follows that our notions of personal identity proceed entirely from the smooth and uninterrupted progress of the thought along a train of connected ideas, according to the principles above explained.

The only question, therefore, which remains is, by what relations this uninterrupted progress of our thought is produced when we consider the successive existence of a mind or thinking person. And here it is evident we must confine ourselves to resemblance and causation and must drop contiguity, which has little or no influence in the present case.

To begin with *resemblance,* suppose we could see clearly into the breast of another and observe that succession of perceptions which constitutes his mind or thinking principle, and suppose that he always preserves the memory of a considerable part of past perceptions, it is evident that nothing could more contribute to the bestowing a relation on this succession amidst all its variations. For what is the memory but a faculty by which we raise up the images of past perceptions? And as an image necessarily resembles its object, must not the frequent placing of these resembling perceptions in the chain of thought convey the imagination more easily from one link to another and make the whole seem like the continuance of one object? In this particular, then, the memory not only discovers the identity but also contributes to its production by producing the relation of resemblance among the perceptions. The case is the same whether we consider ourselves or others.

As to *causation*, we may observe that the true idea of the human mind is to consider it as a system of different perceptions or different existences which are linked together by the relation of cause and effect and mutually produce, destroy, influence, and modify each other. Our impressions give rise to their correspondent ideas; and these ideas, in their turn, produce other impressions. One thought chases another and draws after it a third, by which it is expelled in its turn. In this respect, I cannot compare the soul more properly to anything than to a republic or commonwealth in which the several members are united by the reciprocal ties of government and subordination and give rise to other persons who propagate the same republic in the incessant changes of its parts. And as the same individual republic may not only change its members but also its laws and constitutions, in like manner the same person may vary his character and disposition, as well as his impressions and ideas, without losing his identity. Whatever changes he endures, his several parts are still connected by the relation of causation. And in this view our identity with regard to the passions serves to corroborate that with regard to the imagination, by the making our distant perceptions influence each other and by giving us a present concern for our past or future pains or pleasures.

As memory alone acquaints us with the continuance and extent of this succession of perceptions, it is to be considered, upon that account chiefly, as the source of personal identity. Had we no memory, we never should have any notion of causation nor consequently of that chain of causes and effects which constitute our self or person. But having once acquired this notion of causation from the memory, we can extend the same chain of causes, and consequently the identity of our persons, beyond our memory and can comprehend times, and circumstances, and actions which we have entirely forgot but suppose in general to have existed. For how few of our past actions are there of which we have any memory? Who can tell me, for instance, what were his thoughts and actions on the first of January, 1715, the eleventh of March, 1719, and the third of August, 1733? Or will he affirm, because he has entirely forgot the incidents of these days, that the present self is not the same person with the self of that time, and by that means overturn all the most established notions of personal identity? In this view, therefore, memory does not so much *produce* as *discover* personal identity, by showing us the relation of cause and effect among our different perceptions. It will be incumbent on those who affirm that memory produces entirely our personal identity to give a reason why we can thus extend our identity beyond our memory.

The whole of this doctrine leads us to a conclusion which is of great importance in the present affair, viz. that all the nice and subtle questions concerning personal identity can never possibly be decided and are to be regarded rather as grammatical than as philosophical difficulties. Identity depends on the relations of ideas, and these relations produce identity by means of that easy transition they occasion. But as the relations and the easiness of the transition may diminish by insensible degrees, we have no just standard by which we can decide any dispute concerning the time when they acquire or lose a title to the name of identity. All the disputes concerning the identity of connected objects are merely verbal, except so far as the relation of parts gives rise to some fiction or imaginary principle of union, as we have already observed.

What I have said concerning the first origin and uncertainty of our notion of identity as applied to the human mind may be extended with little or no variation to that of *simplicity*. An object whose different coexistent parts are bound together by a close relation operates upon the imagination after much the same manner as one perfectly simple and indivisible and requires not a much greater stretch of thought in order to its conception. From this similarity of operation we attribute a simplicity to it and feign a principle of union as the support of this simplicity and the center of all the different parts and qualities of the object.

Thus, we have finished our examination of the several systems of philosophy, both of the intellectual and natural world and, in our miscellaneous way of reasoning, have been led into several topics which will either illustrate and confirm some preceding part of this discourse or prepare the way for our following opinions. It is now time to return to a more close examination of our subject and to proceed in the accurate anatomy of human nature, having fully explained the nature of our judgment and understanding.

Section II

CONCLUSION OF THIS BOOK

But before I launch out into those immense depths of philosophy which lie before me, I find myself inclined to stop a moment in my present station and to ponder that voyage which I have undertaken and which undoubtedly requires the utmost art and industry to be brought to a happy conclusion. Methinks I am like a man who, having struck on many shoals, and having narrowly escaped shipwreck in passing a small firth, has yet the temerity to put out to sea in the same leaky weather-beaten vessel, and even carries his ambition so far as to think of compassing the globe under these disadvantageous circumstances. My memory of past errors and perplexities makes me diffident for the future. The wretched condition, weakness, and disorder of the faculties I must employ in my inquiries increase my apprehensions. And the impossibility of amending or correcting these faculties reduces me almost to despair and makes me resolve to perish on the barren rock on which I am at present rather than venture myself upon that boundless ocean which runs out into immensity. This sudden view of my danger strikes me with melancholy; and as it is usual for that passion, above all others, to indulge itself, I cannot forbear feeding my despair with all those desponding reflections which the present subject furnishes me with in such abundance.

I am first affrighted and confounded with that forlorn solitude in which I am placed in my philosophy and fancy myself some strange uncouth monster who, not being able to mingle and unite in society, has been expelled all human commerce and left utterly abandoned and disconsolate. Fain would I run into the crowd for shelter and warmth but cannot prevail with myself to mix with such deformity. I call upon others to join me in order to make a company apart, but no one will hearken to me. Everyone keeps at a distance and dreads that storm which beats upon me from every side. I have exposed myself to the enmity of all metaphysicians, logicians, mathematicians, and even theologians; and can I wonder at the insults I must suffer? I have declared my disapprobation of their systems; and can I be surprised if they should express a hatred of mine and of my person? When I look abroad, I foresee on every side dispute, contradiction, anger, calumny, and detraction. When I turn my eye inward, I find nothing but doubt and ignorance. All the world conspires to oppose and contradict me, though such is my weakness that I feel all my opinions loosen and fall of themselves when unsupported by the approbation of others. Every step I take is with hesitation, and every new reflection makes me dread an error and absurdity in my reasoning.

For with what confidence can I venture upon such bold enterprises, when beside those numberless infirmities peculiar to myself I find so many which are common to human nature? Can I be sure that, in leaving all established opinions, I am following the truth? and by what criterion shall I distinguish her, even if fortune should at last guide me on her footsteps? After the most accurate and exact of my reasonings, I can give no reason why I should assent to it and feel nothing but a *strong* propensity to consider objects *strongly* in that view under which they appear to me. Experience is a principle which instructs me in the several conjunctions of objects for the past. Habit is another principle which determines me to expect the same for the future; and both of them, conspiring to operate upon the imagination, make me form certain ideas in a more intense and lively manner than others which are not attended with the same advantages. Without this quality, by which the mind enlivens some ideas beyond others (which seemingly is so trivial and so little founded on reason), we could never assent to any argument nor carry our view beyond those few objects which are present to our senses. Nay, even to these objects we could never attribute any existence but what was dependent on the senses and must comprehend them entirely in that succession of perceptions which constitutes our self or person. Nay further, even with relation to that succession, we could only admit of those perceptions which are immediately present to our consciousness, nor could those lively images with which the memory presents us be ever received as true pictures of past perceptions. The memory, senses, and understanding are therefore all of them founded on the imagination or the vivacity of our ideas.

No wonder a principle so inconstant and fallacious should lead us into error when implicitly followed (as it must be) in all its variations. It is this principle which makes us reason from cause and effect; and it is the same principle which convinces us of the continued existence of external objects when absent from the senses. But though these two operations be equally natural and necessary in the human mind, yet in some circumstances they are directly contrary; nor is it possible for us to reason justly and regularly from causes and effects and at the same time believe the continued existence of matter. How shall we adjust those principles together? Which of them shall we prefer? Or in case we prefer neither of them but successively assent to both, as is usual among philosophers, with what confidence can we afterward usurp that glorious title when we thus knowingly embrace a manifest contradiction?

This contradiction would be more excusable were it compensated by any degree of solidity and satisfaction in the other parts of our reasoning. But the case is quite contrary. When we trace up the human understanding to its first principles, we find it to lead us into such sentiments as seem to turn into ridicule all our past pains and industry and to discourage us from future inquiries. Nothing is more curiously inquired after by the mind of man than the causes of every phenomenon; nor are we content with knowing the immediate causes but push on our inquiries till we arrive at the original and ultimate principle. We would not willingly stop before we are acquainted with that energy in the cause by which it operates on its effect, that tie which connects them together, and that efficacious quality on which the tie depends. This is our aim in all our studies and reflections; and how must we be disappointed when we learn that this connection, tie, or energy lies merely in ourselves and is nothing but that determination of the mind which is acquired by custom and causes us to make a transition from an object to its usual attendant and from the impression of one to the lively idea of the other? Such a discovery not only cuts off all hope of ever attaining satisfaction but even prevents our very wishes, since it appears that when we say we desire to know the ultimate and operating principle as something which resides in the external object, we either contradict ourselves or talk without a meaning.

This deficiency in our ideas is not, indeed, perceived in common life, nor are we sensible that in the most usual conjunctions of cause and effect we are as ignorant of the ultimate principle which binds them together as in the most unusual and extraordinary. But this proceeds merely from an illusion of the imagination; and the question is, how far we ought to yield to these illusions. This question is very difficult and reduces us to a very dangerous dilemma whichever way we answer it. For if we assent to every trivial suggestion of the fancy, beside that these suggestions are often contrary to each other, they lead us into such errors, absurdities, and obscurities that we must at last become ashamed of our credulity. Nothing is more dangerous to reason than the flights of the imagination, and nothing has been the occasion of more mistakes among philosophers. Men of bright fancies may in this respect be compared to those angels whom the Scripture represents as covering their eyes with their wings. This has already appeared in so many instances that we may spare ourselves the trouble of enlarging upon it any further.

But on the other hand, if the consideration of these instances makes us take a resolution to reject all the trivial suggestions of the fancy and adhere to the understanding, that is, to the general and more established properties of the imagination, even this resolution, if steadily executed, would be dangerous and attended with the most fatal consequences. For I have already shown that the understanding, when it acts alone and according to it most general principles, entirely subverts itself and leaves not the lowest degree of evidence in any proposition, either in philosophy or common life. We save ourselves from this total skepticism only by means of that singular and seemingly trivial property of the fancy by which we enter with difficulty into remote views of things and are not able to accompany them with so sensible an impression as we do those which are more easy and natural. Shall we, then, establish it for a general maxim that no refined or elaborate reasoning is ever to be received? Consider well the consequences of such a principle. By this means, you cut off entirely all science and philosophy; you proceed upon one singular quality of the imagination and by a parity of reason must embrace all of them; and you expressly contradict yourself, since this maxim must be built on the preceding reasoning, which will be allowed to be sufficiently refined and metaphysical. What party, then, shall we choose among these difficulties? If we embrace this principle and condemn all refined reasoning, we run into the most manifest absurdities. If we reject it in favor of these reasonings, we subvert entirely the human understanding. We have therefore no choice left but betwixt a false reason and none at all. For my part, I know not what ought to be done in the present case. I can only observe what is commonly done, which is that this difficulty is seldom or never thought of, and even where it has once been present to the mind, is quickly forgot and leaves but a small impression behind it. Very refined reflections have little or no influence upon us; and yet we do not, and cannot establish it for a rule, that they ought not to have any influence, which implies a manifest contradiction.

But what have I here said, that reflections very refined and metaphysical have little or no influence upon us? This opinion I can scarce forbear retracting, and condemning from my present feeling and experience. The *intense* view of these manifold contradictions and imperfections in human reason has so wrought upon me and heated my brain that I am ready to reject all belief and reasoning, and can look upon no opinion even as more probable or likely than another. Where am I or what? From what causes do I derive my existence and to what condition shall I return? Whose favor shall I court, and whose anger must I dread? What beings surround me? and on whom have I any influence, or who have any influence on me? I am confounded with all these questions and begin to fancy myself in the most deplorable condition imaginable, environed with the deepest darkness and utterly deprived of the use of every member and faculty.

Most fortunately, it happens that since reason is incapable of dispelling these clouds, Nature herself suffices to that purpose and cures me of this philosophical melancholy and delirium, either by relaxing this bent of mind or by some avocation and lively impression of my senses which obliterate all these chimeras. I dine, I play a game of backgammon, I converse and am merry with my friends; and when, after three or four hours' amusement, I would return to these speculations, they appear so cold, and strained, and ridiculous that I cannot find in my heart to enter into them any further.

Here then I find myself absolutely and necessarily determined to live, and talk, and act like other people in the common affairs of life. But notwithstanding that my natural propensity, and the course of my animal spirits and passions reduce me to this indolent belief in the general maxims of the world, I still feel such remains of my former disposition that I am ready to throw all my books and papers into the fire and resolve never more to renounce the pleasures of life for the sake of reasoning and philosophy. For those are my sentiments in that splenetic humor which governs me at present. I may, nay I must yield to the current of nature in submitting to my senses and understanding; and in this blind submission I show most perfectly my skeptical disposition and principles. But does it follow that I must strive against the current of nature, which leads me to indolence and pleasure; that I must seclude myself in some measure from the commerce and society of men, which is so agreeable; and that I must torture my brain with subtleties and sophistries at the very time that I cannot satisfy myself concerning the reasonableness of so painful an application nor have any tolerable prospect of arriving by its means at truth and certainty? Under what obligation do I lie of making such an abuse of time? And to what end can it serve, either for the service of mankind or for my own private interest? No: if I must be a fool, as all those who reason or believe anything *certainly* are, my follies shall at least be natural and agreeable. Where I strive against my inclination, I shall have a good reason for my resistance and will no more be led awandering into such dreary solitudes and rough passages as I have hitherto met with.

These are the sentiments of my spleen and indolence; and indeed, I must confess that philosophy has nothing to oppose to them and expects a victory more from the returns of a serious good-humored disposition than from the force of reason and conviction. In all the incidents of life, we ought still to preserve our skepticism. If we believe that fire warms or water refreshes, it is only because it costs us too much pains to think otherwise. Nay, if we are philosophers, it ought only to be upon skeptical principles and from an inclination which we feel to the employing ourselves after that manner. Where reason is lively and mixes itself with some propensity, it ought to be assented to. Where it does not, it never can have any title to operate upon us.

At the time, therefore, that I am tired with amusement and company and have indulged a *reverie* in my chamber or in a solitary walk by a riverside, I feel my mind all collected within itself and am naturally *inclined* to carry my view into all those subjects about which I have met with so many disputes in the course of my reading and conversation. I cannot forbear having a curiosity to be acquainted with the principles of moral good and evil, the nature and foundation of government and the cause of these several passions and inclinations which actuate and govern me. I am uneasy to think I approve of one object and disapprove of another; call one thing beautiful and another deformed; decide concerning truth and falsehood, reason and folly, without knowing upon what principles I proceed. I am concerned for the condition of the learned world, which lies under such a deplorable ignorance in all these particulars. I feel an ambition to arise in me of contributing to the instruction of mankind and of acquiring a name by my inventions and discoveries. These sentiments spring up naturally in my present disposition, and should I endeavor to banish them by attaching myself to any other business or diversion, I *feel* I should be a loser in point of pleasure; and this is the origin of my philosophy.

But even suppose this curiosity and ambition should not transport me into speculations without the sphere of common life, it would necessarily happen that from my very weakness I must be led into such inquiries. It is certain that superstition is much more bold in its systems and hypotheses than philosophy; and while the latter contents itself with assigning new causes and principles to the phenomena which appear in the visible world, the former opens a world of its own and presents us with scenes, and beings, and objects which are altogether new. Since, therefore, it is almost impossible for the mind of man to rest, like those of beasts, in that narrow circle of objects which are the subject of daily conversation and action, we ought only to deliberate concerning the choice of our guide and ought to prefer that which is safest and most agreeable. And in this respect, I make bold to recommend philosophy and shall not scruple to give it the preference to superstition of every kind or denomination. For as superstition arises naturally and easily from the popular opinions of mankind, it seizes more strongly on the mind and is often able to disturb us in the conduct of our lives and actions. Philosophy, on the contrary, if just, can present us only with mild and moderate sentiments; and if false and extravagant, its opinions are merely the objects of a cold and general speculation and seldom go so far as to interrupt the course of our natural propensities. The *Cynics* are an extraordinary instance of philosophers who, from reasonings purely philosophical, ran into as great extravagancies of conduct as any *monk* or *dervish* that ever was in the world. Generally speaking, the errors in religion are dangerous; those in philosophy only ridiculous.

I am sensible that these two cases of the strength and weakness of the mind will not comprehend all mankind and that there are in England, in particular, many honest gentlemen who, being always employed in their domestic affairs or amusing themselves in common recreations, have carried their thoughts very little beyond those objects which are every day exposed to their senses. And indeed, of such as these I pretend not to make philosophers, nor do I expect them either to be associates in these researches or auditors of these discoveries. They do well to keep themselves in their present situation; and instead of refining them into philosophers, I wish we could communicate to our founders of systems a share of this gross earthy mixture as an ingredient which they commonly stand much in need of and which would serve to temper those fiery particles of which they are composed. While a warm imagination is allowed to enter into philosophy and hypotheses embraced merely for being specious and agreeable we can never have any steady principles nor any sentiments which will suit with common practice and experience. But were these hypotheses once removed, we might hope to establish a system or set of opinions which, if not true (for that, perhaps, is too much to be hoped for), might at least be satisfactory to the human mind and might stand the test of the most critical examination. Nor should we despair of attaining this end because of the many chimerical systems which have successively arisen and decayed away among men, would we consider the shortness of that period wherein these questions have been the subjects of inquiry and reasoning. Two thousand years, with such long interruptions and under such mighty discouragements, are a small space of time to give any tolerable perfection to the sciences; and perhaps we are still in too early an age of the world to discover any principles which will bear the examination of the latest posterity. For my part, my only hope is that I may contribute a little to the advancement of knowledge by giving in some particulars a different turn to the speculations of philosophers and pointing out to them more distinctly those subjects where alone they can expect assurance and conviction. Human Nature is the only science of man and yet has been hitherto the most neglected. It will be sufficient for me if I can bring it a little more into fashion; and the hope of this serves to compose my temper from that spleen and invigorate it from that indolence which sometimes prevail upon me. If the reader finds himself in the same easy disposition, let him follow me in my future speculations. If not, let him follow his inclination and wait the returns of application and good humor. The conduct of a man who studies philosophy in this careless manner is more truly skeptical than that of one who, feeling in himself an inclination to it, is yet so overwhelmed with doubts and scruples as totally to reject it. A true skeptic will be diffident of his philosophical doubts as well as of his philosophical convictions and will never refuse any innocent satisfaction which offers itself upon account of either of them.

Nor is it only proper we should in general indulge our inclination in the most elaborate philosophical researches, notwithstanding our skeptical principles, but also that we should yield to that propensity which inclines us to be positive and certain in *particular points,* according to the light in which we survey them in any *particular instant*. It is easier to forbear all examination and inquiry than to check ourselves in so natural a propensity and guard against that assurance which always arises from an exact and full survey of an object. On such an occasion we are apt not only to forget our skepticism but even our modesty too and make use of such terms as these, *it is evident, it is certain, it is undeniable,* which a due deference to the public ought, perhaps, to prevent. I may have fallen into this fault after the example of others; but I here enter a *caveat* against any objections which may be offered on that head and declare that such expressions were extorted from me by the present view of the object and imply no dogmatical spirit nor conceited idea of my own judgment, which are sentiments that I am sensible can become nobody, and a skeptic still less than any others.

APPENDIX

There is nothing I would more willingly lay hold of than an opportunity of confessing my errors and should esteem such a return to truth and reason to be more honorable than the most unerring judgment. A man who is free from mistakes can pretend to no praises except from the justness of his understanding; but a man who corrects his mistakes shows at once the justness of his understanding and the candor and ingenuity of his temper. I have not yet been so fortunate as to discover any very considerable mistakes in the reasonings delivered in the preceding volumes except on one article; but I have found by experience that some of my expressions have not been so well chosen as to guard against all mistakes in the readers; and it is chiefly to remedy this defect I have subjoined the following Appendix.

We can never be induced to believe any matter of fact except where its cause or its effect is present to us; but what the nature is of that belief which arises from the relation of cause and effect few have had the curiosity to ask themselves. In my opinion, this dilemma is inevitable. Either the belief is some new idea, such as that of *reality* or *existence,* which we join to the simple conception of an object, or it is merely a peculiar *feeling* or *sentiment.* That it is not a new idea annexed to the simple conception may be evinced from these two arguments. *First,* we have no abstract idea of existence distinguishable and separable from the idea of particular objects. It is impossible, therefore, that this idea of existence can be annexed to the idea of any object of form the difference betwixt a simple conception and belief. *Secondly,* the mind has the command over all its ideas and can separate, unite, mix and vary them as it pleases, so that if belief consisted merely in a new idea annexed to the conception, it would be in a man's power to believe what he pleased. We may therefore conclude that belief consists merely in a certain feeling or sentiment, in something that depends not on the will but must arise from certain determinate causes and principles of which we are not masters. When we are convinced of any matter of fact, we do nothing but conceive it, along with a certain feeling, different from what attends the mere *reveries* of the imagination. And when we express our incredulity concerning any fact, we mean that the arguments for the fact produce not that feeling. Did not the belief consist in a sentiment different from our mere conception, whatever objects were presented by the wildest imagination would be on an equal footing with the most established truths founded on history and experience. There is nothing but the feeling or sentiment to distinguish the one from the other.

This, therefore, being regarded as an undoubted truth, *that belief is nothing but a peculiar feeling, different from the simple conception*, the next question that naturally occurs is, *what is the nature of this feeling or sentiment, and whether it be analogous to any other sentiment of the human mind?* This question is important. For if it be not analogous to any other sentiment, we must despair of explaining its causes and must consider it as an original principle of the human mind. If it be analogous, we may hope to explain its causes from analogy and trace it up to more general principles. Now, that there is a greater firmness and solidity in the conceptions which are the objects of conviction and assurance than in the loose and indolent *reveries* of a castle-builder, everyone will readily own. They strike upon us with more force; they are more present to us; the mind has a firmer hold of them and is more actuated and moved by them. It acquiesces in them and, in a manner, fixes and reposes itself on them. In short, they approach nearer to the impressions which are immediately present to us and are therefore analogous to many other operations of the mind.

There is not, in my opinion, any possibility of evading this conclusion but by asserting that belief, beside the simple conception, consists in some impression or feeling distinguishable from the conception. It does not modify the conception and render it more present and intense; it is only annexed to it after the same manner that *will* and *desire* are annexed to particular conceptions of good and pleasure. But the following considerations will, I hope, be sufficient to remove this hypothesis. *First*, it is directly contrary to experience and our immediate consciousness. All men have ever allowed reasoning to be merely an operation of our thoughts or ideas; and however those ideas may be varied to the feeling, there is nothing ever enters into our *conclusions* but ideas or our fainter conceptions. For instance, I hear at present a person's voice with whom I am acquainted, and this sound comes from the next room. This impression of my senses immediately conveys my thoughts to the person, along with all the surrounding objects. I point them out to myself as existent at present with the same qualities and relations that I formerly knew them possessed of. These ideas take faster hold of my mind than the ideas of an enchanted castle. They are different to the feeling; but there is no distinct or separate impression attending them. It is the same case when I recollect the several incidents of a journey or the events of any history. Every particular fact is there the object of belief. Its idea is modified differently from the loose *reveries* of a castle-builder; but no distinct impression attends every distinct idea or conception of matter of fact. This is the subject of plain experience. If ever this experience can be disputed on any occasion, it is when the mind has been agitated with doubts and difficulties, and afterwards, upon taking the object in a new point of view or being presented with a new argument, fixes and reposes itself in one settled conclusion and belief. In this case, there is a feeling distinct and separate from the conception. The passage from doubt and agitation to tranquillity and repose conveys a satisfaction and pleasure to the mind. But take any other case. Suppose I see the legs and thighs of a person in motion, while some interposed object conceals the rest of his body. Here, it is certain, the imagination spreads out the whole figure. I give him a head and shoulders, and breast and neck. These members I conceive and believe him to be possessed of. Nothing can be more evident than that this whole operation is performed by the thought or imagination alone. The transition is immediate. The ideas presently strike us. Their customary connection with the present impression varies them and modifies them in a certain manner but produces no act of the mind distinct from this peculiarity of conception. Let anyone examine his own mind, and he will evidently find this to be the truth.

Secondly, whatever may be the case with regard to this distinct impression, it must be allowed that the mind has a firmer hold or more steady conception of what it takes to be matter of fact than of fictions. Why then look any further or multiply suppositions without necessity?

Thirdly, we can explain the *causes* of the firm conception but not those of any separate impression. And not only so, but the causes of the firm conception exhaust the whole subject, and nothing is left to produce any other effect. An inference concerning a matter of fact is nothing but the idea of an object that is frequently conjoined or is associated with a present impression. This is the whole of it. Every part is requisite to explain, from analogy, the more steady conception; and nothing remains capable of producing any distinct impression.

Fourthly, the *effects* of belief, in influencing the passions and imagination, can all be explained from the firm conception; and there is no occasion to have recourse to any other principle. These arguments, with many others, enumerated in the foregoing volumes, sufficiently prove that belief only modifies the idea or conception and renders it different to the feeling, without producing any distinct impression.

Thus, upon a general view of the subject, there appear to be two questions of importance which we may venture to recommend to the consideration of philosophers, *whether there be anything to distinguish belief from the simple conception, beside the feeling or sentiment? And, whether this feeling be anything but a firmer conception, or a faster hold, that we take of the object?*

If, upon impartial inquiry, the same conclusion that I have formed be assented to by philosophers, the next business is to examine the analogy which there is betwixt belief and other acts of the mind and find the cause of the firmness and strength of conception; and this I do not esteem a difficult task. The transition from a present impression always enlivens and strengthens any idea. When any object is presented, the idea of its usual attendant immediately strikes us as something real and solid. It is *felt* rather than conceived and approaches the impression from which it is derived in its force and influence. This I have proved at large and cannot add any new arguments.

I had entertained some hopes that however deficient our theory of the intellectual world might be, it would be free from those contradictions and absurdities which seem to attend every explication and human reason can give of the material world. But upon a more strict review of the section concerning *personal identity,* I find myself involved in such a labyrinth that, I must confess, I neither know how to correct my former opinions nor how to render them consistent. If this is not a good *general* reason for skepticism, it is at least a sufficient one (if I were not already abundantly supplied) for me to entertain a diffidence and modesty in all my decisions. I shall propose the arguments on both sides, beginning with those that induced me to deny the strict and proper identity and simplicity of a self or thinking being.

When we talk of *self* or *substance,* we must have an idea annexed to these terms, otherwise they are altogether unintelligible. Every idea is derived from preceding impressions; and we have no impression of self or substance as something simple and individual. We have, therefore, no idea of them in that sense.

Whatever is distinct is distinguishable, and whatever is

distinguishable is separable by the thought or imagination. All perceptions are distinct. They are, therefore, distinguishable, and separable, and may be conceived as separately existent, and may exist separately, without any contradiction or absurdity.

When I view this table and that chimney, nothing is present to me but particular perceptions, which are of a like nature with all the other perceptions. This is the doctrine of philosophers. But this table, which is present to me, and that chimney, may and do exist separately. This is the doctrine of the vulgar and implies no contradiction. There is no contradiction, therefore, in extending the same doctrine to all the perceptions.

In general, the following reasoning seems satisfactory. All ideas are borrowed from preceding perceptions. Our ideas of objects, therefore, are derived from that source. Consequently, no proposition can be intelligible or consistent with regard to objects which is not so with regard to perceptions. But it is intelligible and consistent to say that objects exist distinct and independent without any common *simple* substance or subject of inhesion. This proposition, therefore, can never be absurd with regard to perceptions.

When I turn my reflection on *myself,* I never can perceive this *self* without some one or more perceptions: nor can I ever perceive anything but the perceptions. It is the composition of these, therefore, which forms the self.

We can conceive a thinking being to have either many or few perceptions. Suppose the mind to be reduced even below the life of an oyster. Suppose it to have only one perception, as of thirst or hunger. Consider it in that situation. Do you conceive anything but merely that perception? Have you any notion of *self* or *substance?* If not, the addition of other perceptions can never give you that notion.

The annihilation which some people suppose to follow upon death and which entirely destroys this self is nothing but an extinction of all particular perceptions: love and hatred, pain and pleasure, thought and sensation. These, therefore, must be the same with self, since the one cannot survive the other.

Is *self* the same with *substance?* If it be how can that question have place, concerning the subsistence of self, under a change of substance? If they be distinct, what is the difference betwixt them? For my part, I have a notion of neither, when conceived distinct from particular perceptions.

Philosophers begin to be reconciled to the principle *that we have no idea of external substance distinct from the ideas of particular qualities.* This must pave the way for a like principle with regard to the mind, *that we have no notion of it distinct from the particular perception.*

So far I seem to be attended with sufficient evidence. But having thus loosened all our particular perceptions, when I proceed to explain the principles of connection, which binds them together and makes us attribute to them a real simplicity and identity, I am sensible that my account is very defective and that nothing but the seeming evidence of the precedent reasonings could have induced me to receive it. If perceptions are distinct existences, they form a whole only by being connected together. But no connections among distinct existences are ever discoverable by human understanding. We only *feel* a connection or determination of the thought to pass from one object to another. It follows, therefore, that the thought alone feels personal identity when reflecting on the train of past perceptions that compose a mind, the ideas of them are felt to be connected together, and naturally introduce each other. However extraordinary this conclusion may seem, it need not surprise us. Most philosophers seem inclined to think that personal identity *arises* from consciousness and consciousness is nothing but a reflected thought or perception. The present philosophy, therefore, has so far a promising aspect. But all my hopes vanish when I come to explain the principles that unite our successive perceptions in our thought or consciousness. I cannot discover any theory which gives me satisfaction on this head.

In short, there are two principles which I cannot render consistent, nor is it in my power to renounce either of them, viz. *that all our distinct perceptions are distinct existences* and *that the mind never perceives any real connection among distinct existences.* Did our perceptions either inhere in something simple and individual, or did the mind perceive some real connection among them, there would be no difficulty in the case. For my part, I must plead the privilege of a skeptic and confess that this difficulty is too hard for my understanding. I pretend not, however, to pronounce it absolutely insuperable. Others, perhaps, or myself, upon more mature reflections, may discover some hypothesis that will reconcile those contradictions.

I shall also take this opportunity of confessing two other errors of less importance which more mature reflection has discovered to me in my reasoning. The first may be found in Part II., where I say that the distance betwixt two bodies is known, among other things, by the angles which the rays of light flowing from the bodies make with each other. It is certain that these angles are not known to the mind and consequently can never discover the distance. The second error may be found in Part III., where I say two ideas of the same can only be different by their different degrees of force and vivacity. I believe there are other differences among ideas which cannot properly be comprehended under these terms. Had I said that two ideas of the same object can only be different by their different *feeling,* I should have been nearer the truth.

*An Inquiry Concerning
the Principles of Morals*

Section I

OF THE GENERAL PRINCIPLES
OF MORALS

Disputes with men pertinaciously obstinate in their principles are, of all others, the most irksome, except, perhaps,
those with persons entirely disingenuous, who really do not
believe the opinions they defend, but engage in the controversy from affectation, from a spirit of opposition, or from a
desire of showing wit and ingenuity superior to the rest of
mankind. The same blind adherence to their own arguments
is to be expected in both, the same contempt of their antagonists, and the same passionate vehemence in enforcing sophistry and falsehood. And as reasoning is not the source whence
either disputant derives his tenets, it is in vain to expect that
any logic which speaks not to the affections will ever engage
him to embrace sounder principles.

Those who have denied the reality of moral distinctions
may be ranked among the disingenuous disputants; nor is it
conceivable that any human creature could ever seriously believe that all characters and actions were alike entitled to the
affection and regard of everyone. The difference which nature
has placed between one man and another is so wide, and this
difference is still so much further widened by education, example, and habit that, where the opposite extremes come at
once under our apprehension, there is no skepticism so scrupulous, and scarce any assurance so determined, as absolutely
to deny all distinction between them. Let a man's insensibility
be ever so great, he must often be touched with the images of
right and *wrong;* and let his prejudices be ever so obstinate,
he must observe that others are susceptible of like impressions. The only way, therefore, of converting an antagonist of
this kind is to leave him to himself. For, finding that nobody
keeps up the controversy with him, it is probable he will at

last of himself from mere weariness come over to the side of common sense and reason.

There has been a controversy started of late, much better worth examination, concerning the general foundation of *morals;* whether they be derived from *reason* or from *sentiment;* whether we attain the knowledge of them by a chain of argument and induction or by an immediate feeling and finer internal sense; whether, like all sound judgment of truth and falsehood, they should be the same to every rational, intelligent being, or whether, like the perception of beauty and deformity, they be founded entirely on the particular fabric and constitution of the human species.

The ancient philosophers, though they often affirm that virtue is nothing but conformity to reason, yet, in general, seem to consider morals as deriving their existence from taste and sentiment. On the other hand, our modern inquirers, though they also talk much of the beauty of virtue and deformity of vice, yet have commonly endeavored to account for these distinctions by metaphysical reasonings and by deductions from the most abstract principles of the understanding. Such confusion reigned in these subjects that an opposition of the greatest consequence could prevail between one system and another, and even in the parts of almost each individual system, and yet nobody, till very lately, was ever sensible of it. The elegant Lord Shaftesbury, who first gave occasion to remark this distinction, and who, in general, adhered to the principles of the ancients, is not himself entirely free from the same confusion.

It must be acknowledged that both sides of the question are susceptible of specious arguments. Moral distinctions, it may be said, are discernible by pure *reason;* else, whence the many disputes that reign in common life, as well as in philosophy with regard to this subject, the long chain of proofs often produced on both sides, the examples cited, the authorities appealed to, the analogies employed, the fallacies detected, the inferences drawn, and the several conclusions adjusted to their proper principles? Truth is disputable, not taste: what exists in the nature of things is the standard of our judgment; what each man feels within himself is the standard of sentiment. Propositions in geometry may be proved, systems in physics may be controverted, but the harmony of verse, the tenderness of passion, the brilliancy of wit must give immediate pleasure. No man reasons concerning another's beauty, but frequently concerning the justice or injustice of his actions. In every criminal trial, the first object of the prisoner is to disprove the facts alleged and deny the actions imputed to him; the second, to prove that, even if these actions were real, they might be justified as innocent and lawful. It is confessedly by deductions of the understanding that the first point is ascertained; how can we suppose a different faculty of the mind is employed in fixing the other?

On the other hand, those who would resolve all moral determinations into *sentiments* may endeavor to show that it is impossible for reason ever to draw conclusions of this nature. To virtue, say they, it belongs to be *amiable* and vice *odious*. This forms their very nature or essence. But can reason or argumentation distribute these different epithets to any subjects and pronounce beforehand that this must produce love and that hatred? Or what other reason can we ever assign for these affections but the original fabric and formation of the human mind, which is naturally adapted to receive them?

The end of all moral speculations is to teach us our duty, and, by proper representations of the deformity of vice and beauty of virtue, beget correspondent habits and engage us to avoid the one and embrace the other. But is this ever to be expected from inferences and conclusions of the understanding, which of themselves have no hold of the affections or set in motion the active powers of men? They discover truths. But where the truths which they discover are indifferent and beget no desire or aversion, they can have no influence on conduct and behavior. What is honorable, what is fair, what is becoming, what is noble, what is generous takes possession of the heart and animates us to embrace and maintain it. What is intelligible, what is evident, what is probable, what is true procures only the cool assent of the understanding and, gratifying a speculative curiosity, puts an end to our researches.

Extinguish all the warm feelings and prepossessions in favor of virtue, and all disgust or aversion to vice; render men totally indifferent toward these distinctions, and morality is no longer a practical study nor has any tendency to regulate our lives and actions.

These arguments on each side (and many more might be produced) are so plausible that I am apt to suspect they may, the one as well as the other, be solid and satisfactory and that *reason* and *sentiment* concur in almost all moral determinations and conclusions. The final sentence, it is probable, which pronounces characters and actions amiable or odious, praiseworthy or blamable; that which stamps on them the mark of honor or infamy, approbation or censure; that which renders morality an active principle and constitutes virtue our happiness, and vice our misery—it is probable, I say, that this final sentence depends on some internal sense or feeling which nature has made universal in the whole species. For what else can have an influence on this nature? But in order to pave the way for such a sentiment and give a proper discernment of its object, it is often necessary, we find, that much reasoning should precede, that nice distinctions be made, just conclusions drawn, distant comparisons formed, complicated relations examined, and general facts fixed and ascertained. Some species of beauty, especially the natural kinds, on their first appearance command our affection and approbation; and where they fail of this effect, it is impossible for any reasoning to redress their influence or adapt them better to our taste and sentiment. But in many orders of beauty, particularly those of the finer arts, it is requisite to employ much reasoning in order to feel the proper sentiment; and a false relish may frequently be corrected by argument and reflection. There are just grounds to conclude that moral beauty partakes much of this latter species and demands the assistance of our intellectual faculties in order to give it a suitable influence on the human mind.

But though this question concerning the general principles of morals be curious and important, it is needless for us at present to employ further care in our researches concerning it. For if we can be so happy, in the course of this inquiry, as to discover the true origin of morals, it will then easily appear how far either sentiment or reason enters into all determinations of this nature. In order to attain this purpose, we shall endeavor to follow a very simple method: we shall analyze that complication of mental qualities which form what, in common life, we call "personal merit"; we shall consider every attribute of the mind which renders a man an object either of esteem and affection or of hatred and contempt, every habit or sentiment or faculty which, if ascribed to any person, implies either praise or blame and may enter into any panegyric or satire of his character and manners. The quick sensibility, which, on this head, is so universal among mankind, gives a philosopher sufficient assurance that he can never be considerably mistaken in framing the catalogue or incur any danger of misplacing the objects of his contemplation: he needs only enter into his own breast for a moment and consider whether or not he should desire to have this or that quality ascribed to him, and whether such or such an imputation would proceed from a friend or an enemy. The very nature of language guides us almost infallibly in forming a judgment of this nature; and as every tongue possesses one set of words which are taken in a good sense, and another in the opposite, the least acquaintance with the idiom suffices, without any reasoning, to direct us in collecting and arranging the estimable or blamable qualities of men. The only object of reasoning is to discover the circumstances on both sides which are common to these qualities—to observe that particular in which the estimable qualities agree, on the one hand, and the blamable, on the other; and thence to reach the foundation of ethics and find those universal principles from which all censure or approbation is ultimately derived. As this is a question of fact, not of abstract science, we can only expect success by following the experimental method and deducing general maxims from a comparison of particular instances. The other scientifical method, where a general abstract principle is first established and is afterwards branched out into a variety of inferences and conclusions, may be more perfect in itself, but suits less the imperfection of human nature and is a common source of illusion and mistake, in this as well as in other subjects. Men are now cured of their passion for hypotheses and systems in natural philosophy and will hearken to no arguments but those which are derived from experience. It is full time they should attempt a like reformation in all moral disquisitions and reject every system of ethics, however subtle or ingenious, which is not founded on fact and observation.

We shall begin our inquiry on this head by the consideration of the social virtues: Benevolence and Justice. The explication of them will probably give us an opening by which the others may be accounted for.

Section II

OF BENEVOLENCE

Part I

It may be esteemed, perhaps, a superfluous task to prove that the benevolent or softer affections are *estimable* and, wherever they appear, engage the approbation and goodwill of mankind. The epithets *sociable, good-natured, humane, merciful, grateful, friendly, generous, beneficent,* or their equivalents, are known in all languages and universally express the highest merit which human nature is capable of attaining. Where these amiable qualities are attended with birth and power and eminent abilities and display themselves in the good government or useful instruction of mankind, they seem even to raise the possessors of them above the rank of *human nature* and make them approach, in some measure, to the divine. Exalted capacity, undaunted courage, prosperous success—these may only expose a hero or politician to the envy and ill will of the public. But as soon as the praises are added of humane and beneficent, when instances are displayed of lenity, tenderness, or friendship, envy itself is silent or joins the general voice of approbation and applause.

When Pericles, the great Athenian statesman and general, was on his deathbed, his surrounding friends, deeming him now insensible, began to indulge their sorrow for their expiring patron by enumerating his great qualities and successes, his conquests and victories, the unusual length of his administration, and his nine trophies erected over the enemies of the republic. *You forget,* cries the dying hero, who had heard all, *you forget the most eminent of my praises, while you dwell so much on the vulgar advantages in which fortune had a principal share. You have not observed that no citizen has ever yet worn mourning on my account.**

In men of more ordinary talents and capacity, the social virtues become, if possible, still more essentially requisite, there being nothing eminent, in that case, to compensate for the want of them or preserve the person from our severest hatred as well as contempt. A high ambition, an elevated courage is apt, says Cicero, in less perfect characters to degenerate into a turbulent ferocity. The more social and softer virtues are there chiefly to be regarded. These are always good and amiable.†

The principal advantage which Juvenal discovers in the extensive capacity of the human species is that it renders our benevolence also more extensive and gives us larger opportunities of spreading our kindly influence than what are indulged to the inferior creation.‡ It must, indeed, be confessed that by doing good only can a man truly enjoy the advantages of being eminent. His exalted station, of itself, but the more exposes him to danger and tempest. His sole prerogative is to afford shelter to inferiors who repose themselves under his cover and protection.

But I forget that it is not my present business to recommend generosity and benevolence or to paint in their true colors all the genuine charms of the social virtues. These, in-

* Plutarch in *Pericle* 38.
† Cicero, *de Officiis,* lib. i.
‡ Sat. xv. 139f.

162

deed, sufficiently engage every heart on the first apprehension of them; and it is difficult to abstain from some sally or panegyric, as often as they occur in discourse or reasoning. But our object here being more the speculative than the practical part of morals, it will suffice to remark (what will readily, I believe, be allowed) that no qualities are more entitled to the general goodwill and approbation of mankind than beneficence and humanity, friendship and gratitude, natural affection and public spirit, or whatever proceeds from a tender sympathy with others and a generous concern for our kind and species. These, wherever they appear, seem to transfuse themselves, in a manner, into each beholder and to call forth, in their own behalf, the same favorable and affectionate sentiments which they exert on all around.

Part II

We may observe that in displaying the praises of any humane, beneficent man, there is one circumstance which never fails to be amply insisted on—namely, the happiness and satisfaction derived to society from his intercourse and good offices. To his parents, we are apt to say, he endears himself by his pious attachment and duteous care still more than by the connections of nature. His children never feel his authority but when employed for their advantage. With him, the ties of love are consolidated by beneficence and friendship. The ties of friendship approach, in a fond observance of each obliging office, to those of love and inclination. His domestics and dependents have in him a sure resource and no longer dread the power of fortune but so far as she exercises it over him. From him the hungry receive food, the naked clothing, the ignorant and slothful skill and industry. Like the sun, an inferior minister of Providence, he cheers, invigorates, and sustains the surrounding world.

If confined to private life, the sphere of his activity is narrower, but his influence is all benign and gentle. If exalted into a higher station, mankind and posterity reap the fruit of his labors.

As these topics of praise never fail to be employed, and with success, where we would inspire esteem for anyone, may it not thence be concluded that the *utility* resulting from the social virtues forms, at least, a *part* of their merit and is one source of that approbation and regard so universally paid to them?

When we recommend even an animal or a plant as *useful*

and *beneficial*, we give it an applause and recommendation suited to its nature. As, on the other hand, reflection on the baneful influence of any of these inferior beings always inspires us with the sentiment of aversion. The eye is pleased with the prospect of cornfields and loaded vineyards, horses grazing, and flocks pasturing, but flies the view of briars and brambles affording shelter to wolves and serpents.

A machine, a piece of furniture, a vestment, a house well contrived for use and convenience is so far beautiful and is contemplated with pleasure and approbation. An experienced eye is here sensible to many excellences which escape persons ignorant and uninstructed.

Can anything stronger be said in praise of a profession, such as merchandise or manufacture, than to observe the advantages which it procures to society? And is not a monk and inquisitor enraged when we treat his order as useless or pernicious to mankind?

The historian exults in displaying the benefit arising from his labors. The writer of romance alleviates or denies the bad consequences ascribed to his manner of composition.

In general, what praise is implied in the simple epithet "useful!" What reproach in the contrary!

Your gods, says Cicero,* in opposition to the Epicureans, cannot justly claim any worship or adoration with whatever imaginary perfections you may suppose them endowed. They are totally useless and inactive. Even the Egyptians, whom you so much ridicule, never consecrated any animal but on account of its utility.

The skeptics assert,† though absurdly, that the origin of all religious worship was derived from the utility of inanimate objects, as the sun and moon to the support and well-being of mankind. This is also the common reason assigned by historians for the deification of eminent heroes and legislators.‡

To plant a tree, to cultivate a field, to beget children—meritorious acts, according to the religion of Zoroaster.

In all determinations of morality, this circumstance of public utility is ever principally in view; and wherever disputes arise, either in philosophy or common life, concerning the bounds of duty, the question cannot, by any means, be decided with greater certainty than by ascertaining, on any side, the true interests of mankind. If any false opinion, embraced from appearances, has been found to prevail, as soon as further experience and sounder reasoning have given us

* *De Nat. Deor.* lib. i. 36.

† Sext. *Emp. adversus Math.* lib. viii. [ix. 394, 18.]

‡ Diod. Sic. *passim.*

juster notions of human affairs, we retract our first sentiment and adjust anew the boundaries of moral good and evil.

Giving alms to common beggars is naturally praised, because it seems to carry relief to the distressed and indigent. But when we observe the encouragement thence arising to idleness and debauchery, we regard that species of charity rather as a weakness than a virtue.

Tyrannicide, or the assassination of usurpers and oppressive princes, was highly extolled in ancient times, because it both freed mankind from many of these monsters and seemed to keep the others in awe whom the sword or poniard could not reach. But history and experience having since convinced us that this practice increases the jealousy and cruelty of princes, a Timoleon and a Brutus, though treated with indulgence on account of the prejudices of their times, are now considered as very improper models for imitation.

Liberality in princes is regarded as a mark of beneficence. But when it occurs that the homely bread of the honest and industrious is often thereby converted into delicious cates for the idle and the prodigal, we soon retract our heedless praises. The regrets of a prince for having lost a day were noble and generous; but had he intended to have spent it in acts of generosity to his greedy courtiers, it was better lost than misemployed after that manner.

Luxury, or a refinement on the pleasures and conveniences of life, had long been supposed the source of every corruption in government and the immediate cause of faction, sedition, civil wars, and the total loss of liberty. It was therefore universally regarded as a vice and was an object of declamation to all satirists and severe moralists. Those who prove, or attempt to prove, that such refinements rather tend to the increase of industry, civility, and arts regulate anew our *moral* as well as *political* sentiments and represent as laudable or innocent what had formerly been regarded as pernicious and blamable.

Upon the whole, then, it seems undeniable that nothing can bestow more merit on any human creature than the sentiment of benevolence in an eminent degree, and that a *part*, at least, of its merit arises from its tendency to promote the interests of our species and bestow happiness on human society. We carry our view into the salutary consequences of such a character and disposition; and whatever has so benign an influence and forwards so desirable an end is beheld with complacency and pleasure. The social virtues are never regarded without their beneficial tendencies nor viewed as barren and unfruitful. The happiness of mankind, the order of society, the harmony of families, the mutual support of friends are

165

always considered as the result of the gentle dominion over the breasts of men.

How considerable a *part* of their merit we ought to ascribe to their utility will better appear from future disquisitions, as well as the reason why this circumstance has such a command over our esteem and approbation.

Section III

OF JUSTICE

Part I

That Justice is useful to society, and consequently that *part* of its merit, at least, must arise from that consideration, it would be a superfluous undertaking to prove. That public utility is the *sole* origin of Justice, and that reflections on the beneficial consequences of this virtue are the *sole* foundation of its merit, this proposition, being more curious and important, will better deserve our examination and inquiry.

Let us suppose that nature has bestowed on the human race such profuse *abundance* of all *external* conveniences that, without any uncertainty in the event, without any care or industry on our part, every individual finds himself fully provided with whatever his most voracious appetites can want or luxurious imagination wish or desire. His natural beauty, we shall suppose, surpasses all acquired ornaments; the perpetual clemency of the seasons renders useless all clothes or covering; the raw herbage affords him the most delicious fare; the clear fountain the richest beverage. No laborious occupation required: no tillage, no navigation. Music, poetry, and contemplation form his sole business; conversation, mirth, and friendship, his sole amusement.

It seems evident that in such a happy state every other social virtue would flourish and receive tenfold increase; but the cautious, jealous virtue of justice would never once have been dreamed of. For what purpose make a partition of goods where everyone has already more than enough? Why give rise to property where there cannot possibly be any injury? Why call this object *mine* when, upon the seizing of it by another, I need but stretch out my hand to possess myself of what is equally valuable? Justice, in that case, being totally *useless,* would be an idle ceremonial and could never possibly have place in the catalogue of virtues.

We see, even in the present necessitous condition of mankind, that, wherever any benefit is bestowed by nature in an unlimited abundance, we leave it always in common among the whole human race and make no subdivisions of right and property. Water and air, though the most necessary of all objects, are not challenged as the property of individuals; nor can any man commit injustice by the most lavish use and enjoyment of these blessings. In fertile, extensive countries with few inhabitants, land is regarded on the same footing. And no topic is so much insisted on, by those who defend the liberty of the seas, as the unexhausted use of them in navigation. Were the advantages procured by navigation as inexhaustible, these reasoners had never had any adversaries to refute nor had any claims ever been advanced of a separate, exclusive dominion over the ocean.

It may happen in some countries, at some periods, that there be established a property in water, none in land,* if the latter be in greater abundance than can be used by the inhabitants and the former be found with difficulty and in very small quantities.

Again: suppose that, though the necessities of the human race continue the same as at present, yet the mind is so enlarged and so replete with friendship and generosity that every man has the utmost tenderness for every man and feels no more concern for his own interest than for that of his fellows; it seems evident that the *use* of Justice would, in this case, be suspended by such an extensive benevolence, nor would the divisions and barriers of property and obligation have ever been thought of. Why should I bind another, by a deed or promise, to do me any good office when I know that he is already prompted by the strongest inclination to seek my happiness and would of himself perform the desired service, except the hurt he thereby receives be greater than the benefit accruing to me, in which case he knows that, from my innate humanity and friendship, I should be the first to oppose myself to his imprudent generosity? Why raise landmarks between my neighbor's field and mine when my heart has made no division between our interests but shares all his joys and sorrows with the same force and vivacity as if originally my own? Every man, upon this supposition, being a second self to another, would trust all his interests to the discre-

* Genesis, Chaps. 13 and 21.

tion of every man without jealousy, without partition, without distinction. And the whole human race would form only one family where all would lie in common and be used freely, without regard to property, but cautiously too, with an entire regard to the necessities of each individual, as if our own interests were most intimately concerned.

In the present disposition of the human heart, it would perhaps be difficult to find complete instances of such enlarged affections; but still we may observe that the case of families approaches toward it; and the stronger the mutual benevolence is among the individuals, the nearer it approaches, till all distinction of property be, in a great measure, lost and confounded among them. Between married persons, the cement of friendship is by the laws supposed so strong as to abolish all division of possessions and has often, in reality, the force ascribed to it. And it is observable that during the ardor of new enthusiasms, when every principle is inflamed into extravagance, the community of goods has frequently been attempted; and nothing but experience of its inconveniences, from the returning or disguised selfishness of men, could make the imprudent fanatics adopt anew the ideas of justice and of separate property. So true is it that this virtue derives its existence entirely from its necessary *use* to the intercourse and social state of mankind.

To make this truth more evident, let us reverse the foregoing suppositions and, carrying everything to the opposite extreme, consider what would be the effect of these new situations. Suppose a society to fall into such want of all common necessaries that the utmost frugality and industry cannot preserve the greater number from perishing and the whole from extreme misery; it will readily, I believe, be admitted that the strict laws of justice are suspended in such a pressing emergency and give place to the stronger motives of necessity and self-preservation. Is it any crime, after a shipwreck, to seize whatever means or instrument of safety one can lay hold of, without regard to former limitations of property? Or if a city besieged were perishing with hunger, can we imagine that men will see any means of preservation before them and lose their lives from a scrupulous regard to what, in other situations, would be the rules of equity and justice? The *use* and *tendency* of that virtue is to procure happiness and security by preserving order in society. But where the society is ready to perish from extreme necessity, no greater evil can be dreaded from violence and injustice, and every man may now provide for himself by all the means which prudence can dictate or humanity permit. The public, even in less urgent necessities, opens granaries without the consent of proprietors,

168

as justly supposing that the authority of magistracy may, consistent with equity, extend so far. But were any number of men to assemble without the tie of laws or civil jurisdiction, would an equal partition of bread in a famine, though effected by power and even violence, be regarded as criminal or injurious?

Suppose, likewise, that it should be a virtuous man's fate to fall into the society of ruffians, remote from the protection of laws and government, what conduct must he embrace in that melancholy situation? He sees such a desperate rapaciousness prevail, such a disregard to equity, such contempt of order, such stupid blindness to future consequences as must immediately have the most tragical conclusion and must terminate in destruction to the greater number and in a total dissolution of society to the rest. He, meanwhile, can have no other expedient than to arm himself, to whomever the sword he seizes or the buckler may belong, to make provision of all means of defense and security. And his particular regard to justice being no longer of *use* to his own safety or that of others, he must consult the dictates of self-preservation alone, without concern for those who no longer merit his care and attention.

When any man, even in political society, renders himself by his crimes obnoxious to the public, he is punished by the laws in his goods and person, that is, the ordinary rules of justice are, with regard to him, suspended for a moment, and it becomes equitable to inflict on him, for the *benefit* of society, what otherwise he could not suffer without wrong or injury.

The rage and violence of public war, what is it but a suspension of justice among the warring parties who perceive that this virtue is now no longer of any *use* or advantage to them? The laws of war, which then succeed to those of equity and justice, are rules calculated for the *advantage* and *utility* of that particular state in which men are now placed. And were a civilized nation engaged with barbarians who observed no rules even of war, the former must also suspend their observance of them where they no longer serve to any purpose and must render every action or rencounter as bloody and pernicious as possible to the first aggressors.

Thus, the rules of equity or justice depend entirely on the particular state and condition in which men are placed and owe their origin and existence to that *utility* which results to the public from their strict and regular observance. Reverse, in any considerable circumstance, the condition of men, produce extreme abundance or extreme necessity, implant in the human breast perfect moderation and humanity or perfect rapaciousness and malice—by rendering justice totally *useless,* you thereby totally destroy its essence and suspend its obligation upon mankind.

The common situation of society is a medium amidst all these extremes. We are naturally partial to ourselves and to our friends but are capable of learning the advantage resulting from a more equitable conduct. Few enjoyments are given us from the open and liberal hand of nature; but by art, labor, and industry we can extract them in great abundance. Hence, the ideas of property become necessary in all civil society; hence, justice derives its usefulness to the public; and hence alone arises its merit and moral obligation.

These conclusions are so natural and obvious that they have not escaped even the poets in their descriptions of the felicity attending the golden age or the reign of Saturn. The seasons in that first period of nature were so temperate, if we credit these agreeable fictions, that there was no necessity for men to provide themselves with clothes and houses as a security against the violence of heat and cold; the rivers flowed with wine and milk; the oaks yielded honey; and Nature spontaneously produced her greatest delicacies. Nor were these the chief advantages of that happy age. Tempests were not alone removed from nature, but those most furious tempests were unknown to human breasts which now cause such uproar and engender such confusion. Avarice, ambition, cruelty, selfishness were never heard of; cordial affection, compassion, sympathy were the only movements with which the mind was yet acquainted. Even the punctilious distinction of *mine* and *thine* was banished from among that happy race of mortals and carried with it the very notion of property and obligation, justice and injustice.

This *poetical* fiction of the *golden age* is, in some respects, of a piece with the *philosophical* fiction of the *state of nature*, only that the former is represented as the most charming and most peaceable condition which can possibly be imagined, whereas the latter is painted out as a state of mutual war and violence attended with the most extreme necessity. On the first origin of mankind, we are told, their ignorance and savage nature were so prevalent that they could give no mutual trust, but must each depend upon himself and his own force or cunning for protection and security. No law was heard of; no rule of justice known; no distinction of property regarded; power was the only measure of right; and a perpetual war of all against all was the result of men's untamed selfishness and barbarity.*

* This fiction of a state of nature as a state of war was not first started by Mr. Hobbes, as is commonly imagined. Plato endeavors to refute a hypothesis very like it in the 2d, 3d, and 4th books *de Re-*

Whether such a condition of human nature could ever exist or, if it did, could continue so long as to merit the appellation of a state may justly be doubted. Men are necessarily born in a family society at least and are trained up by their parents to some rule of conduct and behavior. But this must be admitted, that, if such a state of mutual war and violence was ever real, the suspension of all laws of justice, from their absolute inutility, is a necessary and infallible consequence.

The more we vary our views of human life, and the newer and more unusual the lights are in which we survey it, the more shall we be convinced that the origin here assigned for the virtue of justice is real and satisfactory.

Were there a species of creatures intermingled with men which, though rational, were possessed of such inferior strength, both of body and mind, that they were incapable of

---

publica. Cicero, on the contrary, supposes it certain and universally acknowledged in the following passage. "Quis enim vestrum, judices, ignorat, ita naturam rerum tulisse, ut quodam tempore homines, nondum neque naturali, neque civili jure descripto, fusi per agros ac dispersi vagarentur, tantumque haberent, quantum manu ac viribus, per caedem ac vulnera, aut eripere, aut retinere potuissent? Qui igitur primi virtute et consilio praestanti exstiterunt, ii perspecto genere humanae docilitatis atque ingenii, dissipatos unum in locum congregarunt, eosque ex feritate illa ad justitiam atque mansuetudinem transduxerunt. Tum res ad communem utilitatem, quas publicas appellamus, tum conventicula hominum, quae postea civitates nominatae sunt, tum domicilia conjuncta, quas urbes dicimus, invento et divino et humano jure, moenibus sepserunt. Atque inter hanc vitam perpolitam humanitate, et illam immanem, nihil tam interest, quam JUS atque VIS. Horum utro uti nolimus, altero est utendum. Vim volumus extingui? Jus valeat necesse est, id est, judicia, quibus omne jus continetur. Judicia displicent, aut nulla sunt? Vis dominetur necesse est. Haec vident omnes."—PRO SEXT, 1. 42.

["Gentlemen of the jury, do any among you not know that there was a time in nature when civil law and natural law had not yet been defined, and mankind roamed abroad possessing only that which they were able to seize and keep through violence and warfare? Thus the most intelligent and virtuous among them recognized man's inherent educability, gathered the wanderers into one place, and changed their state from one of savagery to one of justice and gentleness. Then those affairs which we call public affairs were organized in pursuit of the common good; then men joined with one another into groups which were later called states; then homes were banded together into cities which were enclosed with walls; and all this after divine and human law had been invented. The most striking contrast between our highly civilized life and that early period of disrule is the contrast between law and violence. The two concepts are necessarily related: if we want an end to violence we must accept the rule of law and all those verdicts which we call lawful. If we dislike the verdicts or refuse to enforce them, the only outcome possible is violence. So much is evident to everyone." *Pro P. Sextio (For Publius Sextius),* 1. 42.]

all resistance and could never, upon the highest provocation, make us feel the effects of their resentment, the necessary consequence, I think, is that we should be bound, by the laws of humanity, to give gentle usage to these creatures, but should not, properly speaking, lie under any restraint of justice with regard to them, nor could they possess any right or property exclusive of such arbitrary lords. Our intercourse with them could not be called society, which supposes a degree of equality, but absolute command on the one side and servile obedience on the other. Whatever we covet, they must instantly resign. Our permission is the only tenure by which they hold their possessions, our compassion and kindness the only check by which they curb our lawless will; and as no inconvenience ever results from the exercise of a power so firmly established in nature, the restraints of justice and property, being totally *useless,* would never have place in so unequal a confederacy.

This is plainly the situation of men with regard to animals; and how far these may be said to possess reason I leave it to others to determine. The great superiority of civilized Europeans above barbarous Indians tempted us to imagine ourselves on the same footing with regard to them and made us throw off all restraints of justice, and even of humanity, in our treatment of them. In many nations, the female sex are reduced to like slavery and are rendered incapable of all property, in opposition to their lordly masters. But though the males, when united, have in all countries bodily force sufficient to maintain this severe tyranny, yet such are the insinuations, address, and charms of their fair companions that women are commonly able to break the confederacy and share with the other sex in all the rights and privileges of society.

Were the human species so framed by nature as that each individual possessed within himself every faculty requisite both for his own preservation and for the propagation of his kind, were all society and intercourse cut off between man and man by the primary intention of the Supreme Creator, it seems evident that so solitary a being would be as much incapable of justice as of social discourse and conversation. Where mutual regards and forbearance serve to no manner of purpose, they would never direct the conduct of any reasonable man. The headlong course of the passions would be checked by no reflection on future consequences. And as each man is here supposed to love himself alone and to depend only on himself and his own activity for safety and happiness, he would on every occasion, to the utmost of his power, challenge the preference above every other being, to none of which he is bound by any ties, either of nature or of interest.

But suppose the conjunction of the sexes to be established in nature, a family immediately arises, and particular rules being found requisite for its subsistence, these are immediately embraced, though without comprehending the rest of mankind within their prescriptions. Suppose that several families unite together into one society which is totally disjoined from all others, the rules which preserve peace and order enlarge themselves to the utmost extent of that society, but, becoming then entirely useless, lose their force when carried one step farther. But again, suppose that several distinct societies maintain a kind of intercourse for mutual convenience and advantage, the boundaries of justice still grow larger in proportion to the largeness of men's views and the force of their mutual connnections. History, experience, reason sufficiently instruct us in this natural progress of human sentiments and in the gradual enlargement of our regards to justice in proportion as we become acquainted with the extensive utility of that virtue.

Part II

If we examine the *particular* laws by which justice is directed and property determined, we shall still be presented with the same conclusions. The good of mankind is the only object of all these laws and regulations. Not only is it requisite for the peace and interest of society that men's possessions should be separated, but the rules which we follow in making the separation are such as can best be contrived to serve further the interests of society.

We shall suppose that a creature possessed of reason, but unacquainted with human nature, deliberates with himself what *rules* of justice or property would best promote public interest and establish peace and security among mankind; his most obvious thought would be to assign the largest possessions to the most extensive virtue and give everyone the power of doing good, proportioned to his inclination. In a perfect theocracy, where a being infinitely intelligent governs by particular volitions, this rule would certainly have place and might serve to the wisest purposes. But were mankind to execute such a law, so great is the uncertainty of merit, both from its natural obscurity and from the self-conceit of each individual, that no determinate rule of conduct would ever

173

result from it; and the total dissolution of society must be the immediate consequence. Fanatics may suppose *that dominion is founded on grace* and *that saints alone inherit the earth;* but the civil magistrate very justly puts these sublime theorists on the same footing with common robbers and teaches them, by the severest discipline, that a rule which in speculation may seem the most advantageous to society may yet be found in practice totally pernicious and destructive.

That there were *religious* fanatics of this kind in England during the civil wars we learn from history, though it is probable that the obvious *tendency* of these principles excited such horror in mankind as soon obliged the dangerous enthusiasts to renounce, or at least conceal, their tenets. Perhaps the *levellers,* who claimed an equal distribution of property, were a kind of *political* fanatics which arose from the religious species and more openly avowed their pretensions, as carrying a more plausible appearance of being practicable in themselves as well as useful to human society.

It must, indeed, be confessed that nature is so liberal to mankind that, were all her presents equally divided among the species and improved by art and industry, every individual would enjoy all the necessaries and even most of the comforts of life, nor would ever be liable to any ills but such as might accidentally arise from the sickly frame and constitution of his body. It must also be confessed that wherever we depart from this equality, we rob the poor of more satisfaction than we add to the rich, and that the slight gratification of a frivolous vanity in one individual frequently costs more than bread to many families, and even provinces. It may appear withal that the rule of equality, as it would be highly *useful,* is not altogether *impracticable,* but has taken place, at least in an imperfect degree, in some republics, particularly that of Sparta, where it was attended, it is said, with the most beneficial consequences. Not to mention that the *agrarian* laws, so frequently claimed in Rome, and carried into execution in many Greek cities, proceeded, all of them, from the general idea of the utility of this principle.

But historians, and even common sense, may inform us that, however specious these ideas of *perfect* equality may seem, they are really at bottom *impracticable,* and were they not so, would be extremely *pernicious* to human society. Render possessions ever so equal, men's different degrees of art, care, and industry will immediately break that equality. Or if you check these virtues, you reduce society to the most extreme indigence and, instead of preventing want and beggary in a few, render it unavoidable to the whole community. The most rigorous inquisition, too, is requisite to watch every inequality on its first appearance and the most severe jurisdiction to punish and redress it. But besides that, so much authority must soon degenerate into tyranny and be exerted with great partialities, who can possibly be possessed of it in such a situation as is here supposed? Perfect equality of possessions, destroying all subordination, weakens extremely the authority of magistracy and must reduce all power nearly to a level, as well as property.

We may conclude, therefore, that in order to establish laws for the regulation of property, we must be acquainted with the nature and situation of man, must reject appearances which may be false, though specious, and must search for those rules which are, on the whole, most *useful* and *beneficial:* vulgar sense and slight experience are sufficient for this purpose, where men give not way to too selfish avidity or too extensive enthusiasm.

Who sees not, for instance, that whatever is produced or improved by a man's art or industry ought forever to be secured to him in order to give encouragement to such *useful* habits and accomplishments? That the property ought also to descend to children and relations, for the same *useful* purpose? That it may be alienated by consent in order to beget that commerce and intercourse which is so *beneficial* to human society? And that all contracts and promises ought carefully to be fulfilled in order to secure mutual trust and confidence, by which the general *interest* of mankind is so much promoted?

Examine the writers on the laws of nature and you will always find that, whatever principles they set out with, they are sure to terminate here at last and to assign, as the ultimate reason for every rule which they establish, the convenience and necessities of mankind. A concession thus extorted, in opposition to systems, has more authority than if it had been made in prosecution of them.

What other reason, indeed, could writers ever give why this must be *mine* and that *yours,* since uninstructed nature, surely, never made any such distinction? The objects which receive those appellations are of themselves foreign to us; they are totally disjoined and separated from us; and nothing but the general interests of society can form the connection.

Sometimes the interests of society may require a rule of justice in a particular case but may not determine any particular rule among several which are all equally beneficial. In that case, the *slightest* analogies are laid hold of in order to prevent that indifference and ambiguity which would be the source of perpetual dissension. Thus, possession alone, and first possession, is supposed to convey property where nobody else has any preceding claim and pretension. Many of

175

the reasonings of lawyers are of this analogical nature and depend on very slight connections of the imagination.

Does anyone scruple, in extraordinary cases, to violate all regard to the private property of individuals and sacrifice to public interest a distinction which had been established for the sake of that interest? The safety of the people is the supreme law: all other particular laws are subordinate to it and dependent on it; and if, in the *common* course of things, they be followed and regarded, it is only because the public safety and interest *commonly* demand so equal and impartial an administration.

Sometimes both *utility* and *analogy* fail and leave the laws of justice in total uncertainty. Thus, it is highly requisite that prescription or long possession should convey property; but what number of days or months or years should be sufficient for that purpose it is impossible for reason alone to determine. *Civil laws* here supply the place of the natural *code* and assign different terms for prescription, according to the different *utilit*ies proposed by the legislature. Bills of exchange and promissory notes, by the laws of most countries, prescribe sooner than bonds and mortgages and contracts of a more formal nature.

In general, we may observe that all questions of property are subordinate to the authority of civil laws, which extend, restrain, modify, and alter the rules of natural justice, according to the particular *convenience* of each community. The laws have, or ought to have, a constant reference to the constitution of government, the manners, the climate, the religion, the commerce, the situation of each society. A late author of genius, as well as learning, has prosecuted this subject at large and has established from these principles a system of political knowledge which abounds in ingenious and brilliant thoughts and is not wanting in solidity.*

What is a man's property? Anything which it is lawful for him, and for him alone, to use. *But what rule have we by*

---

* The author of *L'Esprit des Loix* [Montesquieu]. This illustrious writer, however, sets out with a different theory and supposes all right to be founded on certain *rapports* or relations, which is a system that, in my opinion, never will be reconciled with true philosophy. Father Malebranche, as far as I can learn, was the first that started this abstract theory of morals, which was afterwards adopted by Cudworth, Clarke, and others; and as it excludes all sentiment and pretends to found everything on reason, it has not wanted followers in this philosophic age. See Section I, Appendix I. With regard to justice, the virtue here treated of, the inference against this theory seems short and conclusive. Property is allowed to be dependent on civil laws; civil laws are allowed to have no other object but the interest of society. This, therefore, must be allowed to be the sole foundation of property and justice. Not to mention that our obligation

which we can distinguish these objects? Here we must have recourse to statutes, customs, precedents, analogies, and a hundred other circumstances—some of which are constant and inflexible, some variable and arbitrary. But the ultimate point, in which they all professedly terminate, is the interest and happiness of human society. Where this enters not into consideration, nothing can appear more whimsical, unnatural, and even superstitious than all or most of the laws of justice and of property.

Those who ridicule vulgar superstitions and expose the folly of particular regards to meats, days, places, postures, apparel have an easy task, while they consider all the qualities and relations of the objects and discover no adequate cause for that affection or antipathy, veneration or horror, which have so mighty an influence over a considerable part of mankind. A Syrian would have starved rather than taste pigeons; an Egyptian would not have approached bacon; but if these species of food be examined by the senses of sight, smell, or taste, or scrutinized by the sciences of chemistry, medicine, or physics, no difference is ever found between them and any other species, nor can that precise circumstance be pitched on which may afford a just foundation for the religious passion. A fowl on Thursday is lawful food, on Friday abominable; eggs, in this house and in this diocese, are permitted during Lent, a hundred paces farther, to eat them is a damnable sin. This earth or building yesterday was profane; today, by the muttering of certain words, it has become holy and sacred. Such reflections as these, in the mouth of a philosopher, one may safely say, are too obvious to have any influence, because they must always, to every man, occur at first sight; and where they prevail not of themselves, they

itself to obey the magistrate and his laws is founded on nothing but the interests of society.

If the ideas of justice sometimes do not follow the dispositions of civil law, we shall find that these cases, instead of objections, are confirmations of the theory delivered above. Where a civil law is so perverse as to cross all the interests of society, it loses all its authority, and men judge by the ideas of natural justice, which are conformable to those interests. Sometimes also civil laws, for useful purposes, require a ceremony or form to any deed; and where that is wanting, their decrees run contrary to the usual tenor of justice; but one who takes advantage of such chicanes is not commonly regarded as an honest man. Thus, the interests of society require that contracts be fulfilled; and there is not a more material article either of natural or civil justice. But the omission of a trifling circumstance will often, by law, invalidate a contract *in foro humano,* but not *in foro conscientiae,* as divines express themselves. In these cases, the magistrate is supposed only to withdraw his power of enforcing the right, not to have altered the right. Where his intention extends to the right and is conformable to the interests of society, it never fails to alter the right—a clear proof of the origin of justice and of property, as assigned above.

are surely obstructed by education, prejudice, and passion, not by ignorance or mistake.

It may appear to a careless view, or rather a too abstracted reflection, that there enters a like superstition into all the sentiments of justice, and that, if a man expose its object, or what we call property, to the same scrutiny of sense and science, he will not, by the most accurate inquiry, find any foundation for the difference made by moral sentiment. I may lawfully nourish myself from this tree; but the fruit of another of the same species, ten paces off, it is criminal for me to touch. Had I worn this apparel an hour ago, I had merited the severest punishment; but a man by pronouncing a few magical syllables, has now rendered it fit for my use and service. Were this house placed in the neighboring territory, it had been immoral for me to dwell in it, but being built on this side the river, it is subject to a different municipal law, and by its becoming mine I incur no blame or censure. The same species of reasoning, it may be thought, which so successfully exposes superstition is also applicable to justice; nor is it possible, in the one case more than in the other, to point out in the object that precise quality or circumstance which is the foundation of the sentiment.

But there is this material difference between *superstition* and *justice,* that the former is frivolous, useless, and burdensome, the latter is absolutely requisite to the well-being of mankind and existence of society. When we abstract from this circumstance (for it is too apparent ever to be overlooked), it must be confessed that all regards to right and property seem entirely without foundation, as much as the grossest and most vulgar superstition. Were the interests of society nowise concerned, it is as unintelligible why another's articulating certain sounds, implying consent, should change why the reciting of a liturgy by a priest, in a certain habit and posture, should dedicate a heap of brick and timber and render it thenceforth and forever sacred.*

These reflections are far from weakening the obligations of justice or diminishing anything from the most sacred attention to property. On the contrary, such sentiments must ac-

* It is evident that the will or consent alone never transfers property nor causes the obligation of a promise (for the same reasoning extends to both); but the will must be expressed by words or signs in order to impose a tie upon any man. The expression, being once brought in as subservient to the will, soon becomes the principal part of the promise; nor will a man be less bound by his word, though he secretly give a different direction to his intention and withhold the assent of his mind. But though the expression makes, on most occasions, the whole of the promise, yet it does not always so; and one who should make use of any expression of which he knows not the meaning, and which he uses without any sense of the consequences, would not certainly be bound by it. Nay, though he know its meaning,

178

quire new force from the present reasoning. For what stronger foundation can be desired or conceived for any duty than to observe that human society, or even human nature, could not subsist without the establishment of it and will still arrive at greater degrees of happiness and perfection the more inviolable the regard is which is paid to that duty?

The dilemma seems obvious: as justice evidently tends to promote public utility and to support civil society, the sentiment of justice is either derived from our reflecting on that tendency or, like hunger, thirst, and other appetites, resentment, love of life, attachment to offspring, and other passions, arises from a simple original instinct in the human

---

yet if he uses it in jest only, and with such signs as evidently show that he has no serious intentions of binding himself, he would not lie under any obligation of performance; but it is necessary that the words be a perfect expression of the will, without any contrary signs. Nay, even this we must not carry so far as to imagine that one whom, by our quickness of understanding, we conjecture, from certain signs, to have an intention of deceiving us is not bound by his expression or verbal promise, if we accept of it, but must limit this conclusion to those cases where the signs are of a different nature from those of deceit. All these contradictions are easily accounted for if justice arise entirely from its usefulness to society, but will never be explained on any other hypothesis.

It is remarkable that the moral decisions of the *Jesuits,* and other relaxed casuists, were commonly formed in prosecution of some such subtleties of reasoning as are here pointed out and proceeded as much from the habit of scholastic refinement as from any corruption of the heart, if we may follow the authority of Mons. Bayle. See his *Dictionary,* article "Loyola." And why has the indignation of mankind risen so high against these casuists but because everyone perceived that human society could not subsist were such practices authorized and that morals must always be handled with a view to public interest more than philosophical regularity? If the secret direction of the intention, said every man of sense, could invalidate a contract, where is our security? And yet a metaphysical schoolman might think that where an intention was supposed to be requisite, if that intention really had no place, no consequence ought to follow and no obligation be imposed. The casuistical subtleties may not be greater than the subtleties of lawyers, hinted at above; but as the former are *pernicious,* and the latter *innocent* and even *necessary,* this is the reason of the very different reception they meet with from the world.

It is a doctrine of the church of Rome that the priest, by a secret direction of his intention, can invalidate any sacrament. This position is derived from a strict and regular prosecution of the obvious truth, that empty words alone, without any meaning or intention in the speaker, can never be attended with any effect. If the same conclusion be not admitted in reasonings concerning civil contracts, where the affair is allowed to be of so much less consequence than the eternal salvation of thousands, it proceeds entirely from men's sense of the danger and inconvenience of the doctrine in the former case. And we may thence observe that, however positive, arrogant, and dogmatical any superstition may appear, it never can convey any thorough persuasion of the reality of its objects or put them, in any degree, on a balance with the common incidents of life which we learn from daily observation and experimental reasoning.

breast which nature has implanted for like salutary purposes. If the latter be the case, it follows that property, which is the object of justice, is also distinguished by a simple, original instinct and is not ascertained by any argument or reflection. But who is there that ever heard of such an instinct? Or is this a subject in which new discoveries can be made? We may as well expect to discover in the body new senses which had before escaped the observation of all mankind.

But further, though it seems a very simple proposition to say that nature, by an instinctive sentiment, distinguishes property, yet in reality we shall find that there are required for that purpose ten thousand different instincts, and these employed about objects of the greatest intricacy and nicest *discernment*. For when a definition of *property* is required, that relation is found to resolve itself into any possession acquired by occupation, by industry, by prescription, by inheritance, by contract, etc. Can we think that nature, by an original instinct, instructs us in all these methods of acquisition?

These words, too, inheritance and contract, stand for ideas infinitely complicated, and, to define them exactly, a hundred volumes of laws and a thousand volumes of commentators have not been found sufficient. Does nature, whose instincts in men are all simple, embrace such complicated and artificial objects and create a rational creature without trusting anything to the operation of his reason?

But even though all this were admitted, it would not be satisfactory. Positive laws can certainly transfer property. Is it by another original instinct that we recognize the authority of kings and senates and mark all the boundaries of their jurisdiction? Judges, too, even though their sentence be erroneous and illegal, must be allowed, for the sake of peace and order, to have decisive authority and ultimately to determine property. Have we original, innate ideas of praetors, and chancellors, and juries? Who sees not that all these institutions arise merely from the necessities of human society?

All birds of the same species, in every age and country, build their nests alike; in this we see the force of instinct. Men, in different times and places, frame their houses differently; here we perceive the influence of reason and custom. A like inference may be drawn from comparing the instinct of generation and the institution of property.

How great soever the variety of municipal laws, it must be confessed that their chief outlines pretty regularly concur, because the purposes to which they tend are everywhere exactly similar. In like manner, all houses have a roof and walls, windows and chimneys, though diversified in their shape, figure, and materials. The purposes of the latter, directed to the conveniences of human life, discover not more plainly their origin from reason and reflection than do those of the former, which point all to a like end.

I need not mention the variations which all the rules of property receive from the finer turns and connections of the imagination and from the subtleties and abstractions of law topics and reasonings. There is no possibility of reconciling this observation to the notion of original instincts.

What alone will beget a doubt concerning the theory on which I insist is the influence of education and acquired habits, by which we are so accustomed to blame injustice that we are not, in every instance, conscious of any immediate reflection on the pernicious consequences of it. The views the most familiar to us are apt, for that very reason, to escape us; and what we have very frequently performed from certain motives we are apt likewise to continue mechanically, without recalling, on every occasion, the reflections which first determined us. The convenience, or rather necessity, which leads to justice is so universal and everywhere points so much to the same rules that the habit takes place in all societies; and it is not without some scrutiny that we are able to ascertain its true origin. The matter, however, is not so obscure but that, even in common life, we have every moment recourse to the principle of public utility and ask, *What must become of the world, if such practices prevail? How could society subsist under such disorders?* Were the distinction or separation of possessions entirely useless, can anyone conceive that it ever should have obtained in society?

Thus, we seem, upon the whole, to have attained a knowledge of the force of that principle here insisted on and can determine what degree of esteem or moral approbation may result from reflections on public interest and utility. The necessity of justice to the support of society is the *sole* foundation of that virtue; and since no moral excellence is more highly esteemed, we may conclude that this circumstance of usefulness has, in general, the strongest energy and most entire command over our sentiments. It must therefore be the source of a considerable part of the merit ascribed to humanity, benevolence, friendship, public spirit, and other social virtues of that stamp, as it is the *sole* source of the moral approbation paid to fidelity, justice, veracity, integrity, and those other estimable and useful qualities and principles. It is entirely agreeable to the rules of philosophy, and even of common reason, where any principle has been found to have a great force and energy in one instance to ascribe to it a like energy in all similar instances. This indeed is Newton's chief rule of philosophizing.*

* Principia, lib. iii.

Section IV

OF POLITICAL SOCIETY

Had every man sufficient *sagacity* to perceive, at all times, the strong interest which binds him to the observance of justice and equity and *strength of mind* sufficient to persevere in a steady adherence to a general and a distant interest, in opposition to the allurements of present pleasure and advantage, there had never, in that case, been any such thing as government or political society; but each man, following his natural liberty, had lived in entire peace and harmony with all others. What need of positive law where natural justice is of itself a sufficient restraint? Why create magistrates where there never arises any disorder or iniquity? Why abridge our native freedom when, in every instance, the utmost exertion of it is found innocent and beneficial? It is evident that, if government were totally useless, it never could have place, and that the *sole* foundation of the duty of *allegiance* is the *advantage* which it procures to society by preserving peace and order among mankind.

When a number of political societies are erected and maintain a great intercourse together, a new set of rules are immediately discovered to be *useful* in that particular situation, and accordingly take place under the title of "Laws of Nations." Of this kind are the sacredness of the person of ambassadors, abstaining from poisoned arms, quarter in war, with others of that kind which are plainly calculated for the *advantage* of states and kingdoms in their intercourse with each other.

The rules of justice, such as prevail among individuals, are not entirely suspended among political societies. All princes pretend a regard to the rights of other princes, and some, no doubt, without hypocrisy. Alliances and treaties are every day made between independent states, which would only be so much waste of parchment if they were not found, by experience, to have some influence and authority. But here is the difference between kingdoms and individuals. Human nature cannot, by any means, subsist without the association of individuals; and that association never could have place were no regard paid to the laws of equity and justice. Disorder, confusion, the war of all against all are the necessary consequences of such a licentious conduct. But nations can subsist without intercourse. They may even subsist, in some degree, under a general war. The observance of justice, though useful among them, is not guarded by so strong a necessity as among individuals; and the *moral obligation* holds proportion with the *usefulness*. All politicians will allow, and most philosophers, that *reasons of state* may, in particular emergencies dispense with the rules of justice and invalidate any treaty or alliance where the strict observance of it would be prejudicial, in a considerable degree, to either of the contracting parties. But nothing less than the most extreme necessity, it is confessed, can justify individuals in a breach of promise or an invasion of the properties of others.

In a confederated commonwealth, such as the Achaean republic of old or the Swiss Cantons and United Provinces in modern times—as the league has here a peculiar *utility*, the conditions of union have a peculiar sacredness and authority, and a violation of them would be regarded as no less, or even as more, criminal than any private injury or injustice.

The long and helpless infancy of man requires the combination of parents for the subsistence of their young; and that combination requires the virtue of chastity or fidelity to the marriage bed. Without such a *utility*, it will readily be owned that such a virtue would never have been thought of.*

An infidelity of this nature is much more *pernicious* in *women* than in *men*. Hence, the laws of chastity are much stricter over the one sex than over the other.

These rules have all a reference to generation; and yet women past childbearing are no more supposed to be ex-

___

* The only solution which Plato gives to all the objections that might be raised against the community of women established in his imaginary commonwealth is Κάλλιστα γὰρ δὴ τοῦτο καὶ λέγεται καὶ λελέξεται, ὅτι τὸ μὲν ὠφέλιμον καλόν, τὸ δὲ βλαβερὸν αἰσχρόν. Scite enim istud et dicitur et dicetur, Id quod utile sit honestum esse, quod autem inutile sit turpe esse. De Rep. lib. v. p. 457. ex. edit. Serrani. ["Thus the Stoics say that goodness is 'usefulness and nothing but usefulness,' meaning by 'usefulness' virtue and right action." Sextus Empiricus iii.20.] And this maxim will admit of no doubt where public utility is concerned, which is Plato's meaning. And indeed, to what other purpose do all the ideas of chastity and modesty serve? Nisi utile est quod facimus, frustra est gloria, says Phaedrus. ["If our actions are not useful, then glory is of no importance."] Καλὸν τῶν βλαβερῶν οὐδέν says Plutarch, De vitioso pudore. Nihil eorum quae damnosa sunt, pulchrum est. ["Nothing harmful can be good," says Plutarch, (On False Shame).] The same was the opinion of the Stoics. Φασὶν οὖν οἱ Στωικοὶ ἀγαθὸν εἶναι ὠφέλειαν ἢ οὐχ ἕτερον φελείας, ὠφέλειαν μὲν λέγοντες τὴν ἀρετὴν καὶ τὴν σπουδαίαν πρᾶξιν. ["It is well said, now and always, that what is useful is noble, and what is harmful is base."]

empted from them than those in the flower of their youth and beauty. *General rules* are often extended beyond the principle whence they first arise, and this in all matters of taste and sentiment. It is a vulgar story at Paris that during the rage of the Mississippi a humpbacked fellow went every day into the Rue de Quincempoix, where the stockjobbers met in great crowds, and was well paid for allowing them to make use of his hump as a desk in order to sign their contracts upon it. Would the fortune which he raised by this expedient make him a handsome fellow, though it be confessed that personal beauty arises very much from ideas of utility? The imagination is influenced by associations of ideas which, though they arise at first from the judgment, are not easily altered by every particular exception that occurs to us. To which we may add, in the present case of chastity, that the example of the old would be pernicious to the young, and that women, continually foreseeing that a certain time would bring them the liberty of indulgence, would naturally advance that period and think more lightly of this whole duty so requisite to society.

Those who live in the same family have such frequent opportunities of license of this kind that nothing could preserve purity of manners were marriage allowed among the nearest relations or any intercourse of love between them ratified by law and custom. Incest, therefore, being *pernicious* in a superior degree, has also a superior turpitude and moral deformity annexed to it.

What is the reason why, by the Athenian laws, one might marry a half sister by the father but not by the mother? Plainly this: the manners of the Athenians were so reserved that a man was never permitted to approach the women's apartment, even in the same family, unless where he visited his own mother. His stepmother and her children were as much shut up from him as the women of any other family, and there was as little danger of any criminal correspondence between them. Uncles and nieces, for a like reason, might marry at Athens, but neither these, nor half brothers and sisters, could contract that alliance at Rome, where the intercourse was more open between the sexes. Public utility is the cause of all these variations.

To repeat to a man's prejudice anything that escaped him in private conversation or to make any such use of his private letters is highly blamed. The free and social intercourse of minds must be extremely checked where no such rules of fidelity are established.

Even in repeating stories whence we can foresee no ill consequences to result, the giving of one's author is regarded as a piece of indiscretion, if not of immorality. These stories, in passing from hand to hand, and receiving all the usual variations, frequently come about to the persons concerned and produce animosities and quarrels among people whose intentions are the most innocent and inoffensive.

To pry into secrets, to open or even read the letters of others, to play the spy upon their words and looks and actions —what habits more inconvenient in society? What habits, of consequence, more blamable?

This principle is also the foundation of most of the laws of good manners—a kind of lesser morality calculated for the ease of company and conversation. Too much or too little ceremony are both blamed; and everything which promotes ease, without an indecent familiarity, is useful and laudable.

Constancy in friendships, attachments, and familiarities is commendable and is requisite to support trust and good correspondence in society. But in places of general, though casual, concourse, where the pursuit of health and pleasure brings people promiscuously together, public convenience has dispensed with this maxim, and custom there promotes an unreserved conversation for the time by indulging the privilege of dropping afterward every indifferent acquaintance without breach of civility or good manners.

Even in societies which are established on principles the most immoral and the most destructive to the interests of the general society, there are required certain rules which a species of false honor, as well as private interest, engages the members to observe. Robbers and pirates, it has often been remarked, could not maintain their pernicious confederacy did they not establish a new distributive justice among themselves and recall those laws of equity which they have violated with the rest of mankind.

I hate a drinking companion, says the Greek proverb, who never forgets. The follies of the last debauch should be buried in eternal oblivion in order to give full scope to the follies of the next.

Among nations where an immoral gallantry, if covered with a thin veil of mystery, is in some degree authorized by custom, there immediately arises a set of rules calculated for the convenience of that attachment. The famous court or parliament of love in Provence formerly decided all difficult cases of this nature.

In societies for play, there are laws required for the conduct of the game; and these laws are different in each game. The foundation, I own, of such societies is frivolous, and the laws are in a great measure, though not altogether, capricious and arbitrary. So far is there a material difference between them and the rules of justice, fidelity, and loyalty. The general societies of men are absolutely requisite for the subsistence of the species; and the public convenience, which regulates morals, is inviolably established in the nature of man and of the world in which he lives. The comparison, therefore, in these respects is very imperfect. We may only learn from it the necessity of rules wherever men have any intercourse with each other.

They cannot even pass each other on the road without rules. Wagoners, coachmen, and postilions have principles by which they give the way; and these are chiefly founded on mutual ease and convenience. Sometimes also they are arbitrary, at least dependent on a kind of capricious analogy, like many of the reasonings of lawyers.*

To carry the matter further, we may observe that it is impossible for men so much as to murder each other without statutes and maxims and an idea of justice and honor. War has its laws as well as peace; and even that sportive kind of war, carried on among wrestlers, boxers, cudgel players, gladiators, is regulated by fixed principles. Common interest and utility beget infallibly a standard of right and wrong among the parties concerned.

Section V

WHY UTILITY PLEASES

Part I

It seems so natural a thought to ascribe to their utility the praise which we bestow on the social virtues that one would expect to meet with this principle everywhere in moral writers as the chief foundation of their reasoning and inquiry. In common life, we may observe that the circumstances of utility is always appealed to, nor is it supposed that a greater eulogy can be given to any man than to display his usefulness

---

* That the lighter machine yield to the heavier, and in machines of the same kind, that the empty yield to the loaded; this rule is founded on convenience. That those who are going to the capital take place of those who are coming from it—this seems to be founded on some idea of the dignity of the great city—and of the preference of the future to the past. From like reasons, among footwalkers, the right hand entitles a man to the wall and prevents jostling, which peaceable people find very disagreeable and inconvenient.

to the public and enumerate the services which he has performed to mankind and society. What praise, even of an inanimate form, if the regularity and elegance of its parts destroy not its fitness for any useful purpose! And how satisfactory an apology for any disproportion or seeming deformity if we can show the necessity of that particular construction for the use intended! A ship appears more beautiful to an artist, or one moderately skilled in navigation, where its prow is wide and swelling beyond its poop than if it were framed with a precise geometrical regularity, in contradiction to all the laws of mechanics. A building whose doors and windows were exact squares would hurt the eye by that very proportion as ill-adapted to the figure of a human creature, for whose service the fabric was intended. What wonder then that a man whose habits and conduct are hurtful to society and dangerous or pernicious to everyone who has an intercourse with him should, on that account, be an object of disapprobation and communicate to every spectator the strongest sentiment of disgust and hatred? *

But perhaps the difficulty of accounting for these effects of usefulness, or its contrary, has kept philosophers from admitting them into their systems of ethics and has induced them rather to employ any other principle in explaining the origin of moral good and evil. But it is no just reason for rejecting any principle confirmed by experience that we cannot give a satisfactory account of its origin nor are able to resolve it into other, more general principles. And if we would employ a little thought on the present subject we need be at no loss to account for the influence of utility and to deduce it from principles the most known and avowed in human nature.

* We ought not to imagine because an inanimate object may be useful as well as a man that therefore it ought also, according to this system, to merit the appellation of *virtuous.* The sentiments excited by utility are, in the two cases, very different; and the one is mixed with affection, esteem, approbation, etc., and not the other. In like manner, an inanimate object may have good color and proportions as well as a human figure. But can we ever be in love with the former? There are a numerous set of passions and sentiments of which thinking, rational beings are, by the original constitution of nature, the only proper objects, and though the very same qualities be transferred to an insensible, inanimate being, they will not excite the same sentiments. The beneficial qualities of herbs and minerals are, indeed, sometimes called their *virtues;* but this is an effect of the caprice of language, which ought not to be regarded in reasoning. For though there be a species of approbation attending even inanimate objects when beneficial, yet this sentiment is so weak and so different from that which is directed to beneficent magistrates or statesmen that they ought not to be ranked under the same class or appellation.
A very small variation of the object, even where the same qualities are preserved, will destroy a sentiment. Thus, the same beauty, transferred to a different sex, excites no amorous passion where nature is not extremely perverted.

From the apparent usefulness of the social virtues it has readily been inferred by skeptics, both ancient and modern, that all moral distinctions arise from education and were at first invented, and afterwards encouraged, by the art of politicians in order to render men tractable and subdue their natural ferocity and selfishness, which incapacitated them for society. This principle, indeed, of precept and education must so far be owned to have a powerful influence that it may frequently increase or diminish beyond their natural standard the sentiments of approbation or dislike, and may even, in particular instances, create, without any natural principle, a new sentiment of this kind, as is evident in all superstitious practices and observances. But that *all* moral affection or dislike arises from this origin will never surely be allowed by any judicious inquirer. Had nature made no such distinction, founded on the original constitution of the mind, the words *honorable* and *shameful, lovely* and *odious, noble* and *despicable* had never had place in any language, nor could politicians, had they invented these terms, ever have been able to render them intelligible or make them convey any idea to the audience. So that nothing can be more superficial than this paradox of the skeptics; and it were well if, in the abstruser studies of logic and metaphysics, we could as easily obviate the cavils of that sect as in the practical and more intelligible sciences of politics and morals.

The social virtues must, therefore, be allowed to have a natural beauty and amiableness which at first, antecedent to all precept or education, recommends them to the esteem of uninstructed mankind and engages their affections. And as the public utility of these virtues is the chief circumstance whence they derive their merit, it follows that the end which they have a tendency to promote must be some way agreeable to us and take hold of some natural affection. It must please either from considerations of self-interest or from more generous motives and regards.

It has often been asserted that every man has a strong connection with society and perceives the impossibility of his solitary subsistence, he becomes, on that account, favorable to all those habits or principles which promote order in society and insure to him the quiet possession of so inestimable a blessing. As much as we value our own happiness and welfare, as much must we applaud the practice of justice and humanity by which alone the social confederacy can be maintained and every man reap the fruits of mutual protection and assistance.

This deduction of morals from self-love or a regard to private interest is an obvious thought and has not arisen wholly from the wanton sallies and sportive assaults of the skeptics. To mention no others, Polybius, one of the gravest and most judicious as well as most moral writers of antiquity, has assigned this selfish origin of all our sentiments of virtue.* But though the solid, practical sense of that author and his aversion to all vain subtleties render his authority on the present subject very considerable, yet is not this an affair to be decided by authority; and the voice of nature and experience seems plainly to oppose the selfish theory.

We frequently bestow praise on virtuous actions performed in very distant ages and remote countries, where the utmost subtlety of imagination would not discover any appearance of self-interest or find any connection of our present happiness and security with events so widely separated from us.

A generous, a brave, a noble deed performed by an adversary commands our approbation, while, in its consequences, it may be acknowledged prejudicial to our particular interest.

When private advantage concurs with general affection for virtue, we readily perceive and avow the mixture of these distinct sentiments, which have a very different feeling and influence on the mind. We praise, perhaps, with more alacrity where the generous, humane action contributes to our particular interest; but the topics of praise, which we insist on, are very wide of this circumstance. And we may attempt to bring over others to our sentiments, without endeavoring to convince them that they reap any advantage from the actions which we recommend to their approbation and applause.

Frame the model of a praiseworthy character consisting of all the most amiable moral virtues; give instances in which these display themselves after an eminent and extraordinary manner; you readily engage the esteem and approbation of all your audience, who never so much as inquire in what age and country the person lived who possessed these noble qualities—a circumstance, however, of all others the most material to self-love or a concern for our own individual happiness.

Once on a time, a statesman, in the shock and contest of parties, prevailed so far as to procure by his eloquence the banishment of an able adversary, whom he secretly followed, offering him money for his support during his exile and

*Undutifulness to parents is disapproved of by mankind, προορωμένους τὸ μέλλον, καὶ συλλογιζομένους ὅτι τὸ παραπλήσοιν ἑκάστοις αὐτῶν συγκυρήσει. ["looking forward to the future and expecting that the same sort of thing will happen to each of them."] Ingratitude for a like reason (though he seems there to mix a more generous regard) συναγανακτοῦντας μὲν τῷ πέλας, ἀναφέροντας δ' ἐπ' αὐτοὺς τὸ παραπλήσιον, ἐξ ὧν ὑπογίγνεταί τις ἔννοια παρ' ἑκάστῳ τῆς τοῦ καθήκοντος δυνάμεως καὶ θεωρίας. ["becoming irritated along with their neighbor and thinking themselves in a similar situation. In each of them, therefore, arises an idea of the meaning and the theory of the 'fitting.'"] (Ed. Gronovius.) Perhaps the historian only meant that our sympathy and humanity was more enlivened by our considering the similarity of our case with that of the person suffering, which is a just sentiment.

soothing him with topics of consolation in his misfortunes. *Alas!* cries the banished statesman, *with what regret must I leave my friends in this city where even enemies are so generous!* Virtue, though in an enemy, here pleased him; and we also give it the just tribute of praise and approbation; nor do we retract these sentiments when we hear that the action passed at Athens about two thousand years ago and that the persons' names were Aeschines and Demosthenes.

What is that to me? There are few occasions when this question is not pertinent; and had it that universal, infallible influence supposed, it would turn into ridicule every composition and almost every conversation which contain any praise or censure of men and manners.

It is but a weak subterfuge, when pressed by these facts and arguments, to say that we transport ourselves, by the force of imagination, into distant ages and countries and consider the advantage which we should have reaped from these characters had we been contemporaries and had any commerce with the persons. It is not conceivable how a *real* sentiment or passion can ever arise from a known *imaginary* interest, especially when our *real* interest is still kept in view and is often acknowledged to be entirely distinct from the imaginary, and even sometimes opposite to it.

A man brought to the brink of a precipice cannot look down without trembling; and the sentiment of *imaginary* danger actuates him, in opposition to the opinion and belief of *real* safety. But the imagination is here assisted by the presence of a striking object, and yet prevails not, except it be also aided by novelty and the unusual appearance of the object. Custom soon reconciles us to heights and precipices and wears off these false and delusive terrors. The reverse is observable in the estimates which we form of characters and manners; and the more we habituate ourselves to an accurate scrutiny of morals, the more delicate feeling do we acquire of the most minute distinctions between vice and virtue. Such frequent occasion, indeed, have we in common life to pronounce all kinds of moral determinations that no object of this kind can be new or unusual to us, nor could any *false* views or prepossessions maintain their ground against an experience so common and familiar. Experience being chiefly what forms the associations of ideas, it is impossible that any association could establish and support itself in direct opposition to that principle.

Usefulness is agreeable and engages our approbation. This is a matter of fact confirmed by daily observation. But *useful?* For what? For somebody's interest surely. Whose interest then? Not our own only, for our approbation frequently extends further. It must therefore be the interest of those who are served by the character or action approved of; and these, we may conclude, however remote, are not totally indifferent to us. By opening up this principle, we shall discover one great source of moral distinctions.

Part II

Self-love is a principle in human nature of such extensive energy, and the interest of each individual is in general so closely connected with that of the community, that those philosophers were excusable who fancied that all our concern for the public might be resolved into a concern for our own happiness and preservation. They saw, every moment, instances of approbation or blame, satisfaction or displeasure toward characters and actions; they denominated the objects of these sentiments *virtues* or *vices;* they observed that the former had a tendency to increase the happiness and the latter the misery of mankind; they asked whether it were possible that we could have any general concern for society or any distinterested resentment of the welfare or injury of others; they found it simpler to consider all these sentiments as modifications of self-love, and they discovered a pretense at least for this unity of principle in that close union of interest which is so observable between the public and each individual.

But notwithstanding this frequent confusion of interests, it is easy to attain what natural philosophers, after Lord Bacon, have affected to call the *experimentum crucis,* or that experiment which points out the right way in any doubt or ambiguity. We have found instances in which private interest was separate from public, in which it was even contrary, and yet we observed the moral sentiment to continue, notwithstanding this disjunction of interests. And wherever these distinct interests sensibly concurred, we always found a sensible increase of the sentiment and a more warm affection to virtue and detestation of vice, or what we properly call "gratitude" and "revenge." Compelled by these instances, we must renounce the theory which accounts for every moral sentiment by the principle of self-love. We must adopt a more public affection and allow that the interests of society are not, even on their own account, entirely indifferent to us. Usefulness is only a tendency to a certain end; and it is a contradiction in terms that anything pleases as means to an end where the end itself nowise affects us. If usefulness, therefore, be a source of moral sentiment, and if this usefulness be not always considered with a reference to self, it follows that everything which

191

contributes to the happiness of society recommends itself directly to our approbation and goodwill. Here is a principle which accounts, in great part, for the origin of morality; and what need we seek for abstruse and remote systems when there occurs one so obvious and natural? *

Have we any difficulty to comprehend the force of humanity and benevolence? Or to conceive that the very aspect of happiness, joy, prosperity gives pleasure; that of pain, suffering, sorrow communicates uneasiness? The human countenance, says Horace,† borrows smiles or tears from the human countenance. Reduce a person to solitude and he loses all enjoyment, except either of the sensual or speculative kind; and that because the movements of his heart are not forwarded by correspondent movements in his fellow creatures. The signs of sorrow and mourning, though arbitrary, affect us with melancholy, but the natural symptoms, tears and cries and groans, never fail to infuse compassion and uneasiness. And if the effects of misery touch us in so lively a manner, can we be supposed altogether insensible or indifferent toward its causes when a malicious or treacherous character and behavior are presented to us?

We enter, I shall suppose, into a convenient, warm, well-contrived apartment; we necessarily receive a pleasure from its very survey because it presents us with the pleasing ideas of ease, satisfaction, and enjoyment. The hospitable, good-humored, humane landlord appears. This circumstance surely must embellish the whole, nor can we easily forbear reflecting, with pleasure on the satisfaction which results to everyone from his intercourse and good offices.

His whole family, by the freedom, ease, confidence, and calm enjoyment diffused over their countenances, sufficiently express their happiness. I have a pleasing sympathy in the

---

* It is needless to push our researches so far as to ask, why we have humanity or a fellow-feeling with others? It is sufficient that this is experienced to be a principle in human nature. We must stop somewhere in our examination of causes; and there are, in every science, some general principles beyond which we cannot hope to find any principle more general. No man is absolutely indifferent to the happiness and misery of others. The first has a natural tendency to give pleasure, the second pain. This everyone may find in himself. It is not probable that these principles can be resolved into principles more simple and universal, whatever attempts may have been made to that purpose. But if it were possible, it belongs not to the present subject; and we may here safely consider these principles as original—happy if we can render all the consequences sufficiently plain and perspicuous!

† Ut ridentibus arrident, ita flentibus adflent
Humani vultus.   HOR.

["The human face smiles at those who smile, as also it weeps at those who weep." Horace, *The Art of Poetry,* 101–102.]

prospect of so much joy and can never consider the source of it without the most agreeable emotions.

He tells me that an oppressive and powerful neighbor had attempted to dispossess him of his inheritance and had long disturbed all his innocent and social pleasures. I feel an immediate indignation arise in me against such violence and injury.

But it is no wonder, he adds, that a private wrong should proceed from a man who had enslaved provinces, depopulated cities, and made the field and scaffold stream with human blood. I am struck with horror at the prospect of so much misery and am actuated by the strongest antipathy against its author.

In general, it is certain that wherever we go, whatever we reflect on or converse about, everything still presents us with the view of human happiness or misery and excites in our breast a sympathetic movement of pleasure or uneasiness. In our serious occupations, in our careless amusements, this principle still exerts its active energy.

A man who enters the theater is immediately struck with the view of so great a multitude participating of one common amusement and experiences, from their very aspect, a superior sensibility or disposition of being affected with every sentiment which he shares with his fellow creatures.

He observes the actors to be animated by the appearance of a full audience and raised to a degree of enthusiasm which they cannot command in any solitary or calm moment.

Every movement of the theater, by a skillful poet, is communicated, as it were, by magic to the spectators, who weep, tremble, resent, rejoice, and are inflamed with all the variety of passions which actuate the several personages of the drama.

Where any event crosses our wishes and interrupts the happiness of the favorite characters, we feel a sensible anxiety and concern. But where their sufferings proceed from the treachery, cruelty, or tyranny of an enemy, our breasts are affected with the liveliest resentment against the author of these calamities.

It is here esteemed contrary to the rules of art to represent anything cool and indifferent. A distant friend or a confidant who has no immediate interest in the catastrophe ought, if possible, to be avoided by the poet, as communicating a like indifference to the audience and checking the progress of the passions.

Few species of poetry are more entertaining than *pastoral;* and everyone is sensible that the chief source of its pleasure arises from those images of a gentle and tender tranquillity which it represents in its personages and of which it communicates a like sentiment to the reader. Sannazarius, who transferred the scene to the seashore, though he presented the most magnificent object in nature, is confessed to have erred in his choice. The idea of toil, labor, and danger suffered by the fisherman is painful by an unavoidable sympathy which attends every conception of human happiness or misery.

When I was twenty, says a French poet, Ovid was my favorite. Now I am forty, I declare for Horace. We enter, to be sure, more readily into sentiments which resemble those we feel every day; but no passion, when well represented, can be entirely indifferent to us, because there is none of which every man has not within him at least the seeds and first principles. It is the business of poetry to bring every affection near to us by lively imagery and representation and make it look like truth and reality, a certain proof that, wherever the reality is found, our minds are disposed to be strongly affected by it.

Any recent event or piece of news by which the fate of states, provinces, or many individuals is affected is extremely interesting even to those whose welfare is not immediately engaged. Such intelligence is propagated with celerity, heard with avidity, and inquired into with attention and concern. The interest of society appears, on this occasion, to be in some degree the interest of each individual. The imagination is sure to be affected, though the passions excited may not always be so strong and steady as to have great influence on the conduct and behavior.

The perusal of a history seems a calm entertainment, but would be no entertainment at all did not our hearts beat with correspondent movements to those which are described by the historian.

Thucydides and Guicciardin support with difficulty our attention while the former describes the trivial rencounters of the small cities of Greece and the latter the harmless wars of Pisa. The few persons interested, and the small interest, fill not the imagination and engage not the affections. The deep distress of the numerous Athenian army before Syracuse, the danger which so nearly threatens Venice—these excite compassion, these move terror and anxiety.

The indifferent, uninteresting style of Suetonius, equally with the masterly pencil of Tacitus, may convince us of the cruel depravity of Nero or Tiberius; but what a difference of sentiment! While the former coldly relates the facts, the latter sets before our eyes the venerable figures of a Soranus and a Thrasea, intrepid in their fate and only moved by the melting sorrows of their friends and kindred. What sympathy then touches every human heart! What indignation against the tyrant whose causeless fear or unprovoked malice gave rise to such detestable barbarity!

If we bring these subjects nearer, if we remove all suspicion of fiction and deceit, what powerful concern is excited, and how much superior, in many instances, to the narrow attachments of self-love and private interest! Popular sedition, party zeal, a devoted obedience to factious leaders—these are some of the most visible, though less laudable, effects of this social sympathy in human nature.

The frivolousness of the subject, too, we may observe, is not able to detach us entirely from what carries an image of human sentiment and affection.

When a person stutters and pronounces with difficulty, we even sympathize with this trivial uneasiness and suffer for him. And it is a rule in criticism that every combination of syllables or letters which gives pain to the organs of speech in the recital appears also, from a species of sympathy, harsh and disagreeable to the ear. Nay, when we run over a book with our eye, we are sensible of such unharmonious composition because we still imagine that a person recites it to us and suffers from the pronunciation of these jarring sounds. So delicate is our sympathy!

Easy and unconstrained postures and motions are always beautiful; an air of health and vigor is agreeable; clothes which warm, without burdening the body, which cover, without imprisoning the limbs, are well fashioned. In every judgment of beauty, the feelings of the person affected enter into consideration and communicate to the spectator similar touches of pain or pleasure.* What wonder, then, if we can pronounce no judgment concerning the character and conduct of men without considering the tendencies of their actions and the happiness or misery which thence arises to society? What association of ideas would ever operate were that principle here totally inactive? †

* "Decentior equus cujus astricta sunt ilia; sed idem velocior. Pulcher aspectu sit athleta, cujus lacertos exercitatio expressit; idem certamini paratior. Nunquam enim *species* ab *utilitate* dividitur. Sed hoc quidem discernere modici judicii est." Quintilian *Inst.* lib. viii. cap. 3. ["A horse whose flanks are tightly drawn is better-looking, but in addition it is faster. An athlete whose biceps are well-developed may be more handsome; but he is also in better condition for the contest. Appearance can never be separated from utility; to distinguish between them is a sign of mediocre judgment."]

† In proportion to the station which a man possesses, according to the relations in which he is placed, we always expect from him a greater or less degree of good and, when disappointed, blame his inutility; and much more do we blame him if any ill or prejudice arises from his conduct and behavior. When the interests of one coun-

195

If any man, from a cold insensibility or narrow selfishness of temper, is unaffected with the images of human happiness or misery, he must be equally indifferent to the images of vice and virtue; as, on the other hand, it is always found that a warm concern for the interests of our species is attended with a delicate feeling of all moral distinctions—a strong resentment of injury done to men, a lively approbation of their welfare. In this particular, though great superiority is observable of the man above another, yet none are so entirely indifferent to the interest of their fellow creatures as to perceive no distinctions of moral good and evil in consequence of the different tendencies of actions and principles. How, indeed, can we suppose it possible in anyone who wears a human heart that, if there be subjected to his censure one character or system of conduct which is beneficial and another which is pernicious to his species or community, he will not so much as give a cool preference to the former or ascribe to it the smallest merit or regard? Let us suppose a person ever so selfish, let private interest have engrossed ever so much his attention, yet in instances where that is not concerned he must unavoidably feel *some* propensity to the good of mankind and make it an object of choice, if everything else be equal. Would any man who is walking alone tread as willingly on another's gouty toes, whom he has no quarrel with, as on the hard flint and pavement? There is here surely a difference in the case. We surely take into consideration the happiness and misery of others in weighing the several motives of action and incline to the former where no private regards draw us to seek our own promotion or advantage by the injury of our fellow creatures. And if the principles of humanity are capable, in many instances, of influencing our actions, they must, at all times, have *some* authority over our sentiments and give us a general approbation of what is useful to society and blame of what is dangerous or pernicious. The degrees of these sentiments may be the subject of contro-

try interfere with those of another, we estimate the merits of a statesman by the good or ill which results to his own country from his measures and counsels, without regard to the prejudice which he brings on its enemies and rivals. His fellow citizens are the objects which lie nearest the eye while we determine his character. And as nature has implanted in everyone a superior affection to his own country, we never expect any regard to distant nations where a competition arises. Not to mention that while every man consults the good of his own community, we are sensible that the general interest of mankind is better promoted than by any loose indeterminate views to the good of a species, whence no beneficial action could ever result for want of a duly limited object on which they could exert themselves.

versy, but the reality of their existence, one should think, must be admitted in every theory or system.

A creature absolutely malicious and spiteful, were there any such in nature, must be worse than indifferent to the images of vice and virtue. All his sentiments must be inverted and directly opposite to those which prevail in the human species. Whatever contributes to the good of mankind, as it crosses the constant bent of his wishes and desires, must produce uneasiness and disapprobation; and, on the contrary, whatever is the source of disorder and misery in society must, for the same reason, be regarded with pleasure and complacency. Timon, who, probably from his affected spleen more than any inveterate malice, was denominated the man-hater, embraced Alcibiades with great fondness. *Go on, my boy!* cried he, *acquire the confidence of the people: you will one day, I foresee, be the cause of great calamities to them.** Could we admit the two principles of the Manichaeans, it is an infallible consequence that their sentiments of human actions, as well as of everything else, must be totally opposite, and that every instance of justice and humanity, from its necessary tendency, must please the one diety and displease the other. All mankind so far resemble the good principle that where interest or revenge or envy perverts not our disposition, we are always inclined, from our natural philanthropy, to give the preference to the happiness of society and, consequently, to virtue about its opposite. Absolute, unprovoked, disinterested malice has never, perhaps, place in any human breast; or if it had, must there pervert all the sentiments of morals as well as the feelings of humanity. If the cruelty of Nero be allowed entirely voluntary, and not rather the effect of constant fear and resentment, it is evident that Tigellinus, preferably to Seneca or Burrhus, must have possessed his steady and uniform approbation.

A statesman or patriot who serves our own country in our own time has always a more passionate regard paid to him than one whose beneficial influence operated on distant ages or remote nations, where the good resulting from his generous humanity, being less connected with us, seems more obscure and affects us with a less lively sympathy. We may own the merit to be equally great, though our sentiments are not raised to an equal height in both cases. The judgment here corrects the inequalities of our internal emotions and perceptions in like manner as it preserves us from error in the several variations of images presented to our external senses. The same object, at a double distance, really throws on the

* Plutarch in *Vita Alcib.* 16.

eye a picture of but half the bulk, yet we imagine that it appears of the same size in both situations because we know that, on our approach to it, its image would expand on the eye and that the difference consists not in the object itself, but in our position with regard to it. And indeed, without such a correction of appearances, both in internal and external sentiment, men could never think or talk steadily on any subject while their fluctuating situations produce a continual variation on objects and throw them into such different and contrary lights and positions.*

The more we converse with mankind, and the greater social intercourse we maintain, the more shall we be familiarized to these general preferences and distinctions without which our conversation and discourse could scarcely be rendered intelligible to each other. Every man's interest is peculiar to himself, and the aversions and desires which result from it cannot be supposed to affect others in a like degree. General language, therefore, being formed for general use, must be molded on some more general views and must affix the epithets of praise or blame in conformity to sentiments which arise from the general interests of the community. And if these sentiments, in most men, be not so strong as those which have a reference to private good, yet still they must make some distinction, even in persons the most depraved and selfish, and must attach the notion of good to a beneficent conduct and of evil to the contrary. Sympathy, we shall allow, is much fainter than our concern for ourselves, and sympathy with persons remote from us much fainter than that with persons near and contiguous; but for this very reason it is necessary for us, in our calm judgments and discourse concerning the characters of men, to neglect all these differences and render our sentiments more public and social. Besides that, we ourselves often change our situation in this

* For a like reason, the tendencies of actions and characters, not their real accidental consequences, are alone regarded in our moral determinations or general judgments, though in our real feeling or sentiment we cannot help paying greater regard to one whose station, joined to virtue, renders him really useful to society than to one who exerts the social virtues only in good intentions and benevolent affections. Separating the character from the fortune by an easy and necessary effort of thought, we pronounce these persons alike and give them the same general praise. The judgment corrects, or endeavors to correct, the appearance, but is not able entirely to prevail over sentiment.

Why is this peach tree said to be better than that other but because it produces more or better fruit? And would not the same praise be given it, though snails or vermin had destroyed the peaches before they came to full maturity? In morals, too, is not *the tree known by the fruit?* And cannot we easily distinguish between nature and accident in the one case as well as in the other?

particular; we every day meet with persons who are in a situation different from us and who could never converse with us were we to remain constantly in that position and point of view which is peculiar to ourselves. The intercourse of sentiments, therefore, in society and conversation makes us form some general unalterable standard by which we may approve or disapprove of characters and manners. And though the heart takes not part entirely with those general notions, nor regulates all its love and hatred by the universal, abstract differences of vice and virtue without regard to self or the persons with whom we are more intimately connected, yet have these moral differences a considerable influence, and being sufficient, at least, for discourse, serve all our purposes in company, in the pulpit, in the theater, and in the schools.*

Thus, in whatever light we take this subject, the merit ascribed to the social virtues appears still uniform and arises chiefly from that regard which the natural sentiment of benevolence engages us to pay to the interests of mankind and society. If we consider the principles of the human make, such as they appear to daily experience and observation, we must, *a priori*, conclude it impossible for such a creature as man to be totally indifferent to the well- or ill-being of his fellow creatures, and not readily, of himself, to pronounce, where nothing gives him any particular bias, that what promotes their happiness is good, what tends to their misery is evil, without any further regard or consideration. Here then are the faint rudiments at least, or outlines, of a *general* distinction between actions; and in proportion as the humanity of the person is supposed to increase, his connection with those who are injured or benefited, and his lively conception of their misery or happiness, his consequent censure or approbation acquires proportionable vigor. There is no necessity that a generous action, barely mentioned in an old history or remote gazette, should communicate any strong feelings of applause and admiration. Virtue, placed at such a distance, is like a fixed star which, though to the eye of reason it may appear as luminous as the sun in his meridian, is so infinitely removed as to affect the senses neither with light nor heat. Bring this virtue nearer, by our acquaintance or connection

---

* It is wisely ordained by nature that private connections should commonly prevail over universal views and considerations, otherwise our affections and actions would be dissipated and lost for want of a proper limited object. Thus, a small benefit done to ourselves, or our near friends, excites more lively sentiments of love and approbation than a great benefit done to a distant commonwealth; but still we know here, as in all the senses, to correct these inequalities by reflection and retain a general standard of vice and virtue, founded chiefly on general usefulness.

with the persons, or even by an eloquent recital of the case, our hearts are immediately caught, our sympathy enlivened, and our cool approbation converted into the warmest sentiments of friendship and regard. These seem necessary and infallible consequences of the general principles of human nature as discovered in common life and practice.

Again, reverse these views and reasonings; consider the matter *a posteriori;* and, weighing the consequences, inquire if the merit of social virtue be not, in a great measure, derived from the feelings of humanity with which it affects the spectators. It appears to be matter of fact that the circumstance of *utility,* in all subjects, is a source of praise and approbation; that it is constantly appealed to in all moral decisions concerning the merit and demerit of actions; that it is the *sole* source of that high regard paid to justice, fidelity, honor, allegiance, and chastity; that it is inseparable from all the other social virtues, humanity, generosity, charity, affability, lenity, mercy, and moderation; and, in a word, it is a foundation of the chief part of morals which has a reference to mankind and our fellow creatures.

It appears also that in our general approbation of characters and manners the useful tendency of the social virtues moves us not by any regards to self-interest, but has an influence much more universal and extensive. It appears that a tendency to public good and to the promoting of peace, harmony, and order in society does always, by affecting the benevolent principles of our frame, engage us on the side of the social virtues. And it appears, as an additional confirmation, that these principles of humanity and sympathy enter so deeply into all our sentiments and have so powerful an influence as may enable them to excite the strongest censure and applause. The present theory is the simple result of all these inferences, each of which seems founded on uniform experience and observation.

Were it doubtful whether there were any such principle in our nature as humanity or a concern for others, yet when we see, in numberless instances, that whatever has a tendency to promote the interest of society is so highly approved of, we ought thence to learn the force of the benevolent principle, since it is impossible for anything to please as means to an end where the end is totally indifferent. On the other hand, were it doubtful whether there were implanted in our nature any general principle of moral blame and approbation, yet when we see, in numberless instances, the influence of humanity, we ought thence to conclude that it is impossible but that everything which promotes the interests of society must communicate pleasure and what is pernicious give uneasiness.

But when these different reflections and observations concur in establishing the same conclusion, must they not bestow an undisputed evidence upon it?

It is, however, hoped that the progress of this argument will bring a further confirmation of the present theory by showing the rise of other sentiments of esteem and regard from the same or like principles.

Section VI

OF QUALITIES USEFUL TO OURSELVES

Part I

It seems evident that where a quality or habit is subjected to our examination, if it appear in any respect prejudicial to the person possessed of it, or such as incapacitates him for business and action, it is instantly blamed and ranked among his faults and imperfections. Indolence, negligence, want of order and method, obstinacy, fickleness, rashness, credulity —these qualities were never esteemed by anyone indifferent to a character, much less extolled as accomplishments or virtues. The prejudice resulting from them immediately strikes our eye and gives us the sentiment of pain and disapprobation.

No quality, it is allowed, is absolutely either blamable or praiseworthy. It is all according to its degree. A due medium, say the Peripatetics, is the characteristic of virtue. But this medium is chiefly determined by utility. A proper celerity, for instance, and dispatch in business is commendable. When defective, no progress is ever made in the execution of any purpose. When excessive, it engages us in precipitate and ill-concerted measures and enterprises. By such reasonings, we fix the proper and commendable mediocrity in all moral and prudential disquisitions and never lose view of the advantages which result from any character or habit.

Now, as these advantages are enjoyed by the person possessed of the character, it can never be *self-love* which renders the prospect of them agreeable to us, the spectators, and prompts our esteem and approbation. No force of imagination can convert us into another person and make us fancy that we, being that person, reap benefit from those valuable qualities which belong to him. Or if it did, no celerity of imagination could immediately transport us back into ourselves and make us love and esteem the person as different from us. Views and sentiments so opposite to known truth and to each other could never have place, at the same time, in the same person. All suspicion, therefore, of selfish regards is here totally excluded.

It is a quite different principle which actuates our bosom and interests us in the felicity of the person whom we contemplate. Where his natural talents and acquired abilities give us the prospect of elevation, advancement, a figure in life, prosperous success, a steady command over fortune, and the execution of great or advantageous undertakings, we are struck with such agreeable images and feel a complacency and regard immediately arise toward him. The ideas of happiness, joy, triumph, prosperity are connected with every circumstance of his character and diffuse over our minds a pleasing sentiment of sympathy and humanity.*

Let us suppose a person originally framed so as to have no manner of concern for his fellow creatures. but to regard the happiness and misery of all sensible beings with greater indifference than even two contiguous shades of the same color. Let us suppose, if the prosperity of nations were laid on the one hand, and their ruin on the other, and he were desired to choose, that he would stand like the schoolman's ass, irresolute and undetermined between equal motives, or rather like the same ass between two pieces of wood or marble, without any inclination or propensity to either side. The consequence, I believe, must be allowed just that such a person, being absolutely unconcerned either for the public good of a community or the private utility of others, would look on every

* One may venture to affirm that there is no human creature to whom the appearance of happiness (where envy or revenge has no place) does not give pleasure, that of misery, uneasiness. This seems inseparable from our make and constitution. But they are only the more generous minds that are thence prompted to seek zealously the good of others and to have a real passion for their welfare. With men of narrow and ungenerous spirits, this sympathy goes not beyond a slight feeling of the imagination, which serves only to excite sentiments of complacency or censure and makes them apply to the object either honorable or dishonorable appellations. A griping miser, for instance, praises extremely *industry* and *frugality* even in others and sets them, in his estimation, above all the other virtues. He knows the good that results from them and feels that species of happiness with a more lively sympathy than any other you could represent to him, though perhaps he would not part with a shilling to make the fortune of the industrious man whom he praises so highly.

quality, however pernicious or however beneficial to society or to its possessor, with the same indifference as on the most common and uninteresting object.

But if, instead of this fancied monster, we suppose a *man* to form a judgment or determination in the case, there is to him a plain foundation of preference where everything else is equal; and however cool his choice may be, if his heart be selfish or if the persons interested be remote from him, there must still be a choice or distinction between what is useful and what is pernicious. Now this distinction is the same, in all its parts, with the *moral distinction* whose foundation has been so often, and so much in vain, inquired after. The same endowments of the mind, in every circumstance, are agreeable to the sentiment of morals and to that of humanity; the same temper is susceptible of high degrees of the one sentiment and of the other; and the same alteration in the objects, by their nearer approach or by connections, enlivens the one and the other. By all the rules of philosophy, therefore, we must conclude that these sentiments are originally the same, since in each particular, even the most minute, they are governed by the same laws and are moved by the same objects.

Why do philosophers infer, with the greatest certainty, that the moon is kept in its orbit by the same force of gravity that makes bodies fall near the surface of the earth but because these effects are, upon computation, found similar and equal? And must not this argument bring as strong conviction in moral as in natural disquisitions?

To prove, by any long detail, that all the qualities useful to the possessor are approved of, and the contrary censured, would be superfluous. The least reflection on what is every day experienced in life will be sufficient. We shall only mention a few instances in order to remove, if possible, all doubt and hesitation.

The quality the most necessary for the execution of any useful enterprise is *discretion*, by which we carry on a safe intercourse with others, give due attention to our own and to their character, weigh each circumstance of the business which we undertake, and employ the surest and safest means for the attainment of any end or purpose. To a Cromwell, perhaps, or a De Retz, discretion may appear an alderman-like virtue, as Dr. Swift calls it; and being incompatible with those vast designs to which their courage and ambition prompted them, it might really, in them, be a fault or imperfection. But in the conduct of ordinary life, no virtue is more requisite, not only to obtain success, but to avoid the most fatal miscarriages and disappointments. The greatest parts without it, as observed by an elegant writer, may be fatal to their owner, as Polyphemus, deprived of his eye, was only the more exposed on account of his enormous strength and stature.

The best character, indeed, were it not rather too perfect for human nature, is that which is not swayed by temper of any kind, but alternately employs enterprise and caution, as each is *useful* to the particular purpose intended. Such is the excellence which St. Evremond ascribes to Maréchal Turenne, who displayed in every campaign, as he grew older, more temerity in his military enterprises; and being now, from long experience, perfectly acquainted with every incident in war, he advanced with greater firmness and security in a road so well-known to him. Fabius, says Machiavelli, was cautious, Scipio enterprising: and both succeeded because the situation of the Roman affairs, during the command of each, was peculiarly adapted to his genius, but both would have failed had these situations been reversed. He is happy whose circumstances suit his temper; but he is more excellent who can suit his temper to any circumstances.

What need is there to display the praises of *industry* and to extol its advantages in the acquisition of power and riches or in raising what we call a *fortune* in the world? The tortoise, according to the fable, by his perseverance gained the race of the hare, though possessed of much superior swiftness. A man's time, when well husbanded, is, like a cultivated field of which a few acres produce more of what is useful to life than extensive provinces, even of the richest soil, when overrun with weeds and brambles.

But all prospect of success in life, or even of tolerable subsistence, must fail where a reasonable *frugality* is wanting. The heap, instead of increasing, diminishes daily and leaves its possessor so much more unhappy, as, not having been able to confine his expenses to a large revenue, he will still less be able to live contentedly on a small one. The souls of men, according to Plato,* inflamed with impure appetites and losing the body, which alone afforded means of satisfaction, hover about the earth and haunt the places where their bodies are deposited, possessed with a longing desire to recover the lost organs of sensation. So may we see worthless prodigals, having consumed their fortune in wild debauches, thrusting themselves into every plentiful table and every party of pleasure, hated even by the vicious and despised even by fools.

The one extreme of frugality is *avarice*, which, as it both deprives a man of all use of his riches and checks hospitality

* *Phædo* 81.

and every social enjoyment, is justly censured on a double account. *Prodigality,* the other extreme, is commonly more hurtful to a man himself; and each of these extremes is blamed above the other, according to the temper of the person who censures, and according to his greater or less sensibility to pleasure, either social or sensual.

Qualities often derive their merit from complicated sources. *Honesty, fidelity, truth* are praised for their immediate tendency to promote the interests of society; but after those virtues are once established upon this foundation, they are also considered as advantageous to the person himself and as the source of that trust and confidence which can alone give a man any consideration in life. One becomes contemptible, no less than odious, when he forgets the duty which, in this particular, he owes to himself as well as to society.

Perhaps this consideration is one *chief* source of the high blame which is thrown on any instance of failure among women in point of *chastity.* The greatest regard which can be acquired by that sex is derived from their fidelity; and a woman becomes cheap and vulgar, loses her rank, and is exposed to every insult who is deficient in this particular. The smallest failure is here sufficient to blast her character. A female has so many opportunities of secretly indulging these appetites that nothing can give us security but her absolute modesty and reserve; and where a breach is once made, it can scarcely ever be fully repaired. If a man behave with cowardice on one occasion, a contrary conduct reinstates him in his character. But by what action can a woman whose behavior has once been dissolute be able to assure us that she has formed better resolutions and has self-command enough to carry them into execution?

All men, it is allowed, are equally desirous of happiness; but few are successful in the pursuit: one considerable cause is the want of *strength* of *mind,* which might enable them to resist the temptation of present ease or pleasure and carry them forward in the search of more distant profit and enjoyment. Our affections, on a general prospect of their objects, form certain rules of conduct and certain measures of preference of one above another; and these decisions, though really the result of our calm passions and propensities (for what else can pronounce any object eligible, or the contrary), are yet said, by a natural abuse of terms, to be the determinations of pure *reason* and reflection. But when some of these objects approach nearer to us or acquire the advantages of favorable lights and positions which catch the heart or imagination, our general resolutions are frequently confounded, a small enjoyment preferred, and lasting shame and sorrow entailed upon us. And however poets may employ their wit and eloquence in celebrating present pleasure and rejecting all distant views to fame, health, or fortune, it is obvious that this practice is the source of all dissoluteness and disorder, repentance and misery. A man of a strong and determined temper adheres tenaciously to his general resolutions and is neither seduced by the allurements of pleasure nor terrified by the menaces of pain, but keeps still in view those distant pursuits by which he at once insures his happiness and his honor.

Self-satisfaction, at least in some degree, is an advantage which equally attends the *fool* and the *wise man*, but it is the only one; nor is there any other circumstance in the conduct of life where they are upon an equal footing. Business, books, conversation—for all of these a fool is totally incapacitated and, except condemned by his station to the coarsest drudgery, remains a *useless* burden upon the earth. Accordingly, it is found that men are extremely jealous of their character in this particular; and many instances are seen of profligacy and treachery the most avowed and unreserved, none of bearing patiently the imputation of ignorance and stupidity. Dicaearchus, the Macedonian general who, as Polybius tells us,* openly erected one altar to impiety, another to injustice, in order to bid defiance to mankind, even he, I am well assured, would have started at the epithet of *fool* and have meditated revenge for so injurious an appellation. Except the affection of parents, the strongest and most indissoluble bond in nature, no connection has strength sufficient to support the disgust arising from this character. Love itself, which can subsist under treachery, ingratitude, malice, and infidelity, is immediately extinguished by it when perceived and acknowledged; nor are deformity and old age more fatal to the dominion of that passion. So dreadful are the ideas of an utter incapacity for any purpose or undertaking and of continued error and misconduct in life!

When it is asked whether a quick or slow apprehension be most valuable; whether one that at first view penetrates far into a subject, but can perform nothing upon study, or a contrary character which must work out everything by dint of application; whether a clear head or a copious invention; whether a profound genius or a sure judgment—in short, what character or peculiar turn of understanding is more excellent than another, it is evident that we can answer none of these questions without considering which of those qualities capacitates a man best for the world and carries him farthest in any undertaking.

* Lib. xvii, cap. 35.

If refined sense and exalted sense be not so *useful* as common sense, their rarity, their novelty, and the nobleness of their objects make some compensation and render them the admiration of mankind, as gold, though less serviceable than iron, acquires from its scarcity a value which is much superior.

The defects of judgment can be supplied by no art or invention, but those of *memory* frequently may, both in business and in study, by method and industry and by diligence in committing everything to writing; and we scarcely ever hear a short memory given as a reason for a man's failure in any undertaking. But in ancient times, when no man could make a figure without the talent of speaking, and when the audience were too delicate to bear such crude undigested harangues as our extemporary orators offer to public assemblies, the faculty of memory was then of the utmost consequence and was accordingly much more valued than at present. Scarce any great genius is mentioned in antiquity who is not celebrated for this talent; and Cicero enumerates it among the other sublime qualities of Caesar himself.*

Particular customs and manners alter the usefulness of qualities; they also alter their merit. Particular situations and accidents have, in some degree, the same influence. He will always be more esteemed who possesses those talents and accomplishments which suit his station and profession than he whom fortune has misplaced in the part which she has assigned him. The private or selfish virtues are in this respect more arbitrary than the public and social. In other respects, they are, perhaps, less liable to doubt and controversy.

In this kingdom, such continued ostentation of late years has prevailed among men in *active* life with regard to *public spirit*, and among those in *speculative* with regard to *benevolence*, and so many false pretensions to each have been no doubt detected that men of the world are apt, without any bad intention, to discover a sullen incredulity on the head of those moral endowments and even sometimes absolutely to deny their existence and reality. In like manner, I find that of old the perpetual cant of the Stoics and Cynics concerning *virtue*, their magnificent professions and slender performances, bred a disgust in mankind; and Lucian, who, though licentious with regard to pleasure, is yet, in other respects, a very moral writer, cannot sometimes talk of virtue, so much

* Fuit in illo ingenium, ratio, memoria, literae, cura, cogitatio, diligentia, etc. *Philip.* 2. 45. ["There was in him genius, judgment, memory, culture, conscientiousness, thought, diligence," etc. Cicero, *Second Philippic, xlv.* 116.]

boasted, without betraying symptoms of spleen and irony.* But surely this peevish delicacy, whencever it arises, can never be carried so far as to make us deny the existence of every species of merit and all distinction of manners and behavior. Besides *discretion, caution, enterprise, industry, assiduity, frugality, economy, good sense, prudence, discernment* —besides these endowments, I say, whose very names force an avowal of their merit, there are many others to which the most determined skepticism cannot for a moment refuse the tribute of praise and approbation. *Temperance, sobriety, patience, constancy, perseverance, forethought, considerateness, secrecy, order, insinuation, address, presence of mind, quickness of conception, facility of expression*—these and a thousand more of the same kind no man will ever deny to be excellences and perfections. As their merit consists in their tendency to serve the person possessed of them, without any magnificent claim to public and social desert, we are the less jealous of their pretensions and readily admit them into the catalogue of laudable qualities. We are not sensible that, by this concession, we have paved the way for all the other moral excellences and cannot consistently hesitate any longer with regard to disinterested benevolence, patriotism, and humanity.

It seems, indeed, certain that first appearances are here, as usual, extremely deceitful and that it is more difficult, in a speculative way, to resolve into self-love the merit which we ascribe to the selfish virtues above mentioned than that even of the social virtues, justice, and beneficence. For this latter purpose, we need but say that whatever conduct promotes the good of the community is loved, praised, and esteemed by the community on account of that utility and interest of which everyone partakes; and though this affection and regard be, in reality, gratitude, not self-love, yet a distinction, even of this obvious nature, may not readily be made by superficial reasoners; and there is room at least to support the cavil and dispute for a moment. But as qualities which tend only to the utility of their possessor, without any reference to us or to the community, are yet esteemed and valued, by what theory or system can we account for this sentiment from self-love or deduce it from that favorite origin? There seems here a necessity for confessing that the happiness and misery of others are not spectacles entirely indifferent to us, but that the view

*Ἀρετήν τινα, καὶ ἀσώματα, καὶ λήρους μεγάλη τῇ φωνῇ ξυνειρόντων. ["Who hold forth in a loud voice about some sort of virtue, immaterial substances, and such like nonsense." Lucian, *Timon* 9.] Again, Καὶ συναγαγόντες (οἱ φιλόσοφοι) εὖ ἐξαπάτητα μειράκια τήν τε πολυθρύλητον ἀρετὴν τραγῳδοῦσι. ["And bringing together youths who are easily taken in, the philosophers deliver tragic speeches about the hackneyed subject of the former, whether in its causes or effects, like sunshine, or the prospect of well-cultivated plains (to carry our pretensions no higher), communicates a secret joy and satisfaction; the appearance of the latter, like a lowering cloud or barren landscape, throws a melancholy damp over the imagination. And this concession being once made, the difficulty is over, and a natural, unforced interpretation of the phenomena of human life will afterward, we hope, prevail among all speculative inquirers.

Part II

It may not be improper, in this place, to examine the influence of bodily endowments and of the goods of fortune over our sentiments of regard and esteem and to consider whether these phenomena fortify or weaken the present theory. It will naturally be expected that the beauty of the body, as is supposed by all ancient moralists, will be similar in some respects to that of the mind, and that every kind of esteem which is paid to a man will have something similar in its origin, whether it arise from his mental endowments or from the situation of his exterior circumstances.

It is evident that one considerable source of *beauty* in all animals is the advantage which they reap from the particular structure of their limbs and members, suitably to the particular manner of life to which they are by nature destined. The just proportions of a horse described by Xenophon and Virgil are the same that are received at this day by our modern jockeys, because the foundation of them is the same—namely, experience of what is detrimental or useful in the animal.

Broad shoulders, a lank belly, firm joints, taper legs—all these are beautiful in our species, because signs of force and vigor. Ideas of utility and its contrary, though they do not entirely determine what is handsome or deformed, are evidently the source of a considerable part of approbation or dislike.

In ancient times, bodily strength and dexterity, being of greater *use* and importance in war, was also much more esteemed and valued than at present. Not to insist on Homer and the poets, we may observe that historians scruple not to mention *force of body* among the other accomplishments even of Epaminondas, whom they acknowledge to be the

of virtue." *Icaromenippus.* 30] In another place, "Ἡ ποῦ γάρ ἐστιν ἡ πολυθρύλητος ἀρετή, καὶ φύσις, καὶ εἱμαρμένη, καὶ τύχη, ἀνυπόστατα καὶ κενὰ πραγμάτων· ὀνοματα. ["Where then are cliched 'virtue,' and 'nature,' and 'fortune,' all of them empty and meaningless names. (*Deorum concilium,* i.3).]

greatest hero, statesman, and general of all the Greeks.* A like praise is given to Pompey, one of the greatest of the Romans.† This instance is similar to what we observed above with regard to memory.

What derision and contempt, with both sexes, attend *impotence*, while the unhappy object is regarded as one deprived of so capital a pleasure in life and at the same time as disabled from communicating it to others. *Barrenness* in women, being also a species of *inutility*, is a reproach, but not in the same degree, of which the reason is very obvious, according to the present theory.

There is no rule in painting or statuary more indispensable than that of balancing the figures and placing them with the greatest exactness on their proper center of gravity. A figure which is not justly balanced is ugly, because it conveys the disagreeable ideas of fall, harm, and pain.‡

A disposition or turn of mind which qualifies a man to rise in the world and advance his fortune is entitled to esteem and regard, as has already been explained. It may, therefore, naturally be supposed that the actual possession of riches and authority will have a considerable influence over these sentiments.

Let us examine any hypothesis by which we can account for the regard paid to the rich and powerful; we shall find none satisfactory but that which derives it from the enjoyment communicated to the spectator by the images of prosperity, happiness, ease, plenty, authority, and the gratification

---

* Diodorus Siculus, lib. xv, 88. It may not be improper to give the character of Epaminondas, as drawn by the historian, in order to show the ideas of perfect merit which prevailed in those ages. In other illustrious men, says he, you will observe that each possessed some one shining quality which was the foundation of his fame; in Epaminondas all the *virtues* are found united, force of body, eloquence of expression, vigor of mind, contempt of riches, gentleness of disposition, and, *what is chiefly to be regarded,* courage and conduct in war.

† Cum alacribus, saltu; cum velocibus, cursu; cum validis recte-certabat. SALLUST apud VEGET. *De Re Mil.* 19. ["With the spirited, he jumped; with the swift he raced; and with the strong he competed in the proper manner."]

‡ All men are equally liable to pain and disease and sickness and may again recover health and ease. These circumstances, as they make no distinction between one man and another, are no source of pride or humility, regard or contempt. But comparing our own species to superior ones, it is a very mortifying consideration that we should all be so liable to diseases and infirmities; and divines accordingly employ this topic in order to depress self-conceit and vanity. They would have more success if the common bent of our thoughts were not perpetually turned to compare ourselves with others. The infirmities of old age are mortifying because a comparison with the young may take place. The king's evil is industriously concealed because it affects others and is often transmitted to posterity. The case is nearly the same with such diseases as convey any nauseous or frightful images, the epilepsy, for instance, ulcers, sores, scabs, etc.

of every appetite. Self-love, for instance, which some affect so much to consider as the source of every sentiment, is plainly insufficient for this purpose. Where no goodwill or friendship appears, it is difficult to conceive on what we can found our hope of advantage from the riches of others, though we naturally respect the rich, even before they discover any such favorable disposition toward us.

We are affected with the same sentiments when we lie so much out of the sphere of their activity that they cannot even be supposed to possess the power of serving us. A prisoner of war, in all civilized nations, is treated with a regard suited to his condition; and riches, it is evident, go far toward fixing the condition of any person. If birth and quality enter for a share, this still affords us an argument to our present purpose. For what is it we call a man of birth but one who is descended from a long succession of rich and powerful ancestors and who acquires our esteem by his connection with persons whom we esteem? His ancestors, therefore, though dead, are respected in some measure on account of their riches and, consequently, without any kind of expectation.

But not to go so far as prisoners of war or the dead to find instances of this disinterested regard for riches, we may only observe, with a little attention, those phenomena which occur in common life and conversation. A man who is himself, we shall suppose, of a competent fortune and of no profession, being introduced to a company of strangers, naturally treats them with different degrees of respect as he is informed of their different fortunes and conditions, though it is impossible that he can so suddenly propose, and perhaps he would not accept of, any pecuniary advantage from them. A traveler is always admitted into company, and meets with civility, in proportion as his train and equipage speak him a man of great or moderate fortune. In short, the different ranks of men are, in a great measure, regulated by riches, and that with regard to superiors as well as inferiors, strangers as well as acquaintance.

What remains, therefore, but to conclude that as riches are desired for ourselves only as the means of gratifying our appetites, either at present or in some imaginary future period, they beget esteem in others merely from their having that influence. This indeed is their very nature or essence: they have a direct reference to the commodities, conveniences, and pleasures of life; the bill of a banker who is broke or gold in a desert island would otherwise be full as valuable. When we approach a man who is, as we say, at his ease, we are presented with the pleasing ideas of plenty, satisfaction, cleanliness, warmth: a cheerful house, elegant furniture, ready service, and whatever is desirable in meat, drink, or apparel. On

211

the contrary, when a poor man appears, the disagreeable images of want, penury, hard labor, dirty furniture, coarse or ragged clothes, nauseous meat, and distasteful liquor immediately strike our fancy. What else do we mean by saying that one is rich, the other poor? And as regard or contempt is the natural consequence of those different situations in life, it is easily seen what additional light and evidence this throws on our preceding theory with regard to all moral distinctions.*

A man who has cured himself of all ridiculous prepossessions and is fully, sincerely, and steadily convinced, from experience as well as philosophy, that the difference of fortune makes less difference in happiness than is vulgarly imagined —such a one does not measure out degrees of esteem according to the rentrolls of his acquaintance. He may, indeed, externally pay a superior deference to the great lord above the vassal, because riches are the most convenient, being the most fixed and determinate source of distinction; but his internal sentiments are more regulated by the personal characters of men than by the accidental and capricious favors of fortune.

In most countries of Europe, family, that is, hereditary riches, marked with titles and symbols from the sovereign, is the chief source of distinction. In England, more regard is paid to present opulence and plenty. Each practice has its advantages and disadvantages. Where birth is respected, unactive, spiritless minds remain in haughty indolence and dream of nothing but pedigrees and genealogies; the generous and ambitious seek honor and authority and reputation and favor. Where riches are the chief idol, corruption, venality, rapine prevail; arts, manufactures, commerce, agriculture flourish. The former prejudice, being favorable to military virtue, is more suited to monarchies. The latter, being the chief spur to industry, agrees better with a republican government. And we accordingly find that each of these forms of government, by varying the *utility* of those customs, has commonly a proportionable effect on the sentiments of mankind.

* There is something extraordinary, and seemingly unaccountable, in the operation of our passions when we consider the fortune and situation of others. Very often another's advancement and prosperity produces envy, which has a strong mixture of hatred, and arises chiefly from the comparison of ourselves with the person. At the very same time, or at least in very short intervals, we may feel the passion of respect, which is a species of affection or goodwill with a mixture of humility. On the other hand, the misfortunes of our fellows often cause pity, which has in it a strong mixture of goodwill. This sentiment of pity is nearly allied to contempt, which is a species of dislike with a mixture of pride. I only point out these phenomena as a subject of speculation to such as are curious with regard to moral inquiries. It is sufficient for the present purpose to observe, in general, that power and riches commonly cause respect, poverty and meanness contempt, though particular views and incidents may sometimes raise the passions of envy and of pity.

Section VII

OF QUALITIES IMMEDIATELY AGREEABLE TO OURSELVES

Whoever has passed an evening with serious, melancholy people and has observed how suddenly the conversation was animated and what sprightliness diffused itself over the countenance, discourse, and behavior of everyone on the accession of a good-humored, lively companion, such a one will easily allow that *cheerfulness* carries great merit with it and naturally conciliates the goodwill of mankind. No quality, indeed, more readily communicates itself to all around, because no one has a greater propensity to display itself in jovial talk and pleasant entertainment. The flame spreads through the whole circle, and the most sullen and morose are often caught by it. That the melancholy hate the merry, even though Horace says it, I have some difficulty to allow, because I have always observed that, where the jollity is moderate and decent, serious people are so much the more delighted, as it dissipates the gloom with which they are commonly oppressed and gives them an unusual enjoyment.

From this influence of cheerfulness, both to communicate itself and to engage approbation, we may perceive that there is another set of mental qualities which, without any utility or any tendency to further good, either of the community or of the possessor, diffuse a satisfaction on the beholders and procure friendship and regard. Their immediate sensation to the person possessed of them is agreeable; others enter into the same humor and catch the sentiment by a contagion or natural sympathy; and as we cannot forbear loving whatever pleases, a kindly emotion arises toward the person who communicates so much satisfaction. He is a more animating spectacle; his presence diffuses over us more serene complacency and enjoyment; our imagination, entering into his feelings and disposition, is affected in a more agreeable manner than if a melancholy, dejected, sullen, anxious temper were presented to us. Hence, the affection and approbation which attend the

213

former, the aversion and disgust with which we regard the latter.*

Few men would envy the character which Caesar gives of Cassius:

> He loves no play,
> As thou do'st, Anthony: He hears no music:
> Seldom he smiles; and smiles in such a sort,
> As if he mocked himself, and scorned his spirit
> That could be moved to smile at any thing.

Not only such men, as Caesar adds, are commonly *dangerous*, but also, having little enjoyment within themselves, they can never become agreeable to others or contribute to social entertainment. In all polite nations and ages, a relish for pleasure, if accompanied with temperance and decency, is esteemed a considerable merit, even in the greatest men, and becomes still more requisite in those of inferior rank and character. It is an agreeable representation which a French writer gives of the situation of his own mind in this particular: *Virtue I love*, says he, *without austerity, pleasure without effeminacy, and life without fearing its end.*†

Who is not struck with any signal instance of *greatness of mind* or dignity of character, with elevation of sentiment, disdain of slavery, and with that noble pride and spirit which arises from conscious virtue? The sublime, says Longinus, is often nothing but the echo or image of magnanimity; and where this quality appears in anyone, even though a syllable be not uttered, it excites our applause and admiration, as may be observed of the famous silence of Ajax in the *Odyssey*, which expresses more noble disdain and resolute indignation than any language can convey.‡

"Were I Alexander," said Parmenio, "I would accept of these offers made by Darius." — "So would I, too," replied

---

* There is no man who, on particular occasions, is not affected with all the disagreeable passions: fear, anger, dejection, grief, melancholy, anxiety, etc. But these, so far as they are natural and universal, make no difference between one man and another and can never be the object of blame. It is only when the disposition gives a *propensity* to any of these disagreeable passions that they disfigure the character and, by giving uneasiness, convey the sentiment of disapprobation to the spectator.

> † "J'aime la vertue, sans rudesse;
> J'aime le plaisir, sans molesse;
> J'aime la vie, et n'en crains point la fin."
>   St. Evremond.

‡ Cap 9.

214

Alexander, "were I Parmenio." This saying is admirable, says Longinus, from a like principle.*

"Go!" cries the same hero to his soldiers, when they refused to follow him to the Indies, "go, tell your countrymen that you left Alexander completing the conquest of the world." — "Alexander," said the Prince of Condé, who always admired this passage, "abandoned by his soldiers among barbarians not yet fully subdued, felt in himself such a dignity and right of empire that he could not believe it possible that anyone would refuse to obey him. Whether in Europe or in Asia, among Greeks or Persians, all was indifferent to him: wherever he found men, he fancied he should find subjects."

The confidant of Medea in the tragedy recommends caution and submission and, enumerating all the distresses of that unfortunate heroine, asks her what she has to support her against her numerous and implacable enemies? "Myself," replies she: "Myself, I say, and it is enough." Boileau justly recommends this passage as an instance of true sublime.†

When Phocion, the modest, the gentle Phocion, was led to execution, he turned to one of his fellow sufferers, who was lamenting his own hard fate, "Is it not glory enough for you," says he, "that you die with Phocion?" ‡

Place in opposition the picture which Tacitus draws of Vitellius, fallen from empire, prolonging his ignominy from a wretched love of life, delivered over to the merciless rabble —tossed, buffeted, and kicked about; constrained, by their holding a poniard under his chin, to raise his head and expose himself to every contumely. What abject infamy! What low humiliation! Yet even here, says the historian, he discovered some symptoms of a mind not wholly degenerate. To a tribune who insulted him, he replied, "I am still your emperor." §

We never excuse the absolute want of spirit and dignity of character or a proper sense of what is due to one's self in

* *Idem.*

† *Réflexion* X. sur Longin.

‡ Plutarch in *Phoc.* 36.

§ Tacit. *Hist.* lib. iii. 85. The author, entering upon the narration, says, *Laniata veste, foedum spectaculum ducebatur, multis increpantibus, nullo inlacrimante: deformitas exitus misericordiam abstulerat.* [Tacitus, *Histories.* iii. 85 . . . "With torn robe, he was led along, a filthy sight. Many yelled at him, though no one wept. The ugliness of his end had removed any pity."] To enter thoroughly into this method of thinking, we must make allowance for the ancient maxims, that no one ought to prolong his life after it became dishonorable; but, as he had always a right to dispose of it, it then became a duty to part with it.

society and the common intercourse of life. This vice constitutes what we properly call "meanness"—when a man can submit to the basest slavery in order to gain his ends, fawn upon those who abuse him, and degrade himself by intimacies and familiarities with undeserving inferiors. A certain degree of generous pride or self-value is so requisite that the absence of it in the mind displeases, after the same manner as the want of a nose, eye, or any of the most material features of the face or members of the body.*

The utility of *courage*, both to the public and to the person possessed of it, is an obvious foundation of merit; but to anyone who duly considers of the matter, it will appear that this quality has a peculiar luster which it derives wholly from itself and from that noble elevation inseparable from it. Its figure, drawn by painters and by poets, displays in each feature a sublimity and daring confidence which catches the eye, engages the affections, and diffuses by sympathy a like sublimity of sentiment over every spectator.

Under what shining colors does Demosthenes † represent Philip, where the orator apologizes for his own administration and justifies that pertinacious love of liberty with which he had inspired the Athenians! "I beheld Philip," says he, "he with whom was your contest, resolutely, while in pursuit of empire and dominion, exposing himself to every wound; his eye gored, his neck wrested, his arm, his thigh pierced; whatever part of his body fortune should seize on, that cheerfully relinquishing, provided that, with what remained, he might live in honor and renown. And shall it be said that he, born in Pella, a place heretofore mean and ignoble, should be inspired with so high an ambition and thirst of fame, while you, Athenians," etc. These praises excite the most lively admiration, but the views presented by the orator carry us not, we see, beyond the hero himself, nor ever regard the future advantageous consequences of his valor.

The martial temper of the Romans, inflamed by continual wars, had raised their esteem of courage so high that in their

---

* The absence of virtue may often be a vice, and that of the highest kind, as in the instance of ingratitude as well as meanness. Where we expect a beauty, the disappointment gives an uneasy sensation and produces a real deformity. An abjectness of character, likewise, is disgustful and contemptible in another view. Where a man has no sense of value in himself, we are not likely to have any higher esteem of him. And if the same person who crouches to his superiors is insolent to his inferiors (as often happens), this contrariety of behavior, instead of correcting the former vice, aggravates it extremely by the addition of a vice still more odious. See Sect. viii, "Of Qualities Immediately Agreeable to Others."

† *Pro corona.* 247.

language it was called *virtue*, by way of excellence and of distinction from all other moral qualities. *"The Suevi,"* in the opinion of Tacitus,* *"dressed their hair with a laudable intent; not for the purpose of loving or being loved; they adorned themselves only for their enemies, and in order to appear more terrible"*—a sentiment of the historian which would sound a little oddly in other nations and other ages.

The Scythians, according to Herodotus,† after scalping their enemies, dressed the skin like leather and used it as a towel; and whoever had the most of those towels was most esteemed among them. So much had martial bravery, in that nation as well as in many others, destroyed the sentiments of humanity —a virtue surely much more useful and engaging.

It is indeed observable that, among all uncultivated nations who have not, as yet, had full experience of the advantages attending beneficence, justice, and the social virtues, courage is the predominant excellence, what is most celebrated by poets, recommended by parents and instructors, and admired by the public in general. The ethics of Homer are, in this particular, very different from those of Fénelon, his elegant imitator, and such as were well suited to an age when one hero, as remarked by Thucydides,‡ could ask another, without offense, whether he were a robber or not. Such also, very lately, was the system of ethics which prevailed in many barbarous parts of Ireland, if we may credit Spencer in his judicious account of the state of that kingdom.§

Of the same class of virtues with courage is that undisturbed philosophical *tranquillity*, superior to pain, sorrow, anxiety, and each assault of adverse fortune. Conscious of his own virtue, say the philosophers, the sage elevates himself above every accident of life and, securely placed in the temple of wisdom, looks down on inferior mortals engaged in pursuit of honors, riches, reputation, and every frivolous enjoyment. These pretensions, no doubt, when stretched to the utmost, are by far too magnificent for human nature. They carry, however, a grandeur with them which seizes the spectator and strikes him with admiration. And the nearer we can

* *De moribus Germanorum* 38.

† Lib. iv. 64.

‡ Lib. i. 5.

§ It is a common use, says he, amongst their gentlemen's sons, that, as soon as they are able to use their weapons, they strait gather to themselves three or four stragglers or kern, with whom wandering a while up and down idly the country, taking only meat, he at last falleth into some bad occasion that shall be offered; which being once made known, he is thenceforth counted a man of worth in whom there is courage.

approach in practice to this sublime tranquillity and indifference (for we must distinguish it from a stupid insensibility), the more secure enjoyment shall we attain within ourselves and the more greatness of mind shall we discover to the world. The philosophical tranquillity may indeed be considered only as a branch of magnanimity.

Who admires not Socrates his perpetual serenity and contentment amidst the greatest poverty and domestic vexations, his resolute contempt of riches, and his magnanimous care of preserving liberty, while he refused all assistance from his friends and disciples and avoided even the dependence of an obligation? Epictetus had not so much as a door to his little house or hovel and therefore soon lost his iron lamp, the only furniture which he had worth taking. But resolving to disappoint all robbers for the future, he supplied its place with an earthen lamp, of which he very peaceably kept possession ever after.

Among the ancients, the heroes in philosophy as well as those in war and patriotism have a grandeur and force of sentiment which astonishes our narrow souls and is rashly rejected as extravagant and supernatural. They, in their turn, I allow, would have had equal reason to consider as romantic and incredible the degree of humanity, clemency, order, tranquillity, and other social virtues to which, in the administration of government, we have attained in modern times had anyone been then able to have made a fair representation of them. Such is the compensation which nature, or rather education, has made in the distribution of excellences and virtues in those different ages.

The merit of *benevolence,* arising from its utility and its tendency to promote the good of mankind, has been already explained and is, no doubt, the source of a *considerable* part of that esteem which is so universally paid to it. But it will also be allowed that the very softness and tenderness of the sentiment, its engaging endearments, its fond expressions, its delicate attentions, and all that flow of mutual confidence and regard which enters into a warm attachment of love and friendship—it will be allowed, I say, that these feelings, being delightful in themselves, are necessarily communicated to the spectators and melt them into the same fondness and delicacy. The tear naturally starts in our eye on the apprehension of a warm sentiment of this nature; our breast heaves, our heart is agitated, and every humane, tender principle of our frame is set in motion and gives us the purest and most satisfactory enjoyment.

When poets form descriptions of Elysian fields, where the blessed inhabitants stand in no need of each other's assistance, they yet represent them as maintaining a constant intercourse of love and friendship and soothe our fancy with the pleasing image of these soft and gentle passions. The idea of tender tranquillity in a pastoral Arcadia is agreeable from a like principle, as has been observed above.*

Who would live amidst perpetual wrangling and scolding and mutual reproaches? The roughness and harshness of these emotions disturb and displease us; we suffer by contagion and sympathy, nor can we remain indifferent spectators, even though certain that no pernicious consequences would ever follow from such angry passions.

As a certain proof that the whole merit of benevolence is not derived from its usefulness, we may observe that, in a kind way of blame, we say "a person is *too good*" when he exceeds his part in society and carries his attention for others beyond the proper bounds. In like manner, we say "a man is *too high-spirited, too intrepid, too indifferent about fortune*" —reproaches which really at bottom imply more esteem than many panegyrics. Being accustomed to rate the merit and demerit of characters chiefly by their useful or pernicious tendencies, we cannot forbear applying the epithet of blame when we discover a sentiment which rises to a degree that is hurtful; but it may happen, at the same time, that its noble elevation, or its engaging tenderness, so seizes the heart as rather to increase our friendship and concern for the person.†

The amours and attachments of Harry IV of France, during the civil wars of the League, frequently hurt his interest and his cause, but all the young, at least, and amorous who can sympathize with the tender passions will allow that this very weakness (for they will readily call it such) chiefly endears that hero and interests them in his fortunes.

The excessive bravery and resolute inflexibility of Charles XII ruined his own country and infested all his neighbors, but have such splendor and greatness in their appearance as strikes us with admiration, and they might in some degree be even approved of, if they betrayed not sometimes too evident symptoms of madness and disorder.

The Athenians pretended to the first invention of agriculture and of laws and always valued themselves extremely on the benefit thereby procured to the whole race of mankind. They also boasted, and with reason, of their warlike enterprises, particularly against those innumerable fleets and ar-

---

* Sect. v, Part 2, "Why Utility Pleases."

† Cheerfulness could scarce admit of blame from its excess were it not that dissolute mirth, without a proper cause or subject, is a sure symptom and characteristic of folly and on that account disgustful.

mies of Persians which invaded Greece during the reigns of Darius and Xerxes. But though there be no comparison, in point of utility, between these peaceful and military honors, yet we find that the orators who have written such elaborate panegyrics on that famous city have chiefly triumphed in displaying the warlike achievements. Lysias, Thucydides, Plato, and Isocrates discover, all of them, the same partiality which, though condemned by calm reason and reflection, appears so natural in the mind of man.

It is observable that the great charm of poetry consists in lively pictures of the sublime passions, magnanimity, courage, disdain of fortune, or those of the tender affections, love, and friendship which warm the heart and diffuse over it similar sentiments and emotions. And though all kinds of passion, even the most disagreeable, such as grief and anger, are observed, when excited by poetry, to convey a satisfaction from a mechanism of nature not easy to be explained, yet those more elevated or softer affections have a peculiar influence and please from more than one cause or principle. Not to mention that they alone interest us in the fortune of the persons represented or communicate any esteem and affection for their character.

And can it possibly be doubted that this talent itself of poets to move the passions, this *pathetic* and *sublime* of sentiment is a very considerable merit and, being enhanced by its extreme rarity, may exalt the person possessed of it above every character of the age in which he lives? The prudence, address, steadiness and benign government of Augustus, adorned with all the splendor of his noble birth and imperial crown, render him but an unequal competitor for fame with Virgil, who lays nothing into the opposite scale but the divine beauties of his poetical genius.

The very sensibility to these beauties, or a *delicacy* of taste, is itself a beauty in any character, as conveying the purest, the most durable, and most innocent of all enjoyments.

These are some instances of the several species of merit that are valued for the immediate pleasure which they communicate to the person possessed of them. No views of utility or of future beneficial consequences enter into this sentiment of approbation, yet is it of a kind similar to that other sentiment which arises from views of a public or private utility. The same social sympathy, we may observe, or fellow-feeling with human happiness or misery, gives rise to both; and this analogy, in all the parts of the present theory, may justly be regarded as a confirmation of it.

Section VIII

OF QUALITIES IMMEDIATELY AGREEABLE TO OTHERS*

As the mutual shocks in *society* and the oppositions of interest and self-love have constrained mankind to establish the laws of *justice* in order to preserve the advantages of mutual assistance and protection, in like manner the eternal contrarieties in *company* of men's pride and self-conceit have introduced the rules of *good manners* or *politeness* in order to facilitate the intercourse of minds and an undisturbed commerce and conversation. Among well-bred people, a mutual deference is affected; contempt of others disguised; authority concealed; attention given to each in his turn; and an easy stream of conversation maintained, without vehemence, without interruption, without eagerness for victory, and without any airs of superiority. These attentions and regards are immediately *agreeable* to others, abstracted from any consideration of utility or beneficial tendencies: they conciliate affection, promote esteem, and extremely enhance the merit of the person who regulates his behavior by them.

Many of the forms of breeding are arbitrary and casual; but the thing expressed by them is still the same. A Spaniard goes out of his own house before his guest to signify that he leaves him master of all. In other countries, the landlord walks out last as a common mark of deference and regard.

But, in order to render a man perfect *good company*, he must have *wit* and *ingenuity* as well as good manners. What wit is it may not be easy to define, but it is easy surely to determine that it is a quality immediately *agreeable* to others and communicating, on its first appearance, a lively joy and satisfaction to everyone who has any comprehension of it.

* It is the nature, and indeed the definition of virtue, that it is a quality of the mind agreeable to or approved of by everyone who considers or contemplates it. But some qualities produce pleasure because they are useful to society or useful or agreeable to the person himself; others produce it more immediately, which is the case with the class of virtues here considered.

The most profound metaphysics, indeed, might be employed in explaining the various kinds and species of wit; and many classes of it, which are now received on the sole testimony of taste and sentiment, might perhaps be resolved into more general principles. But this is sufficient for our present purpose, that it does affect taste and sentiment; and bestowing an immediate enjoyment is a sure source of approbation and affection.

In countries where men pass most of their time in conversation and visits and assemblies, these *companionable* qualities, so to speak, are of high estimation and form a chief part of personal merit. In countries where men live a more domestic life and either are employed in business or amuse themselves in a narrower circle of acquaintance, the more solid qualities are chiefly regarded. Thus, I have often observed that among the French the first questions with regard to a stranger are, *Is he polite? Has he wit?* In our own country, the chief praise bestowed is always that of a *good-natured, sensible fellow*.

In conversation, the lively spirit of dialogue is *agreeable*, even to those who desire not to have any share in the discourse; hence, the teller of long stories, or the pompous declaimer, is very little approved of. But most men desire likewise their turn in the conversation and regard, with a very evil eye, that *loquacity* which deprives them of a right they are naturally so jealous of.

There is a sort of harmless *liars* frequently to be met with in company who deal much in the marvelous. Their usual intention is to please and entertain; but as men are most delighted with what they conceive to be truth, these people mistake extremely the means of pleasing and incur universal blame. Some indulgence, however, to lying or fiction is given in *humorous* stories, because it is there really agreeable and entertaining and truth is not of any importance.

Eloquence, genius of all kinds, even good sense and sound reasoning, when it rises to an eminent degree and is employed upon subjects of any considerable dignity and nice discernment—all these endowments seem immediately agreeable and have a merit distinct from their usefulness. Rarity, likewise, which so much enhances the price of everything, must set an additional value on these noble talents of the human mind.

Modesty may be understood in different senses, even abstracted from chastity, which has been already treated of. It sometimes means that tenderness and nicety of honor, that apprehension of blame, that dread of intrusion or injury toward others, that *pudor* which is the proper guardian of

222

every kind of virtue and a sure preservative against vice and corruption. But its most usual meaning is when it is opposed to *impudence* and *arrogance* and expresses a diffidence of our own judgment and a due attention and regard for others. In young men, chiefly, this quality is a sure sign of good sense and is also the certain means of augmenting that endowment by preserving their ears open to instruction and making them still grasp after new attainments. But it has a further charm to every spectator by flattering every man's vanity and presenting the appearance of a docile pupil who receives, with proper attention and respect, every word they utter.

Men have, in general, a much greater propensity to overvalue than undervalue themselves, notwithstanding the opinion of Aristotle.* This makes us more jealous of the excess on the former side and causes us to regard, with a peculiar indulgence, all tendency to modesty and self-diffidence as esteeming the danger less of falling into any vicious extreme of that nature. It is thus, in countries where men's bodies are apt to exceed in corpulency, personal beauty is placed in a much greater degree of slenderness than in countries where that is the most usual defect. Being so often struck with instances of one species of deformity, men think they can never keep at too great a distance from it and wish always to have a leaning to the opposite side. In like manner, were the door opened to self-praise and were Montaigne's maxim observed, that one should say as frankly, *I have sense, I have learning, I have courage, beauty or wit,* as it is sure we often think so —were this the case, I say, everyone is sensible that such a flood of impertinence would break in upon us as would render society wholly intolerable. For this reason, custom has established it as a rule in common societies that men should not indulge themselves in self-praise or even speak much of themselves; and it is only among intimate friends, or people of very manly behavior, that one is allowed to do himself justice. Nobody finds fault with Maurice, Prince of Orange, for his reply to one who asked him whom he esteemed the first general of the age: *The Marquis of Spinola,* said he, *is the second.* Though it is observable that the self-praise implied is here better implied than if it had been directly expressed without any cover or disguise.

He must be a very superficial thinker who imagines that all instances of mutual deferences are to be understood in earnest and that a man would be more estimable for being ignorant of his own merits and accomplishments. A small bias toward modesty, even in the internal sentiment, is favorably re-

* *Ethic. ad Nicomachum.* iv. 3, 37.

garded, especially in young people; and a strong bias is required in the outward behavior; but this excludes not a noble pride and spirit which may openly display itself in its full extent when one lies under calumny or oppression of any kind. The generous contumacy of Socrates, as Cicero calls it, has been highly celebrated in all ages and, when joined to the usual modesty of his behavior, forms a shining character. Iphicrates, the Athenian, being accused of betraying the interests of his country, asked his accuser, *Would you,* says he, *have on a like occasion been guilty of that crime? By no means,* replied the other. *And can you then imagine,* cried the hero, *that Iphicrates would be guilty?* * In short, a generous spirit and self-value, well founded, decently disguised, and courageously supported under distress and calumny, is a great excellence and seems to derive its merit from the noble elevation of its sentiment or its immediate agreeableness to its possessor. In ordinary characters, we approve of a bias toward modesty, which is a quality immediately agreeable to others. The vicious excess of the former virtue, namely, insolence or haughtiness, is immediately disagreeable to others; the excess of the latter is so to the possessor. Thus are the boundaries of these duties adjusted.

A desire of fame, reputation, or a character with others is so far from being blamable that it seems inseparable from virtue, genius, capacity, and a generous or noble disposition. An attention even to trivial matters, in order to please, is also expected and demanded by society; and no one is surprised if he find a man in company to observe a greater elegance of dress and more pleasant flow of conversation than when he passes his time at home and with his own family. Wherein then consists *vanity* which is so justly regarded as a fault or imperfection? It seems to consist chiefly in such an intemperate display of our advantages, honors, and accomplishments, in such an importunate and open demand of praise and admiration as is offensive to others and encroaches too far on *their* secret vanity and ambition. It is besides a sure symptom of the want of true dignity and elevation of mind, which is so great an ornament in any character. For why that impatient desire of applause, as if you were not justly entitled to it and might not reasonably expect that it would forever attend you? Why so anxious to inform us of the great company which you have kept, the obliging things which were said to you, the honors, the distinctions which you met with, as if these were not things of course and what

* Quintil. lib. v. cap. 12.

we could readily, of ourselves, have imagined, without being told of them?

Decency, or a proper regard to age, sex, character, and station in the world, may be ranked among the qualities which are immediately agreeable to others and which, by that means, acquire praise and approbation. An effeminate behavior in a man, a rough manner in a woman—these are ugly because unsuitable to each character and different from the qualities which we expect in the sexes. It is as if a tragedy abounded in comic beauties, or a comedy in tragic. The disproportions hurt the eye and convey a disagreeable sentiment to the spectators, the source of blame and disapprobation. This is that *indecorum* which is explained so much at large by Cicero in his *Offices.*

Among the other virtues we may also give *cleanliness* a place, since it naturally renders us agreeable to others and is no inconsiderable source of love and affection. No one will deny that a negligence in this particular is a fault; and as faults are nothing but smaller vices, and this fault can have no other origin than the uneasy sensation which it excites in others, we may in this instance, seemingly so trivial, clearly discover the origin of moral distinctions about which the learned have involved themselves in such mazes of perplexity and error.

But besides all the *agreeable* qualities the origin of whose beauty we can in some degree explain and account for, there still remains something mysterious and inexplicable which conveys an immediate satisfaction to the spectator, but how, or why, or for what reason, he cannot pretend to determine. There is a *manner,* a grace, an ease, a genteelness, an I-know-not-what, which some men possess above others, which is very different from external beauty and comeliness, and which, however, catches our affection almost as suddenly and powerfully. And though this *manner* be chiefly talked of in the passion between the sexes, where the concealed magic is easily explained, yet surely much of it prevails in all our estimation of characters and forms no inconsiderable part of personal merit. This class of accomplishments, therefore, must be trusted entirely to the blind but sure testimony of taste and sentiment and must be considered as a part of ethics left by nature to baffle all the pride of philosophy and make her sensible of her narrow boundaries and slender acquisitions.

We approve of another because of his wit, politeness, modesty, decency, or any agreeable quality which he possesses, although he be not of our acquaintance nor has ever given us any entertainment by means of these accomplishments. The

225

idea which we form of their effect on his acquaintance has an agreeable influence on our imagination and gives us the sentiment of approbation. This principle enters into all the judgments which we form concerning manners and characters.

Section IX

CONCLUSION

Part I

It may justly appear surprising that any man in so late an age should find it requisite to prove, by elaborate reasoning, that *personal merit* consists altogether in the possession of mental qualities *useful* or *agreeable* to the *person himself* or to *others*. It might be expected that this principle would have occurred even to the first, rude, unpracticed inquirers concerning morals and been received from its own evidence without any argument or disputation. Whatever is valuable in any kind so naturally classes itself under the division of *useful* or *agreeable*, the *utile* or the *dulce*, that it is not easy to imagine why we should ever seek further or consider the question as a matter of nice research or inquiry. And as everything useful or agreeable must possess these qualities with regard either to the *person himself* or to *others*, the complete delineation or description of merit seems to be performed as naturally as a shadow is cast by the sun or an image is reflected upon water. If the ground on which the shadow is cast be not broken and uneven, nor the surface from which the image is reflected disturbed and confused, a just figure is immediately presented without any art or attention. And it seems a reasonable presumption that systems and hypotheses have perverted our natural understanding when a theory so simple and obvious could so long have escaped the most elaborate examination.

But however the case may have fared with philosophy, in common life these principles are still implicitly maintained; nor is any other topic of praise or blame ever recurred to when we employ any panegyric or satire, any applause or censure of human action and behavior. If we observe men in every intercourse of business or pleasure, in every discourse and conversation, we shall find them nowhere, except in the schools, at any loss upon this subject. What so natural, for instance, as the following dialogue? You are very happy, we shall suppose one to say, addressing himself to another, that you have given your daughter to Cleanthes. He is a man of honor and humanity. Everyone who has any intercourse with him is sure of *fair* and *kind* treatment.* I congratulate you, too, says another, on the promising expectations of this son-in-law, whose assiduous application to the study of the laws, whose quick penetration and early knowledge both of men and business prognosticate the greatest honors and advancement.† You surprise me, replies a third, when you talk of Cleanthes as a man of business and application. I met him lately in a circle of the gayest company, and he was the very life and soul of our conversation: so much wit with good manners, so much gallantry without affectation, so much ingenious knowledge so genteelly delivered, I have never before observed in anyone.‡ You would admire him still more, says a fourth, if you knew him more familiarly. That cheerfulness which you might remark in him is not a sudden flash struck out by company; it runs through the whole tenor of his life and preserves a perpetual serenity on his countenance and tranquillity in his soul. He has met with severe trials, misfortunes as well as dangers, and by his greatness of mind was still superior to all of them.§ The image, gentlemen, which you have here delineated of Cleanthes, cried I, is that of accomplished merit. Each of you has given a stroke of the pencil to his figure; and you have unawares exceeded all the pictures drawn by Gratian or Castiglione. A philosopher might select this character as a model of perfect virtue.

And as every quality which is useful or agreeable to ourselves or others is, in common life, allowed to be a part of personal merit, so no other will ever be received where men judge of things by their natural, unprejudiced reason, without the delusive glosses of superstition and false religion. Celibacy, fasting, penance, mortification, self-denial, humility, silence, solitude, and the whole train of monkish virtues—for what reason are they everywhere rejected by men of sense but because they serve to no manner of purpose; neither advance a man's fortune in the world, nor render him a more

* Qualities useful to others.
† Qualities useful to the person himself.
‡ Qualities immediately agreeable to others.
§ Qualities immediately agreeable to the person himself.

valuable member of society; neither qualify him for the entertainment of company, nor increase his power of self-enjoyment? We observe, on the contrary, that they cross all these desirable ends, stupefy the understanding and harden the heart, obscure the fancy and sour the temper. We justly, therefore, transfer them to the opposite column and place them in the catalogue of vices; nor has any superstition force sufficient among men of the world to pervert entirely these natural sentiments. A gloomy, hair-brained enthusiast, after his death, may have a place in the calendar but will scarcely ever be admitted when alive into intimacy and society, except by those who are as delirious and dismal as himself.

It seems a happiness in the present theory that it enters not into that vulgar dispute concerning the *degrees* of benevolence or self-love which prevail in human nature—a dispute which is never likely to have any issue, both because men who have taken part are not easily convinced and because the phenomena which can be produced on either side are so dispersed, so uncertain, and subject to so many interpretations that it is scarcely possible accurately to compare them or draw from them any determinate inference or conclusion. It is sufficient for our present purpose if it be allowed what surely, without the greatest absurdity, cannot be disputed, that there is some benevolence, however small, infused into our bosom; some spark of friendship for humankind; some particle of the dove kneaded into our frame, along with the elements of the wolf and serpent. Let these generous sentiments be supposed ever so weak, let them be insufficient to move even a hand or finger of our body, they must still direct the determinations of our mind and, where everything else is equal, produce a cool preference of what is useful and serviceable to mankind above what is pernicious and dangerous. A *moral distinction,* therefore, immediately arises; a general sentiment of blame and approbation; a tendency, however faint, to the objects of the one and a proportionable aversion to those of the other. Nor will those reasoners who so earnestly maintain the predominant selfishness of humankind be anywise scandalized at hearing of the weak sentiments of virtue implanted in our nature. On the contrary, they are found as ready to maintain the one tenet as the other; and their spirit of satire (for such it appears, rather than of corruption) naturally gives rise to both opinions, which have, indeed, a great and almost an indissoluble connection together.

Avarice, ambition, vanity, and all passions vulgarly, though improperly, comprised under the denomination of *self-love* are here excluded from our theory concerning the origin of morals, not because they are too weak, but because they have

228

not a proper direction for that purpose. The notion of morals implies some sentiment common to all mankind which recommends the same object to general approbation and makes every man, or most men, agree in the same opinion or decision concerning it. It also implies some sentiment so universal and comprehensive as to extend to all mankind and render the actions and conduct, even of the persons the most remote, an object of applause or censure, according as they agree or disagree with that rule of right which is established. These two requisite circumstances belong alone to the sentiment of humanity here insisted on. The other passions produce, in every breast, many strong sentiments of desire and aversion, affection and hatred, but these neither are felt so much in common nor are so comprehensive as to be the foundation of any general system and established theory of blame or approbation.

When a man denominates another his *enemy,* his *rival,* his *antagonist,* his *adversary,* he is understood to speak the language of self-love and to express sentiments peculiar to himself and arising from his particular circumstances and situation. But when he bestows on any man the epithets of *vicious* or *odious* or *depraved,* he then speaks another language and expresses sentiments in which he expects all his audience are to concur with him. He must here, therefore, depart from his private and particular situation and must choose a point of view common to him with others: he must move some universal principle of the human frame and touch a string to which all mankind have an accord and symphony. If he mean, therefore, to express that this man possesses qualities whose tendency is pernicious to society, he has chosen this common point of view and has touched the principle of humanity in which every man, in some degree, concurs. While the human heart is compounded of the same elements as at present, it will never be wholly indifferent to public good nor entirely unaffected with the tendency of characters and manners. And though this affection of humanity may not generally be esteemed so strong as vanity or ambition, yet being common to all men, it can alone be the foundation of morals or of any general system of blame or praise. One man's ambition is not another's ambition, nor will the same event or object satisfy both; but the humanity of one man is the humanity of everyone; and the same object touches this passion in all human creatures.

But the sentiments which arise from humanity are not only the same in all human creatures and produce the same approbation or censure, but they also comprehend all human creatures; nor is there anyone whose conduct or character is not, by their means, an object, to everyone, of censure or approbation. On the contrary, those other passions, commonly denominated selfish, both produce different sentiments in each individual, according to his particular situation, and also contemplate the greater part of mankind with the utmost indifference and unconcern. Whoever has a high regard and esteem for me flatters my vanity; whoever expresses contempt mortifies and displeases me. But as my name is known but to a small part of mankind, there are few who come within the sphere of this passion or excite, on its account, either my affection or disgust. But if you represent a tyrannical, insolent, or barbarous behavior, in any country or in any age of the world, I soon carry my eye to the pernicious tendency of such a conduct and feel the sentiment of repugnance and displeasure toward it. No character can be so remote as to be, in this light, wholly indifferent to me. What is beneficial to society or to the person himself must still be preferred. And every quality or action of every human being must by this means be ranked under some class or denomination expressive of general censure or applause.

What more, therefore, can we ask to distinguish the sentiments dependent on humanity from those connected with any other passion or to satisfy us why the former are the origin of morals, not the latter? Whatever conduct gains my approbation by touching my humanity procures also the applause of all mankind by affecting the same principle in them; but what serves my avarice or ambition pleases these passions in me alone and affects not the avarice and ambition of the rest of mankind. There is no circumstance of conduct in any man, provided it have a beneficial tendency, that is not agreeable to my humanity, however remote the person; but every man, so far removed as neither to cross nor serve my avarice and ambition, is regarded as wholly indifferent by those passions. The distinction, therefore, between these species of sentiment being so great and evident, language must soon be molded upon it and must invent a peculiar set of terms in order to express those universal sentiments of censure or approbation which arise from humanity or from views of general usefulness and its contrary. *Virtue* and *vice* become then known; morals are recognized; certain general ideas are framed of human conduct and behavior; such measures are expected from men in such situations: this action is determined to be conformable to our abstract rule; that other, contrary. And by such universal principles are the particular sentiments of self-love frequently controlled and limited.*

* It seems certain, both from reason and experience, that a rude,

From instances of popular tumults, seditions, factions, panics, and of all passions which are shared with a multitude, we may learn the influence of society in exciting and supporting any emotion; while the most ungovernable disorders are raised, we find by that means, from the slightest and most frivolous occasions. Solon was no very cruel, though perhaps an unjust, legislator, who punished neuters in civil wars; and few, I believe, would in such cases incur the penalty were their affection and discourse allowed sufficient to absolve them. No selfishness, and scarce any philosophy, have there force sufficient to support a total coolness and indifference; and he must be more or less than man who kindles not in the common blaze. What wonder, then, that moral sentiments are found of such influence in life, though springing from principles which may appear at first sight somewhat small and delicate? But these principles, we must remark, are social and universal: they form, in a manner, the *party* of humankind against vice or disorder, its common enemy; and as the benevolent concern for others is diffused in a greater or less degree over all men, and is the same in all, it occurs more frequently in discourse, is cherished by society and conversation, and the blame and approbation consequent on it are thereby roused from that lethargy into which they are probably lulled in solitary and uncultivated nature. Other passions, though perhaps originally stronger, yet being selfish and private, are often overpowered by its force and yield the dominion of our breast to those social and public principles.

Another spring of our constitution that brings a great addition of force to moral sentiment is the love of fame, which rules with such uncontrolled authority in all generous minds

---

untaught savage regulates chiefly his love and hatred by the ideas of private utility and injury and has but faint conceptions of a general rule or system of behavior. The man who stands opposite to him in battle he hates heartily, not only for the present moment, which is almost unavoidable, but forever after; nor is he satisfied without the most extreme punishment and vengeance. But we, accustomed to society and to more enlarged reflections, consider that this man is serving his own country and community; that any man, in the same situation, would do the same; that we ourselves, in like circumstances, observe a like conduct; that, in general, human society is best supported on such maxims. And by these suppositions and views, we correct, in some measure, our ruder and narrower passions. And though much of our friendship and enmity be still regulated by private considerations of benefit and harm, we pay at least this homage to general rules, which we are accustomed to respect, that we commonly pervert our adversary's conduct by imputing malice or injustice to him in order to give vent to those passions which arise from self-love and private interest. When the heart is full of rage, it never wants pretense of this nature, though sometimes as frivolous as those from which Horace, being almost crushed by the fall of a tree, affects to accuse of parricide the first planter of it.

and is often the grand object of all their designs and undertakings. By our continual and earnest pursuit of a character, a name, a reputation in the world, we bring our own deportment and conduct frequently in review and consider how they appear in the eyes of those who approach and regard us. This constant habit of surveying ourselves, as it were in reflection, keeps alive all the sentiments of right and wrong and begets in noble natures a certain reverence for themselves as well as others, which is the surest guardian of every virtue. The animal conveniences and pleasures sink gradually in their value, while every inward beauty and moral grace is studiously acquired and the mind is accomplished in every perfection which can adorn or embellish a rational creature.

Here is the most perfect morality with which we are acquainted; here is displayed the force of many sympathies. Our moral sentiment is itself a feeling chiefly of that nature; and our regard to a character with others seems to arise only from a care of preserving a character with ourselves; and in order to attain this end, we find it necessary to prop our tottering judgment on the correspondent approbation of mankind.

But that we may accommodate matters and remove, if possible, every difficulty, let us allow all these reasonings to be false. Let us allow that, when we resolve the pleasure which arises from views of utility into the sentiments of humanity and sympathy, we have embraced a wrong hypothesis. Let us confess it necessary to find some other explication of that applause which is paid to objects, whether inanimate, animate, or rational, if they have a tendency to promote the welfare and advantage of mankind. However difficult it be to conceive that an object is approved of on account of its tendency to a certain end, while the end itself is totally indifferent, let us swallow this absurdity and consider what are the consequences. The preceding delineation or definition of *personal merit* must still retain its evidence and authority: it must still be allowed that every quality of the mind which is *useful* or *agreeable* to the *person himself* or to *others* communicates a pleasure to the spectator, engages his esteem, and is admitted under the honorable denomination of virtue or merit. Are not justice, fidelity, honor, veracity, allegiance, chastity esteemed solely on account of their tendency to promote the good of society? Is not that tendency inseparable from humanity, benevolence, lenity, generosity, gratitude, moderation, tenderness, friendship, and all the other social virtues? Can it possibly be doubted that industry, discretion, frugality, secrecy, order, perseverance, forethought, judgment, and this whole class of virtues and accomplishments of which many pages would not contain the catalogue—can it be doubted, I say, that the tendency of these qualities to promote the interest and happiness of their possessor is the sole foundation of their merit? Who can dispute that a mind which supports a perpetual serenity and cheerfulness, a noble dignity and undaunted spirit, a tender affection and goodwill to all around, as it has more enjoyment within itself is also a more animating and rejoicing spectacle than if dejected with melancholy, tormented with anxiety, irritated with rage, or sunk into the most abject baseness and degeneracy? And as to the qualities immediately *agreeable to others,* they speak sufficiently for themselves; and he must be unhappy indeed, either in his own temper or in his situation and company, who has never perceived the charms of a facetious wit or flowing affability, of a delicate modesty or decent genteelness of address and manner.

I am sensible that nothing can be more unphilosophical than to be positive or dogmatical on any subject and that, even if *excessive* skepticism could be maintained, it would not be more destructive to all just reasoning and inquiry. I am convinced that where men are the most sure and arrogant, they are commonly the most mistaken and have there given reins to passion without that proper deliberation and suspense which can alone secure them from the grossest absurdities. Yet I must confess that this enumeration puts the matter in so strong a light that I cannot, *at present,* be more assured of any truth which I learn from reasoning and argument than that personal merit consists entirely in the usefulness or agreeableness of qualities to the person himself possessed of them or to others who have any intercourse with him. But when I reflect that though the bulk and figure of the earth have been measured and delineated, though the motions of the tides have been accounted for, the order and economy of the heavenly bodies subjected to their proper laws, and *infinite* itself reduced to calculation, yet men still dispute concerning the foundation of their moral duties—when I reflect on this, I say, I fall back into diffidence and skepticism and suspect that an hypothesis so obvious, had it been a true one, would long ere now have been received by the unanimous suffrage and consent of mankind.

Part II

Having explained the moral *approbation* attending merit or virtue, there remains nothing but briefly to consider our interested *obligation* to it and to inquire whether every man who has any regard to his own happiness and welfare will not best find his account in the practice of every moral duty. If this can be clearly ascertained from the foregoing theory, we shall have the satisfaction to reflect that we have advanced principles which not only, it is hoped, will stand the test of reasoning and inquiry, but may contribute to the amendment of men's lives and their improvement in morality and social virtue. And though the philosophical truth of any proposition by no means depends on its tendency to promote the interests of society, yet a man has but a bad grace who delivers a theory, however true, which he must confess leads to a practice dangerous and pernicious. Why rake into those corners of nature which spread a nuisance all around? Why dig up the pestilence from the pit in which it is buried? The ingenuity of your researches may be admired, but your systems will be detested, and mankind will agree, if they cannot refute them, to sink them at least in eternal silence and oblivion. Truths which are *pernicious* to society, if any such there be, will yield to errors which are salutary and *advantageous*.

But what philosophical truths can be more advantageous to society than those here delivered, which represent virtue in all her genuine and most engaging charms and make us approach her with ease, familiarity, and affection? The dismal dress falls off, with which many divines and some philosophers have covered her, and nothing appears but gentleness, humanity, beneficence, affability, nay, even at proper intervals, play, frolic, and gaiety. She talks not of useless austerities and rigors, suffering, and self-denial. She declares that her sole purpose is to make her votaries, and all mankind, during every instant of their existence, if possible, cheerful and happy; nor does she ever willingly part with any pleasure but in hopes of ample compensation in some other period of their lives. The sole trouble which she demands is that of just calculation and a steady preference of the greater happiness. And if any austere pretenders approach her, enemies to joy and pleasure, she either rejects them as hypocrites and deceivers, or, if she admit them in her train, they are ranked, however, among the least favored of her votaries.

And, indeed, to drop all figurative expression, what hopes can we ever have of engaging mankind to a practice which we confess full of austerity and rigor? Or what theory of morals can ever serve any useful purpose unless it can show, by a particular detail, that all the duties which it recommends are also the true interest of each individual? The peculiar advantage of the foregoing system seems to be that it furnishes proper mediums for that purpose.

That the virtues which are immediately *useful* or *agreeable*

234

to the person possessed of them are desirable in a view to self-interest, it would surely be superfluous to prove. Moralists, indeed, may spare themselves all the pains which they often take in recommending these duties. To what purpose collect arguments to evince that temperance is advantageous and the excesses of pleasure hurtful? When it appears that these excesses are only denominated such because they are hurtful and that if the unlimited use of strong liquors, for instance, no more impaired health or the faculties of mind and body than the use of air or water, it would not be a whit more vicious or blamable.

It seeems equally superfluous to prove that the companionable virtues of good manners and wit, decency and genteelness are more desirable than the contrary qualities. Vanity alone, without any other consideration, is a sufficient motive to make us wish for the possession of these accomplishments. No man was ever willingly deficient in this particular. All our failures here proceed from bad education, want of capacity, or a perverse and unpliable disposition. Would you have your company coveted, admired, followed rather than hated, despised, avoided? Can anyone seriously deliberate in the case? As no enjoyment is sincere without some reference to company and society, so no society can be agreeable, or even tolerable, where a man feels his presence unwelcome and discovers all around him symptoms of disgust and aversion.

But why, in the greater society or confederacy of mankind, should not the case be the same as in particular clubs and companies? Why is it more doubtful that the enlarged virtues of humanity, generosity, beneficence are desirable, with a view to happiness and self-interest, than the limited endowments of ingenuity and politeness? Are we apprehensive lest those social affections interfere in a greater and more immediate degree than any other pursuits with private utility and cannot be gratified without some important sacrifice of honor and advantage? If so, we are but ill instructed in the nature of the human passions and are more influenced by verbal distinctions than by real differences.

Whatever contradiction may vulgarly be supposed between the *selfish* and *social* sentiments or dispositions, they are really no more opposite than selfish and ambitious, selfish and revengeful, selfish and vain. It is requisite that there be an original propensity of some kind, in order to be a basis to self-love, by giving a relish to the objects of its pursuit—and none more fit for this purpose than benevolence or humanity. The goods of fortune are spent in one gratification or another: the miser who accumulates his annual income and lends it out at interest has really spent it in the gratification of his avarice.

And it would be difficult to show why a man is more a loser by a generous action than by any other method of expense, since the utmost which he can attain by the most elaborate selfishness is the indulgence of some affection.

Now, if life without passion must be altogether insipid and tiresome, let a man suppose that he has full power of modeling his own disposition, and let him deliberate what appetite or desire he would choose for the foundation of his happiness and enjoyment. Every affection, he would observe, when gratified by success, gives a satisfaction proportioned to its force and violence; but besides this advantage, common to all, the immediate feeling of benevolence and friendship, humanity and kindness is sweet, smooth, tender, and agreeable, independent of all fortune and accidents. These virtues are, besides, attended with a pleasing consciousness or remembrance and keep us in humor with ourselves as well as others, while we retain the agreeable reflection of having done our part toward mankind and society. And though all men show a jealousy of our success in the pursuits of avarice and ambition, yet are we almost sure of their goodwill and good wishes so long as we persevere in the paths of virtue and employ ourselves in the execution of generous plans and purposes. What other passion is there where we shall find so many advantages united: an agreeable sentiment, a pleasing consciousness, a good reputation? But of these truths, we may observe, men are of themselves pretty much convinced; nor are they deficient in their duty to society because they would not wish to be generous, friendly, and humane, but because they do not feel themselves such.

Treating vice with the greatest candor and making it all possible concessions, we must acknowledge that there is not, in any instance, the smallest pretext for giving it the preference above virtue with a view to self-interest, except, perhaps, in the case of justice, where a man, taking things in a certain light, may often seem to be a loser by his integrity. And though it is allowed that, without a regard to property, no society could subsist, yet, according to the imperfect way in which human affairs are conducted, a sensible knave, in particular incidents, may think that an act of iniquity or infidelity will make a considerable addition to his fortune without causing any considerable breach in the social union and confederacy. That *honesty is the best policy* may be a good general rule, but is liable to many exceptions. And he, it may perhaps be thought, conducts himself with most wisdom who observes the general rule and takes advantage of all the exceptions.

I must confess that if a man think that this reasoning

much requires an answer, it will be a little difficult to find any which will to him appear satisfactory and convincing. If his heart rebel not against such pernicious maxims, if he feel no reluctance to the thoughts of villainy or baseness, he has indeed lost a considerable motive to virtue; and we may expect that his practice will be answerable to his speculation. But in all ingenuous natures, the antipathy to treachery and roguery is too strong to be counterbalanced by any views of profit or pecuniary advantage. Inward peace of mind, consciousness of integrity, a satisfactory review of our own conduct—these are circumstances very requisite to happiness and will be cherished and cultivated by every honest man who feels the importance of them.

Such a one has, besides, the frequent satisfaction of seeing knaves, with all their pretended cunning and abilities, betrayed by their own maxims; and while they purpose to cheat with moderation and secrecy, a tempting incident occurs—nature is frail—and they give in to the snare, whence they can never extricate themselves without a total loss of reputation and the forfeiture of all future trust and confidence with mankind.

But were they ever so secret and successful, the honest man, if he has any tincture of philosophy, or even common observation and reflection, will discover that they themselves are, in the end, the greatest dupes and have sacrificed the invaluable enjoyment of a character, with themselves at least, for the acquisition of worthless toys and gewgaws. How little is requisite to supply the *necessities* of nature? And in a view to *pleasure*, what comparison between the unbought satisfaction of conversation, society, study, even health and the common beauties of nature, but above all, the peaceful reflection on one's own conduct? What comparison, I say, between these and the feverish, empty amusements of luxury and expense? These natural pleasures, indeed, are really without price, both because they are below all price in their attainment and above it in their enjoyment.

237

Appendix I

CONCERNING MORAL SENTIMENT

If the foregoing hypothesis be received, it will now be easy for us to determine the question first started, concerning the general principles of morals; and though we postponed the decision of that question lest it should then involve us in intricate speculations which are unfit for moral discourses, we may resume it at present and examine how far either *reason* or *sentiment* enters into all decisions of praise or censure.

One principal foundation of moral praise being supposed to lie in the usefulness of any quality or action, it is evident that *reason* must enter for a considerable share in all decisions of this kind, since nothing but that faculty can instruct us in the tendency of qualities and actions and point out their beneficial consequences to society and to their possessor. In many cases, this is an affair liable to great controversy: doubts may arise; opposite interests may occur; and a preference must be given to one side, from very nice views and a small overbalance of utility. This is particularly remarkable in questions with regard to justice, as is, indeed, natural to suppose from that species of utility which attends this virtue. Were every single instance of justice, like that of benevolence, useful to society, this would be a more simple state of the case and seldom liable to great controversy. But as single instances of justice are often pernicious in their first and immediate tendency, and as the advantage to society results only from the observance of the general rule and from the concurrence and combination of several persons in the same equitable conduct, the case here becomes more intricate and involved. The various circumstances of society, the various consequences of any practice, the various interests which may be proposed—these, on many occasions, are doubtful and subject to great discussion and inquiry. The object of municipal laws is to fix all the questions with regard to justice: the debates of civilians, the reflections of politicians, the precedents of history and public records are all directed to the same purpose. And a very accurate *reason* or *judgment* is

238

often requisite to give the true determination amidst such intricate doubts arising from obscure or opposite utilities.

But though reason, when fully assisted and improved, be sufficient to instruct us in the pernicious or useful tendency of qualities and actions, it is not alone sufficient to produce any moral blame or approbation. Utility is only a tendency to a certain end; and were the end totally indifferent to us, we should feel the same indifference toward the means. It is requisite a *sentiment* should here display itself in order to give a preference to the useful above the pernicious tendencies. This sentiment can be no other than a feeling for the happiness of mankind and a resentment of their misery, since these are the different ends which virtue and vice have a tendency to promote. Here, therefore, *reason* instructs us in the several tendencies of actions, and *humanity* makes a distinction in favor of those which are useful and beneficial.

This partition between the faculties of understanding and sentiment, in all moral decisions, seems clear from the preceding hypothesis; but I shall suppose that hypothesis false. It will then be requisite to look out for some other theory that may be satisfactory; and I dare venture to affirm that none such will ever be found so long as we suppose reason to be the sole source of morals. To prove this, it will be proper to weigh the five following considerations:

I. It is easy for a false hypothesis to maintain some appearance of truth, while it keeps wholly in generals, makes use of undefined terms, and employs comparisons instead of instances. This is particularly remarkable in that philosophy which ascribes the discernment of all moral distinctions to reason alone, without the concurrence of sentiment. It is impossible that, in any particular instance, this hypothesis can so much as be rendered intelligible, whatever specious figure it may make in general declamations and discourses. Examine the crime of *ingratitude*, for instance, which has place wherever we observe goodwill, expressed and known, together with good offices performed on the one side and a return of ill will or indifference, with ill offices or neglect, on the other; anatomize all these circumstances and examine, by your reason alone, in what consists the demerit or blame: you never will come to any issue or conclusion.

Reason judges either of *matter of fact* or of *relations*. Inquire then, first, where is that matter of fact which we here call *crime;* point it out; determine the time of its existence; describe its essence or nature; explain the sense or faculty to which it discovers itself. It resides in the mind of the person who is ungrateful. He must, therefore, feel it and be conscious of it. But nothing is there except the passion of ill will or absolute indifference. You cannot say that these of themselves always, and in all circumstances, are crimes. No; they are only crimes when directed toward persons who have before expressed and displayed goodwill toward us. Consequently, we may infer that the crime of ingratitude is not any particular individual *fact,* but arises from a complication of circumstances which, being presented to the spectator, excites the *sentiment* of blame by the particular structure and fabric of his mind.

This representation, you say, is false. Crime, indeed, consists not in a particular *fact* of whose reality we are assured by *reason,* but it consists in certain *moral relations* discovered by reason, in the same manner as we discover by reason the truths of geometry or algebra. But what are the relations, I ask, of which you here talk? In the case stated above, I see, first, goodwill and good offices in one person; then, ill will and ill offices in the other. Between these, there is the relation of *contrariety.* Does the crime consist in that relation? But suppose a person bore me ill will or did me ill offices, and I, in return, were indifferent toward him or did him good offices —here is the same relation of *contrariety;* and yet, my conduct is often highly laudable. Twist and turn this matter as much as you will, you can never rest the morality on relation but must have recourse to the decisions of sentiment.

When it is affirmed that two and three are equal to the half of ten, this relation of equality I understand perfectly. I conceive that if ten be divided into two parts, of which one has as many units as the other, and if any of these parts be compared to two added to three, it will contain as many units as that compound number. But when you draw thence a comparison to moral relations, I own that I am altogether at a loss to understand you. A moral action, a crime, such as ingratitude, is a complicated object. Does the morality consist in the relation of its parts to each other? How? After what manner? Specify the relation; be more particular and explicit in your propositions; and you will easily see their falsehood.

No, say you, the morality consists in the relation of actions to the rule of right; and they are denominated good or ill, according as they agree or disagree with it. What then is this rule of right? In what does it consist? How is it determined? By reason, you say, which examines the moral relations of actions. So that moral relations are determined by the comparison of actions to a rule. And that rule is determined by considering the moral relations of objects. Is not this fine reasoning?

All this is metaphysics, you cry. That is enough; there

needs nothing more to give a strong presumption of false-hood. Yes, replied I, here are metaphysics, surely; but they are all on your side, who advance an abstruse hypothesis which can never be made intelligible nor quadrate with any particular instance or illustration. The hypothesis which we embrace is plain. It maintains that morality is determined by sentiment. It defines virtue to be *whatever mental action or quality gives to a spectator the pleasing sentiment of appro-bation;* and vice the contrary. We then proceed to examine a plain matter of fact—to wit, what actions have this influence, we consider all the circumstances in which these actions agree, and thence endeavor to extract some general observa-tions with regard to these sentiments. If you call this meta-physics and find anything abstruse here, you need only con-clude that your turn of mind is not suited to the moral sci-ences.

II. When a man at any time deliberates concerning his own conduct (as whether he had better, in a particular emer-gency, assist a brother or a benefactor), he must consider these separate relations, with all the circumstances and situa-tions of the persons, in order to determine the superior duty and obligation. And in order to determine the proportion of lines in any triangle, it is necessary to examine the nature of that figure and the relations which its several parts bear to each other. But notwithstanding this appearing similarity in the two cases, there is at bottom an extreme difference be-tween them. A speculative reasoner concerning triangles or circles considers the several known and given relations of the parts of these figures and thence infers some unknown rela-tion which is dependent on the former. But in moral delibera-tions, we must be acquainted, beforehand, with all the objects and all their relations to each other and from a comparison of the whole fix our choice or approbation. No new fact to be ascertained, no new relation to be discovered. All the cir-cumstances of the case are supposed to be laid before us ere we can fix any sentence of blame or approbation. If any material circumstance be yet unknown or doubtful, we must first employ our inquiry or intellectual faculties to assure us of it and must suspend for a time all moral decision or senti-ment. While we are ignorant whether a man were aggressor or not, how can we determine whether the person who killed him be criminal or innocent? But after every circumstance, every relation is known, the understanding has no further room to operate nor any object on which it could employ it-self. The approbation or blame which then ensues cannot be the work of the judgment but of the heart; and it is not a speculative proposition or affirmation, but an active feeling or

241

sentiment. In the disquisitions of the understanding, from known circumstances and relations we infer some new and unknown. In moral decisions, all the circumstances and relations must be previously known; and the mind, from the contemplation of the whole, feels some new impression of affection or disgust, esteem or contempt, approbation or blame.

Hence, the great difference between a mistake of *fact* and one of *right;* and hence, the reason why the one is commonly criminal and not the other. When Oedipus killed Laius, he was ignorant of the relation and from circumstances, innocent and involuntary, formed erroneous opinions concerning the action which he committed. But when Nero killed Agrippina, all the relations between himself and the person, and all the circumstances of the fact, were previously known to him; but the motive of revenge or fear or interest prevailed in his savage heart over the sentiments of duty and humanity. And when we express that detestation against him to which he himself in a little time became insensible, it is not that we see any relations of which he was ignorant, but that, from the rectitude of our disposition, we feel sentiments against which he was hardened, from flattery and a long perseverance in the most enormous crimes. In these sentiments then, not in a discovery of relations of any kind, do all moral determinations consist. Before we can pretend to form any decision of this kind, everything must be known and ascertained on the side of the object or action. Nothing remains but to feel, on our part, some sentiment of blame or approbation, whence we pronounce the action criminal or virtuous.

III. This doctrine will become still more evident if we compare moral beauty with natural, to which in many particulars it bears so near a resemblance. It is on the proportion, relation, and positions of parts that all natural beauty depends, but it would be absurd thence to infer that the perception of beauty, like that of truth in geometrical problems, consists wholly in the perception of relations and was performed entirely by the understanding or intellectual faculties. In all the sciences, our mind, from the known relations, investigates the unknown; but in all decisions of taste or external beauty, all the relations are beforehand obvious to the eye; and we thence proceed to feel a sentiment of complacency or disgust, according to the nature of the object and disposition of our organs.

Euclid has fully explained all the qualities of the circle, but has not, in any proposition, said a word of its beauty. The reason is evident. The beauty is not a quality of the circle. It lies not in any part of the line whose parts are equally distant from a common center. It is only the effect which that figure

242

produces upon the mind, whose peculiar fabric or structure renders it susceptible of such sentiments. In vain would you look for it in the circle or seek it, either by your senses or by mathematical reasonings, in all the properties of that figure.

Attend to Palladio and Perrault while they explain all the parts and proportions of a pillar: they talk of the cornice and frieze, and base and entablature, and shaft and architrave, and give the description and position of each of these members. But should you ask the description and position of its beauty, they would readily reply that the beauty is not in any of the parts or members of a pillar but results from the whole when that complicated figure is presented to an intelligent mind susceptible to those finer sensations. Till such a spectator appear, there is nothing but a figure of such particular dimensions and proportions—from his sentiments alone arise its elegance and beauty.

Again, attend to Cicero while he paints the crimes of a Verres or a Catiline; you must acknowledge that the moral turpitude results, in the same manner, from the contemplation of the whole when presented to a being whose organs have such a particular structure and formation. The orator may paint rage, insolence, barbarity, on the one side; meekness, suffering, sorrow, innocence, on the other. But if you feel no indignation or compassion arise in you from this complication of circumstances, you would in vain ask him in what consists the crime or villainy which he so vehemently exclaims against; at what time or on what subject it first began to exist; and what has a few months afterwards become of it, when every disposition and thought of all the actors is totally altered or annihilated. No satisfactory answer can be given to any of these questions upon the abstract hypothesis of morals; and we must at last acknowledge that the crime or immorality is no particular fact or relation which can be the object of the understanding, but arises entirely from the sentiment of disapprobation which, by the structure of human nature, we unavoidably feel on the apprehension of barbarity or treachery.

IV. Inanimate objects may bear to each other all the same relations which we observe in moral agents, though the former can never be the object of love or hatred nor are consequently susceptible of merit or iniquity. A young tree which overtops and destroys its parent stands in all the same relations with Nero when he murdered Agrippina and, if morality consisted merely in relations, would, no doubt, be equally criminal.

V. It appears evident that the ultimate ends of human actions can never, in any case, be accounted for by *reason*, but recommend themselves entirely to the sentiments and affections of mankind without any dependence on the intellectual faculties. Ask a man *why he uses exercise;* he will answer, *because he desires to keep his health.* If you then inquire *why he desires health,* he will readily reply, *because sickness is painful.* If you push your inquiries further and desire a reason *why he hates pain,* it is impossible he can ever give any. This is an ultimate end and is never referred to any other object.

Perhaps to your second question, *why he desires health,* he may also reply that *it is necessary for the exercise of his calling.* If you ask *why he is anxious on that head,* he will answer, *because he desires to get money.* If you demand, *why? It is the instrument of pleasure,* says he. And beyond this, it is an absurdity to ask for a reason. It is impossible there can be a progress *in infinitum* and that one thing can always be a reason why another is desired. Something must be desirable on its own account and because of its immediate accord or agreement with human sentiment and affection.

Now, as virtue is an end and is desirable on its own account, without fee or reward, merely for the immediate satisfaction which it conveys, it is requisite that there should be some sentiment which it touches—some internal taste or feeling, or whatever you please to call it, which distinguishes moral good and evil and which embraces the one and rejects the other.

Thus, the distinct boundaries and offices of *reason* and of *taste* are easily ascertained. The former conveys the knowledge of truth and falsehood; the latter gives the sentiment of beauty and deformity, vice and virtue. The one discovers objects as they really stand in nature, without addition or diminution; the other has a productive faculty; and gilding or straining all natural objects with the colors borrowed from internal sentiment, raises, in a manner, a new creation. Reason, being cool and disengaged, is no motive to action and directs only the impulse received from appetite or inclination by showing us the means of attaining happiness or avoiding misery. Taste, as it gives pleasure or pain, and thereby constitutes happiness or misery, becomes a motive to action and is the first spring or impulse to desire and volition. From circumstances and relations, known or supposed, the former leads us to the discovery of the concealed and unknown. After all circumstances and relations are laid before us, the latter makes us feel from the whole a new sentiment of blame or approbation. The standard of the one, being founded on the nature of things, is eternal and inflexible, even by the will of the Supreme Being; the standard of the other, arising from the internal frame and constitution of animals, is ultimately derived from that Supreme Will which bestowed on each being its peculiar nature and arranged the several classes and orders of existence.

Appendix II

OF SELF-LOVE

There is a principle, supposed to prevail among many, which is utterly incompatible with all virtue or moral sentiment; and as it can proceed from nothing but the most depraved disposition, so in its turn it tends still further to encourage that depravity. This principle is that all *benevolence* is mere hypocrisy, friendship a cheat, public spirit a farce, fidelity a snare to procure trust and confidence, and that while all of us, at bottom, pursue only our private interest, we wear these fair disguises in order to put others off their guard and expose them the more to our wiles and machinations. What heart one must be possessed of who professes such principles, and who feels no internal sentiment that belies so pernicious a theory, it is easy to imagine, and also, what degree of affection and benevolence he can bear to a species whom he represents under such odious colors and supposes so little susceptible of gratitude or any return of affection. Or, if we should not ascribe these principles wholly to a corrupted heart, we must at least account for them from the most careless and precipitate examination. Superficial reasoners, indeed, observing many false pretenses among mankind, and feeling, perhaps, no very strong restraint in their own disposition, might draw a general and a hasty conclusion that all is equally corrupted and that men, different from all other animals, and indeed from all other species of existence, admit of no degrees of good or bad, but are, in every instance, the same creatures under different disguises and appearances.

There is another principle, somewhat resembling the former, which has been much insisted on by philosophers and has been the foundation of many a system—that, whatever affection one may feel or imagine he feels for others, no pas-

245

sion is, or can be, disinterested; that the most generous friendship, however sincere, is a modification of self-love; and that, even unknown to ourselves, we seek only our own gratification while we appear the most deeply engaged in schemes for the liberty and happiness of mankind. By a turn of imagination, by a refinement of reflection, by an enthusiasm of passion, we seem to take part in the interests of others and imagine ourselves divested of all selfish considerations. But, at bottom, the most generous patriot, and most niggardly miser, the bravest hero, and most abject coward have, in every action, an equal regard to their own happiness and welfare.

Whoever concludes from the seeming tendency of this opinion that those who make profession of it cannot possibly feel the true sentiments of benevolence, or have any regard for genuine virtue, will often find himself, in practice, very much mistaken. Probity and honor were no strangers to Epicurus and his sect. Atticus and Horace seem to have enjoyed from nature, and cultivated by reflection, as generous and friendly dispositions as any disciple of the austerer schools; and among the modern, Hobbes and Locke, who maintained the selfish system of morals, lived irreproachable lives, though the former lay not under any restraint of religion which might supply the defects of his philosophy. An Epicurean or a Hobbist readily allows that there is such a thing as friendship in the world without hypocrisy or disguise, though he may attempt, by a philosophical chemistry, to resolve the elements of this passion, if I may so speak, into those of another and explain every affection to be self-love twisted and molded by a particular turn of imagination into a variety of appearances. But as the same turn of imagination prevails not in every man, nor gives the same direction to the original passion, this is sufficient, even according to the selfish system, to make the widest difference in human characters and denominate one man virtuous and humane, another vicious and meanly interested. I esteem the man whose self-love, by whatever means, is so directed as to give him a concern for others and render him serviceable to society, as I hate or despise him who has no regard to anything beyond his own gratifications and enjoyments. In vain would you suggest that these characters, though seemingly opposite, are at bottom the same, and that a very inconsiderable turn of thought forms the whole difference between them. Each character, notwithstanding these inconsiderable differences, appears to me, in practice, pretty durable and untransmutable; and I find not in this more than in other subjects that the natural sentiments, arising from the general appearances of things, are easily destroyed by subtle reflections concerning the minute origin of these appearances. Does not the lively, cheerful color of a countenance inspire me with complacency and pleasure, even though I learn from philosophy that all difference of complexion arises from the most minute differences of thickness in the most minute parts of the skin, by means of which a superficies is qualified to reflect one of the original colors of light and absorb the others?

But though the question concerning the universal or partial selfishness of man be not so material, as is usually imagined, to morality and practice, it is certainly of consequence in the speculative science of human nature and is a proper object of curiosity and inquiry. It may not, therefore, be unsuitable, in this place, to bestow a few reflections upon it.*

The most obvious objection to the selfish hypothesis is that as it is contrary to common feeling and our most unprejudiced notions, there is required the highest stretch of philosophy to establish so extraordinary a paradox. To the most careless observer, there appear to be such dispositions as benevolence and generosity, such affections as love, friendship, compassion, gratitude. These sentiments have their causes, effects, objects, and operations marked by common language and observation and plainly distinguished from those of the selfish passions. And as this is the obvious appearance of things, it must be admitted till some hypothesis be discovered which, by penetrating deeper into human nature, may prove the former affections to be nothing but modifications of the latter. All attempts of this kind have hitherto proved fruitless and seem to have proceeded entirely from that love of *simplicity* which has been the source of much false reasoning in philosophy. I shall not here enter into any detail on the present subject. Many able philosophers have shown the insufficiency of these systems; and I shall take for granted what, I believe, the smallest reflection will make evident to every impartial inquirer.

But the nature of the subject furnishes the strongest presumption that no better system will ever, for the future, be in-

---

* Benevolence naturally divides into two kinds, the *general* and the *particular*. The first is where we have no friendship, or connection, or esteem for the person, but feel only a general sympathy with him, or a compassion for his pains, and a congratulation with his pleasures. The other species of benevolence is founded on an opinion of virtue, on services done us, or on some particular connections. Both these sentiments must be allowed real in human nature; but whether they will resolve into some nice considerations of self-love is a question more curious than important. The former sentiment, to wit, that of general benevolence, or humanity, or sympathy, we shall have occasion frequently to treat of in the course of this inquiry; and I assume it as real from general experience, without any other proof.

vented in order to account for the origin of the benevolent from the selfish affections and reduce all the various emotions of the human mind to a perfect simplicity. The case is not the same in this species of philosophy as in physics. Many a hypothesis in nature, contrary to first appearances, has been found on more accurate scrutiny solid and satisfactory. Instances of this kind are so frequent that a judicious as well as witty philosopher * has ventured to affirm, if there be more than one way in which any phenomenon may be produced, that there is a general presumption for its arising from the causes which are the least obvious and familiar. But the presumption always lies on the other side in all inquiries concerning the origin of our passions and of the internal operations of the human mind. The simplest and most obvious cause which can there be assigned for any phenomenon is probably the true one. When a philosopher, in the explication of his system, is obliged to have recourse to some very intricate and refined reflections and to suppose them essential to the production of any passion or emotion, we have reason to be extremely on our guard against so fallacious a hypothesis. The affections are not susceptible of any impression from the refinements of reason or imagination; and it is always found that a vigorous exertion of the latter faculties, necessarily from the narrow capacity of the human mind, destroys all activity in the former. Our predominant motive or intention is, indeed, frequently concealed from ourselves when it is mingled and confounded with other motives which the mind, from vanity or self-conceit, is desirous of supposing more prevalent. But there is no instance that a concealment of this nature has ever arisen from the abstruseness and intricacy of the motive. A man that has lost a friend and patron may flatter himself that all his grief arises from generous sentiments, without any mixture of narrow or interested considerations; but a man that grieves for a valuable friend who needed his patronage and protection—how can we suppose that his passionate tenderness arises from some metaphysical regards to a self-interest which has no foundation or reality? We may as well imagine that minute wheels and springs, like those of a watch, give motion to a loaded wagon as account for the origin of passion from such abstruse reflections.

Animals are found susceptible of kindness, both to their own species and to ours; nor is there, in this case, the least suspicion of disguise or artifice. Shall we account for all *their* sentiments, too, from refined deductions of self-interest? Or if

* Mons. Fontenelle.

we admit a distinterested benevolence in the inferior species, by what rule of analogy can we refuse it in the superior?

Love between the sexes begets a complacency and goodwill very distinct from the gratification of an appetite. Tenderness to their offspring, in all sensible beings, is commonly able alone to counterbalance the strongest motives of self-love and has no manner of dependence on that affection. What interest can a fond mother have in view who loses her health by assiduous attendance on her sick child and afterwards languishes and dies of grief when freed, by its death, from the slavery of that attendance?

Is gratitude no affection of the human breast, or is that a word merely without any meaning or reality? Have we no satisfaction in one man's company above another's and no desire of the welfare of our friend, even though absence or death should prevent us from all participation in it? Or what is it commonly that gives us any participation in it, even while alive and present, but our affection and regard to him?

These and a thousand other instances are marks of a general benevolence in human nature, where no *real* interest binds us to the object. And how an *imaginary* interest, known and avowed for such, can be the origin of any passion or emotion seems difficult to explain. No satisfactory hypothesis of this kind has yet been discovered, nor is there the smallest probability that the future industry of men will ever be attended with more favorable success.

But further, if we consider rightly of the matter, we shall find that the hypothesis which allows of a disinterested benevolence, distinct from self-love, has really more *simplicity* in it and is more conformable to the analogy of nature than that which pretends to resolve all friendship and humanity into this latter principle. There are bodily wants or appetites acknowledged by everyone which necessarily precede all sensual enjoyment and carry us directly to seek possession of the object. Thus, hunger and thirst have eating and drinking for their end; and from the gratification of these primary appetites arises a pleasure which may become the object of another species of desire or inclination that is secondary and interested. In the same manner, there are mental passions by which we are impelled immediately to seek particular objects, such as fame, or power, or vengeance, without any regard to interest; and when these objects are attained, a pleasing enjoyment ensues as the consequence of our indulged affections. Nature must, by the internal frame and constitution of the mind, give an original propensity to fame ere we can reap any pleasure from that acquisition or pursue it from motives of self-love and a desire of happiness. If I have no vanity, I take no delight in praise; if I be void of ambition, power gives me no enjoyment; if I be not angry, the punishment of an adversary is totally indifferent to me. In all these cases, there is a passion which points immediately to the object and constitutes it our good or happiness, as there are other secondary passions which afterwards arise and pursue it as a part of our happiness when once it is constituted such by our original affections. Were there no appetite of any kind antecedent to self-love, that propensity could scarcely ever exert itself, because we should, in that case, have felt few and slender pains or pleasures and have little misery or happiness to avoid or to pursue.

Now, where is the difficulty in conceiving that this may likewise be the case with benevolence and friendship and that, from the original frame of our temper, we may feel a desire of another's happiness or good which, by means of that affection, becomes our own good and is afterwards pursued from the combined motives of benevolence and self-enjoyment? Who sees not that vengenace, from the force alone of passion, may be so eagerly pursued as to make us knowingly neglect every consideration of ease, interest, or safety, and, like some vindictive animals, infuse our very souls into the wounds we give an enemy? * And what a malignant philosophy must it be that will not allow to humanity and friendship the same privileges which are indisputably granted to the darker passions of enmity and resentment? Such a philosophy is more like a satire than a true delineation or description of human nature, and may be a good foundation for paradoxical wit and raillery, but it is a very bad one for any serious argument or reasoning.

* *Animasque in vulnere ponunt.* VIRG. *Geor.* 4, 238. ["They put their souls in the wound." Virgil, *Georgics* 4, 238.] *Dum alteri noceat, sui negligens,* says Seneca of anger. *De ira.* i. 1. ["It inflicts harm on another while neglecting itself." Seneca, *On Anger,* i. 1.]

Appendix III

SOME FURTHER CONSIDERATIONS WITH REGARD TO JUSTICE

The intention of this Appendix is to give some more particular explication of the origin and nature of Justice and to mark some differences between it and the other virtues.

The social virtues of humanity and benevolence exert their influence immediately by a direct tendency or instinct which chiefly keeps in view the simple object, moving the affections, and comprehends not any scheme or system nor the consequences resulting from the concurrence, imitation, or example of others. A parent flies to the relief of his child, transported by that natural sympathy which actuates him and which affords no leisure to reflect on the sentiments or conduct of the rest of mankind in like circumstances. A generous man cheerfully embraces an opportunity of serving his friend because he then feels himself under the dominion of the beneficent affections; nor is he concerned whether any other person in the universe were ever before actuated by such noble motives or will ever afterwards prove their influence. In all these cases, the social passions have in view a single individual object and pursue the safety or happiness alone of the person loved and esteemed. With this they are satisfied; in this they acquiesce. And as the good resulting from their benign influence is in itself complete and entire, it also excites the moral sentiment of approbation without any reflection on further consequences and without any more enlarged views of the concurrence or imitation of the other members of society. On the contrary, were the generous friend or disinterested patriot to stand alone in the practice of beneficence, this would rather enhance his value in our eyes and join the praise of rarity and novelty to his other, more exalted merits.

The case is not the same with the social virtues of justice and fidelity. They are highly useful or, indeed, absolutely necessary to the well-being of mankind. But the benefit resulting from them is not the consequence of every individual single act, but arises from the whole scheme or system concurred in by the whole or the greater part of the society. General peace and order are the attendants of justice or a general abstinence from the possessions of others; but a particular regard to the particular right of one individual citizen may frequently, considered in itself, be productive of pernicious consequences. The result of the individual acts is here, in many instances, directly opposite to that of the whole system of actions; and the former may be extremely hurtful, while the latter is, to the highest degree, advantageous. Riches inherited from a parent are in a bad man's hand the instrument of mischief. The right of succession may, in one instance, be hurtful. Its benefit arises only from the observance of the general rule; and it is sufficient if compensation be thereby made for all the ills and inconveniences which flow from particular characters and situations.

Cyrus, young and inexperienced, considered only the individual case before him and reflected on a limited fitness and convenience when he assigned the long coat to the tall boy and the short coat to the other of smaller size. His governor instructed him better, while he pointed out more enlarged views and consequences and informed his pupil of the general, inflexible rules necessary to support general peace and order in society.

The happiness and prosperity of mankind arising from the social virtue of benevolence and its subdivisions may be compared to a wall built by many hands—which still rises by each stone that is heaped upon it and receives increase proportional to the diligence and care of each workman. The same happiness, raised by the social virtue of justice and its subdivisions, may be compared to the building of a vault where each individual stone would of itself fall to the ground; nor is the whole fabric supported but by the mutual assistance and combination of its corresponding parts.

All the laws of nature which regulate property as well as all civil laws are general and regard alone some essential circumstances of the case, without taking into consideration the characters, situations, and connections of the person concerned or any particular consequences which may result from the determination of these laws in any particular case which offers. They deprive, without scruple, a beneficent man of all his possessions if acquired by mistake, without a good title, in order to bestow them on a selfish miser who has already heaped up immense stores of superfluous riches. Public utility requires that property should be regulated by general inflexible rules; and though such rules are adopted as best serve the same end of public utility, it is impossible for them to prevent all particular hardships or make beneficial consequences result from every individual case. It is sufficient if the whole plan or scheme be necessary to the support of civil society and if the balance of good, in the main, do thereby preponderate much above that of evil. Even the general laws of the universe, though planned by Infinite Wisdom, cannot exclude all evil or inconvenience in every particular operation.

It has been asserted by some that justice arises from *human conventions* and proceeds from the voluntary choice, consent, or combination of mankind. If by *convention* be here meant a *promise* (which is the most usual sense of the word), nothing can be more absurd than this position. The observance of promises is itself one of the most considerable parts of justice; and we are not surely bound to keep our word because we have given our word to keep it. But if by convention be meant a sense of common interest, which sense each man feels in his own breast, which he remarks in his fellows, and which carries him, in concurrence with others, into a general plan or system of actions which tends to public utility, it must be owned that in this sense justice arises from human conventions. For if it be allowed (what is indeed evident) that the particular consequences of a particular act of justice may be hurtful to the public as well as to individuals, it follows that every man, in embracing that virtue, must have an eye to the whole plan or system and must expect the concurrence of his fellows in the same conduct and behavior. Did all his views terminate in the consequences of each act of his own, his benevolence and humanity, as well as his self-love, might often prescribe to him measures of conduct very different from those which are agreeable to the strict rules of right and justice.

Thus, two men pull the oars of a boat by common convention, for common interest, without any promise or contract; thus, gold and silver are made the measures of exchange; thus, speech, and words, and language are fixed by human convention and agreement. Whatever is advantageous to two or more persons if all perform their part, but what loses all advantage if only one perform, can arise from no other principle. There would otherwise be no motive for any one of them to enter into that scheme of conduct.*

* This theory concerning the origin of property and consequently of justice is in the main the same with that hinted at and adopted by Grotius. "Hinc discimus, quae fuerit causa, ob quam a primaeva communione rerum primo mobilium, deinde et immobilium discessum est: nimirum quod cum non contenti homines vesci sponte natis, antra habitare, corpore aut nudo agere, aut corticibus arborum ferarumve pellibus vestito, vitae genus exquisitus, delegissent, industria opus fuit, quàm singuli rebus singulis adhiberent: quo minus autem fructus in commune conferrentur, primum obstitit locorum, in quae homines

The word *natural* is commonly taken in so many senses and is of so loose a signification that it seems vain to dispute whether justice be natural or not. If self-love, if benevolence be natural to man, if reason and forethought be also natural, then may the same epithet be applied to justice, order, fidelity, property, society. Men's inclination, their necessities, lead them to combine, their understanding and experience tell them that this combination is impossible where each governs himself by no rule and pays no regard to the possessions of others. And from these passions and reflections conjoined, as soon as we observe like passions and reflections in others, the sentiment of justice, throughout all ages, has infallibly and certainly had place, to some degree or other, in every individual of the human species. In so sagacious an animal, what necessarily arises from the exertion of his intellectual faculties may justly be esteemed natural.*

Among all civilized nations, it has been the constant en-

---

discesserunt, distantia, deinde justitiae et amoris defectus, per quem fiebat, ut nec in labore, nec in consumptione fructuum quae debebat, aequalitas servaretur. Simul discimus, quomodo res in proprietatem iverint; non animi actu solo, neque enim scire alii poterant, quid alii suum esse vellent, ut eo abstinerent, et idem velle plures poterant; sed pacto quodam aut expresso, ut per divisionem, aut tacito, ut per occupationem." *De jure belli et pacis,* lib. ii. cap. 2 § 2. art. 4–5.

["We discover from this why the primitive communal ownership, first of movable property but then also of immovable property, was given up. It is not surprising, for when men were no longer willing to eat unprocessed food, to live in caves, to go naked or clad only in tree bark or wild animal skins, and when they had opted for a more refined way of life, it was necessary that each person work at a different pursuit. The first obstacle to accumulating a common store of the product was the distance between the places to which men had scattered; the second was a diminishing of justice and love, which resulted in equality being maintained neither in work nor in the consumption of the fruits of the work as necessary. We learn also how the development of private property came about. It was not by means of a single mental act, for how could people know what other men desired for themselves and thus what to keep their hands off; what is more, it was possible for several people to want the same thing. The establishment of private property came about rather by an agreement of some sort, either overt, as in a division of property, or tacit, as by seizure." *On the Law of War and Peace.* ii. 2, 2, 4 and 5.]

---

* Natural may be opposed either to what is *unusual, miraculous,* or *artificial.* In the two former senses, justice and property are undoubtedly natural. But as they suppose reason, forethought, design, and a social union and confederacy among men, perhaps that epithet cannot strictly, in the last sense, be applied to them. Had men lived without society, property had never been known, and neither justice nor injustice had ever existed. But society among human creatures had been impossible without reason and forethought. Inferior animals that unite are guided by instinct, which supplies the place of reason. But all these disputes are merely verbal.

deavor to remove everything arbitrary and partial from the decision of property and to fix the sentence of judges by such general views and considerations as may be equal to every member of the society. For besides that nothing could be more dangerous than to accustom the bench, even in the smallest instance, to regard private friendship or enmity, it is certain that men, where they imagine that there was no other reason for the preference of their adversary but personal favor, are apt to entertain the strongest ill will against the magistrates and judges. When natural reason, therefore, points out no fixed view of public utility by which a controversy of property can be decided, positive laws are often framed to supply its place and direct the procedure of all courts of judicature. Where these two fail, as often happens, precedents are called for; and a former decision, though given itself without any sufficient reason, justly becomes a sufficient reason for a new decision. If direct laws and precedents be wanting, imperfect and indirect ones are brought in aid, and the controverted case is ranged under them by analogical reasonings, and comparisons, and similitudes, and correspondences which are often more fanciful than real. In general, it may safely be affirmed that jurisprudence is, in this respect, different from all the sciences, and that in many of its nicer questions there cannot properly be said to be truth or falsehood on either side. If one pleader bring the case under any former law or precedent by a refined analogy or comparison, the opposite pleader is not at a loss to find an opposite analogy or comparison; and the preference given by the judge is often founded more on taste and imagination than on any solid argument. Public utility is the general object of all courts of judicature; and this utility, too, requires a stable rule in all controversies; but where several rules, nearly equal and indifferent, present themselves, it is a very slight turn of thought which fixes the decision in favor of either party.*

---

* That there be a separation or distinction of possessions, and that this separation be steady and constant, this is absolutely required by the interests of society, and hence the origin of justice and property. What possessions are assigned to particular persons, this is, generally speaking, pretty indifferent and is often determined by very frivolous views and considerations. We shall mention a few particulars.

Were a society formed among several independent members, the most obvious rule which could be agreed on would be to annex property to *present* possession and leave everyone a right to what he at present enjoys. The relation of possession, which takes place between the person and the object, naturally draws on the relation of property.

For a like reason, occupation or first possession becomes the foundation of property.

Where a man bestows labor and industry upon any object which

255

We may just observe, before we conclude this subject, that, after the laws of justice are fixed by views of general utility, the injury, the hardship, the harm which result to any individual from a violation of them enter very much into consideration and are a great source of that universal blame which attends every wrong or iniquity. By the laws of society, this coat, this horse is mine and *ought* to remain perpetually in

---

before belonged to nobody, as in cutting down and shaping a tree, in cultivating a field, etc., the alteration which he produces causes a relation between him and the object and naturally engages us to annex it to him by the new relation of property. This cause here concurs with the public utility, which consists in the encouragement given to industry and labor.

Perhaps, too, private humanity toward the possessor concurs, in this instance, with the other motives and engages us to leave with him what he has acquired by his sweat and labor, and what he has flattered himself in the constant enjoyment of. For though private humanity can by no means be the origin of justice, since the latter virtue so often contradicts the former, yet when the rule of separate and constant possession is once formed by the indispensable necessities of society, private humanity and an aversion to the doing a hardship to another may, in a particular instance, give rise to a particular rule of property.

I am much inclined to think that the right of succession or inheritance much depends on those connections of the imagination and that the relation to a former proprietor begetting a relation to the object is the cause why the property is transferred to a man after the death of his kinsman. It is true, industry is more encouraged by the transference of possession to children or near relations; but this consideration will only have place in a cultivated society, whereas the right of succession is regarded even among the greatest barbarians.

Acquisition of property by *accession* can be explained noway but by having recourse to the relations and connections of the imagination.

The property of rivers, by the laws of most nations, and by the natural turn of our thought, is attributed to the proprietors of their banks, excepting such vast rivers as the Rhine or the Danube, which seem too large to follow as an accession to the property of the neighboring fields. Yet even these rivers are considered as the property of that nation through whose dominions they run, the idea of a nation being of a suitable bulk to correspond with them and bear them such a relation in the fancy.

The accessions which are made to land bordering upon rivers follow the land, say the Civilians, provided it be made by what they call *alluvion,* that is, insensibly and imperceptibly—which are circumstances that assist the imagination in the conjunction.

Where there is any considerable portion torn at once from one bank and added to another, it becomes not *his* property whose land it falls on till it unite with the land and till the trees and plants have spread their roots into both. Before that, the thought does not sufficiently join them.

In short, we must ever distinguish between the necessity of a separation and constancy in men's possession and the rules which assign particular objects to particular persons. The first necessity is obvious, strong, and invincible; the latter may depend on a public utility more light and frivolous, on the sentiment of private humanity and aversion to private hardship, on positive laws, on precedents, analogies, and very fine connections and turns of the imagination.

my possession; I reckon on the secure enjoyment of it; by depriving me of it, you disappoint my expectations and doubly displease me and offend every bystander. It is a public wrong so far as the rules of equity are violated; it is a private harm so far as an individual is injured. And though the second consideration could have no place were not the former previously established—for otherwise the distinction of *mine* and *thine* would be unknown in society—yet there is no question but the regard to general good is much enforced by the respect to particular. What injures the community without hurting any individual is often more lightly thought of; but where the greatest public wrong is also conjoined with a considerable private one, no wonder the highest disapprobation attends so iniquitous a behavior.

Appendix IV

OF SOME VERBAL DISPUTES

Nothing is more usual than for philosophers to encroach upon the province of grammarians and to engage in disputes of words, while they imagine that they are handing controversies of the deepest importance and concern. It was in order to avoid altercations, so frivolous and endless, that I endeavored to state with the utmost caution the object of our present inquiry and proposed simply to collect, on the one hand, a list of those mental qualities which are the object of love or esteem and form a part of personal merit and, on the other hand, a catalogue of those qualities which are the object of censure or reproach and which detract from the character of the person possessed of them, subjoining some reflections concerning the origin of these sentiments of praise or blame. On all occasions where there might arise the least hesitation, I avoided the terms *virtue* and *vice*, because some of those qualities which I classed among the objects of praise receive in the English language the appellation of *talents* rather than of virtues, as some of the blamable or censurable qualities are often called *defects* rather than vices. It may now perhaps be expected that, before we conclude this moral inquiry, we should exactly separate the one from the other, should mark the precise boundaries of virtues and talents, vices and defects, and should explain the reason and origin of that distinction. But in order to excuse myself from this undertaking, which would at last prove only a grammatical inquiry, I shall subjoin the four following reflections which shall contain all that I intend to say on the present subject.

First, I do not find that in the English or any other modern tongue the boundaries are exactly fixed between virtues and talents, vices and defects or that a precise definition can be given of the one as contradistinguished from the other. Were we to say, for instance, that the esteemable qualities alone which are voluntary are entitled to the appellation of virtues, we should soon recollect the qualities of courage, equanimity, patience, self-command, with many others, which almost every language classes under this appellation, though they depend little or not at all on our choice. Should we affirm that the qualities alone which prompt us to act our part in society are entitled to that honorable distinction, it must immediately occur that these are indeed the most valuable qualities and are commonly denominated the *social* virtues; but that this very epithet supposes that there are also virtues of another species. Should we lay hold of the distinction between *intellectual* and *moral* endowments and affirm the last alone to be the real and genuine virtues, because they alone lead to action, we should find that many of those qualities usually called intellectual virtues, such as prudence, penetration, discernment, discretion, had also a considerable influence on conduct. The distinction between the *heart* and the *head* may also be adopted: the qualities of the first may be defined such as, in their immediate exertion, are accompanied with a feeling or sentiment, and these alone may be called the genuine virtues; but industry, frugality, temperance, secrecy, perseverance, and many other laudable powers or habits, generally styled virtues, are exerted without any immediate sentiment in the person possessed of them and are only known to him by their effects. It is fortunate, amidst all this seeming perplexity, that the question, being merely verbal, cannot possibly be of any importance. A moral, philosophical discourse needs not enter into all those caprices of language which are so variable in different dialects and in different ages of the same dialect. But, on the whole, it seems to me that though it is always allowed that there are virtues of many different kinds, yet, when a man is called *virtuous,* or is denominated a man of virtue, we chiefly regard his social qualities, which are indeed the most valuable. It is at the same time certain that any remarkable defect in courage, temperance, economy, industry, understanding, dignity of mind would bereave even a very good-natured, honest man of this honorable appellation. Who did ever say, except by way of irony, that such a one was a man of great virtue but an egregious blockhead?

But, *secondly,* it is no wonder that languages should not be very precise in marking the boundaries between virtues and talents, vices and defects, since there is so little distinction made in our internal estimation of them. It seems, indeed, certain that the *sentiment* of conscious worth, the self-satisfaction proceeding from a review of a man's own conduct and character—it seems certain, I say, that this sentiment which, though the most common of all others, has no proper name in our language,* arises from the endowments of courage and capacity, industry and ingenuity, as well as from any other mental excellences. Who, on the other hand, is not deeply mortified with reflecting on his own folly and dissoluteness and feels not a secret sting or compunction whenever his memory presents any past occurrence where he behaved with stupidity or ill manners? No time can efface the cruel ideas of a man's own foolish conduct or of affronts which cowardice or imprudence has brought upon him. They still haunt his solitary hours, damp his most aspiring thoughts, and show him, even to himself, in the most contemptible and most odious colors imaginable.

What is there, too, we are more anxious to conceal from others than such blunders, infirmities, and meannesses, or more dread to have exposed by raillery and satire? And is not the chief object of vanity our bravery or learning, our wit or breeding, our eloquence or address, our taste or abilities? These we display with care, if not with ostentation; and we commonly show more ambition of excelling in them than even in the social virtues themselves, which are in reality of such superior excellence. Good nature and honesty, especially the latter, are so indispensably required that, though the greatest censure attends any violation of these duties, no eminent praise follows such common instances of them as seem essential to the support of human society. And hence the reason, in my opinion, why, though men often extol so liberally the qualities of their heart, they are shy in commending the endowments of their head; because the latter virtues, being supposed more rare and extraordinary, are observed to be the more usual objects of pride and self-conceit

* The term pride is commonly taken in a bad sense; but this sentiment seems indifferent and may be either good or bad, according as it is well or ill founded, and according to the other circumstances which accompany it. The French express this sentiment by the term *amour propre;* but as they also express self-love as well as vanity by the same term, there arises thence a great confusion in Rochefoucauld and many of their moral writers.

and when boasted of, beget a strong suspicion of these sentiments.

It is hard to tell whether you hurt a man's character most by calling him a knave or a coward and whether a beastly glutton or drunkard be not as odious and contemptible as a selfish, ungenerous miser. Give me my choice, and I would rather, for my own happiness and self-enjoyment, have a friendly, humane heart than possess all the other virtues of Demosthenes and Philip united. But I would rather pass with the world for one endowed with extensive genius and intrepid courage and should thence expect stronger instances of general applause and admiration. The figure which a man makes in life, the reception which he meets with in company, the esteem paid him by his acquaintance—all these advantages depend as much upon his good sense and judgment as upon any other part of this character. Had a man the best intentions in the world and were the farthest removed from all injustice and violence, he would never be able to make himself be much regarded without a moderate share at least of parts and understanding.

What is it then we can here dispute about? If sense and courage, temperance and industry, wisdom and knowledge confessedly form a considerable part of *personal merit,* if a man possessed of these qualities is both better satisfied with himself and better entitled to the goodwill, esteem, and services of others than one entirely destitute of them—if, in short, the *sentiments* are similar which arise from these endowments and from the social virtues, is there any reason for being so extremely scrupulous about a *word* or disputing whether they be entitled to the denomination of virtues? It may, indeed, be pretended that the sentiment of approbation, which those accomplishments produce, besides its being *inferior,* is also somewhat *different* from that which attends the virtues of justice and humanity. But this seems not a sufficient reason for ranking them entirely under different classes and appellations. The character of Caesar and that of Cato, as drawn by Sallust, are both of them virtuous, in the strictest and most limited sense of the word, but in a different way; nor are the sentiments entirely the same which arise from them. The one produces love, the other esteem; the one is amiable, the other awful. We should wish to meet the one character in a friend, the other we should be ambitious of in ourselves. In like manner, the approbation which attends temperance, or industry, or frugality may be somewhat different from that which is paid to the social virtues, without making them entirely of a different species. And, indeed, we may observe that these endowments, more than the other virtues,

260

produce not, all of them, the same kind of approbation. Good sense and genius beget esteem and regard; wit and humor excite love and affection.*

Most people, I believe, will naturally, without premeditation, assent to the definition of the elegant and judicious poet!

> Virtue (for mere good nature is a fool)
> Is sense and spirit with humanity.†

What pretensions has a man to our generous assistance or good offices who has dissipated his wealth in profuse expenses, idle vanities, chimerical projects, dissolute pleasures, or extravagant gaming? These vices (for we scruple not to call them such) bring misery unpitied and contempt on everyone addicted to them.

Achaeus, a wide and prudent prince, fell into a fatal snare which cost him his crown and life, after having used every reasonable precaution to guard himself against it. On that account, says the historian, he is a just object of regard and compassion, his betrayers alone of hatred and contempt.‡

The precipitate flight and improvident negligence of Pompey, at the beginning of the civil wars, appeared such notorious blunders to Cicero as quite palled his friendship toward that great man. *In the same manner,* says he, *as want of cleanliness, decency, or discretion in a mistress are found to alienate our affections.* For so he expresses himself where he

---

* Love and esteem are nearly the same passion and arise from similar causes. The qualities which produce both are such as communicate pleasure. But where this pleasure is severe and serious; or where its object is great and makes a strong impression; or where it produces any degree of humility and awe—in all these cases, the passion which arises from the pleasure is more properly denominated esteem than love. Benevolence attends both, but is connected with love in a more eminent degree. There seems to be still a stronger mixture of pride in contempt than of humility in esteem; and the reason would not be difficult to one who studied accurately the passions. All these various mixtures, and compositions, and appearances of sentiment form a very curious subject of speculation but are wide of our present purpose. Throughout this inquiry, we always consider, in general, what qualities are a subject of praise or of censure, without entering into all the minute differences of sentiment which they excite. It is evident that whatever is condemned is also disliked, as well as what is hated; and we here endeavor to take objects according to their most simple views and appearances. These sciences are but too apt to appear abstract to common readers, even with all the precautions which we can take to clear them from superfluous speculations and bring them down to every capacity.

† [Armstrong:] *The Art of Preserving Health.* Book IV.

‡ Polybius, lib. viii. cap. 2, 8, and 9.

talks, not in the character of a philosopher, but in that of a statesman and man of the world, to his friend Atticus.*

But the same Cicero, in imitation of all the ancient moralists, when he reasons as a philosopher, enlarges very much his ideas of virtue and comprehends every laudable quality or endowment of the mind under that honorable appellation. This leads to the *third* reflection which we proposed to make, to wit, that the ancient moralists, the best models, made no material distinction among the different species of mental endowments and defects, but treated all alike under the appellation of virtues and vices and made them indiscriminately the object of their moral reasonings. The *prudence* explained in Cicero's *Offices* † is that sagacity which leads to the discovery of truth and preserves us from error and mistake. *Magnanimity, temperance, decency* are there also at large discoursed of. And as that eloquent moralist followed the common received division of the four cardinal virtues, our social duties form but one head in the general distribution of his subject.‡

* Lib. ix. epist. 10, 2.

† Lib. i. cap. 6.

‡ The following passage of Cicero is worth quoting, as being the most clear and express to our purpose that anything can be imagined and, in a dispute which is chiefly verbal must, on account of the author, carry an authority from which there can be no appeal.

"Virtus autem, quae est per se ipsa laudabilis, et sine qua nihil laudari potest, tamen habet plures partes, quarum alia est aliâ ad laudationem aptior. Sunt enim aliae virtutes, quae videntur in moribus hominum, et quadam comitate ac beneficentia positae: aliae quae in ingenii aliqua facultate, aut animi magnitudine ac robore. Nam clementia, justitia, benignitas, fides, fortitudo in periculis communibus, jucunda est auditu in laudationibus. Omnes enim hae virtutes non tam ipsis, qui eas in se habent, quam generi hominum fructuosae putantur. Sapientia et magnitudo animi, qua omnes res humanae, tenues et pro nihilo putantur; et in cogitando vis quaedam ingenii, et ipsa eloquentia admirationis habet non minus, jucunditatis minus. Ipsos enim magis videtur, quos laudamus, quam illos, apud quos laudamus, ornare ac tueri: sed tamen in laudando jungenda sunt etiam haec genera virtutum. Ferunt enim aures hominum, cum illa quae jucunda et grata, tum etiam illa quae mirabilia sunt in virtute, laudari." De orat. lib. ii. cap. 84.

I suppose, if Cicero were now alive, it would be found difficult to fetter his moral sentiments by narrow systems or persuade him that no qualities were to be admitted as *virtues*, or acknowledged to be a part of *personal merit*, but what were recommended by *The Whole Duty of Man.*

["But although virtue is praiseworthy for itself, and is that without which nothing else is praiseworthy, still it has several parts, some of which are more praiseworthy than others. Some virtues inhere in men's manner, as in some kind of amiability and beneficence; others inhere in a capacity of the mind, such as largeness of soul and strength of mind. For we like to hear of mercy, justice, kindness, loyalty, and courage in common dangers when men are praised. These virtues are all considered as benefiting men in general rather than

262

We need only peruse the titles of chapters in Aristotle's *Ethics* to be convinced that he ranks courage, temperance, magnificence, magnanimity, modesty, prudence, and a manly openness among the virtues, as well as justice and friendship.

To *sustain* and to *abstain*, that is, to be patient and continent, appeared to some of the ancients a summary comprehension of all morals.

Epictetus has scarcely ever mentioned the sentiment of humanity and compassion but in order to put his disciples on their guard against it. The virtue of the *Stoics* seems to consist chiefly in a firm temper and a sound understanding. With them, as with Solomon and the Eastern moralists, folly and wisdom are equivalent to vice and virtue.

Men will praise thee, says David, * when thou dost well unto thyself. I hate a wise man, says the Greek poet, who is not wise to himself.†

Plutarch is no more cramped by systems in his philosophy than in his history. Where he compares the great men of Greece and Rome, he fairly sets in opposition all their blemishes and accomplishments of whatever kind and omits nothing considerable which can either depress or exalt their characters. His moral discourses contain the same free and natural censure of men and manners.

The character of Hannibal, as drawn by Livy,‡ is esteemed partial, but allows him many eminent virtues. Never was there a genius, says the historian, more equally fitted for those opposite offices of commanding and obeying; and it were, therefore, difficult to determine whether he rendered himself *dearer* to the general or to the army. To none would Hasdrubal entrust more willingly the conduct of any dangerous enterprise; under none did the soldiers discover more courage and confidence, great boldness in facing danger, great prudence in the midst of it. No labor could fatigue his body or subdue his mind. Cold and heat were indifferent to him. Meat and drink he sought as supplies to the necessities

---

merely those who have them. Wisdom and largeness of soul, which make the affairs of men seem valueless and of no importance, are more a cause for admiration than for pleasure, as also is true for a certain intellectual power of thought and even for eloquence itself. For they seem more ornaments to those whom we praise than to those before whom they are praised. Nevertheless, even these sorts of virtue must be mentioned when praise is being given, for the ears of men are willing to hear praised that which is admirable, as well as that which is enjoyable and pleasant, in virtue."] *De oratore* (*Of the Orator*). ii 84.]

* Psalm 49.

†Μισῶ σοφιστὴν ὅστις οὐδ' αὐτῷ σοφός. Euripides [Fragment 905.]

‡ Lib. xxi. cap. 4.

of nature, not as gratifications of his voluptuous appetites. Waking or rest he used indiscriminately, by night or by day. These great *virtues* were balanced by great *vices:* inhuman cruelty; perfidy more than *punic:* no truth, no faith, no regard to oaths, promises, or religion.

The character of Alexander the Sixth, to be found in Guicciardin,* is pretty similar, but juster, and is a proof that even the moderns, where they speak naturally, hold the same language with the ancients. In this pope, says he, there was a singular capacity and judgment: admirable prudence, a wonderful talent of persuasion, and in all momentous enterprises a diligence and dexterity incredible. But these *virtues* were infinitely overbalanced by his *vices:* no faith, no religion, insatiable avarice, exorbitant ambition, and a more than barbarous cruelty.

Polybius,† reprehending Timaeus for his partiality against Agathocles, whom he himself allows to be the most cruel and impious of all tyrants, says, If he took refuge in Syracuse, as asserted by that historian, flying the dirt and smoke and toil of his former profession of a potter; and if, proceeding from such slender beginnings, he became master in a little time of all Sicily, brought the Carthaginian state into the utmost danger, and at last died in old age and in possession of sovereign dignity—must he not be allowed something prodigious and extraordinary and to have possessed great talents and capacity for business and action? His historian, therefore, ought not to have alone related what tended to his reproach and infamy, but also what might redound to his *praise* and *honor.*

In general, we may observe that the distinction of voluntary or involuntary was little regarded by the ancients in their moral reasonings, where they frequently treated the question as very doubtful *whether virtue could be taught or not?* ‡ They justly considered that cowardice, meanness, levity, anxiety, impatience, folly, and many other qualities of the mind might appear ridiculous and deformed, contemptible and odious, though independent of the will. Nor could it be supposed at all times in every man's power to attain every kind of mental more than of exterior beauty.

And here there occurs the *fourth* reflection which I pur-

* Lib. i.

† Lib. xii. 15.

‡ *Vid.* Plato in *Menone,* Seneca in *de otio sap.* cap. 31. So also Horace, *Virtutem doctrina paret, naturane donet. Epist.* lib. i. ep. 18, 100. [See Plato in *Meno;* Seneca in *De otio sapientis* ("On the Leisure of the Wise Man") 31.] Aeschines Socraticus, *Dial.* i. ["Whether virtue follows in the path of learning or is given by nature." *Epistles.* i. 18, 100.) Aeschines Socraticus, *Dialogue* i.]

posed to make in suggesting the reason why modern philosophers have often followed a course in their moral inquiries so different from that of the ancients. In later times, philosophy of all kinds, especially ethics, have been more closely united with theology than ever they were observed to be among the heathens; and as this latter science admits of no terms of composition, but bends every branch of knowledge to its own purpose without much regard to the phenomena of nature or to the unbiased sentiments of the mind, hence reasoning and even language have been warped from their natural course, and distinctions have been endeavored to be established where the difference of the objects was, in a manner, imperceptible. Philosophers, or rather divines under that disguise, treating all morals as on a like footing with civil laws guarded by the sanctions of reward and punishment, were necessarily led to render this circumstance of *voluntary* or *involuntary* the foundation of their whole theory. Everyone may employ *terms* in what sense he pleases; but this, in the meantime, must be allowed, that *sentiments* are every day experienced of blame and praise which have objects beyond the dominion of the will or choice and of which it behooves us, if not as moralists as speculative philosophers at least, to give some satisfactory theory and explication.

A blemish, a fault, a vice, a crime—these expressions seem to denote different degrees of censure and disapprobation which are, however, all of them, at the bottom pretty nearly of the same kind or species. The explication of one will easily lead us into a just conception of the others; and it is of greater consequence to attend to things than to verbal appellations. That we owe a duty to ourselves is confessed even in the most vulgar system of morals; and it must be of consequence to examine that duty in order to see whether it bears any affinity to that which we owe to society. It is probable that the approbation attending the observance of both is of a similar nature and arises from similar principles, whatever appellation we may give to either of these excellences.

A Dialogue

My friend Palamedes, who is as great a rambler in his principles as in his person, and who has run over, by study and travel, almost every region of the intellectual and material world, surprised me lately with an account of a nation with whom, he told me, he had passed a considerable part of his life, and whom he found, in the main, a people extremely civilized and intelligent.

There is a country, said he, in the world called Fourli, no matter for its longitude or latitude, whose inhabitants have ways of thinking in many things, particularly in morals, diametrically opposite to ours. When I came among them, I found that I must submit to double pains: first, to learn the meaning of the terms in their language and, then, to know the import of those terms and the praise or blame attached to them. After a word had been explained to me and a character which it expressed had been described, I concluded that such an epithet must necessarily be the greatest reproach in the world and was extremely surprised to find one in a public company apply it to a person with whom he lived in the strictest intimacy and friendship. *You fancy*, said I one day to an acquaintance, *that Changuis is your mortal enemy: I love to extinguish quarrels, and I must therefore tell you that I heard him talk of you in the most obliging manner.* But to my great astonishment, when I repeated Changuis's words, though I had both remembered and understood them perfectly, I found that they were taken for the most mortal affront and that I had very innocently rendered the breach between these persons altogether irreparable.

As it was my fortune to come among this people on a very advantageous footing, I was immediately introduced to the best company; and being desired by Alcheic to live with him, I readily accepted of his invitation, as I found him universally esteemed for his personal merit and indeed regarded by everyone in Fourli as a perfect character.

One evening, he invited me, as an amusement, to bear him company in a serenade which he intended to give to Gulki, with whom, he told me, he was extremely enamored; and I soon found that his taste was not singular, for we met many of his rivals who had come on the same errand. I very naturally concluded that this mistress of his must be one of the finest women in town, and I already felt a secret inclination to see her and be acquainted with her. But as the moon began to rise, I was much surprised to find that we were in the midst of the university where Gulki studied; and I was somewhat ashamed for having attended my friend on such an errand.

I was afterwards told that Alcheic's choice of Gulki was very much approved of by all the good company in town and that it was expected, while he gratified his own passion, he would perform to that young man the same good office which he had himself owed to Elcouf. It seems Alcheic had been very handsome in his youth, had been courted by many lovers, but had bestowed his favors chiefly on the sage Elcouf, to whom he was supposed to owe, in a great measure, the astonishing progress which he had made in philosophy and virtue.

It gave me some surprise that Alcheic's wife (who by-the-by happened also to be his sister) was nowise scandalized at this species of infidelity.

Much about the same time, I discovered (for it was not attempted to be kept a secret from me or anybody) that Alcheic was a murderer and a parricide and had put to death an innocent person, the most nearly connected with him and whom he was bound to protect and defend by all the ties of nature and humanity. When I asked, with all the caution and deference imaginable, what was his motive for this action, he replied coolly that he was not then so much at ease in his circumstances as he is at present and that he had acted, in that particular, by the advice of all his friends.

Having heard Alcheic's virtue so extremely celebrated, I pretended to join in the general voice of acclamation and only asked, by way of curiosity, as a stranger, which of all his noble actions was most highly applauded; and I soon found that all sentiments were united in giving the preference to the assassination of Usbek. This Usbek had been to the last moment Alcheic's intimate friend, had laid many high obligations upon him, had even saved his life on a certain occasion, and had, by his will, which was found after the murder, made him heir to a considerable part of his fortune. Alcheic, it seems, conspired with about twenty or thirty more, most of them also Usbek's friends; and falling all together on that unhappy man when he was not aware, they had torn him with a hundred wounds and given him that reward for all his past favors and obligations. Usbek, said the general voice of the people, had many great and good qualities—his very vices were shining, magnificent, and generous—but this action of Alcheic's sets him far above Usbek in the eyes of all judges of merit and is one of the noblest that ever perhaps the sun shone upon.

Another part of Alcheic's conduct, which I also found highly applauded, was his behavior toward Calish, with whom he was joined in a project or undertaking of some importance. Calish, being a passionate man, gave Alcheic one day a sound drubbing, which he took very patiently, waited the return of Calish's good humor, kept still a fair correspondence with him, and by that means brought the affair in which they were joined to a happy issue and gained to himself immortal honor by his remarkable temper and moderation.

I have lately received a letter from a correspondent in Fourli, by which I learn that, since my departure, Alcheic, falling into a bad state of health, has fairly hanged himself and has died, universally regretted and applauded in that country. So virtuous and noble a life, says each Fourlian, could not be better crowned than by so noble an end; and Alcheic has proved by this, as well as by all his other actions, what was his constant principle during his life, and what he boasted of near his last moments, that a wise man is scarcely inferior to the great god Vitzli. This is the name of the supreme deity among the Fourlians.

The notions of this people, continued Palamedes, are as extraordinary with regard to good manners and sociableness as with regard to morals. My friend Alcheic formed once a party for my entertainment composed of all the prime wits and philosophers of Fourli, and each of us brought his mess along with him to the place where we assembled. I observed one of them to be worse provided than the rest and offered him a share of my mess, which happened to be a roasted pullet; and I could not but remark that he and all the rest of the company smiled at my simplicity. I was told that Alcheic had once so much interest with his club as to prevail with them to eat in common and that he had made use of an artifice for that purpose. He persuaded those whom he observed to be *worst* provided to offer their mess to the company, after which the others, who had brought more delicate fare, were ashamed not to make the same offer. This is regarded as so extraordinary an event that it has since, as I learn, been recorded in the history of Alcheic's life, composed by one of the greatest geniuses of Fourli.

Pray, said I, Palamedes, when you were at Fourli, did you

also learn the art of turning your friends into ridicule by telling them strange stories and then laughing at them if they believed you? I assure you, replied he, had I been disposed to learn such a lesson, there was no place in the world more proper. My friend, so often mentioned, did nothing from morning to night but sneer, and banter, and rally; and you could scarcely ever distinguish whether he were in jest or earnest. But you think, then, that my story is improbable and that I have used, or rather abused, the privilege of a traveler. To be sure, said I, you were but in jest. Such barbarous and savage manners are not only incompatible with a civilized, intelligent people, such as you said these were, but are scarcely compatible with human nature. They exceed all we ever read of among the Mingrelians and Topinamboues.

Have a care, cried he, have a care! You are not aware that you are speaking blasphemy and are abusing your favorites, the Greeks, especially the Athenians, whom I have couched, all along, under these bizarre names I employed. If you consider aright, there is not one stroke of the foregoing character which might not be found in the man of highest merit at Athens, without diminishing in the least from the brightness of his character. The amours of the Greeks, their marriages,* and the exposing of their children cannot but strike you immediately. The death of Usbeck is an exact counterpart to that of Caesar.

All to a trifle, said I, interrupting him; you did not mention that Usbek was a usurper.

I did not, replied he, lest you should discover the parallel I aimed at. But even adding this circumstance, we should make no scruple, according to our sentiments of morals, to denominate Brutus and Cassius ungrateful traitors and assassins, though you know that they are, perhaps, the highest characters of all antiquity; and the Athenians erected statues to them, which they placed near those of Harmodius and Aristogiton, their own deliverers. And if you think this circumstance which you mention so material to absolve these patriots, I shall compensate it by another, not mentioned, which will equally aggravate their crime. A few days before the execution of their fatal purpose, they all swore fealty to Caesar; and protesting to hold his person ever sacred, they touched the altar with those hands which they had already armed for his destruction.†

I need not remind you of the famous and applauded story

---

* The laws of Athens allowed a man to marry his sister by the father. Solon's law forbids pederasty to slaves, as being an act of too great dignity for such mean persons.

† Appian. *Bell. civ.* lib. iii. Suetonius in *Vita Caesaris* 84.

of Themistocles and of his patience toward Eurybiades the Spartan, his commanding officer, who, heated by debate, lifted his cane to him in a council of war (the same thing as if he had cudgeled him). *Strike!* cries the Athenian, *strike! but hear me.*

You are too good a scholar not to discover the ironical Socrates and his Athenian club in my last story; and you will certainly observe that it is exactly copied from Xenophon, with a variation only of the names; * and I think I have fairly made it appear that an Athenian man of high merit might be such a one as with us would pass for incestuous, a parricide, an assassin, an ungrateful, perjured traitor, and something else too abominable to be named, not to mention his rusticity and ill manners; and having lived in this manner, his death might be entirely suitable. He might conclude the scene by a desperate act of self-murder and die with the most absurd blasphemies in his mouth. And notwithstanding all this, he shall have statues if not altars erected to his memory; poems and orations shall be composed in his praise; great sects shall be proud of calling themselves by his name; and the most distant posterity shall blindly continue their admiration, though, were such a one to arise among themselves, they would justly regard him with horror and execration.

I might have been aware, replied I, of your artifice. You seem to take pleasure in this topic and are, indeed, the only man I ever knew who was well acquainted with the ancients and did not extremely admire them. But instead of attacking their philosophy, their eloquence, or poetry, the usual subjects of controversy between us, you now seem to impeach their morals and accuse them of ignorance in a science which is the only one, in my opinion, in which they are not surpassed by the moderns. Geometry, physics, astronomy, anatomy, botany, geography, navigation—in these we justly claim the superiority; but what have we to oppose to their moralists? Your representation of things is fallacious. You have no indulgence for the manners and customs of different ages. Would you try a Greek or Roman by the common law of England? Hear him defend himself by his own maxims, and then pronounce.

There are no manners so innocent or reasonable but may be rendered odious or ridiculous if measured by a standard unknown to the persons, especially if you employ a little art or eloquence in aggravating some circumstances and extenuating others, as best suits the purpose of your discourse. All these artifices may easily be retorted on you. Could I inform

* *Mem. Soc.* lib. iii. 14, 1.

the Athenians, for instance, that there was a nation in which adultery, both active and passive, so to speak, was in the highest vogue and esteem, in which every man of education chose for his mistress a married woman, the wife, perhaps, of his friend and companion, and valued himself upon these infamous conquests as much as if he had been several times a conqueror in boxing or wrestling at the Olympic games; in which every man also took a pride in his tameness and facility with regard to his own wife and was glad to make friends or gain interest by allowing her to prostitute her charms, and even, without any such motive, gave her full liberty and indulgence—I ask what sentiments the Athenians would entertain of such a people, they who never mentioned the crime of adultery but in conjunction with robbery and poisoning? Which would they admire most, the villainy or the meanness of such a conduct?

Should I add that the same people were as proud of their slavery and dependence as the Athenians of their liberty; and though a man among them were oppressed, disgraced, impoverished, insulted, or imprisoned by the tyrant, he would still regard it as the highest merit to love, serve, and obey him, and even to die for his smallest glory or satisfaction. These noble Greeks would probably ask me whether I spoke of a human society or of some inferior servile species.

It was then I might inform my Athenian audience that these people, however, wanted not spirit and bravery. If a man, say I, though their intimate friend, should throw out, in a private company, a raillery against them nearly approaching any of those with which your generals and demagogues every day regale each other in the face of the whole city, they never can forgive him; but in order to revenge themselves, they oblige him immediately to run them through the body or be himself murdered. And if a man who is an absolute stranger to them should desire them, at the peril of their own life, to cut the throat of their bosom companion, they immediately obey and think themselves highly obliged and honored by the commission. These are their maxims of honor; this is their favorite morality.

But though so ready to draw their sword against their friends and countrymen, no disgrace, no infamy, no pain, no poverty will ever engage these people to turn the point of it against their own breast. A man of rank would row in the galleys, would beg his bread, would languish in prison, would suffer any tortures and still preserve his wretched life. Rather than escape his enemies by a generous contempt of death, he would infamously receive the same death from his enemies, aggravated by their triumphant insults and by the most exquisite sufferings.

It is very usual too, continue I, among this people, to erect jails where every art of plaguing and tormenting the unhappy prisoners is carefully studied and practiced. And in these jails, it is usual for a parent voluntarily to shut up several of his children in order that another child whom he owns to have no greater or rather less merit than the rest may enjoy his whole fortune and wallow in every kind of voluptuousness and pleasure. Nothing so virtuous in their opinion as this barbarous partiality.

But what is more singular in this whimsical nation, say I to the Athenians, is that a frolic of yours during the Saturnalia,* when the slaves are served by their masters, is seriously continued by them throughout the whole year, and throughout the whole course of their lives, accompanied, too, with some circumstances which still further augment the absurdity and ridicule. Your sport only elevates for a few days those whom fortune has thrown down and whom she, too, in sport, may really elevate forever above you; but this nation gravely exalts those whom nature has subjected to them and whose inferiority and infirmities are absolutely incurable. The women, though without virtue, are their masters and sovereigns: these they reverence, praise, and magnify; to these they pay the highest deference and respect; and in all places and all times, the superiority of the females is readily acknowledged and submitted to by everyone who has the least pretensions to education and politeness. Scarce any crime would be so universally detested as an infraction of this rule.

You need go no farther, replied Palamedes. I can easily conjecture the people whom you aim at. The strokes with which you have painted them are pretty just, and yet you must acknowledge that scarce any people are to be found, either in ancient or modern times, whose national character is, upon the whole, less liable to exception. But I give you thanks for helping me out with my argument. I had no intention of exalting the moderns at the expense of the ancients. I only meant to represent the uncertainty of all these judgments concerning characters and to convince you that fashion, vogue, custom, and law were the chief foundation of all moral determinations. The Athenians, surely, were a civilized, intelligent people, if ever there were one; and yet their man of merit might, in this age, be held in horror and execration. The French are also, without doubt, a very civilized, intelligent people; and yet their man of merit might, with the Athe-

* The Greeks kept the feast of Saturn, or Cronus, as well as the Romans. See Lucian. *Epist. Saturn.*

nians, be an object of the highest contempt and ridicule and even hatred. And what renders the matter more extraordinary, these two people are supposed to be the most similar in their national character of any in ancient and modern times; and while the English flatter themselves that they resemble the Romans, their neighbors on the Continent draw the parallel between themselves and those polite Greeks. What wide difference, therefore, in the sentiments of morals must be found between civilized nations and barbarians or between nations whose characters have little in common? How shall we pretend to fix a standard for judgments of this nature?

By tracing matters, replied I, a little higher and examining the first principles which each nation establishes of blame or censure. The Rhine flows north, the Rhone south; yet both spring from the *same* mountain and are also actuated, in their opposite directions, by the *same* principle of gravity. The different inclinations of the ground on which they run cause all the difference of their courses.

In how many circumstances would an Athenian and a Frenchman of merit certainly resemble each other? Good sense, knowledge, wit, eloquence, humanity, fidelity, truth, justice, courage, temperance, constancy, dignity of mind—these you have all omitted in order to insist only on the points in which they may by accident differ. Very well; I am willing to comply with you and shall endeavor to account for these differences from the most universal, established principles of morals.

The Greek loves I care not to examine more particularly. I shall only observe that, however blamable, they arose from a very innocent cause, the frequency of the gymnastic exercises among that people, and were recommended, though absurdly, as the source of friendship, sympathy, mutual attachment, and fidelity *—qualities esteemed in all nations and all ages.

The marriage of half brothers and sisters seems no great difficulty. Love between the nearer relations is contrary to reason and public utility; but the precise point where we are to stop can scarcely be determined by natural reason and is therefore a very proper subject for municipal law or custom. If the Athenians went a little too far on the one side, the canon law has surely pushed matters a great way into the other extreme.†

Had you asked a parent at Athens why he bereaved his child of that life which he had so lately given it, It is because I love it, he would reply, and regard the poverty which it

* Plat. *Symp.* p. 182. Ex edit. Seranir.
† See *Inquiry*, Sect. IV, "Of Political Society."

must inherit from me as a greater evil than death, which it is not capable of dreading, feeling, or resenting.*

How is public liberty, the most valuable of all blessings, to be recovered from the hands of a usurper or tyrant if his power shields him from public rebellion and our scruples from private vengeance? That his crime is capital by law, you acknowledge; and must the highest aggravation of his crime, the putting of himself above law, form his full security? You can reply nothing but by showing the great inconveniences of assassination; which, could anyone have proved clearly to the ancients, he had reformed their sentiments in this particular.

Again, to cast your eye on the picture which I have drawn of modern manners, there is almost as great difficulty, I acknowledge, to justify French as Greek gallantry, except only that the former is much more natural and agreeable than the latter. But our neighbors, it seems, have resolved to sacrifice some of the domestic to the social pleasures and to prefer ease, freedom, and an open commerce to a strict fidelity and constancy. These ends are both good and are somewhat difficult to reconcile; nor need we be surprised if the customs of nations incline too much, sometimes to the one side, sometimes to the other.

The most inviolable attachment to the laws of our country is everywhere acknowledged a capital virtue; and where the people are not so happy as to have any legislature but a single person, the strictest loyalty is, in that case, the truest patriotism.

Nothing surely can be more absurd and barbarous than the practice of dueling; but those who justify it say that it begets civility and good manners. And a duelist, you may observe, always values himself upon his courage, his sense of honor, his fidelity and friendship—qualities which are here indeed very oddly directed, but which have been esteemed universally since the foundation of the world.

Have the gods forbidden self-murder? An Athenian allows that it ought to be forborne. Has the Deity permitted it? A Frenchman allows that death is preferable to pain and infamy.

You see then, continued I, that the principles upon which men reason in morals are always the same, though the conclusions which they draw are often very different. That they all reason aright with regard to this subject more than with regard to any other it is not incumbent on any moralist to show. It is sufficient that the original principles of censure or blame are uniform and that erroneous conclusions can be

* Plut. *De amore prolis, sub fine.*

corrected by sounder reasoning and larger experience. Though many ages have elapsed since the fall of Greece and Rome, though many changes have arrived in religion, language, laws, and customs, none of these revolutions has ever produced any considerable innovation in the primary sentiments of morals more than in those of external beauty. Some minute differences, perhaps, may be observed in both. Horace * celebrates a low forehead and Anacreon joined eyebrows; † but the Apollo and the Venus of antiquity are still our models for male and female beauty, in like manner as the character of Scipio continues our standard for the glory of heroes and that of Cornelia for the honor of matrons.

It appears that there never was any quality recommended by anyone as a virtue or moral excellence but on account of its being *useful* or *agreeable* to a man *himself* or to *others*. For what other reason can ever be assigned for praise or approbation? Or where would be the sense of extolling a *good* character or action which, at the same time, is allowed to be *good for nothing*? All the differences, therefore, in morals may be reduced to this one general foundation and may be accounted for by the different views which people take of these circumstances.

Sometimes men differ in their judgment about the usefulness of any habit or action; sometimes also the peculiar circumstances of things render one moral quality more useful than others and give it a peculiar preference.

It is not surprising that during a period of war and disorder the military virtues should be more celebrated than the pacific and attract more the admiration and attention of mankind.

How usual is it (says Tully [Cicero]) to find Cimbrians, Celtiberians, and other barbarians, who bear with inflexible constancy all the fatigues and dangers of the field, but are immediately dispirited under the pain and hazard of a languishing distemper; while, on the other hand, the Greeks patiently endure the slow approaches of death, when armed with sickness and disease, but timorously fly his presence when he attacks them violently with swords and falchions! ‡

So different is even the same virtue of courage among warlike or peaceful nations! And indeed we may observe that, as the

* *Epist.* lib. i. epist. 7, 26. Also lib. i. ode 3.

† Ode 28. Petronius (cap. 86) joins both these circumstances as beauties.

‡ *Tusc. Quaest*, lib. ii, 27.

difference between war and peace is the greatest that arises among nations and public societies, it produces also the greatest variations in moral sentiment and diversifies the most our ideas of virtue and personal merit.

Sometimes, too, magnanimity, greatness of mind, disdain of slavery, inflexible rigor and integrity may better suit the circumstances of one age than those of another and have a more kindly influence, both on public affairs and on a man's own safety and advancement. Our idea of merit, therefore, will also vary a little with these variations and Labeo, perhaps, be censured for the same qualities which procured Cato the highest approbation.

A degree of luxury may be ruinous and pernicious in a native of Switzerland, which only fosters the arts, and encourages industry in a Frenchman or Englishman. We are not, therefore, to expect either the same sentiments or the same laws in Berne which prevail in London or Paris.

Different customs have also some influence as well as different utilities and by giving an early bias to the mind may produce a superior propensity either to the useful or the agreeable qualities to those which regard self or those which extend to society. These four sources of moral sentiment still subsist, but particular accidents may, at one time, make any one of them flow with greater abundance than at another.

The customs of some nations shut up the women from all social commerce. Those of others make them so essential a part of society and conversation that, except where business is transacted, the male sex alone are supposed almost wholly incapable of mutual discourse and entertainment. As this difference is the most material that can happen in private life, it must also produce the greatest variation in our moral sentiments.

Of all nations in the world where polygamy was not allowed, the Greeks seem to have been the most reserved in their commerce with the fair sex and to have imposed on them the strictest laws of modesty and decency. We have a strong instance of this in an oration of Lysias.* A widow, injured, ruined, undone, calls a meeting of a few of her nearest friends and relations; and though never before accustomed, says the orator, to speak in the presence of men, the distress of her circumstances constrained her to lay the case before them. The very opening of her mouth in such company required, it seems, an apology.

When Demosthenes prosecuted his tutors to make them refund his patrimony, it became necessary for him, in the

* *Orat.* 33.

course of the lawsuit, to prove that the marriage of Aphobus' sister with Onetor was entirely fraudulent and that, notwithstanding her sham marriage, she had lived with her brother at Athens for two years past, ever since her divorce from her former husband. And it is remarkable that though these were people of the first fortune and distinction in the city, the orator could prove this fact noway but by calling for her female slaves to be put to the question and by the evidence of one physician who had seen her in her brother's house during her illness.* So reserved were Greek manners.

We may be assured that an extreme purity of manners was the consequence of this reserve. Accordingly, we find that, except the fabulous stories of a Helen and a Clytemnestra, there scarcely is an instance of any event in the Greek history which proceeded from the intrigues of women. On the other hand, in modern times, particularly in a neighboring nation, the females enter into all transactions and all management of church and state; and no man can expect success who takes not care to obtain their good graces. Harry the Third, by incurring the displeasure of the fair, endangered his crown and lost his life as much as by his indulgence to heresy.

It is needless to dissemble: the consequence of a very free commerce between the sexes, and of their living much together, will often terminate in intrigues and gallantry. We must sacrifice somewhat of the *useful* if we be very anxious to obtain all the *agreeable* qualities and cannot pretend to reach alike every kind of advantage. Instances of license, daily multiplying, will weaken the scandal with the one sex and teach the other, by degrees, to adopt the famous maxim of La Fontaine with regard to female infidelity, *that if one knows it, it is but a small matter: if one knows it not, it is nothing.*†

Some people are inclined to think that the best way of adjusting all differences and of keeping the proper medium between the *agreeable* and the *useful* qualities of the sex is to live with them after the manner of the Romans and the English (for the customs of these two nations seem similar in this respect) ‡—that is, without gallantry § and without jeal-

---

* In *Onetorem*, [873–4].

† Quand on le sçait c'est peu de chose;
Quand on l'ignore, ce n'est rien.

‡ During the time of the emperors, the Romans seem to have been more given to intrigues and gallantry than the English are at present; and the women of condition, in order to retain their lovers, endeavored to fix a name of reproach on those who were addicted to wenching and low amours. They were called *Ancillarioli*. See Seneca *de beneficiis*, lib. i. cap. 9. See also Martial. lib. xii. epig. 58.

§ The gallantry here meant is that of amours and attachments, not

ousy. By a parity of reason, the customs of the Spaniards and of the Italians of an age ago (for the present are very different) must be the worst of any because they favor both gallantry and jealousy.

Nor will these different customs of nations affect the one sex only; their idea of personal merit in the males must also be somewhat different with regard at least to conversation, address, and humor. The one nation where the men live much apart will naturally more approve of prudence, the other of gaiety. With the one, simplicity of manners will be in the highest esteem, with the other, politeness. The one will distinguish themselves by good sense and judgment, the other by taste and delicacy. The eloquence of the former will shine most in the senate, that of the other on the theater.

These, I say, are the *natural* effects of such customs. For it must be confessed that chance has a great influence on national manners; and many events happen in society which are not to be accounted for by general rules. Who could imagine, for instance, that the Romans, who lived freely with their women, should be very indifferent about music and esteem dancing infamous, while the Greeks, who never almost saw a woman but in their own houses, were continually piping, singing, and dancing?

The differences of moral sentiment which naturally arise from a republican or monarchical government are also very obvious, as well as those which proceed from general riches or poverty, union or faction, ignorance or learning. I shall conclude this long discourse with observing that different customs and situations vary not the original ideas of merit (however they may some consequences) in any very essential point and prevail chiefly with regard to young men, who can aspire to the agreeable qualities and may attempt to please. The *manner*, the *ornaments*, the *graces* which succeed in this shape are more arbitrary and casual; but the merit of riper years is almost everywhere the same and consists chiefly in integrity, humanity, ability, knowledge, and the other more solid and useful qualities of the human mind.

What you insist on, replied Palamedes, may have some foundation when you adhere to the maxims of common life and ordinary conduct. Experience and the practice of the world readily correct any great extravagance on either side. But what say you to *artificial* lives and manners? How do you reconcile the maxims on which, in different ages and nations, these are founded?

What do you understand by *artificial* lives and manners?

---

that of complaisance, which is as much paid to the fair sex in England as in any other country.

said I. I explain myself, replied he. You know that religion had, in ancient times, very little influence on common life, and that, after men had performed their duty in sacrifices and prayers at the temple, they thought that the gods left the rest of their conduct to themselves and were little pleased or offended with those virtues or vices which only affected the peace and happiness of human society. In those ages, it was the business of philosophy alone to regulate men's ordinary behavior and deportment; and, accordingly, we may observe that this being the sole principle by which a man could elevate himself above his fellows, it acquired a mighty ascendant over many and produced great singularities of maxims and of conduct. At present, when philosophy has lost the allurement of novelty, it has no such extensive influence but seems to confine itself mostly to speculations in the closet, in the same manner as the ancient religion was limited to sacrifices in the temple. Its place is now supplied by the modern religion, which inspects our whole conduct and prescribes a universal rule to our actions, to our words, to our very thoughts and inclinations—a rule so much the more austere as it is guarded by infinite, though distant, rewards and punishments, and no infraction of it can ever be concealed or disguised.

Diogenes is the most celebrated model of extravagant philosophy. Let us seek a parallel to him in modern times. We shall not disgrace any philosophic name by a comparison with the Dominics or Loyolas or any canonized monk or friar. Let us compare him to Pascal, a man of parts and genius as well as Diogenes himself, and perhaps, too, a man of virtue had he allowed his virtuous inclinations to have exerted and displayed themselves.

The foundation of Diogenes' conduct was an endeavor to render himself an independent being as much as possible and to confine all his wants and desires and pleasures within himself and his own mind. The aim of Pascal was to keep a perpetual sense of his dependence before his eyes and never to forget his numberless wants and infirmities. The ancient supported himself by magnanimity, ostentation, pride, and the idea of his own superiority above his fellow creatures. The modern made constant profession of humility and abasement, of the contempt and hatred of himself, and endeavored to attain these supposed virtues as far as they are attainable. The austerities of the Greek were in order to inure himself to hardships and prevent his ever suffering; those of the Frenchman were embraced merely for their own sake and in order to suffer as much as possible. The philosopher indulged himself in the most beastly pleasures, even in public; the saint refused himself the most innocent, even in private. The former

280

thought it his duty to love his friends, and to rail at them, and reprove them, and scold them; the latter endeavored to be absolutely indifferent toward his nearest relations and to love and speak well of his enemies. The great object of Diogenes' wit was every kind of supersititon, that is, every kind of religion known in his time. The mortality of the soul was his standard principle; and even his sentiments of a Divine Providence seem to have been licentious. The most ridiculous superstitions directed Pascal's faith and practice; and an extreme contempt of this life, in comparison of the future, was the chief foundation of his conduct.

In such a remarkable contrast do these two men stand, yet both of them have met with general admiration in their different ages and have been proposed as models of imitation. Where, then, is the universal standard of morals which you talk of? And what rule shall we establish for the many different, nay, contrary sentiments of mankind?

An experiment, said I, which succeeds in the air will not always succeed in a vacuum. When men depart from the maxims of common reason and affect these *artificial* lives, as you call them, no one can answer for what will please or displease them. They are in a different element from the rest of mankind, and the natural principles of their mind play not with the same regularity as if left to themselves, free from the illusions of religious superstition or philosophical enthusiasm.

Dialogues Concerning
Natural Religion

Pamphilus To Hermippus

It has been remarked, my Hermippus, that, though the ancient philosophers conveyed most of their instruction in the form of dialogue, this method of composition has been little practiced in later ages and has seldom succeeded in the hands of those who have attempted it. Accurate and regular argument, indeed, such as is now expected of philosophical inquirers, naturally throws a man into the methodical and didactic manner, where he can immediately, without preparation, explain the point at which he aims and thence proceed, without interruption, to deduce the proofs on which it is established. To deliver a *system* in conversation scarcely appears natural; and, while the dialogue writer desires, by departing from the direct style of composition, to give a freer air to his performance and avoid the appearance of *author* and *reader*, he is apt to run into a worse inconvenience and convey the image of *pedagogue* and *pupil*. Or, if he carries on the dispute in the natural spirit of good company by throwing in a variety of topics and preserving a proper balance among the speakers, he often loses so much time in preparations and transitions that the reader will scarcely think himself compensated by all the graces of dialogue for the order, brevity, and precision which are sacrificed to them.

There are some subjects, however, to which dialogue-writing is peculiarly adapted and where it is still preferable to the direct and simple method of composition.

Any point of doctrine which is so *obvious* that it scarcely admits of dispute, but at the same time so *important* that it cannot be too often inculcated, seems to require some such method of handling it—where the novelty of the manner may compensate the triteness of the subject; where the vivacity of conversation may enforce the precept; and where the variety of lights, presented by various personages and characters, may appear neither tedious nor redundant.

Any question of philosophy, on the other hand, which is so *obscure* and *uncertain* that human reason can reach no fixed determination with regard to it—if it should be treated at all

—seems to lead us naturally into the style of dialogue and conversation. Reasonable men may be allowed to differ where no one can reasonably be positive. Opposite sentiments, even without any decision, afford an agreeable amusement; and if the subject be curious and interesting, the book carries us, in a manner, into company and unites the two greatest and purest pleasures of human life—study and society.

Happily, these circumstances are all to be found in the subject of *natural religion*. What truth so obvious, so certain as the being of a God, which the most ignorant ages have acknowledged, for which the most refined geniuses have ambitiously striven to produce new proofs and arguments? What truth so important as this, which is the ground of all our hopes, the surest foundation of morality, the firmest support of society, and the only principle which ought never to be a moment absent from our thoughts and meditations? But, in treating of this obvious and important truth, what obscure questions occur concerning the nature of that Divine Being, his attributes, his decrees, his plan of providence? These have been always subjected to the disputations of men; concerning these human reason has not reached any certain determination. But these are topics so interesting that we cannot restrain our restless inquiry with regard to them, though nothing but doubt, uncertainty, and contradiction have as yet been the result of our most accurate researches.

This I had lately occasion to observe while I passed, as usual, part of the summer season with Cleanthes and was present at those conversations of his with Philo and Demea, of which I gave you lately some imperfect account. Your curiosity, you then told me, was so excited that I must, of necessity, enter into a more exact detail of their reasonings and display those various systems which they advanced with regard to so delicate a subject as that of natural religion. The remarkable contrast in their characters still further raised your expectations, while you opposed the accurate philosophical turn of Cleanthes to the careless skepticism of Philo or compared either of their dispositions with the rigid inflexible orthodoxy of Demea. My youth rendered me a mere auditor of their disputes; and that curiosity, natural to the early season of life, has so deeply imprinted in my memory the whole chain and connection of their arguments that, I hope, I shall not omit or confound any considerable part of them in the recital.

Part I

After I joined the company whom I found sitting in Cleanthes' library, Demea paid Cleanthes some compliments on the great care which he took of my education and on his unwearied perseverance and constancy in all his friendships. The father of Pamphilus, said he, was your intimate friend; the son is your pupil and may indeed be regarded as your adopted son, were we to judge by the pains which you bestow in conveying to him every useful branch of literature and science. You are no more wanting, I am persuaded, in prudence than in industry. I shall, therefore, communicate to you a maxim which I have observed with regard to my own children, that I may learn how far it agrees with your practice. The method I follow in their education is founded on the saying of an ancient, "That students of philosophy ought first to learn logics, then ethics, next physics, last of all the nature of the gods." * This science of natural theology, according to him, being the most profound and abstruse of any, required the maturest judgment in its students; and none but a mind enriched with all the other sciences can safely be entrusted with it.

Are you so late, says Philo, in teaching your children the principles of religion? Is there no danger of their neglecting or rejecting altogether those opinions of which they have heard so little during the whole course of their education? It is only as a science, replied Demea, subjected to human reasoning and disputation, that I postpone the study of natural theology. To season their minds with early piety is my chief care; and by continual precept and instruction and, I hope, too, by example, I imprint deeply on their tender minds an habitual reverence for all the principles of religion. While they pass through every other science, I still remark the uncertainty of each part; the eternal disputations of men; the obscurity of all philosophy; and the strange, ridiculous conclusions which some of the greatest geniuses have derived from the principles of mere human reason. Having thus tamed their mind to a proper submission and self-diffidence, I have no longer any scruple of opening to them the greatest mysteries of religion nor apprehend any danger from that assuming arrogance of philosophy which may lead them to reject the most established doctrines and opinions.

* Chrysippus *a pud* Plut., *De repug. Stoicorum.*

Your precaution, says Philo, of seasoning your children's minds early with piety is certainly very reasonable and no more than is requisite in this profane and irreligious age. But what I chiefly admire in your plan of education is your method of drawing advantage from the very principles of philosophy and learning which, by inspiring pride and self-sufficiency, have commonly, in all ages, been found so destructive to the principles of religion. The vulgar, indeed, we may remark, who are unacquainted with science and profound inquiry, observing the endless disputes of the learned, have commonly a thorough contempt for philosophy and rivet themselves the faster, by that means, in the great points of theology which have been taught them. Those who enter a little into study and inquiry, finding many appearances of evidence in doctrines the newest and most extraordinary, think nothing too difficult for human reason and, presumptuously breaking through all fences, profane the inmost sanctuaries of the temple. But Cleanthes will, I hope, agree with me that, after we have abandoned ignorance, the surest remedy, there is still one expedient left to prevent this profane liberty. Let Demea's principles be improved and cultivated; let us become thoroughly sensible of the weakness, blindness, and narrow limits of human reason; let us duly consider its uncertainty and endless contrarieties, even in the subjects of common life and practice; let the errors and deceits of our very senses be set before us; the insuperable difficulties which attend first principles in all systems; the contradictions which adhere to the very ideas of matter, cause and effect, extension, space, time, motion, and, in a word, quantity of all kinds, the object of the only science that can fairly pretend to any certainty or evidence—when these topics are displayed in their full light, as they are by some philosophers and almost all divines, who can retain such confidence in this frail faculty of reason as to pay any regard to its determinations in points so sublime, so abstruse, so remote from common life and experience? When the coherence of the parts of a stone, or even that composition of parts which renders it extended—when these familiar objects, I say, are so inexplicable and contain circumstances so repugnant and contradictory, with what assurance can we decide concerning the origin of worlds or trace their history from eternity to eternity?

While Philo pronounced these words, I could observe a smile in the countenance both of Demea and Cleanthes. That of Demea seemed to imply an unreserved satisfaction in the doctrines delivered; but in Cleanthes' features I could distinguish an air of finesse, as if he perceived some raillery or artificial malice in the reasonings of Philo.

You propose then, Philo, said Cleanthes, to erect religious faith on philosophical skepticism; and you think that, if certainty or evidence be expelled from every other subject of inquiry, it will all retire to these theological doctrines, and there acquire a superior force and authority. Whether your skepticism be as absolute and sincere as you pretend, we shall learn by and by, when the company breaks up; we shall then see whether you go out at the door or the window, and whether you really doubt if your body has gravity or can be injured by its fall, according to popular opinion derived from our fallacious senses and more fallacious experience. And this consideration, Demea, may, I think, fairly serve to abate our ill will to this humorous sect of the skeptics. If they be thoroughly in earnest, they will not long trouble the world with their doubts, cavils, and disputes; if they be only in jest, they are, perhaps, bad railers, but can never be very dangerous, either to the state, to philosophy, or to religion.

In reality, Philo, continued he, it seems certain that, though a man, in a flush of humor, after intense reflection on the many contradictions and imperfections of human reason, may entirely renounce all belief and opinion, it is impossible for him to persevere in this total skepticism or make it appear in his conduct for a few hours. External objects press in upon him; passions solicit him; his philosophical melancholy dissipates; and even the utmost violence upon his own temper will not be able, during any time, to preserve the poor appearance of skepticism. And for what reason impose on himself such a violence? This is a point in which it will be impossible for him ever to satisfy himself consistently with his skeptical principles. So that, upon the whole, nothing could be more ridiculous than the principles of the ancient Pyrrhonians, if in reality, they endeavored, as is pretended, to extend throughout the same skepticism which they had learned from the declamations of their schools, and which they ought to have confined to them.

In this view, there appears a great resemblance between the sects of the Stoics and Pyrrhonians, though perpetual antagonists; and both of them seem founded on this erroneous maxim that what a man can perform sometimes and in some dispositions, he can perform always and in every disposition. When the mind, by Stoical reflections, is elevated into a sublime enthusiasm of virtue and strongly smit with any *species* of honor or public good, the utmost bodily pain and sufferings will not prevail over such a high sense of duty; and it is possible, perhaps, by its means, even to smile and exult in the midst of tortures. If this sometimes may be the case in fact and reality, much more may a philosopher, in his school or even in his closet, work himself up to such an enthusiasm and support, in imagination, the acutest pain or most calamitous event which he can possibly conceive. But how shall he support this enthusiasm itself? The bent of his mind relaxes and cannot be recalled at pleasure; avocations lead him astray; misfortunes attack him unawares; and the *philosopher* sinks, by degrees, into the *plebeian*.

I allow of your comparison between the Stoics and Skeptics, replied Philo. But you may observe, at the same time, that though the mind cannot, in Stoicism, support the highest flights of philosophy, yet, even when it sinks lower, it still retains somewhat of its former disposition; and the effects of the Stoic's reasoning will appear in his conduct in common life and through the whole tenor of his actions. The ancient schools, particularly that of Zeno, produced examples of virtue and constancy which seem astonishing to present times.

> Vain Wisdom all and false Philosophy.
> Yet with a pleasing sorcery could charm
> Pain, for a while, or anguish; and excite
> Fallacious Hope, or arm the obdurate breast
> With stubborn Patience, as with triple steel.

In like manner, if a man has accustomed himself to skeptical considerations on the uncertainty and narrow limits of reason, he will not entirely forget them when he turns his reflection on other subjects; but in all his philosophical principles and reasoning, I dare not say in his common conduct, he will be found different from those who either never formed any opinions in the case or have entertained sentiments more favorable to human reason.

To whatever length anyone may push his speculative principles of skepticism, he must act, I own, and live, and converse like other men; and for this conduct, he is not obliged to give any other reason than the absolute necessity he lies under of so doing. If he ever carries his speculations farther than this necessity constrains him and philosophizes either on natural or moral subjects, he is allured by a certain pleasure and satisfaction which he finds in employing himself after that manner. He considers, besides, that everyone, even in common life, is constrained to have more or less of this philosophy; that from our earliest infancy we make continual advances in forming more general principles of conduct and reasoning; that the larger experience we acquire, and the stronger reason we are endued with, we always render our principles the more general and comprehensive; and that what we call *philosophy* is nothing but a more regular and methodical operation of the same kind. To philosophize on such subjects is nothing essentially different from reasoning on common life, and we may only expect greater stability, if not greater truth, from our philosophy on account of its exacter and more scrupulous method of proceeding.

But when we look beyond human affairs and the properties of the surrounding bodies; when we carry our speculations into the two eternities, before and after the present state of things, into the creation and formation of the universe, the existence and properties of spirits, the powers and operations of one universal Spirit existing without beginning and without end, omnipotent, omniscient, immutable, infinite, and incomprehensible—we must be far removed from the smallest tendency to skepticism not to be apprehensive that we have here got quite beyond the reach of our faculties. So long as we confine our speculations to trade, or morals, or politics, or criticism, we make appeals, every moment, to common sense and experience, which strengthen our philosophical conclusions and remove, at least in part, the suspicion which we so justly entertain with regard to every reasoning that is very subtle and refined. But, in theological reasonings, we have not this advantage, while at the same time, we are employed upon objects which, we must be sensible, are too large for our grasp and, of all others, require most to be familiarized to our apprehension. We are like foreigners in a strange country to whom everything must seem suspicious and who are in danger every moment of transgressing against the laws and customs of the people with whom they live and converse. We know not how far we ought to trust our vulgar methods of reasoning in such a subject, since, even in common life, and in that province which is peculiarly appropriated to them, we cannot account for them and are entirely guided by a kind of instinct or necessity in employing them.

All skeptics pretend that, if reason be considered in an abstract view, it furnishes invincible arguments against itself, and that we could never retain any conviction or assurance, on any subject, were not the skeptical reasonings so refined and subtle that they are not able to counterpoise the more solid and more natural arguments derived from the senses and experience. But it is evident, whenever our arguments lose this advantage and run wide of common life, that the most refined skepticism comes to be upon a footing with them and is able to oppose and counterbalance them. The one has no more weight than the other. The mind must remain in suspense between them; and it is that very suspense or balance which is the triumph of skepticism.

But I observe, says Cleanthes, with regard to you, Philo,

and all speculative skeptics, that your doctrine and practice are as much at variance in the most abstruse points of theory as in the conduct of common life. Wherever evidence discovers itself, you adhere to it, notwithstanding your pretended skepticism; and I can observe, too, some of your sect to be as decisive as those who make greater professions of certainty and assurance. In reality, would not a man be ridiculous who pretended to reject Newton's explication of the wonderful phenomenon of the rainbow because the explication gives a minute anatomy of the rays of light—a subject, forsooth, too refined for human comprehension? And what would you say to one, who, having nothing particular to object to the arguments of Copernicus and Galileo for the motion of the earth, should withhold his assent on that general principle that these subjects were too magnificent and remote to be explained by the narrow and fallacious reason of mankind?

There is indeed a kind of brutish and ignorant skepticism, as you well observed, which gives the vulgar a general prejudice against what they do not easily understand and makes them reject every principle which requires elaborate reasoning to prove and establish it. This species of skepticism is fatal to knowledge, not to religion, since we find that those who make greatest profession of it give often their assent not only to the great truths of theism and natural theology, but even to the most absurd tenets which a traditional superstition has recommended to them. They firmly believe in witches, though they will not believe nor attend to the most simple proposition of Euclid. But the refined and philosophical skeptics fall into an inconsistency of an opposite nature. They push their researches into the most abstruse corners of science, and their assent attends them in every step, proportioned to the evidence which they meet with. They are even obliged to acknowledge that the most abstruse and remote objects are those which are best explained by philosophy. Light is in reality anatomized; the true system of the heavenly bodies is discovered and ascertained. But the nourishment of bodies by food is still an inexplicable mystery; the cohesion of the parts of matter is still incomprehensible. These skeptics, therefore, are obliged in every question, to consider each particular evidence apart and proportion their assent to the precise degree of evidence which occurs. This is their practice in all natural, mathematical, moral, and political science. And why not the same, I ask, in the theological and religious? Why must conclusions of this nature be alone rejected on the general presumption of the insufficiency of human reason, without any particular discussion of the evidence? Is not such an unequal conduct a plain proof of prejudice and passion?

Our senses, you say, are fallacious; our understanding erroneous; our ideas, even of the most familiar objects—extension, duration, motion—full of absurdities and contradictions. You defy me to solve the difficulties or reconcile the repugnancies which you discover in them. I have not capacity for so great an undertaking; I have not leisure for it. I perceive it to be superfluous. Your own conduct, in every circumstance, refutes your principles and shows the firmest reliance on all the received maxims of science, morals, prudence, and behavior.

I shall never assent to so harsh an opinion as that of a celebrated writer,* who says that the Skeptics are not a sect of philosophers, they are only a sect of liars. I may, however, affirm (I hope without offense) that they are a sect of jesters or railers. But for my part, whenever I find myself disposed to mirth and amusement, I shall certainly choose my entertainment of a less perplexing and abstruse nature. A comedy, a novel, or, at most, a history seems a more natural recreation than such metaphysical subtleties and abstractions.

In vain would the skeptic make a distinction between science and common life or between one science and another. The arguments employed in all, if just, are of a similar nature and contain the same force and evidence. Or if there be any difference among them, the advantage lies entirely on the side of theology and natural religion. Many principles of mechanics are founded on very abstruse reasoning, yet no man who has any pretensions to science, even no speculative skeptic, pretends to entertain the least doubt with regard to them. The Copernican system contains the most surprising paradox and the most contrary to our natural conceptions, to appearances, and to our very senses, yet even monks and inquisitors are now constrained to withdraw their opposition to it. And shall Philo, a man of so liberal a genius and extensive knowledge, entertain any general undistinguished scruples with regard to the religious hypothesis, which is founded on the simplest and most obvious arguments and, unless it meets with artificial obstacles, has such easy access and admission into the mind of man?

And here we may observe, continued he, turning himself towards Demea, a pretty curious circumstance in the history of the sciences. After the union of philosophy with the popular religion, upon the first establishment of Christianity, noth-

* *L'art de penser* [Antoine (the great) Arnauld and others: *La Logique ou l'art de penser (Port-Royal Logic)*, 1662.]

ing was more usual, among all religious teachers, than declamations against reason, against the senses, against every principle derived merely from human research and inquiry. All the topics of the ancient Academics were adopted by the Fathers and thence propagated for several ages in every school and pulpit throughout Christendom. The Reformers embraced the same principles of reasoning, or rather declamation; and all panegyrics on the excellence of faith were sure to be interlarded with some severe strokes of satire against natural reason. A celebrated prelate, too,* of the Romish communion, a man of the most extensive learning, who wrote a demonstration of Christianity, has also composed a treatise which contains all the cavils of the boldest and most determined Pyrrhonism. Locke seems to have been the first Christian who ventured openly to assert that *faith* was nothing but a species of *reason;* that religion was only a branch of philosophy; and that a chain of arguments, similar to that which established any truth in morals, politics, or physics, was always employed in discovering all the principles of theology, natural and revealed. The ill use which Bayle and other libertines made of the philosophical skepticism of the Fathers and first Reformers still further propagated the judicious sentiment of Mr. Locke. And it is now in a manner avowed, by all pretenders to reasoning and philosophy, that *atheist* and *skeptic* are almost synonymous. And as it is certain that no man is in earnest when he professes the latter principle, I would fain hope that there are as few who seriously maintain the former.

Don't you remember, said Philo, the excellent saying of Lord Bacon on this head? That a little philosophy, replied Cleanthes, makes a man an Atheist; a great deal converts him to religion. That is a very judicious remark, too, said Philo. But what I have in my eye is another passage, where, having mentioned David's fool, who said in his heart there is no God, this great philosopher observes that the atheists nowadays have a double share of folly, for they are not contented to say in their hearts there is no God, but they also utter that impiety with their lips and are thereby guilty of multiplied indiscretion and imprudence. Such people, though they were ever so much in earnest, cannot, methinks, be very formidable.

But though you should rank me in this class of fools, I cannot forbear communicating a remark that occurs to me, from the history of the religious and irreligious skepticism with which you have entertained us. It appears to me that

---

* Mons. Huet.

there are strong symptoms of priestcraft in the whole progress of this affair. During ignorant ages, such as those which followed the dissolution of the ancient schools, the priests perceived that atheism, deism, or heresy of any kind could only proceed from the presumptuous questioning of received opinions and from a belief that human reason was equal to everything. Education had then a mighty influence over the minds of men and was almost equal in force to those suggestions of the senses and common understanding by which the most determined skeptic must allow himself to be governed. But at present, when the influence of education is much diminished and men, from a more open commerce of the world, have learned to compare the popular principles of different nations and ages, our sagacious divines have changed their whole system of philosophy and talk the language of Stoics, Platonists, and Peripatetics, not that of Pyrrhonians and Academics. If we distrust human reason, we have now no other principle to lead us into religion. Thus, skeptics in one age, dogmatists in another—whichever system best suits the purpose of these reverend gentlemen in giving them an ascendant over mankind—they are sure to make it their favorite principle and established tenet.

It is very natural, said Cleanthes, for men to embrace those principles by which they find they can best defend their doctrines, nor need we have any recourse to priestcraft to account for so reasonable an expedient. And surely nothing can afford a stronger presumption that any set of principles are true and ought to be embraced than to observe that they tend to the confirmation of true religion and serve to confound the cavils of atheists, libertines, and freethinkers of all denominations.

Part II

I must own, Cleanthes, said Demea, that nothing can more surprise me than the light in which you have all along put this argument. By the whole tenor of your discourse, one would imagine that you were maintaining the Being of a God against the cavils of atheists and infidels and were necessitated to become a champion for that fundamental principle of all religion. But this, I hope, is not by any means a question among us. No man, no man at least of common sense, I am persuaded, ever entertained a serious doubt with regard to a truth so certain and self-evident. The question is not concerning the *being* but the *nature* of GOD. This I affirm, from the infirmities of human understanding, to be altogether incomprehensible and unknown to us. The essence of that supreme Mind, his attributes, the manner of his existence, the very nature of his duration—these and every particular which regards so divine a Being are mysterious to men. Finite, weak, and blind creatures, we ought to humble ourselves in his august presence and, conscious of our frailties, adore in silence his infinite perfections which eye hath not seen, ear hath not heard, neither hath it entered into the heart of man to conceive. They are covered in a deep cloud from human curiosity; it is profaneness to attempt penetrating through these sacred obscurities, and, next to the impiety of denying his existence, is the temerity of prying into his nature and essence, decrees and attributes.

But lest you should think that my *piety* has here got the better of my *philosophy*, I shall support my opinion, if it needs any support, by a very great authority. I might cite all the divines, almost from the foundation of Christianity, who have ever treated of this or any other theological subject; but I shall confine myself, at present, to one equally celebrated for piety and philosophy. It is Father Malebranche who, I remember, thus expresses himself.* "One ought not so much," says he, "to call God a spirit in order to express positively what he is, as in order to signify that he is not matter. He is a Being infinitely perfect—of this we cannot doubt. But in the same manner as we ought not to imagine, even supposing him corporeal, that he is clothed with a human body, as the anthropomorphites asserted, under color that that figure was the most perfect of any, so neither ought we to imagine that the spirit of God has human ideas or bears any resemblance to our spirit, under color that we know nothing more perfect than a human mind. We ought rather to believe that as he comprehends the perfections of matter without being material . . . he comprehends also the perfections of created spirits without being spirit, in the manner we conceive spirit; that his true name is *He that is,* or, in other words, Being without restrictions, All Being, the Being infinite and universal."

After so great an authority, Demea, replied Philo, as that which you have produced, and a thousand more which you might produce, it would appear ridiculous in me to add any sentiment or express my approbation of your doctrine. But surely, where reasonable men treat these subjects, the question can never be concerning the *being* but only the *nature* of the Deity. The former truth, as you well observe, is unquestionable and self-evident. Nothing exists without a cause; and

* *Recherche de la Vérité,* liv. 3, cap. 9.

the original cause of this universe (whatever it be) we call God and piously ascribe to him every species of perfection. Whoever scruples this fundamental truth deserves every punishment which can be inflicted among philosophers, to wit, the greatest ridicule, contempt, and disapprobation. But as all perfection is entirely relative, we ought never to imagine that we comprehend the attributes of this divine Being or to suppose that his perfections have any analogy or likeness to the perfections of a human creature. Wisdom, thought, design, knowledge—these we justly ascribe to him because these words are honorable among men, and we have no other language or other conceptions by which we can express our adoration of him. But let us beware lest we think that our ideas anywise correspond to his perfections or that his attributes have any resemblance to these qualities among men. He is infinitely superior to our limited view and comprehension and is more the object of worship in the temple than of disputation in the schools.

In reality, Cleanthes, continued he, there is no need of having recourse to that affected skepticism so displeasing to you in order to come at this determination. Our ideas reach no farther than our experience. We have no experience of divine attributes and operations. I need not conclude my syllogism: you can draw the inference yourself. And it is a pleasure to me (and I hope to you, too) that just reasoning and sound piety here concur in the same conclusion, and both of them establish the adorably mysterious and incomprehensible nature of the Supreme Being.

Not to lose any time in circumlocutions, said Cleanthes, addressing himself to Demea, much less in replying to the pious declamations of Philo, I shall briefly explain how I conceive this matter. Look round the world, contemplate the whole and every part of it: you will find it to be nothing but one great machine subdivided into an infinite number of lesser machines, which again admit of subdivisions to a degree beyond what human senses and faculties can trace and explain. All these various machines, and even their most minute parts, are adjusted to each other with an accuracy which ravishes into admiration all men who have ever contemplated them. The curious adapting of means to ends, throughout all nature, resembles exactly, though it much exceeds, the productions of human contrivance—of human design, thought, wisdom, and intelligence. Since therefore the effects resemble each other, we are led to infer, by all the rules of analogy, that the causes also resemble and that the Author of nature is somewhat similar to the mind of man, though possessed of much larger faculties, proportioned to the grandeur of the work which he has executed. By this argument *a posteriori*, and by this argument alone, do we prove at once the existence of a Deity and his similarity to human mind and intelligence.

I shall be so free, Cleanthes, said Demea, as to tell you that from the beginning I could not approve of your conclusion concerning the similarity of the Deity to men, still less can I approve of the mediums by which you endeavor to establish it. What! No demonstration of the Being of God! No abstract arguments! No proofs *a priori!* Are these which have hitherto been so much insisted on by philosophers all fallacy, all sophism? Can we reach no farther in this subject than experience and probability? I will not say that this is betraying the cause of a Deity; but surely, by this affected candor, you give advantages to atheists which they never could obtain by the mere dint of argument and reasoning.

What I chiefly scruple in this subject, said Philo, is not so much that all religious arguments are by Cleanthes reduced to experience as that they appear not to be even the most certain and irrefragable of that inferior kind. That a stone will fall, that fire will burn, that the earth has solidity, we have observed a thousand and a thousand times; and when any new instance of this nature is presented, we draw without hesitation the accustomed inference. The exact similarity of the cases gives us a perfect assurance of a similar event, and a stronger evidence is never desired nor sought after. But wherever you depart, in the least, from the similarity of the cases, you diminish proportionably the evidence and may at last bring it to a very weak *analogy,* which is confessedly liable to error and uncertainty. After having experienced the circulation of the blood in human creatures, we make no doubt that it takes place in *Titius* and *Maevius;* but from its circulation in frogs and fishes, it is only a presumption, though a strong one, from analogy that it takes place in men and other animals. The analogical reasoning is much weaker when we infer the circulation of the sap in vegetables from our experience that the blood circulates in animals; and those who hastily followed that imperfect analogy are found, by more accurate experiments, to have been mistaken.

If we see a house, Cleanthes, we conclude, with the greatest certainty, that it had an architect or builder, because this is precisely that species of effect which we have experienced to proceed from that species of cause. But surely you will not affirm that the universe bears such a resemblance to a house that we can with the same certainty infer a similar cause or that the analogy is here entire and perfect. The dissimilitude is so striking that the utmost you can here pretend to is a guess, a conjecture, a presumption concerning a similar cause; and how that pretension will be received in the world, I leave you to consider.

It would surely be very ill received, replied Cleanthes; and I should be deservedly blamed and detested did I allow that the proofs of a Deity amounted to no more than a guess or conjecture. But is the whole adjustment of means to ends in a house and in the universe so slight a resemblance? the economy of final causes? the order, proportion, and arrangement of every part? Steps of a stair are plainly contrived that human legs may use them in mounting; and this inference is certain and infallible. Human legs are also contrived for walking and mounting; and this inference, I allow, is not altogether so certain because of the dissimilarity which you remark; but does it, therefore, deserve the name only of presumption or conjecture?

Good God! cried Demea, interrupting him, where are we? Zealous defenders of religion allow that the proofs of a Deity fall short of perfect evidence! And you, Philo, on whose assistance I depended in proving the adorable mysteriousness of the Divine Nature, do you assert to all these extravagant opinions of Cleanthes? For what other name can I give them? or, why spare my censure when such principles are advanced, supported by such an authority, before so young a man as Pamphilus?

You seem not to apprehend, replied Philo, that I argue with Cleanthes in his own way and, by showing him the dangerous consequences of his tenets, hope at last to reduce him to our opinion. But what sticks most with you, I observe, is the representation which Cleanthes has made of the argument *a posteriori;* and, finding that that argument is likely to escape your hold and vanish into air, you think it so disguised that you can scarcely believe it to be set in its true light. Now, however much I may dissent, in other respects, from the dangerous principle of Cleanthes, I must allow that he has fairly represented that argument, and I shall endeavor so to state the matter to you that you will entertain no further scruples with regard to it.

Were a man to abstract from everything which he knows or has seen, he would be altogether incapable, merely from his own ideas, to determine what kind of scene the universe must be or to give the preference to one state or situation of things above another. For as nothing which he clearly conceives could be esteemed impossible or implying a contradiction, every chimera of his fancy would be upon an equal footing; nor could he assign any just reason why he adheres to one idea or system and rejects the others which are equally possible.

Again, after he opens his eyes and contemplates the world as it really is, it would be impossible for him at first to assign the cause of any one event, much less of the whole of things or of the universe. He might set his fancy a rambling, and she might bring him in an infinite variety of reports and representations. These would all be possible, but, being all equally possible, he would never of himself give a satisfactory account for his preferring one of them to the rest. Experience alone can point out to him the true cause of any phenomenon.

Now, according to this method of reasoning, Demea, it follows (and is, indeed, tacitly allowed by Cleanthes himself) that order, arrangement or the adjustment of final causes, is not of itself any proof of design, but only so far as it has been experienced to proceed from that principle. For aught we can know *a priori*, matter may contain the source or spring of order originally within itself as well as mind does; and there is no more difficulty in conceiving that the several elements, from an internal unknown cause, may fall into the most exquisite arrangement than to conceive that their ideas, in the great universal mind, from a like internal unknown cause, fall into that arrangement. The equal possibility of both these suppositions is allowed. But, by experience, we find (according to Cleanthes) that there is a difference between them. Throw several pieces of steel together, without shape or form, they will never arrange themselves so as to compose a watch. Stone and mortar and wood, without an architect, never erect a house. But the ideas in a human mind, we see, by an unknown, inexplicable economy, arrange themselves so as to form the plan of a watch or house. Experience, therefore, proves that there is an original principle of order in mind, not in matter. From similar effects we infer similar causes. The adjustment of means to ends is alike in the universe as in a machine of human contrivance. The causes, therefore, must be resembling.

I was from the beginning scandalized, I must own, with this resemblance which is asserted between the Deity and human creatures and must conceive it to imply such a degradation of the Supreme Being as no sound theist could endure. With your assistance, therefore, Demea, I shall endeavor to defend what you justly call the adorable mysteriousness of the Divine Nature and shall refute this reasoning of Cleanthes, provided he allows that I have made a fair representation of it.

When Cleanthes had assented, Philo, after a short pause, proceeded in the following manner.

That all inferences, Cleanthes, concerning fact are founded on experience, and that all experimental reasonings are founded on the supposition that similar causes prove similar effects and similar effects similar causes, I shall not at present much dispute with you. But observe, I entreat you, with what extreme caution all just reasoners proceed in the transferring of experiments to similar cases. Unless the cases be exactly similar, they repose no perfect confidence in applying their past observation to any particular phenomenon. Every alteration of circumstances occasions a doubt concerning the event; and it requires new experiments to prove certainly that the new circumstances are of no moment or importance. A change in bulk, situation, arrangement, age, disposition of the air, or surrounding bodies—any of these particulars may be attended with the most unexpected consequences. And unless the objects be quite familiar for us, it is the highest temerity to expect with assurance, after any of these changes, an event similar to that which before fell under our observation. The slow and deliberate steps of philosophers here, if anywhere, are distinguished from the precipitate march of the vulgar, who, hurried on by the smallest similitude, are incapable of all discernment or consideration.

But can you think, Cleanthes, that your usual phlegm and philosophy have been preserved in so wide a step as you have taken when you compared to the universe houses, ships, furniture, machines and, from their similarity in some circumstances, inferred a similarity in their causes? Thought, design, intelligence, such as we discover in men and other animals, is no more than one of the springs and principles of the universe, as well as heat or cold, attraction or repulsion, and a hundred others which fall under daily observation. It is an active cause by which some particular parts of nature, we find, produce alterations on other parts. But can a conclusion, with any propriety, be transferred from parts to the whole? Does not the great disproportion bar all comparison and inference? From observing the growth of a hair, can we learn anything concerning the generation of a man? Would the manner of a leaf's blowing, even though perfectly known, afford us any instruction concerning the vegetation of a tree?

But allowing that we were to take the *operations* of one part of nature upon another for the foundation of our judgment concerning the *origin* of the whole (which never can be admitted), yet why select so minute, so weak, so bounded a principle as the reason and design of animals is found to be upon this planet? What peculiar privilege has this little agitation of the brain which we call *thought* that we must thus make it the model of the whole universe? Our partiality in our own favor does indeed present it on all occasions, but sound philosophy ought carefully to guard against so natural an illusion.

So far from admitting, continued Philo, that the operations of a part can afford us any just conclusion concerning the origin of the whole, I will not allow any one part to form a rule for another part if the latter be very remote from the former. Is there any reasonable ground to conclude that the inhabitants of other planets possess thought, intelligence, reason, or anything similar to these faculties in men? When nature has so extremely diversified her manner of operation in this small globe, can we imagine that she incessantly copies herself throughout so immense a universe? And if thought, as we may well suppose, be confined merely to this narrow corner and has even there so limited a sphere of action, with what propriety can we assign it for the original cause of all things? The narrow views of a peasant who makes his domestic economy the rule for the government of kingdoms is in comparison a pardonable sophism.

But were we ever so much assured that a thought and reason resembling the human were to be found throughout the whole universe, and were its activity elsewhere vastly greater and more commanding that it appears in this globe, yet I cannot see why the operations of a world constituted, arranged, adjusted, can with any propriety be extended to a world which is in its embryo state and is advancing towards that constitution and arrangement. By observation, we know somewhat of the economy, action, and nourishment of a finished animal, but we must transfer with great caution that observation to the growth of a fetus in the womb, and still more to the formation of an animalcule in the loins of its male parent. Nature, we find, even from our limited experience, possesses an infinite number of springs and principles which incessantly discover themselves on every change of her position and situation. And what new and unknown principles would actuate her in so new and unknown a situation as that of the formation of a universe, we cannot, without the utmost temerity, pretend to determine.

A very small part of this great system, during a very short time, is very imperfectly discovered to us; and do we thence pronounce decisively concerning the origin of the whole?

Admirable conclusion! Stone, wood, brick, iron, brass have not, at this time, in this minute globe of earth, an order or arrangement without human art and contrivance; therefore, the universe could not originally attain its order and arrangement without something similar to human art. But is a part of nature a rule for another part very wide of the former? Is it a rule for the whole? Is a very small part a rule for the universe? Is nature in one situation a certain rule for nature in another situation vastly different from the former?

And can you blame me, Cleanthes, if I here imitate the prudent reserve of Simonides, who, according to the noted story, being asked by Hiero, *what God was?* desired a day to think of it, and then two days more, and after that manner continually prolonged the term, without ever bringing in his definition or description? Could you even blame me if I had answered, at first, *that I did not know* and was sensible that this subject lay vastly beyond the reach of my faculties? You might cry out skeptic and railer as much as you pleased; but, having found in so many other subjects much more familiar the imperfections and even contradictions of human reason, I never should expect any success from its feeble conjectures in a subject so sublime and so remote from the sphere of our observation. When two *species* of objects have always been observed to be conjoined together, I can *infer,* by custom, the existence of one wherever I *see* the existence of the other; and this I call an argument from experience. But how this argument can have place where the objects, as in the present case, are single, individual, without parallel or specific resemblance may be difficult to explain. And will any man tell me with a serious countenance that an orderly universe must arise from some thought and art like the human because we have experience of it? To ascertain this reasoning, it were requisite that we had experience of the origin of worlds; and it is not sufficient, surely, that we have seen ships and cities arise from human art and contrivance.

Philo was proceeding in this vehement manner, somewhat between jest and earnest, as it appeared to me, when he observed some signs of impatience in Cleanthes and then immediately stopped short. What I had to suggest, said Cleanthes, is only that you would not abuse terms or make use of popular expressions to subvert philosophical reasonings. You know that the vulgar often distinguish reason from experience, even where the question relates only to matter of fact and existence, though it is found, where that *reason* is properly analyzed, that it is nothing but a species of experience. To prove by experience the origin of the universe from mind is not more contrary to common speech than to prove the motion of the earth from the same principle. And a caviller might raise all the same objections to the Copernican system which you have urged against my reasonings. Have you other earths, might he say, which you have seen to move? Have . . .

Yes! cried Philo, interrupting him, we have other earths. Is not the moon another earth, which we see to turn round its center? Is not Venus another earth, where we observe the same phenomenon? Are not the revolutions of the sun also a confirmation, from analogy, of the same theory? All the planets, are they not earths which revolve about the sun? Are not the satellites moons which move round Jupiter and Saturn and along with these primary planets round the sun? These analogies and resemblances, with others which I have not mentioned, are the sole proofs of the Copernican system; and to you it belongs to consider whether you have any analogies of the same kind to support your theory.

In reality, Cleanthes, continued he, the modern system of astronomy is now so much received by all inquirers and has become so essential a part even of our earliest education that we are not commonly very scrupulous in examining the reasons upon which it is founded. It is now become a matter of mere curiosity to study the first writers on that subject, who had the full force of prejudice to encounter and were obliged to turn their arguments on every side in order to render them popular and convincing. But if we peruse Galileo's famous *Dialogues* concerning the system of the world, we shall find that that great genius, one of the sublimest that ever existed, first bent all his endeavors to prove that there was no foundation for the distinction commonly made between elementary and celestial substances. The schools, proceeding from the illusions of sense, had carried this distinction very far and had established the latter substances to be ingenerable, incorruptible, unalterable, impassible and had assigned all the opposite qualities to the former. But Galileo, beginning with the moon, proved its similarity in every particular to the earth: its convex figure, its natural darkness when not illuminated, its density, its distinction into solid and liquid, the variations of its phases, the mutual illuminations of the earth and moon, their mutual eclipses, the inequalities of the lunar surface, etc. After many instances of this kind, with regard to all the planets, men plainly saw that these bodies became proper objects of experience and that the similarity of their nature enabled us to extend the same arguments and phenomena from one to the other.

In this cautious proceeding of the astronomers, you may read your own condemnation, Cleanthes, or rather may see that the subject in which you are engaged exceeds all human reason and inquiry. Can you pretend to show any such similarity between the fabric of a house and the generation of a universe? Have you ever seen nature in any such situation as resembles the first arrangement of the elements? Have worlds ever been formed under your eye, and have you had leisure to observe the whole progress of the phenomenon, from the first appearance of order to its final consummation? If you have, then cite your experience, and deliver your theory.

Part III

How the most absurd argument, replied Cleanthes, in the hands of a man of ingenuity and invention may acquire an air of probability! Are you not aware, Philo, that it became necessary for Copernicus and his first disciples to prove the similarity of the terrestrial and celestial matter because several philosophers, blinded by old systems and supported by some sensible appearances, had denied this similarity? But that it is by no means necessary that theists should prove the similarity of the works of *nature* to those of *art,* because this similarity is self-evident and undeniable? The same matter, a like form—what more is requisite to show an analogy between their causes and to ascertain the origin of all things from a divine purpose and intention? Your objections, I must freely tell you, are no better than the abstruse cavils of those philosophers who denied motion and ought to be refuted in the same manner—by illustrations, examples, and instances rather than by serious argument and philosophy.

Suppose, therefore, that an articulate voice were heard in the clouds, much louder and more melodious than any which human art could ever reach; suppose that this voice were extended in the same instant over all nations and spoke to each nation in its own language and dialect; suppose that the words delivered not only contain a just sense and meaning, but convey some instruction altogether worthy of a benevolent Being superior to mankind—could you possibly hesitate a moment concerning the cause of this voice, and must you not instantly ascribe it to some design or purpose? Yet I cannot see but all the same objections (if they merit that appellation) which lie against the system of theism may also be produced against this inference.

Might you not say that all conclusions concerning fact were founded on experience; that, when we hear an articulate voice in the dark and thence infer a man, it is only the resemblance of the effects which leads us to conclude that there is a like resemblance in the cause; but that this extraordinary voice, by its loudness, extent, and flexibility to all languages, bears so little analogy to any human voice that we have no reason to suppose any analogy in their causes; and, consequently, that a rational, wise, coherent speech proceeded, you know not whence, from some accidental whistling of the winds, not from any divine reason or intelligence? You see clearly your own objections in these cavils, and I hope too you see clearly that they cannot possibly have more force in the one case than in the other.

But to bring the case still nearer the present one of the universe, I shall make two suppositions which imply not any absurdity or impossibility. Suppose that there is a natural, universal, invariable language, common to every individual of human race, and that books are natural productions which perpetuate themselves in the same manner with animals and vegetables, by descent and propagation. Several expressions of our passions contain a universal language: all brute animals have a natural speech, which, however limited, is very intelligible to their own species. And as there are infinitely fewer parts and less contrivance in the finest composition of eloquence than in the coarsest organized body, the propagation of an *Iliad* or *Æneid* is an easier supposition than that of any plant or animal.

Suppose, therefore, that you enter into your library thus peopled by natural volumes containing the most refined reason and most exquisite beauty; could you possibly open one of them and doubt that its original cause bore the strongest analogy to mind and intelligence? When it reasons and discourses; when it expostulates, argues, and enforces its views and topics; when it applies sometimes to the pure intellect, sometimes to the affections; when it collects, disperses, and adorns every consideration suited to the subject—could you persist in asserting that all this, at the bottom, had really no meaning and that the first formation of this volume in the loins of its original parent proceeded not from thought and design? Your obstinacy, I know, reaches not that degree of firmness; even your skeptical play and wantonness would be abashed at so glaring an absurdity.

But if there be any difference, Philo, between this supposed case and the real one of the universe, it is all to the advantage of the latter. The anatomy of an animal affords many stronger instances of design than the perusal of Livy or Tacitus; and any objection which you start in the former case, by carrying me back to so unusual and extraordinary a scene as the first formation of worlds, the same objection has place on the supposition of our vegetating library. Choose, then, your party, Philo, without ambiguity or evasion; assert either that a rational volume is no proof of a rational cause, or admit of a similar cause to all the works of nature.

Let me here observe, too, continued Cleanthes, that this religious argument, instead of being weakened by that skepticism so much affected by you, rather acquires force from it and becomes more firm and undisputed. To exclude all argument or reasoning of every kind is either affectation or madness. The declared profession of every reasonable skeptic is only to reject abstruse, remote, and refined arguments; to adhere to common sense and the plain instincts of nature; and to assent, wherever any reasons strike him with so full a force that he cannot, without the greatest violence, prevent it. Now, the arguments for natural religion are plainly of this kind; and nothing but the most perverse, obstinate metaphysics can reject them. Consider, anatomize the eye, survey its structure and contrivance, and tell me, from your own feeling, if the idea of a contriver does not immediately flow in upon you with a force like that of sensation. The most obvious conclusion, surely is in favor of design; and it requires time, reflection, and study to summon up those frivolous though abstruse objections which can support infidelity. Who can behold the male and female of each species, the correspondence of their parts and instincts, their passions and whole course of life before and after generation but must be sensible that the propagation of the species is intended by nature? Millions and millions of such instances present themselves through every part of the universe, and no language can convey a more intelligible irresistible meaning than the curious adjustment of final causes. To what degree, therefore, of blind dogmatism must one have attained to reject such natural and such convincing arguments?

Some beauties in writing we may meet with which seem contrary to rules and which gain the affections and animate the imagination in opposition to all the precepts of criticism and to the authority of the established masters of art. And if the argument for theism be, as you pretend, contradictory to the principles of logic, its universal, its irresistible influence proves clearly that there may be arguments of a like irregular nature. Whatever cavils may be urged, an orderly world, as well as a coherent, articulate speech, will still be received as an incontestable proof of design and intention.

It sometimes happens, I own, that the religious arguments have not their due influence on an ignorant savage and barbarian, not because they are obscure and difficult, but because he never asks himself any question with regard to them. Whence arises the curious structure of an animal? From the copulation of its parents. And these whence? From *their* parents? A few removes set the objects at such a distance that to him they are lost in darkness and confusion; nor is he actuated by any curiosity to trace them farther. But this is neither dogmatism nor skepticism, but stupidity: a state of mind very different from your sifting, inquisitive disposition, my ingenious friend. You can trace causes from effects; you can compare the most distant and remote objects; and your greatest errors proceed not from barrenness of thought and invention, but from too luxuriant a fertility, which suppresses your natural good sense by a profusion of unnecessary scruples and objections.

Here I could observe, Hermippus, that Philo was a little embarrassed and confounded; but, while he hesitated in delivering an answer, luckily for him, Demea broke in upon the discourse and saved his countenance.

Your instance, Cleanthes, said he, drawn from books and language, being familiar, has, I confess, so much more force on that account; but is there not some danger, too, in this very circumstance, and may it not render us presumptuous, by making us imagine we comprehend the Deity and have some adequate idea of his nature and attributes? When I read a volume, I enter into the mind and intention of the author; I become him, in a manner, for the instant, and have an immediate feeling and conception of those ideas which revolved in his imagination while employed in that composition. But so near an approach we never surely can make to the Deity. His ways are not our ways. His attributes are perfect but incomprehensible. And this volume of nature contains a great and inexplicable riddle, more than any intelligible discourse of reasoning.

The ancient Platonists, you know, were the most religious and devout of all the pagan philosophers, yet many of them, particularly Plotinus, expressly declare that intellect or understanding is not to be ascribed to the Deity and that our most perfect worship of him consists not in acts of veneration, reverence, gratitude, or love, but in a certain mysterious self-annihilation or total extinction of all our faculties. These ideas are, perhaps, too far stretched, but still it must be acknowledged that, by representing the Deity as so intelligible and comprehensible, and so similar to a human mind, we are guilty of the grossest and most narrow partiality and make ourselves the model of the whole universe.

All the *sentiments* of the human mind, gratitude, resentment, love, friendship, approbation, blame, pity, emulation, envy, have a plain reference to the state and situation of man and are calculated for preserving the existence and promoting the activity of such a being in such circumstances. It seems, therefore, unreasonable to transfer such sentiments to a supreme existence or to suppose him actuated by them; and the phenomena, besides, of the universe will not support us in such a theory. All our *ideas* derived from the senses are confessedly false and illusive and cannot therefore be supposed to have place in a supreme intelligence. And as the ideas of internal sentiment, added to those of the external senses, compose the whole furniture of human understanding, we may conclude that none of the *materials* of thought are in any respect similar in the human and in the divine intelligence. Now, as to the *manner* of thinking, how can we make any comparison between them or suppose them anywise resembling? Our thought is fluctuating, uncertain, fleeting, successive, and compounded; and were we to remove these circumstances, we absolutely annihilate its essence, and it would in such a case be an abuse of terms to apply to it the name of thought or reason. At least, if it appear more pious and respectful (as it really is) still to retain these terms when we mention the Supreme Being, we ought to acknowledge that their meaning, in that case, is totally incomprehensible and that the infirmities of our nature do not permit us to reach any ideas which in the least correspond to the ineffable sublimity of the Divine attributes.

Part IV

It seems strange to me, said Cleanthes, that you, Demea, who are so sincere in the cause of religion, should still maintain the mysterious, incomprehensible nature of the Deity and should insist so strenuously that he has no manner of likeness or resemblance to human creatures. The Deity, I can readily allow, possesses many powers and attributes of which we can have no comprehension; but, if our ideas, so far as they go, be not just and adequate and correspondent to his real nature, I know not what there is in this subject worth insisting on. Is the name, without any meaning, of such mighty importance? Or how do you mystics, who maintain the absolute incomprehensibility of the Deity, differ from skeptics or atheists, who assert that the first cause of all is unknown and unintelligible? Their temerity must be very great if, after rejecting the production by a mind—I mean a mind resembling the human (for I know of no other)—they pretend to assign, with certainty, any other specific intelligible cause; and their conscience must be very scrupulous, indeed, if they refuse to call the universal unknown cause a God or Deity and to bestow on him as many sublime eulogies and unmeaning epithets as you shall please to require of them.

Who could imagine, replied Demea, that Cleanthes, the calm philosophical Cleanthes, would attempt to refute his antagonists by affixing a nickname to them and, like the common bigots and inquisitors of the age, have recourse to invective and declamation instead of reasoning? Or does he not perceive that these topics are easily retorted and that *anthropomorphite* is an appellation as invidious and implies as dangerous consequences as the epithet of *mystic* with which he has honored us? In reality, Cleanthes, consider what it is you assert when you represent the Deity as similar to a human mind and understanding. What is the soul of man? A composition of various faculties, passions, sentiments, ideas—united, indeed, into one self or person, but still distinct from each other. When it reasons, the ideas which are the parts of its discourse arrange themselves in a certain form or order which is not preserved entire for a moment, but immediately gives place to another arrangement. New opinions, new passions, new affections, new feelings arise which continually diversify the mental scene and produce in it the greatest variety and most rapid succession imaginable. How is this compatible with that perfect immutability and simplicity which all true theists ascribe to the Deity? By the same act, say they, he sees past, present, and future; his love and hatred, his mercy and justice, are one individual operation; he is entire in every point of space and complete in every instant of duration. No succession, no change, no acquisition, no diminution. What he is implies not in it any shadow of distinction or diversity. And what he is this moment, he ever has been and ever will be, without any new judgment, sentiment, or operation. He stands fixed in one simple, perfect state; nor can you ever say, with any propriety, that this act of his is different from that other or that this judgment or idea has been lately formed and will give place, by succession, to any different judgment or idea.

I can readily allow, said Cleanthes, that those who maintain the perfect simplicity of the Supreme Being, to the extent in which you have explained it, are complete mystics and chargeable with all the consequences which I have drawn from their opinion. They are, in a word, atheists without knowing it. For though it be allowed that the Deity possesses attributes of which we have no comprehension, yet ought we never to ascribe to him any attributes which are absolutely incompatible with that intelligent nature essential to him. A mind whose acts and sentiments and ideas are not distinct and successive, one that is wholly simple and totally immutable, is a mind which has no thought, no reason, no will, no sentiment, no love, no hatred, or, in a word, is no mind at all. It is an abuse of terms to give it that appellation, and we may as well speak of limited extension without figure or of number without composition.

Pray consider, said Philo, whom you are at present inveighing against. You are honoring with the appellation of *atheist* all the sound, orthodox divines, almost, who have treated of this subject; and you will at last be, yourself, found, according to your reckoning, the only sound theist in the world. But if idolators be atheists, as, I think, may justly be asserted, and Christian theologians the same, what becomes of the argument, so much celebrated, derived from the universal consent of mankind?

But, because I know you are not much swayed by names and authorities, I shall endeavor to show you, a little more distinctly, the inconveniences of that anthropomorphism which you have embraced and shall prove that there is no ground to suppose a plan of the world to be formed in the Divine mind, consisting of distinct ideas, differently arranged, in the same manner as an architect forms in his head the plan of a house which he intends to execute.

It is not easy, I own, to see what is gained by this supposition, whether we judge of the matter by *reason* or by *experience*. We are still obliged to mount higher in order to find the cause of this cause which you had assigned as satisfactory and conclusive.

If *reason* (I mean abstract reason derived from inquiries *a priori*) be not alike mute with regard to all questions concerning cause and effect, this sentence at least it will venture to pronounce: that a mental world or universe of ideas requires a cause as much as does a material world or universe of objects and, if similar in its arrangement, must require a similar cause. For what is there in this subject which should occasion a different conclusion or inference? In an abstract view, they are entirely alike; and no difficulty attends the one supposition which is not common to both of them.

Again, when we will needs force *experience* to pronounce some sentence, even on these subjects which lie beyond her sphere, neither can she perceive any material difference in this particular between these two kinds of worlds, but finds them to be governed by similar principles and to depend upon an equal variety of causes in their operations. We have specimens in miniature of both of them. Our own mind resembles the one, a vegetable or animal body the other. Let experience, therefore, judge from these samples. Nothing seems more delicate, with regard to its causes, than thought; and as these causes never operate in two persons after the same manner, so we never find two persons who think exactly alike. Nor indeed does the same person think exactly alike at any two different periods of time. A difference of age, of the disposition of his body, of weather, of food, of company, of books, of passions—any of these particulars, or others more minute, are sufficient to alter the curious machinery of thought and communicate to it very different movements and operations. As far as we can judge, vegetables and animal bodies are not more delicate in their motions nor depend upon a greater variety or more curious adjustment of springs and principles.

How, therefore, shall we satisfy ourselves concerning the cause of that Being whom you suppose the Author of nature, or, according to your system of anthropomorphism, the ideal world into which you trace the material? Have we not the same reason to trace that ideal world into another ideal world or new intelligent principle? But if we stop and go no farther, why go so far? Why not stop at the material world? How can we satisfy ourselves without going on *in infinitum?* And, after all, what satisfaction is there in that infinite progression? Let us remember the story of the Indian philosopher and his elephant. It was never more applicable than to the present subject. If the material world rests upon a similar ideal world, this ideal world must rest upon some other, and so on without end. It were better, therefore, never to look beyond the present material world. By supposing it to contain the principle of its order within itself, we really assert it to be God; and the sooner we arrive at that Divine Being, so much the better. When you go one step beyond the mundane system, you only excite an inquisitive humor which it is impossible ever to satisfy.

To say that the different ideas which compose the reason of the Supreme Being fall into order of themselves and by their own nature is really to talk without any precise meaning. If it has a meaning, I would fain know why it is not as good sense to say that the parts of the material world fall into order of themselves and by their own nature. Can the one opinion be intelligible, while the other is not so?

We have, indeed, experience of ideas which fall into order of themselves and without any *known* cause. But, I am sure, we have a much larger experience of matter which does the same, as in all instances of generation and vegetation, where the accurate analysis of the cause exceeds all human comprehension. We have also experience of particular systems of thought and of matter which have no order: of the first in madness, of the second in corruption. Why, then, should we think that order is more essential to one than the other? And if it requires a cause in both, what do we gain by your system in tracing the universe of objects into a similar universe of ideas? The first step which we make leads us on forever. It were, therefore, wise in us to limit all our inquiries to the present world, without looking farther. No satisfaction can ever be attained by these speculations which so far exceed the narrow bounds of human understanding.

It was usual with the Peripatetics, you know, Cleanthes, when the cause of any phenomenon was demanded, to have recourse to their *faculties* or *occult qualities* and to say, for instance, that bread nourished by its nutritive faculty and senna purged by its purgative. But it has been discovered that this subterfuge was nothing but the disguise of ignorance and that these philosophers, though less ingenuous, really said the same thing with the skeptics or the vulgar who fairly confessed that they knew not the cause of these phenomena. In like manner, when it is asked what cause produces order in the ideas of the Supreme Being, can any other reason be assigned by you, anthropomorphites, than that it is a *rational* faculty and that such is the nature of the Deity? But why a similar answer will not be equally satisfactory in accounting for the order of the world, without having recourse to any such intelligent creator as you insist on, may be difficult to determine. It is only to say that *such* is the nature of material objects and that they are all originally possessed of a *faculty* of order and proportion. These are only more learned and elaborate ways of confessing our ignorance; nor has the one hypothesis any real advantage above the other, except in its greater conformity to vulgar prejudices.

You have displayed this argument with great emphasis, replied Cleanthes. You seem not sensible how easy it is to answer it. Even in common life, if I assign a cause for any event, is it any objection, Philo, that I cannot assign the cause of that cause and answer every new question which may incessantly be started? And what philosophers could possibly submit to so rigid a rule?—philosophers who confess ultimate causes to be totally unknown and are sensible that the most refined principles into which they trace the phenomena are still to them as inexplicable as these phenomena themselves are to the vulgar. The order and arrangement of nature, the curious adjustment of final causes, the plain use and intention of every part and organ—all these bespeak in the clearest language and intelligent cause or author. The heavens and the earth join in the same testimony: the whole chorus of nature raises one hymn to the praises of its Creator. You alone, or almost alone, disturb this general harmony. You start abstruse doubts, cavils, and objections; you ask me what is the cause of this cause? I know not; I care not; that concerns not me. I have found a Deity; and here I stop my inquiry. Let those go farther who are wiser or more enterprising.

I pretend to be neither, replied Philo, and for that very reason I should never, perhaps, have attempted to go so far, especially when I am sensible that I must at last be contented to sit down with the same answer which, without further trouble, might have satisfied me from the beginning. If I am still to remain in utter ignorance of causes and can absolutely give an explication of nothing, I shall never esteem it any advantage to shove off for a moment a difficulty which you acknowledge must immediately, in its full force, recur upon me. Naturalists indeed very justly explain particular effects by more general causes, though these general causes themselves should remain in the end totally inexplicable, but they never surely thought it satisfactory to explain a particular effect by a particular cause which was no more to be accounted for than the effect itself. An ideal system, arranged of itself, without a precedent design, is not a whit more explicable than a material one which attains its order in a like manner; nor is there anymore difficulty in the latter supposition than in the former.

Part V

But to show you still more inconveniences, continued Philo, in your anthropomorphism, please to take a new survey of your principles. *Like effects prove like causes.* This is the experimental argument; and this, you say too, is the sole theological argument. Now, it is certain that the liker the effects are which are seen and the liker the causes which are inferred, the stronger is the argument. Every departure on either side diminishes the probability and renders the experiment less conclusive. You cannot doubt of the principle; neither ought you to reject its consequences.

All the new discoveries in astronomy which prove the immense grandeur and magnificence of the works of nature are so many additional arguments for a Deity, according to the true system of theism; but, according to your hypothesis of experimental theism, they become so many objections by removing the effect still farther from all resemblance to the effects of human art and contrivance. For if Lucretius, even following the old system of the world, could exclaim:

Quis regere immensi summam, quis habere profundi
Indu manu validas potis est moderanter habenas?
Quis pariter cœlos omnes convertere? et omnes
Ignibus ætheriis terras suffire feraces?
Omnibus inque locis esse omni tempore præsto? *

If Tully [Cicero] esteemed this reasoning so natural as to put
into the mouth of his Epicurean:

Quibus enim oculis animi intueri potuit vester Plato fa-
bricam illam tanti operis, qua construi a Deo atque
ædificari mundum facit? quæ molitio? quæ ferramenta?
qui vectes? quæ machinæ? qui minstri tanti muneris fu-
erunt? quemadmodum autem obedire et parere voluntati
architecti aer, ignis, aqua, terra potuerunt? †

If this argument, I say, had any force in former ages, how
much greater must it have at present, when the bounds of
Nature are so infinitely enlarged and such a magnificent
scene is opened to us? It is still more unreasonable to form
our idea of so unlimited a cause from our experience of the
narrow productions of human design and invention.

The discoveries by microscopes, as they open a new universe in miniature, are still objections, according to you, arguments, according to me. The further we push our researches of this kind, we are still led to infer the universal
cause of all to be vastly different from mankind or from any
object of human experience and observation.

And what say you to the discoveries in anatomy, chemistry, botany? . . . These surely are no objections, replied
Cleanthes; they only discover new instances of art and contrivance. It is still the image of mind reflected on us from innumerable objects. Add a mind *like the human,* said Philo. I
know of no other, replied Cleanthes. And the liker, the better, insisted Philo. To be sure, said Cleanthes.

Now, Cleanthes, said Philo, with an air of alacrity and
triumph, mark the consequences. *First,* by this method of

* [*De Rerum Natura*], lib. XI [II], 1094. ["Who can rule the sum,
who hold in his hand with controlling force the strong reins, of the
immeasurable deep? Who can at once make all the different heavens
to roll and warm with ethereal fires all the fruitful earths, or be
present in all places at all times?" (Translation by H. A. J. Munro,
G. Bell & Sons, 1920.)]

† *De Natura Deorum,* lib. I [cap. VIII]. ["How could your Plato, in his
mind's eye, see the construction of so great a work, by whose means God
sought to erect the edifice of the world? What materials, what imple-
ments, what bars, what machines, what workers did He employ in so
great a work? How did the architect bend to his will air, earth, fire,
and water and exact obedience from them?"]

reasoning you renounce all claim to infinity in any of the attributes of the Deity. For, as the cause ought only to be proportioned to the effect, and the effect, so far as it falls under our cognizance, is not infinite, what pretensions have we, upon your suppositions, to ascribe that attribute to the Divine Being? You will still insist that, by removing him so much from all similarity to human creatures, we give in to the most arbitrary hypothesis and at the same time weaken all proofs of his existence.

Secondly, you have no reason, on your theory, for ascribing perfection to the Deity, even in his finite capacity, or for supposing him free from every error, mistake, or incoherence in his undertakings. There are many inexplicable difficulties in the works of nature which, if we allow a perfect author to be proved *a priori,* are easily solved and become only seeming difficulties from the narrow capacity of man, who cannot trace infinite relations. But according to your method of reasoning, these difficulties become all real and, perhaps, will be insisted on as new instances of likeness to human art and contrivance. At least, you must acknowledge that it is impossible for us to tell, from our limited views, whether this system contains any great faults or deserves any considerable praise if compared to other possible and even real systems. Could a peasant, if the *Æneid* were read to him, pronounce that poem to be absolutely faultless or even assign to it its proper rank among the productions of human wit, he who had never seen any other production?

But were this world ever so perfect a production, it must still remain uncertain whether all the excellences of the work can justly be ascribed to the workman. If we survey a ship, what an exalted idea must we form of the ingenuity of the carpenter who framed so complicated, useful, and beautiful a machine? And what surprise must we feel when we find him a stupid mechanic who imitated others and copied an art which, through a long succession of ages, after multiplied trials, mistakes, corrections, deliberations, and controversies, had been gradually improving? Many worlds might have been botched and bungled, throughout an eternity, ere this system was struck out, much labor lost, many fruitless trials made, and a slow but continued improvement carried on during infinite ages in the art of world-making. In such subjects, who can determine where the truth, nay, who can conjecture where the probability lies amidst a great number of hypotheses which may be proposed, and a still greater which may be imagined?

And what shadow of an argument, continued Philo, can you produce from your hypothesis to prove the unity of the

Deity? A great number of men join in building a house or ship, in rearing a city, in framing a commonwealth; why may not several deities combine in contriving and framing a world? This is only so much greater similarity to human affairs. By sharing the work among several, we may so much further limit the attributes of each and get rid of that extensive power and knowledge which must be supposed in one deity, and which, according to you, can only serve to weaken the proof of his existence. And if such foolish, such vicious creatures as man can yet often unite in framing and executing one plan, how much more those deities or demons, whom we may suppose several degrees more perfect!

To multiply causes without necessity is indeed contrary to true philosophy, but this principle applies not to the present case. Were one deity antecedently proved by your theory who were possessed of every attribute requisite to the production of the universe, it would be needless, I own (though not absurd), to suppose any other deity existent. But while it is still a question whether all these attributes are united in one subject or dispersed among several independent beings, by what phenomena in nature can we pretend to decide the controversy? Where we see a body raised in a scale, we are sure that there is in the opposite scale, however concealed from sight, some counterpoising weight equal to it; but it is still allowed to doubt whether that weight be an aggregate of several distinct bodies or one uniform united mass. And if the weight requisite very much exceeds anything which we have ever seen conjoined in any single body, the former supposition becomes still more probable and natural. An intelligent being of such vast power and capacity as is necessary to produce the universe or, to speak in the language of ancient philosophy, so prodigious an animal exceeds all analogy and even comprehension.

But further, Cleanthes; men are mortal and renew their species by generation; and this is common to all living creatures. The two great sexes of male and female, says Milton, animate the world. Why must this circumstance, so universal, so essential, be excluded from those numerous and limited deities? Behold, then, the theogeny of ancient times brought back upon us.

And why not become a perfect anthropomorphite? Why not assert the deity or deities to be corporeal and to have eyes, a nose, mouth, ears, etc.? Epicurus maintained that no man had ever seen reason but in a human figure; therefore, the gods must have a human figure. And this argument, which is deservedly so much ridiculed by Cicero, becomes, according to you, solid and philosophical.

In a word, Cleanthes, a man who follows your hypothesis is able, perhaps, to assert or conjecture that the universe sometime arose from something like design; but beyond that position he cannot ascertain one single circumstance and is left afterwards to fix every point of his theology by the utmost license of fancy and hypothesis. This world, for aught he knows, is very faulty and imperfect compared to a superior standard and was only the first rude essay of some infant deity who afterwards abandoned it, ashamed of his lame performance; it is the work only of some dependent, inferior deity and is the object of derision to his superiors; it is the production of old age and dotage in some superannuated deity and, ever since his death, has run on at adventures from the first impulse and active force which it received from him. You justly give signs of horror, Demea, at these strange suppositions; but these, and a thousand more of the same kind, are Cleanthes' suppositions, not mine. From the moment the attributes of the Deity are supposed finite, all these have place. And I cannot, for my part, think that so wild and unsettled a system of theology is, in any respect, preferable to none at all.

These suppositions I absolutely disown, cried Cleanthes. They strike me, however, with no horror, especially when proposed in that rambling way in which they drop from you. On the contrary, they give me pleasure when I see that, by the utmost indulgence of your imagination, you never get rid of the hypothesis of design in the universe, but are obliged at every turn to have recourse to it. To this concession I adhere steadily; and this I regard as a sufficient foundation for religion.

Part VI

It must be a slight fabric, indeed, said Demea, which can be erected on so tottering a foundation. While we are uncertain whether there is one deity or many, whether the deity or deities, to whom we owe our existence, be perfect or imperfect, subordinate or supreme, dead or alive, what trust or confidence can we repose in them? What devotion or worship address to them? What veneration or obedience pay them? To all the purposes of life, the theory of religion becomes altogether useless; and even with regard to speculative consequences, its uncertainty, according to you, must render it totally precarious and unsatisfactory.

To render it still more unsatisfactory, said Philo, there occurs to me another hypothesis which must acquire an air of probability from the method of reasoning so much insisted on by Cleanthes. That like effects arise from like causes—this principle he supposes the foundation of all religion. But there is another principle of the same kind, no less certain and derived from the same source of experience, that, where several known circumstances are observed to be similar, the unknown will also be found similar. Thus, if we see the limbs of a human body, we conclude that it is also attended with a human head, though hid from us. Thus, if we see, through a chink in a wall, a small part of the sun, we conclude that were the wall removed we should see the whole body. In short, this method of reasoning is so obvious and familiar that no scruple can ever be made with regard to its solidity.

Now, if we survey the universe, so far as it falls under our knowledge, it bears a great resemblance to an animal or organized body and seems actuated with a like principle of life and motion. A continual circulation of matter in it produces no disorder; a continual waste in every part is incessantly repaired; the closest sympathy is perceived throughout the entire system; and each part or member, in performing its proper offices, operates both to its own preservation and to that of the whole. The world, therefore, I infer, is an animal; and the Deity is the *soul* of the world, actuating it, and actuated by it.

You have too much learning, Cleanthes, to be at all surprised at this opinion, which, you know, was maintained by almost all the theists of antiquity and chiefly prevails in their discourses and reasonings. For though, sometimes, the ancient philosophers reason from final causes, as if they thought the world the workmanship of God, yet it appears rather their favorite notion to consider it as his body whose organization renders it subservient to him. And it must be confessed that, as the universe resembles more a human body than it does the works of human art and contrivance, if our limited analogy could ever, with any propriety, be extended to the whole of nature, the inference seems juster in favor of the ancient than the modern theory.

There are many other advantages, too, in the former theory which recommended it to the ancient theologians. Nothing more repugnant to all their notions because nothing more repugnant to common experience than mind without body, a mere spiritual substance which fell not under their senses nor comprehension and of which they had not observed one single instance throughout all nature. Mind and body they knew because they felt both; an order, arrangement, organization, or internal machinery in both they likewise knew, after the same manner; and it could not but seem reasonable to transfer this experience to the universe and to suppose the divine mind and body to be also coeval and to have, both of them, order and arrangement naturally inherent in them and inseparable from them.

Here, therefore, is a new species of *anthropomorphism*, Cleanthes, on which you may deliberate, and a theory which seems not liable to any considerable difficulties. You are too much superior, surely, to *systematical prejudices* to find anymore difficulty in supposing an animal body to be, originally, of itself or from unknown causes, possessed of order and organization than in supposing a similar order to belong to mind. But the *vulgar prejudice* that body and mind ought always to accompany each other ought not, one should think, to be entirely neglected, since it is founded on *vulgar experience*, the only guide which you profess to follow in all these theological inquiries. And if you assert that our limited experience is an unequal standard by which to judge of the unlimited extent of nature, you entirely abandon your own hypothesis and must thenceforward adopt our mysticism, as you call it, and admit of the absolute incomprehensibility of the Divine Nature.

This theory, I own, replied Cleanthes, has never before occurred to me, though a pretty natural one; and I cannot readily, upon so short an examination and reflection, deliver any opinion with regard to it. You are very scrupulous, indeed, said Philo. Were I to examine any system of yours, I should not have acted with half that caution and reserve in starting objections and difficulties to it. However, if anything occur to you, you will oblige us by proposing it.

Why then, replied Cleanthes, it seems to me that, though the world does, in many circumstances, resemble an animal body, yet is the analogy also defective in many circumstances the most material: no organs of sense; no seat of thought or reason; no one precise origin of motion and action. In short, it seems to bear a stronger resemblance to a vegetable than to an animal, and your inference would be so far inconclusive in favor of the soul of the world.

But, in the next place, your theory seems to imply the eternity of the world; and that is a principal which, I think, can be refuted by the strongest reasons and probabilities. I shall suggest an argument to this purpose which, I believe, has not been insisted on by any writer. Those who reason from the late origin of arts and sciences, though their inference wants not force, may perhaps be refuted by considerations derived from the nature of human society, which is in continual revolution between ignorance and knowledge, liberty and slavery, riches and poverty, so that it is impossible for us, from our limited experience, to foretell with assurance what events may or may not be expected. Ancient learning and history seem to have been in great danger of entirely perishing after the inundation of the barbarous nations; and had these convulsions continued a little longer or been a little more violent, we should not probably have now known what passed in the world a few centuries before us. Nay, were it not for the superstition of the popes, who preserved a little jargon of Latin in order to support the appearance of an ancient and universal church, that tongue must have been utterly lost; in which case, the Western world, being totally barbarous, would not have been in a fit disposition for receiving the Greek language and learning, which was conveyed to them after the sacking of Constantinople. When learning and books had been extinguished, even the mechanical arts would have fallen considerably to decay; and it is easily imagined that fable or tradition might ascribe to them a much later origin than the true one. This vulgar argument, therefore, against the eternity of the world seems a little precarious.

But here appears to be the foundation of a better argument. Lucullus was the first that brought cherry trees from Asia to Europe, though that tree thrives so well in many European climates that it grows in the woods without any culture. Is it possible that, throughout a whole eternity, no European had ever passed into Asia and thought of transplanting so delicious a fruit into his own country? Or if the tree was once transplanted and propagated, how could it ever afterwards perish? Empires may rise and fall, liberty and slavery succeed alternately, ignorance and knowledge give place to each other; but the cherry tree will still remain in the woods of Greece, Spain, and Italy and will never be affected by the revolutions of human society.

It is not two thousand years since vines were transplanted into France, though there is no climate in the world more favorable to them. It is not three centuries since horses, cows, sheep, swine, dogs, corn were known in America. Is it possible that during the revolutions of a whole eternity there never arose a Columbus who might open the communication between Europe and that continent? We may as well imagine that all men would wear stockings for ten thousand years and never have the sense to think of garters to tie them. All these seem convincing proofs of the youth or rather infancy of the world, as being founded on the operation of principles more constant and steady than those by which human society is governed and directed. Nothing less than a total convulsion of the elements will ever destroy all the European animals

321

and vegetables which are now to be found in the Western world.

And what argument have you against such convulsions? replied Philo. Strong and almost incontestable proofs may be traced over the whole earth that every part of this globe has continued for many ages entirely covered with water. And though order were supposed inseparable from matter, and inherent in it, yet may matter be susceptible of many and great revolutions through the endless periods of eternal duration. The incessant changes to which every part of it is subject seem to intimate some such general transformations, though, at the same time, it is observable that all the changes and corruptions of which we have ever had experience are but passages from one state of order to another; nor can matter ever rest in total deformity and confusion. What we see in the parts, we may infer in the whole; at least, that is the method of reasoning on which you rest your whole theory. And were I obliged to defend any particular system of this nature, which I never willingly should do, I esteem none more plausible than that which ascribes an eternal inherent principle of order to the world, though attended with great and continual revolutions and alterations. This at once solves all difficulties; and if the solution, by being so general, is not entirely complete and satisfactory, it is at least a theory that we must sooner or later have recourse to, whatever system we embrace. How could things have been as they are, were there not an original inherent principle of order somewhere, in thought or in matter? And it is very indifferent to which of these we give the preference. Chance has no place on any hypothesis, skeptical or religious. Everything is surely governed by steady, inviolable laws. And were the inmost essence of things laid open to us, we should then discover a scene of which, at present, we can have no idea. Instead of admiring the order of natural beings, we should clearly see that it was absolutely impossible for them, in the smallest article, ever to admit of any other disposition.

Were anyone inclined to revive the ancient pagan theology which maintained, as we learn from Hesiod, that this globe was governed by 30,000 deities, who arose from the unknown powers of nature, you would naturally object, Cleanthes, that nothing is gained by this hypothesis and that it is as easy to suppose all men animals, being more numerous but less perfect, to have sprung immediately from a like origin. Push the same inference a step further, and you will find a numerous society of deities as explicable as one universal deity who possesses within himself the powers and perfections of the whole society. All these systems, then, of Skepticism, Polytheism, and Theism, you must allow, on your principles, to be on a like footing and that no one of them has any advantage over the others. You may thence learn the fallacy of your principles.

Part VII

But here, continued Philo, in examining the ancient system of the soul of the world, there strikes me, all on a sudden, a new idea which, if just, must go near to subvert all your reasoning and destroy even your first inferences on which you repose such confidence. If the universe bears a greater likeness to animal bodies and to vegetables than to the works of human art, it is more probable that its cause resembles the cause of the former than that of the latter, and its origin ought rather to be ascribed to generation or vegetation than to reason or design. Your conclusion, even according to your own principles, is therefore lame and defective.

Pray open up this argument a little further, said Demea, for I do not rightly apprehend it in that concise manner in which you have expressed it.

Our friend Cleanthes, replied Philo, as you have heard, asserts that, since no question of fact can be proved otherwise than by experience, the existence of a Deity admits not of proof from any other medium. The world, says he, resembles the works of human contrivance; therefore, its cause must also resemble that of the other. Here we may remark that the operation of one very small part of nature, to wit, man, upon another very small part, to wit, that inanimate matter lying within his reach, is the rule by which Cleanthes judges of the origin of the whole; and he measures objects, so widely disproportioned, by the same individual standard. But to waive all objections drawn from this topic, I affirm that there are other parts of the universe (besides the machines of human invention) which bear still a greater resemblance to the fabric of the world and which, therefore, afford a better conjecture concerning the universal origin of this system. These parts are animals and vegetables. The world plainly resembles more an animal or a vegetable than it does a watch or a knitting-loom. Its cause, therefore, it is more probable, resembles the cause of the former. The cause of the former is generation or vegetation. The cause, therefore, of the world we may infer to be something similar or analogous to generation or vegetation.

But how is it conceivable, said Demea, that the world can arise from anything similar to vegetation or generation?

Very easily, replied Philo. In like manner as a tree sheds its seed into the neighboring fields and produces other trees, so the great vegetable, the world, or this planetary system, produces within itself certain seeds which, being scattered into the surrounding chaos, vegetate into new worlds. A comet, for instance, is the seed of a world; and after it has been fully ripened, by passing from sun to sun, and star to star, it is, at last, tossed into the unformed elements which everywhere surround this universe and immediately sprouts up into a new system.

Or if, for the sake of variety (for I see no other advantage), we should suppose this world to be an animal: a comet is the egg of this animal; and in like manner as an ostrich lays its egg in the sand, which, without any further care, hatches the egg and produces a new animal, so . . . I understand you, says Demea. But what wild, arbitrary suppositions are these! What *data* have you for such extraordinary conclusions? And is the slight, imaginary resemblance of the world to a vegetable or an animal sufficient to establish the same inference with regard to both? Objects which are in general so widely different, ought they to be a standard for each other?

Right, cries Philo. This is the topic on which I have all along insisted. I have still asserted that we have no *data* to establish any system of cosmogony. Our experience, so imperfect in itself and so limited both in extent and duration, can afford us no probable conjecture concerning the whole of things. But if we must needs fix on some hypothesis, by what rule, pray, ought we to determine our choice? Is there any other rule than the greater similarity of the objects compared? And does not a plant or an animal, which springs from vegetation or generation, bear a stronger resemblance to the world than does any artificial machine, which arises from reason and design?

But what is this vegetation and generation of which you talk? said Demea. Can you explain their operations and anatomize that fine internal structure on which they depend?

As much, at least, replied Philo, as Cleanthes can explain the operations of reason or anatomize the internal structure on which it depends. But without any such elaborate disquisitions, when I see an animal, I infer that it sprang from generation, and that with as great certainty as you conclude a house to have been reared by design. These words *generation, reason* mark only certain powers and energies in nature whose effects are known but whose essence is incomprehensible; and one of these principles more than the other has no privilege for being made a standard to the whole of nature.

In reality, Demea, it may reasonably be expected that the larger the views are which we take of things, the better will they conduct us in our conclusions concerning such extraordinary and such magnificent subjects. In this little corner of the world alone, there are four principles, *reason, instinct, generation, vegetation,* which are similar to each other and are the causes of similar effects. What a number of other principles may we naturally suppose in the immense extent and variety of the universe could we travel from planet to planet, and from system to system, in order to examine each part of this mighty fabric? Any one of these four principles above mentioned (and a hundred others which lie open to our conjecture) may afford us a theory by which to judge of the origin of the world; and it is a palpable and egregious partiality to confine our view entirely to that principle by which our own minds operate. Were this principle more intelligible on that account, such a partiality might be somewhat excusable; but reason, in its internal fabric and structure, is really as little known to us as instinct or vegetation; and, perhaps, even that vague, undeterminate word *nature* to which the vulgar refer everything is not at the bottom more inexplicable. The effects of these principles are all known to us from experience; but the principles themselves and their manner of operation are totally unknown; nor is it less intelligible or less conformable to experience to say that the world arose by vegetation, from a seed shed by another world, than to say that it arose from a divine reason or contrivance, according to the sense in which Cleanthes understands it.

But methinks, said Demea, if the world had a vegetative quality and could sow the seeds of new worlds into the infinite chaos, this power would be still an additional argument for design in its author. For whence could arise so wonderful a faculty but from design? Or how can order spring from anything which perceives not that order which it bestows?

You need only look around you, replied Philo, to satisfy yourself with regard to this question. A tree bestows order and organization on that tree which springs from it, without knowing the order; an animal in the same manner on its offspring; a bird on its nest; and instances of this kind are even more frequent in the world than those of order which arise from reason and contrivance. To say that all this order in animals and vegetables proceeds ultimately from design is begging the question; nor can that great point be ascertained otherwise than by proving, *a priori,* both that order is, from its nature, inseparably attached to thought and that it can never of itself or from original unknown principles belong to matter.

But further, Demea, this objection which you urge can never be made use of by Cleanthes, without renouncing a defence which he has already made against one of my objections. When I inquired concerning the cause of that supreme reason and intelligence into which he resolves everything, he told me that the impossibility of satisfying such inquiries could never be admitted as an objection in any species of philosophy. *We must stop somewhere,* says he, *nor is it ever within the reach of human capacity to explain ultimate causes or show the last connections of any objects. It is sufficient if any steps, so far as we go, are supported by experience and observation.* Now, that vegetation and generation, as well as reason, are experienced to be principles of order in nature is undeniable. If I rest my system of cosmogony on the former, preferably to the latter, it is at my choice. The matter seems entirely arbitrary. And when Cleanthes asks me what is the cause of my great vegetative or generative faculty, I am equally entitled to ask him the cause of his great reasoning principle. These questions we have agreed to forbear on both sides; and it is chiefly his interest on the present occasion to stick to this agreement. Judging by our limited and imperfect experience, generation has some privileges above reason, for we see every day the latter arise from the former, never the former from the latter.

Compare, I beseech you, the consequences on both sides. The world, say I, resembles an animal; therefore it is an animal, therefore it arose from generation. The steps, I confess, are wide, yet there is some small appearance of analogy in each step. The world, says Cleanthes, resembles a machine; therefore it is a machine, therefore it arose from design. The steps are here equally wide and the analogy less striking. And if he pretends to carry on *my* hypothesis a step further and to infer design or reason from the great principle of generation on which I insist, I may, with better authority, use the same freedom to push further *his* hypothesis and infer a divine generation or theogony from his principle of reason. I have at least some faint shadow of experience, which is the utmost that can ever be attained in the present subject. Reason, in innumerable instances, is observed to arise from the principle of generation and never to arise from any other principle.

Hesiod and all the ancient mythologists were so struck with this analogy that they universally explained the origin of nature from an animal birth and copulation. Plato, too, so far as he is intelligible, seems to have adopted some such notion in his *Timaeus.*

The Brahmins assert that the world arose from an infinite spider, who spun this whole complicated mass from his bowels and annihilates afterwards the whole or any part of it by absorbing it again and resolving it into his own essence. Here is a species of cosmogony which appears to us ridiculous, because a spider is a little contemptible animal whose operations we are never likely to take for a model of the whole universe. But still, here is a new species of analogy, even in our globe. And were there a planet wholly inhabited by spiders (which is very possible), this inference would there appear as natural and irrefragable as that which in our planet ascribes the origin of all things to design and intelligence, as explained by Cleanthes. Why an orderly system may not be spun from the belly as well as from the brain it will be difficult for him to give a satisfactory reason.

I must confess, Philo, replied Cleanthes, that, of all men living, the task which you have undertaken, of raising doubts and objections, suits you best and seems, in a manner, natural and unavoidable to you. So great is your fertility of invention that I am not ashamed to acknowledge myself unable, on a sudden, to solve regularly such out-of-the-way difficulties as you incessantly start upon me, though I clearly see, in general, their fallacy and error. And I question not but you are yourself, at present, in the same case and have not the solution so ready as the objection, while you must be sensible that common sense and reason are entirely against you and that such whimsies as you have delivered may puzzle but never can convince us.

Part VIII

What you ascribe to the fertility of my invention, replied Philo, is entirely owing to the nature of the subject. In subjects adapted to the narrow compass of human reason, there is commonly but one determination which carries probability or conviction with it; and to a man of sound judgment, all other suppositions but that one appear entirely absurd and chimerical. But in such questions as the present, a hundred contradictory views may preserve a kind of imperfect analogy, and invention has here full scope to exert itself. Without any great effort of thought, I believe that I could, in an instant, propose other systems of cosmogony which would have some faint appearance of truth, though it is a thousand, a million to one if either yours or any one of mine be the true system.

For instance, what if I should revive the old Epicurean hypothesis? This is commonly, and I believe justly, esteemed the most absurd system that has yet been proposed; yet I know not whether, with a few alterations, it might not be brought to bear a faint appearance of probability. Instead of supposing matter infinite, as Epicurus did, let us suppose it finite. A finite number of particles is only susceptible of finite transpositions; and it must happen, in an eternal duration, that every possible order or position must be tried an infinite number of times. This world, therefore, with all its events, even the most minute, has before been produced and destroyed, and will again be produced and destroyed without any bounds and limitations. No one who has a conception of the powers of infinite, in comparison of finite, will ever scruple this determination.

But this supposes, said Demea, that matter can acquire motion without any voluntary agent or first mover.

And where is the difficulty, replied Philo, of that supposition? Every event, before experience, is equally difficult and incomprehensible; and every event, after experience, is equally easy and intelligible. Motion, in many instances, from gravity, from elasticity, from electricity, begins in matter, without any known voluntary agent; and to suppose always, in these cases, an unknown voluntary agent is mere hypothesis, and hypothesis attended with no advantages. The beginning of motion in matter itself is as conceivable *a priori* as its communication from mind and intelligence.

Besides, why may not motion have been propagated by impulse through all eternity, and the same stock of it, or nearly the same, be still upheld in the universe? As much is lost by the composition of motion, as much is gained by its resolution. And whatever the causes are, the fact is certain that matter is and always has been in continual agitation, as far as human experience or tradition reaches. There is not probably, at present, in the whole universe, one particle of matter at absolute rest.

And this very consideration, too, continued Philo, which we have stumbled on in the course of the argument suggests a new hypothesis of cosmogony that is not absolutely absurd and improbable. Is there a system, an order, an economy of things, by which matter can preserve that perpetual agitation which seems essential to it and yet maintain a constancy in the forms which it produces? There certainly is such an economy, for this is actually the case with the present world. The continual motion of matter, therefore, in less than infinite transpositions, must produce this economy or order, and, by its very nature, that order, when once established, supports itself for many ages if not to eternity. But wherever matter is so poised, arranged, and adjusted as to continue in perpetual motion and yet preserve a constancy in the forms, its situation must, of necessity, have all the same appearance of art and contrivance which we observe at present. All the parts of each form must have a relation to each other and to the whole; and the whole itself must have a relation to the other parts of the universe, to the element in which the form subsists, to the materials with which it repairs its waste and decay, and to every other form which is hostile or friendly. A defect in any of these particulars destroys the form, and the matter of which it is composed is again set loose and is thrown into irregular motions and fermentations till it unite itself to some other regular form. If no such form be prepared to receive it, and if there be a great quantity of this corrupted matter in the universe, the universe itself is entirely disordered, whether it be the feeble embryo of a world in its first beginnings that is thus destroyed or the rotten carcass of one languishing in old age and infirmity. In either case, a chaos ensues till finite though innumerable revolutions produce, at last, some forms whose parts and organs are so adjusted as to support the forms amidst a continued succession of matter.

Suppose (for we shall endeavor to vary the expression) that matter were thrown into any position by a blind, unguided force; it is evident that this first position must, in all probability, be the most confused and most disorderly imaginable, without any resemblance to those works of human contrivance which, along with a symmetry of parts, discover an adjustment of means to ends and a tendency to self-preservation. If the actuating force cease after this operation, matter must remain forever in disorder and continue an immense chaos, without any proportion or activity. But suppose that the actuating force, whatever it be, still continues in matter, this first position will immediately give place to a second, which will likewise, in all probability, be as disorderly as the first, and so on through many successions of changes and revolutions. No particular order or position ever continues a moment unaltered. The original force, still remaining in activity, gives a perpetual restlessness to matter. Every possible situation is produced and instantly destroyed. If a glimpse or dawn of order appears for a moment, it is instantly hurried away and confounded by that never-ceasing force which actuates every part of matter.

Thus, the universe goes on for many ages in a continued succession of chaos and disorder. But is it not possible that it may settle at last, so as not to lose its motion and active force (for that we have supposed inherent in it), yet so as to preserve an uniformity of appearance amidst the continual motion and fluctuation of its parts? This we find to be the case with the universe at present. Every individual is perpetually changing, and every part of every individual; and yet the whole remains, in appearance, the same. May we not hope for such a position or rather be assured of it from the eternal revolutions of unguided matter; and may not this account for all the appearing wisdom and contrivance which is in the universe? Let us contemplate the subject a little, and we shall find that this adjustment if attained by matter of a seeming stability in the forms, with a real and perpetual revolution or motion of parts, affords a plausible, if not a true, solution of the difficulty.

It is in vain, therefore, to insist upon the uses of the parts in animals and vegetables and their curious adjustment to each other. I would fain know how an animal could subsist unless its parts were so adjusted? Do we not find that it immediately perishes whenever this adjustment ceases, and that its matter, corrupting, tries some new form? It happens indeed that the parts of the world are so well adjusted that some regular form immediately lays claim to this corrupted matter; and if it were not so, could the world subsist? Must it not dissolve, as well as the animal, and pass through new positions and situations till in great but finite succession it fall, at last, into the present or some such order?

It is well, replied Cleanthes, you told us that this hypothesis was suggested on a sudden, in the course of the argument. Had you had leisure to examine it, you would soon have perceived the insuperable objections to which it is exposed. No form, you say, can subsist unless it possess those powers and organs requisite for its subsistence; some new order or economy must be tried, and so on, without intermission, till at last some order which can support and maintain itself is fallen upon. But according to this hypothesis, whence arise the many conveniences and advantages which men and all animals possess? Two eyes, two ears are not absolutely necessary for the subsistence of the species. Human race might have been propagated and preserved without horses, dogs, cows, sheep, and those innumerable fruits and products which serve to our satisfaction and enjoyment. If no camels had been created for the use of man in the sandy deserts of Africa and Arabia, would the world have been dissolved? If no loadstone had been framed to give that wonderful and useful direction to the needle, would human society and the human kind have been immediately extinguished? Though the maxims of nature be in general very frugal, yet instances of this

330

kind are far from being rare; and any one of them is a sufficient proof of design—and of a benevolent design—which gave rise to the order and arrangement of the universe.

At least, you may safely infer, said Philo, that the foregoing hypothesis is so far incomplete and imperfect, which I shall not scruple to allow. But can we ever reasonably expect greater success in any attempts of this nature? Or can we ever hope to erect a system of cosmogony that will be liable to no exceptions and will contain no circumstance repugnant to our limited and imperfect experience of the analogy of nature? Your theory itself cannot surely pretend to any such advantage, even though you have run into *anthropomorphism,* the better to preserve a conformity to common experience. Let us once more put it to trial. In all instances which we have ever seen, ideas are copied from real objects and are ectypal, not archetypal, to express myself in learned terms. You reverse this order and give thought the precedence. In all instances which we have ever seen, thought has no influence upon matter except where that matter is so conjoined with it as to have an equal reciprocal influence upon it. No animal can move immediately anything but the members of its own body; and, indeed, the equality of action and reaction seems to be an universal law of nature; but your theory implies a contradiction to this experience. These instances, with many more which it were easy to collect (particularly the supposition of a mind or system of thought that is eternal or, in other words, an animal ingenerable and immortal)—these instances, I say, may teach all of us sobriety in condemning each other and let us see that as no system of this kind ought ever to be received from a slight analogy, so neither ought any to be rejected on account of a small incongruity. For that is an inconvenience from which we can justly pronounce no one to be exempted.

All religious systems, it is confessed, are subject to great and insuperable difficulties. Each disputant triumphs in his turn, while he carries on an offensive war, and exposes the absurdities, barbarities, and pernicious tenets of his antagonist. But all of them, on the whole, prepare a complete triumph for the *skeptic,* who tells them that no system ought ever to be embraced with regard to such subjects, for this plain reason, that no absurdity ought ever to be assented to with regard to any subject. A total suspense of judgment is here our only reasonable resource. And if every attack, as is commonly observed, and no defense among the theologians is successful, how complete must be *his* victory who remains always, with all mankind, on the offensive and has himself no

331

fixed station or abiding city which he is ever, on any occasion, obliged to defend?

Part IX

But if so many difficulties attend the argument *a posteriori*, said Demea, had we not better adhere to that simple and sublime argument *a priori* which, by offering to us infallible demonstration, cuts off at once all doubt and difficulty? By this argument, too, we may prove the *infinity* of the Divine attributes, which, I am afraid, can never be ascertained with certainty from any other topic. For how can an effect which either is finite or, for aught we know, may be so—how can such an effect, I say, prove an infinite cause? The unity, too, of the Divine Nature it is very difficult, if not absolutely impossible, to deduce merely from contemplating the works of nature; nor will the uniformity alone of the plan, even were it allowed, give us any assurance of that attribute. Whereas the argument *a priori* . . .

You seem to reason, Demea, interposed Cleanthes, as if those advantages and conveniences in the abstract argument were full proofs of its solidity. But it is first proper, in my opinion, to determine what argument of this nature you choose to insist on; and we shall afterwards, from itself, better than from its *useful* consequences, endeavor to determine what value we ought to put upon it.

The argument, replied Demea, which I would insist on is the common one. Whatever exists must have a cause or reason of its existence, it being absolutely impossible for anything to produce itself or be the cause of its own existence. In mounting up, therefore, from effects to causes, we must either go on in tracing an infinite succession, without any ultimate cause at all, or must at last have recourse to some ultimate cause that is *necessarily* existent. Now that the first supposition is absurd may be thus proved. In the infinite chain or succession of causes and effects, each single effect is determined to exist by the power and efficacy of that cause which immediately preceded; but the whole eternal chain or succession, taken together, is not determined or caused by anything, and yet it is evident that it requires a cause or reason as much as any particular object which begins to exist in time. The question is still reasonable why this particular succession of causes existed from eternity and not any other succession or no succession at all. If there be no necessarily existent being, any supposition which can be formed is equally possible; nor is there anymore absurdity in *nothing's* having existed from eternity than there is in that succession of causes which constitutes the universe. What was it, then, which determined *something* to exist rather than *nothing* and bestowed being on a particular possibility, exclusive of the rest? *External causes*, there are supposed to be none. *Chance* is a word without a meaning. Was it *nothing*? But that can never produce anything. We must, therefore, have recourse to a necessarily existent Being who carries the *reason* of his existence in himself and who cannot be supposed not to exist, without an express contradiction. There is, consequently, such a Being— that is, there is a Deity.

I shall not leave it to Philo, said Cleanthes, though I know that the starting objections is his chief delight, to point out the weakness of this metaphysical reasoning. It seems to me so obviously ill grounded, and at the same time of so little consequence to the cause of true piety and religion, that I shall myself venture to show the fallacy of it.

I shall begin with observing that there is an evident absurdity in pretending to demonstrate a matter of fact or to prove it by any arguments *a priori*. Nothing is demonstrable unless the contrary implies a contradiction. Nothing that is distinctly conceivable implies a contradiction. Whatever we conceive as existent, we can also conceive as nonexistent. There is no being, therefore, whose nonexistence implies a contradiction. Consequently, there is no being whose existence is demonstrable. I propose this argument as entirely decisive and am willing to rest the whole controversy upon it.

It is pretended that the Deity is a necessarily existent being; and this necessity of his existence is attempted to be explained by asserting that, if we knew his whole essence or nature, we should perceive it to be as impossible for him not to exist as for twice two not to be four. But it is evident that this can never happen, while our faculties remain the same as at present. It will still be possible for us, at any time, to conceive the nonexistence of what we formerly conceived to exist; nor can the mind ever lie under a necessity of supposing any object to remain always in being, in the same manner as we lie under a necessity of always conceiving twice two to be four. The words, therefore, *necessary existence* have no meaning or, which is the same thing, none that is consistent.

But further, why may not the material universe be the necessarily existent Being, according to this pretended explication of necessity? We dare not affirm that we know all the qualities of matter; and, for aught we can determine, it may contain some qualities which, were they known, would make its nonexistence appear as great a contradiction as that twice two is five. I find only one argument employed to prove that the material world is not the necessarily existent Being; and this argument is derived from the contingency both of the matter and the form of the world. "Any particle of matter," it is said, "may be *conceived* to be annihilated, and any form may be *conceived* to be altered. Such an annihilation or alteration, therefore, is not impossible." * But it seems a great partiality not to perceive that the same argument extends equally to the Deity, so far as we have any conception of him, and that the mind can at least imagine him to be nonexistent or his attributes to be altered. It must be some unknown, inconceivable qualities which can make his nonexistence appear impossible or his attributes unalterable; and no reason can be assigned why these qualities may not belong to matter. As they are altogether unknown and inconceivable, they can never be proved incompatible with it.

Add to this that in tracing an eternal succession of objects it seems absurd to inquire for a general cause or first author. How can anything that exists from eternity have a cause, since that relation implies a priority in time and a beginning of existence?

In such a chain, too, or succession of objects, each part is caused by that which preceded it and causes that which succeeds it. Where then is the difficulty? But the *whole,* you say, wants a cause. I answer that the uniting of these parts into a whole, like the uniting of several distinct countries into one kingdom, or several distinct members into one body, is performed merely by an arbitrary act of the mind and has no influence on the nature of things. Did I show you the particular causes of each individual in a collection of twenty particles of matter, I should think it very unreasonable should you afterwards ask me what was the cause of the whole twenty. This is sufficiently explained in explaining the cause of the parts.

Though the reasonings which you have urged, Cleanthes, may well excuse me, said Philo, from starting any further difficulties, yet I cannot forbear insisting still upon another topic. It is observed by arithmeticians that the products of 9 compose always either 9 or some lesser product if you add together all the characters of which any of the former products is composed. Thus, of 18, 27, 36, which are products of 9, you make 9 by adding 1 to 8, 2 to 7, 3 to 6. Thus 369 is a product also of 9; and if you add 3, 6, and 9, you make 18, a lesser product of 9.† To a superficial observer, so wonder-

* Dr. Clarke
† *Republique des Lettres,* Aut 1685.

ful a regularity may be admired as the effect either of chance or design; but a skillful algebraist immediately concludes it to be the work of necessity and demonstrates that it must for ever result from the nature of these numbers. Is it not probable, I ask, that the whole economy of the universe is conducted by a like necessity, though no human algebra can furnish a key which solves the difficulty? And instead of admiring the order of natural beings, may it not happen that, could we penetrate into the intimate nature of bodies, we should clearly see why it was absolutely impossible they could ever admit of any other disposition? So dangerous is it to introduce this idea of necessity into the present question! and so naturally does it afford an inference directly opposite to the religious hypothesis!

But dropping all these abstractions, continued Philo, and confining ourselves to more familiar topics, I shall venture to add an observation that the argument *a priori* has seldom been found very convincing, except to people of a metaphysical head who have accustomed themselves to abstract reasoning and who, finding from mathematics that the understanding frequently leads to truth through obscurity, and contrary to first appearances, have transferred the same habit of thinking to subjects where it ought not to have place. Other people, even of good sense and the best inclined to religion, feel always some deficiency in such arguments, though they are not perhaps able to explain distinctly where it lies—a certain proof that men ever did and ever will derive their religion from other sources than from this species of reasoning.

Part X

It is my opinion, I own, replied Demea, that each man feels, in a manner, the truth of religion within his own breast and, from a consciousness of his imbecility and misery rather than from any reasoning, is led to seek protection from that Being on whom he and all nature is dependent. So anxious or so tedious are even the best scenes of life that futurity is still the object of all our hopes and fears. We incessantly look forward and endeavor, by prayers, adoration, and sacrifice, to appease those unknown powers whom we find, by experience, so able to afflict and oppress us. Wretched creatures that we are! What resource for us amidst the innumerable ills of life, did not religion suggest some methods of atonement and appease those terrors with which we are incessantly agitated and tormented?

I am indeed persuaded, said Philo, that the best and indeed the only method of bringing everyone to a due sense of religion is by just representations of the misery and wickedness of men. And for that purpose, a talent of eloquence and strong imagery is more requisite than that of reasoning and argument. For is it necessary to prove what everyone feels within himself? It is only necessary to make us feel it, if possible, more intimately and sensibly.

The people, indeed, replied Demea, are sufficiently convinced of this great and melancholy truth. The miseries of life, the unhappiness of man, the general corruptions of our nature, the unsatisfactory enjoyment of pleasures, riches, honors—these phrases have become almost proverbial in all languages. And who can doubt of what all men declare from their own immediate feeling and experience?

In this point, said Philo, the learned are perfectly agreed with the vulgar; and in all letters, *sacred* and *profane,* the topic of human misery has been insisted on with the most pathetic eloquence that sorrow and melancholy could inspire. The poets, who speak from sentiment, without a system, and whose testimony has therefore the more authority, abound in images of this nature. From Homer down to Dr. Young, the whole inspired tribe have ever been sensible that no other representation of things would suit the feeling and observation of each individual.

As to authorities, replied Demea, you need not seek them. Look round this library of Cleanthes. I shall venture to affirm that, except authors of particular sciences, such as chemistry or botany, who have no occasion to treat of human life, there is scarce one of those innumerable writers from whom the sense of human misery has not, in some passage or other, extorted a complaint and confession of it. At least, the chance is entirely on that side; and no one author has ever, so far as I can recollect, been so extravagant as to deny it.

There you must excuse me, said Philo. Leibniz has denied it and is perhaps the first * who ventured upon so bold and paradoxical an opinion; at least, the first who made it essential to his philosophical system.

And by being the first, replied Demea, might he not have been sensible of his error? For is this a subject in which philosophers can propose to make discoveries, especially in so late an age? And can any man hope by a simple denial (for the subject scarcely admits of reasoning) to bear down the

* That sentiment had been maintained by Dr. King and some few others before Leibniz, though by none of so great fame as that German philosopher.

united testimony of mankind, founded on sense and consciousness?

And why should man, added he, pretend to an exemption from the lot of all other animals? The whole earth, believe me, Philo, is cursed and polluted. A perpetual war is kindled amongst all living creatures. Necessity, hunger, want stimulate the strong and courageous; fear, anxiety, terror agitate the weak and infirm. The first entrance into life gives anguish to the newborn infant and to its wretched parent; weakness, impotence, distress attend each stage of that life, and it is, at last, finished in agony and horror.

Observe, too, says Philo, the curious artifices of nature in order to embitter the life of every living being. The stronger prey upon the weaker and keep them in perpetual terror and anxiety. The weaker, too, in their turn, often prey upon the stronger, and vex and molest them without relaxation. Consider that innumerable race of insects, which either are bred on the body of each animal or, flying about, infix their stings in him. These insects have others still less than themselves which torment them. And thus on each hand, before and behind, above and below, every animal is surrounded with enemies which incessantly seek his misery and destruction.

Man alone, said Demea, seems to be, in part, an exception to this rule. For by combination in society, he can easily master lions, tigers, and bears, whose greater strength and agility naturally enable them to prey upon him.

On the contrary, it is here chiefly, cried Philo, that the uniform and equal maxims of nature are most apparent. Man, it is true, can, by combination, surmount all his *real* enemies and become master of the whole animal creation; but does he not immediately raise up to himself *imaginary* enemies, the demons of his fancy, who haunt him with superstitious terrors and blast every enjoyment of life? His pleasure, as he imagines, becomes in their eyes a crime; his food and repose give them umbrage and offence; his very sleep and dreams furnish new materials to anxious fear; and even death, his refuge from every other ill, presents only the dread of endless and innumerable woes. Nor does the wolf molest more the timid flock than superstititon does the anxious breast of wretched mortals.

Besides, consider, Demea: this very society by which we surmount those wild beasts, our natural enemies, what new enemies does it not raise to us? What woe and misery does it not occasion? Man is the greatest enemy of man. Oppression, injustice, contempt, contumely, violence, sedition, war, calumny, treachery, fraud—by these, they mutually torment each other, and they would soon dissolve that society which they had formed were it not for the dread of still greater ills which must attend their separation.

But though these external insults, said Demea, from animals, from men, from all the elements, which assault us form a frightful catalogue of woes, they are nothing in comparison of those which arise within ourselves, from the distempered condition of our mind and body. How many lie under the lingering torment of diseases? Hear the pathetic enumeration of the great poet.

> Intestine stone and ulcer, colic-pangs,
> Demoniac frenzy, moping melancholy,
> And moon-struck madness, pining atrophy,
> Marasmus, and wide-wasting pestilence.
> Dire was the tossing, deep the groans: *Despair*
> Tended the sick, busiest from couch to couch.
> And over them triumphant *Death* his dart
> Shook: but delay'd to strike, though oft invok'd
> With vows, as their chief good and final hope.

The disorders of the mind, continued Demea, though more secret, are not perhaps less dismal and vexatious. Remorse, shame, anguish, rage, disappointment, anxiety, fear, dejection, despair—who has ever passed through life without cruel inroads from these tormentors? How many have scarcely ever felt any better sensations? Labor and poverty, so abhorred by everyone, are the certain lot of the far greater number; and those few privileged persons who enjoy ease and opulence never reach contentment or true felicity. All the goods of life united would not make a very happy man, but all the ills united would make a wretch indeed; and any one of them almost (and who can be free from every one?), nay, often the absence of one good (and who can possess all?) is sufficient to render life ineligible.

Were a stranger to drop on a sudden into this world, I would show him, as a specimen of its ills, an hospital full of diseases, a prison crowded with malefactors and debtors, a field of battle strewed with carcasses, a fleet foundering in the ocean, a nation languishing under tyranny, famine, or pestilence. To turn the gay side of life to him and give him a notion of its pleasures—whither should I conduct him? To a ball, to an opera, to court? He might justly think that I was only showing him a diversity of distress and sorrow.

There is no evading such striking instances, said Philo, but by apologies which still further aggravate the charge. Why have all men, I ask, in all ages, complained incessantly of the miseries of life? . . . They have no just reason, says one:

these complaints proceed only from their discontented, repining, anxious disposition. . . And can there possibly, I reply, be a more certain foundation of misery than such a wretched temper?

But if they were really as unhappy as they pretend, says my antagonist, why do they remain in life? . . .

Not satisfied with life, afraid of death—

this is the secret chain, say I, that holds us. We are terrified, not bribed to the continuance of our existence.

It is only a false delicacy, he may insist, which a few refined spirits indulge and which has spread these complaints among the whole race of mankind. . . And what is this delicacy, I ask, which you blame? Is it anything but a greater sensibility to all the pleasures and pains of life? And if the man of a delicate, refined temper, by being so much more alive than the rest of the world, is only so much more unhappy, what judgment must we form in general of human life?

Let men remain at rest, says our adversary, and they will be easy. They are willing artificers of their own misery. . . No! reply I: an anxious languor follows their repose; disappointment, vexation, trouble, their activity and ambition.

I can observe something like what you mention in some others, replied Cleanthes, but I confess I feel little or nothing of it in myself and hope that it is not so common as you represent it.

If you feel not human misery yourself, cried Demea, I congratulate you on so happy a singularity. Others, seemingly the most prosperous, have not been ashamed to vent their complaints in the most melancholy strains. Let us attend to the great, the fortunate emperor, Charles V, when, tired with human grandeur, he resigned all his extensive dominions into the hands of his son. In the last harangue which he made on that memorable occasion, he publicly avowed *that the greatest prosperities which he had ever enjoyed had been mixed with so many adversities that he might truly say he had never enjoyed any satisfaction or contentment.* But did the retired life in which he sought for shelter afford him any greater happiness? If we may credit his son's account, his repentance commenced the very day of his resignation.

Cicero's fortune, from small beginnings, rose to the greatest luster and renown; yet what pathetic complaints of the ills of life do his familiar letters, as well as philosophical discourses, contain? And suitably to his own experience, he introduces Cato, the great, the fortunate Cato protesting in his old age that had he a new life in his offer, he would reject the present.

Ask yourself, ask any of your acquaintance, whether they would live over again the last ten or twenty years of their life. No! but the next twenty, they say, will be better:

> And from the dregs of life, hope to receive
> What the first sprightly running could not give.

Thus, at last, they find (such is the greatness of human misery, it reconciles even contradictions) that they complain at once of the shortness of life and of its vanity and sorrow.

And is it possible, Cleanthes, said Philo, that after all these reflections, and infinitely more which might be suggested, you can still persevere in your anthropomorphism and assert the moral attributes of the Deity, his justice, benevolence, mercy, and rectitude, to be of the same nature with these virtues in human creatures? His power, we allow, is infinite; whatever he wills is executed; but neither man nor any other animal is happy; therefore, he does not will their happiness. His wisdom is infinite; he is never mistaken in choosing the means to any end; but the course of nature tends not to human or animal felicity; therefore, it is not established for that purpose. Through the whole compass of human knowledge, there are no inferences more certain and infallible than these. In what respect, then, do his benevolence and mercy resemble the benevolence and mercy of men?

Epicurus' old questions are yet unanswered.

Is he willing to prevent evil, but not able? Then is he impotent. Is he able, but not willing? Then is he malevolent. Is he both able and willing? Whence then is evil?

You ascribe, Cleanthes (and I believe justly), a purpose and intention to nature. But what, I beseech you, is the object of that curious artifice and machinery which she has displayed in all animals—the preservation alone of individuals and propagation of the species? It seems enough for her purpose, if such a rank be barely upheld in the universe, without any care or concern for the happiness of the members that compose it. No resource for this purpose; no machinery in order merely to give pleasure or ease; no fund of pure joy and contentment; no indulgence without some want or necessity accompanying it. At least, the few phenomena of this nature are overbalanced by opposite phenomena of still greater importance.

Our sense of music, harmony, and indeed beauty of all kinds, gives satisfaction, without being absolutely necessary to the preservation and propagation of the species. But what racking pains, on the other hand, arise from gouts, gravels, megrims, toothaches, rheumatisms, where the injury to the animal machinery is either small or incurable? Mirth, laughter, play, frolic seem gratuitous satisfactions which have no further tendency; spleen, melancholy, discontent, superstition are pains of the same nature. How then does the Divine benevolence display itself, in the sense of you anthropomorphites? None but we mystics, as you were pleased to call us, can account for this strange mixture of phenomena, by deriving it from attributes infinitely perfect but incomprehensible.

And have you, at last, said Cleanthes smiling, betrayed your intentions, Philo? Your long agreement with Demea did indeed a little surprise me, but I find you were all the while erecting a concealed battery against me. And I must confess that you have now fallen upon a subject worthy of your noble spirit of opposition and controversy. If you can make out the present point and prove mankind to be unhappy or corrupted, there is an end at once of all religion. For to what purpose establish the natural attributes of the Deity, while the moral are still doubtful and uncertain?

You take umbrage very easily, replied Demea, at opinions the most innocent and the most generally received, even amongst the religious and devout themselves; and nothing can be more surprising than to find a topic like this—concerning the wickedness and misery of man—charged with no less than atheism and profaneness. Have not all pious divines and preachers who have indulged their rhetoric on so fertile a subject, have they not easily, I say, given a solution of any difficulties which may attend it? This world is but a point in comparison of the universe; this life but a moment in comparison of eternity. The present evil phenomena, therefore, are rectified in other regions and in some future period of existence. And the eyes of men, being then opened to larger views of things, see the whole connection of general laws and trace, with adoration, the benevolence and rectitude of the Deity through all the mazes and intricacies of his providence.

No! replied Cleanthes, no! These arbitrary suppositions can never be admitted, contrary to matter of fact, visible and uncontroverted. Whence can any cause be known but from its known effects? Whence can any hypothesis be proved but from the apparent phenomena? To establish one hypothesis upon another is building entirely in the air; and the utmost we ever attain by these conjectures and fictions is to ascertain the bare possibility of our opinion, but never can we, upon such terms, establish its reality.

The only method of supporting Divine benevolence—and it is what I willingly embrace—is to deny absolutely the misery and wickedness of man. Your representations are exaggerated; your melancholy views mostly fictitious; your inferences contrary to fact and experience. Health is more common than sickness; pleasure than pain; happiness than misery. And for one vexation which we meet with, we attain, upon computation, a hundred enjoyments.

Admitting your position, replied Philo, which yet is extremely doubtful, you must at the same time allow that, if pain be less frequent than pleasure, it is infinitely more violent and durable. One hour of it is often able to outweigh a day, a week, a month of our common insipid enjoyments; and how many days, weeks, and months are passed by several in the most acute torments? Pleasure, scarcely in one instance, is ever able to reach ecstasy and rapture; and in no one instance can it continue for any time at its highest pitch and altitude. The spirits evaporate, the nerves relax, the fabric is disordered, and the enjoyment quickly degenerates into fatigue and uneasiness. But pain often—good God, how often!—rises to torture and agony; and the longer it continues, it becomes still more genuine agony and torture. Patience is exhausted, courage languishes, melancholy seizes us, and nothing terminates our misery but the removal of its cause or another event which is the sole cure of all evil, but which, from our natural folly, we regard with still greater horror and consternation.

But not to insist upon these topics, continued Philo, though most obvious, certain, and important, I must use the freedom to admonish you, Cleanthes, that you have put the controversy upon a most dangerous issue and are unawares introducing a total skepticism into the most essential articles of natural and revealed theology. What! no method of fixing a just foundation for religion unless we allow the happiness of human life and maintain a continued existence even in this world, with all our present pains, infirmities, vexations, and follies, to be eligible and desirable! But this is contrary to everyone's feeling and experience; it is contrary to an authority so established as nothing can subvert. No decisive proofs can ever be produced against this authority; nor is it possible for you to compute, estimate, and compare all the pains and all the pleasures in the lives of all men and of all animals; and thus, by your resting the whole system of religion on a point which, from its very nature, must for ever be uncertain, you tacitly confess that that system is equally uncertain.

But allowing you what never will be believed, at least, what you never possibly can prove, that animal or, at least, human happiness in this life exceeds its misery, you have yet done nothing, for this is not, by any means, what we expect from infinite power, infinite wisdom, and infinite goodness. Why is there any misery at all in the world? Not by chance, surely. From some cause then. Is it from the intention of the Deity? But he is perfectly benevolent. Is it contrary to his intention? But he is almighty. Nothing can shake the solidity of this reasoning, so short, so clear, so decisive, except we assert that these subjects exceed all human capacity and that our common measures of truth and falsehood are not applicable to them—a topic which I have all along insisted on, but which you have, from the beginning, rejected with scorn and indignation.

But I will be contented to retire still from this intrenchment, for I deny that you can ever force me in it. I will allow that pain or misery in man is *compatible* with infinite power and goodness in the Deity, even in your sense of these attributes: what are you advanced by all these concessions? A mere possible compatibility is not sufficient. You must *prove* these pure, unmixed, and uncontrollable attributes from the present mixed and confused phenomena, and from these alone. A hopeful undertaking! Were the phenomena ever so pure and unmixed, yet, being finite, they would be insufficient for that purpose. How much more, where they are also so jarring and discordant!

Here, Cleanthes, I find myself at ease in my argument. Here I triumph. Formerly, when we argued concerning the natural attributes of intelligence and design, I needed all my skeptical and metaphysical subtlety to elude your grasp. In many views of the universe and of its parts, particularly the latter, the beauty and fitness of final causes strike us with such irresistible force that all objections appear (what I believe they really are) mere cavils and sophisms; nor can we then imagine how it was ever possible for us to repose any weight on them. But there is no view of human life or of the condition of mankind from which, without the greatest violence, we can infer the moral attributes or learn that infinite benevolence, conjoined with infinite power and infinite wisdom, which we must discover by the eyes of faith alone. It is your turn now to tug the laboring oar and to support your philosophical subtleties against the dictates of plain reason and experience.

Part XI

I scruple not to allow, said Cleanthes, that I have been apt to suspect the frequent repetition of the word *infinite*, which we meet with in all theological writers, to savor more of panegyric than of philosophy, and that any purposes of reasoning, and even of religion, would be better served were we to rest contented with more accurate and more moderate expressions. The terms *admirable, excellent, superlatively great, wise,* and *holy*—these sufficiently fill the imaginations of men, and anything beyond, besides that it leads into absurdities, has no influence on the affections or sentiments. Thus, in the present subject, if we abandon all human analogy, as seems your intention, Demea, I am afraid we abandon all religion and retain no conception of the great object of our adoration. If we preserve human analogy, we must forever find it impossible to reconcile any mixture of evil in the universe with infinite attributes; much less can we ever prove the latter from the former. But supposing the Author of nature to be finitely perfect, though far exceeding mankind, a satisfactory account may then be given of natural and moral evil and every untoward phenomenon be explained and adjusted. A less evil may then be chosen in order to avoid a greater; inconveniences be submitted to in order to reach a desirable end; and, in a word, benevolence, regulated by wisdom and limited by necessity, may produce just such a world as the present. You, Philo, who are so prompt at starting views and reflections and analogies, I would gladly hear, at length, without interruption, your opinion of this new theory; and if it deserve our attention, we may afterwards, at more leisure, reduce it into form.

My sentiments, replied Philo, are not worth being made a mystery of; and, therefore, without any ceremony, I shall deliver what occurs to me with regard to the present subject. It must, I think, be allowed that, if a very limited intelligence whom we shall suppose utterly unacquainted with the universe were assured that it were the production of a very good, wise, and powerful Being, however finite, he would, from his conjectures, form *beforehand* a different notion of it from what we find it to be by experience; nor would he ever imagine, merely from these attributes of the cause of which he is informed, that the effect could be so full of vice and misery and disorder as it appears in this life. Supposing now that this person were brought into the world, still assured that it was the workmanship of such a sublime and benevolent Being, he might, perhaps, be surprised at the disappointment, but would never retract his former belief if founded on any very solid argument, since such a limited intelligence must be sensible of his own blindness and ignorance and must allow that there may be many solutions of those phenomena which will for ever escape his comprehension. But supposing, which is the real case with regard to man, that this creature is not antecedently convinced of a supreme intelligence, benevolent, and powerful, but is left to gather such a belief from the appearances of things—this entirely alters the case, nor will he ever find any reason for such a conclusion. He may be fully convinced of the narrow limits of his understanding, but this will not help him in forming an inference concerning the goodness of superior powers, since he must form that inference from what he knows; not from what he is ignorant of. The more you exaggerate his weakness and ignorance, the more diffident you render him and give him the greater suspicion that such subjects are beyond the reach of his faculties. You are obliged, therefore, to reason with him merely from the known phenomena and to drop every arbitrary supposition or conjecture.

Did I show you a house or palace where there was not one apartment convenient or agreeable, where the windows, doors, fires, passages, stairs, and the whole economy of the building were the source of noise, confusion, fatigue, darkness, and the extremes of heat and cold, you would certainly blame the contrivance, without any further examination. The architect would in vain display his subtlety and prove to you that, if this door or that window were altered, greater ills would ensue. What he says may be strictly true: the alteration of one particular, while the other parts of the building remain, may only augment the inconveniences. But still you would assert in general that, if the architect had had skill and good intentions, he might have formed such a plan of the whole and might have adjusted the parts in such a manner as would have remedied all or most of these inconveniences. His ignorance, or even your own ignorance of such a plan, will never convince you of the impossibility of it. If you find any inconveniences and deformities in the building, you will always, without entering into any detail, condemn the architect.

In short, I repeat the question: Is the world, considered in general and as it appears to us in this life, different from what a man or such a limited being would, *beforehand,* expect from a very powerful, wise, and benevolent Deity? It must be strange prejudice to assert the contrary. And from thence I conclude that, however consistent the world may be, allowing certain suppositions and conjectures with the idea of such a Deity, it can never afford us an inference concerning his existence. The consistency is not absolutely denied, only the inference. Conjectures, especially where infinity is excluded from the Divine attributes, may perhaps be sufficient to prove a consistency, but can never be foundations for any inference.

There seem to be *four* circumstances on which depend all or the greatest part of the ills that molest sensible creatures; and it is not impossible but all these circumstances may be necessary and unavoidable. We know so little beyond common life, or even of common life, that, with regard to the economy of a universe, there is no conjecture, however wild, which may not be just, nor any one, however plausible, which may not be erroneous. All that belongs to human understanding, in this deep ignorance and obscurity, is to be sceptical, or at least cautious, and not to admit of any hypothesis whatever, much less of any which is supported by no appearance of probability. Now this I assert to be the case with regard to all the causes of evil and the circumstances on which it depends. None of them appear to human reason in the least degree necessary or unavoidable, nor can we suppose them such, without the utmost license of imagination.

The *first* circumstance which introduces evil is that contrivance or economy of the animal creation by which pains, as well as pleasures, are employed to excite all creatures to action and make them vigilant in the great work of self-preservation. Now, pleasure alone, in its various degrees, seems to human understanding sufficient for this purpose. All animals might be constantly in a state of enjoyment; but when urged by any of the necessities of nature, such as thirst, hunger, weariness, instead of pain, they might feel a diminution of pleasure by which they might be prompted to seek that object which is necessary to their subsistence. Men pursue pleasure as eagerly as they avoid pain; at least, they might have been so constituted. It seems, therefore, plainly possible to carry on the business of life without any pain. Why then is any animal ever rendered susceptible of such a sensation? If animals can be free from it an hour, they might enjoy a perpetual exemption from it, and it required as particular a contrivance of their organs to produce that feeling as to endow them with sight, hearing, or any of the senses. Shall we conjecture that such a contrivance was necessary, without any appearance of reason, and shall we build on that conjecture as on the most certain truth?

But a capacity of pain would not alone produce pain were it not for the *second* circumstance, viz. the conducting of the world by generals laws; and this seems nowise necessary to a very perfect Being. It is true, if everything were conducted by particular volitions, the course of nature would be perpetually broken, and no man could employ his reason in the conduct of life. But might not other particular volitions remedy this inconvenience? In short, might not the Deity exterminate all ill, wherever it were to be found, and produce all good, without any preparation or long progress of causes and effects?

Besides, we must consider that, according to the present economy of the world, the course of nature, though supposed exactly regular, yet to us appears not so, and many events are uncertain, and many disappoint our expectations. Health and sickness, calm and tempest, with an infinite number of other accidents whose causes are unknown and variable, have a great influence both on the fortunes of particular persons and on the prosperity of public societies; and indeed, all human life, in a manner, depends on such accidents. A being, therefore, who knows the secret springs of the universe might easily, by particular volitions, turn all these accidents to the good of mankind and render the whole world happy, without discovering himself in any operation. A fleet whose purposes were salutary to society might always meet with a fair wind; good princes enjoy sound health and long life; persons born to power and authority be framed with good tempers and virtuous dispositions. A few such events as these, regularly and wisely conducted, would change the face of the world and yet would no more seem to disturb the course of nature or confound human conduct than the present economy of things, where the causes are secret and variable and compounded. Some small touches given to Caligula's brain in his infancy might have converted him into a Trajan. One wave, a little higher than the rest, by burying Caesar and his fortune in the bottom of the ocean, might have restored liberty to a considerable part of mankind. There may, for aught we know, be good reasons why Providence interposes not in this manner, but they are unknown to us; and, though the mere supposition that such reasons exist may be sufficient to *save* the conclusion concerning the Divine attributes, yet surely it can never be sufficient to *establish* that conclusion.

If everything in the universe be conducted by general laws, and if animals be rendered susceptible of pain, it scarcely seems possible but some ill must arise in the various shocks of matter and the various concurrence and opposition of general laws; but this ill would be very rare were it not for the *third* circumstance which I proposed to mention, viz. the great frugality with which all powers and faculties are distributed to every particular being. So well adjusted are the organs and capacities of all animals, and so well fitted to their preservation, that, as far as history or tradition reaches, there appears not to be any single species which has yet been extinguished in the universe. Every animal has the requisite endowments, but these endowments are bestowed with so scrupulous an economy that any considerable diminution must

347

entirely destroy the creature. Wherever one power is increased, there is a proportional abatement in the others. Animals which excel in swiftness are commonly defective in force. Those which possess both are either imperfect in some of their senses or are oppressed with the most craving wants. The human species, whose chief excellence is reason and sagacity, is of all others the most necessitous and the most deficient in bodily advantages, without clothes, without arms, without food, without lodging, without any convenience of life, except what they owe to their own skill and industry. In short, nature seems to have formed an exact calculation of the necessities of her creatures and, like a *rigid master,* has afforded them little more powers or endowments than what are strictly sufficient to supply those necessities. An *indulgent parent* would have bestowed a large stock in order to guard against accidents and secure the happiness and welfare of the creature in the most unfortunate concurrence of circumstances. Every course of life would not have been so surrounded with precipices that the least departure from the true path, by mistake or necessity, must involve us in misery and ruin. Some reserve, some fund, would have been provided to ensure happiness, nor would the powers and the necessities have been adjusted with so rigid an economy. The Author of nature is conceivably powerful; his force is supposed great, if not altogether inexhaustible, nor is there any reason, as far as we can judge, to make him observe this strict frugality in his dealings with his creatures. It would have been better, were his power extremely limited, to have created fewer animals and to have endowed these with more faculties for their happiness and preservation. A builder is never esteemed prudent who undertakes a plan beyond what his stock will enable him to finish.

In order to cure most of the ills of human life, I require not that man should have the wings of the eagle, the swiftness of the stag, the force of the ox, the arms of the lion, the scales of the crocodile or rhinoceros; much less do I demand the sagacity of an angel or cherubim. I am contented to take an increase in one single power or faculty of his soul. Let him be endowed with a greater propensity to industry and labor, a more vigorous spring and activity of mind, a more constant bent to business and application. Let the whole species possess naturally an equal diligence with that which many individuals are able to attain by habit and reflection, and the most beneficial consequences, without any allay of ill, is the immediate and necessary result of this endowment. Almost all the moral as well as natural evils of human life arise from idleness; and were our species, by the original constitution of their frame, exempt from this vice or infirmity, the perfect cultivation of land, the improvement of arts and manufactures, the exact execution of every office and duty, immediately follow; and men at once may fully reach that state of society which is so imperfectly attained by the best regulated government. But as industry is a power, and the most valuable of any, nature seems determined, suitably to her usual maxims, to bestow it on men with a very sparing hand and rather to punish him severely for his deficiency in it than to reward him for his attainments. She has so contrived his frame that nothing but the most violent necessity can oblige him to labor; and she employs all his other wants to overcome, at least in part, the want of diligence and to endow him with some share of a faculty of which she has thought fit naturally to bereave him. Here our demands may be allowed very humble and therefore the more reasonable. If we required the endowments of superior penetration and judgment, of a more delicate taste of beauty, of a nicer sensibility to benevolence and friendship, we might be told that we impiously pretend to break the order of nature, that we want to exalt ourselves into a higher rank of being, that the presents which we require, not being suitable to our state and condition, would only be pernicious to us. But it is hard, I dare to repeat it, it is hard that, being placed in a world so full of wants and necessities, where almost every being and element is either our foe or refuses its assistance . . . we should also have our own temper to struggle with and should be deprived of that faculty which can alone fence against these multiplied evils.

The *fourth* circumstance whence arises the misery and ill of the universe is the inaccurate workmanship of all the springs and principles of the great machine of nature. It must be acknowledged that there are few parts of the universe which seem not to serve some purpose and whose removal would not produce a visible defect and disorder in the whole. The parts hang all together, nor can one be touched without affecting the rest, in a greater or less degree. But at the same time, it must be observed that none of these parts or principles, however useful, are so accurately adjusted as to keep precisely within those bounds in which their utility consists; but they are, all of them, apt, on every occasion, to run into the one extreme or the other. One would imagine that this grand production had not received the last hand of the maker —so little finished is every part and so coarse are the strokes with which it is executed. Thus, the winds are requisite to convey the vapors along the surface of the globe and to assist men in navigation; but how often, rising up to tempests and hurricanes, do they become pernicious? Rains are necessary to nourish all the plants and animals of the earth; but how often are they defective? how often excessive? Heat is requisite to all life and vegetation but is not always found in the due proportion. On the mixture and secretion of the humors and juices of the body depend the health and prosperity of the animal; but the parts perform not regularly their proper function. What more useful than all the passions of the mind, ambition, vanity, love, anger? But how often do they break their bounds and cause the greatest convulsions in society? There is nothing so advantageous in the universe but what frequently becomes pernicious, by its excess or defect; nor has nature guarded, with the requisite accuracy, against all disorder or confusion. The irregularity is never perhaps so great as to destroy any species, but is often sufficient to involve the individuals in ruin and misery.

On the concurrence, then, of these *four* circumstances does all or the greatest part of natural evil depend. Were all living creatures incapable of pain, or were the world administered by particular volitions, evil never could have found access into the universe; and were animals endowed with a large stock of powers and faculties, beyond what strict necessity requires, or were the several springs and principles of the universe so accurately framed as to preserve always the just temperament and medium, there must have been very little ill in comparison of what we feel at present. What then shall we pronounce on this occasion? Shall we say that these circumstances are not necessary, and that they might easily have been altered in the contrivance of the universe? This decision seems too presumptuous for creatures so blind and ignorant. Let us be more modest in our conclusions. Let us allow that, if the goodness of the Deity (I mean a goodness like the human) could be established on any tolerable reasons *a priori*, these phenomena, however untoward, would not be sufficient to subvert that principle, but might easily, in some unknown manner, be reconcilable to it. But let us still assert that, as this goodness is not antecedently established but must be inferred from the phenomena, there can be no grounds for such an inference while there are so many ills in the universe and while these ills might so easily have been remedied, as far as human understanding can be allowed to judge on such a subject. I am skeptic enough to allow that the bad appearances, notwithstanding all my reasonings, may be compatible with such attributes as you suppose, but surely they can never prove these attributes. Such a conclusion cannot result from skepticism, but must arise from the phenomena and from our confidence in the reasonings which we deduce from these phenomena.

Look round this universe. What an immense profusion of beings, animated and organized, sensible and active! You admire this prodigious variety and fecundity. But inspect a little more narrowly these living existences, the only beings worth regarding. How hostile and destructive to each other! How insufficient all of them for their own happiness! How contemptible or odious to the spectator! The whole presents nothing but the idea of a blind nature, impregnated by a great vivifying principle, and pouring forth from her lap, without discernment or parental care, her maimed and abortive children!

Here the Manichaean system occurs as a proper hypothesis to solve the difficulty; and, no doubt, in some respects it is very specious and has more probability than the common hypothesis, by giving a plausible account of the strange mixture of good and ill which appears in life. But if we consider, on the other hand, the perfect uniformity and agreement of the parts of the universe, we shall not discover in it any marks of the combat of a malevolent with a benevolent being. There is indeed an opposition of pains and pleasures in the feelings of sensible creatures; but are not all the operations of nature carried on by an opposition of principles, of hot and cold, moist and dry, light and heavy? The true conclusion is that the original Source of all things is entirely indifferent to all these principles and has no more regard to good above ill than to heat above cold, or to drought above moisture, or to light above heavy.

There may *four* hypotheses be framed concerning the first causes of the universe: that they are endowed with perfect goodness; that they have perfect malice; that they are opposite and have both goodness and malice; that they have neither goodness nor malice. Mixed phenomena can never prove the two former unmixed principles; and the uniformity and steadiness of general laws seem to oppose the third. The fourth, therefore, seems by far the most probable.

What I have said concerning natural evil will apply to moral with little or no variation; and we have no more reason to infer that the rectitude of the Supreme Being resembles human rectitude than that his benevolence resembles the human. Nay, it will be thought that we have still greater cause to exclude from him moral sentiments, such as we feel them, since moral evil, in the opinion of many, is much more predominant above moral good than natural evil above natural good.

But even though this should not be allowed, and though

351

the virtue which is in mankind should be acknowledged much superior to the vice, yet, so long as there is any vice at all in the universe, it will very much puzzle you anthropomorphites how to account for it. You must assign a cause for it, without having recourse to the first cause. But as every effect must have a cause, and that cause another, you must either carry on the progression *in infinitum* or rest on that original principle, who is the ultimate cause of all things. . . .

Hold! hold! cried Demea. Whither does your imagination hurry you? I joined in alliance with you in order to prove the incomprehensible nature of the Divine Being and refute the principles of Cleanthes, who would measure everything by human rule and standard. But I now find you running into all the topics of the greatest libertines and infidels and betraying that holy cause which you seemingly espoused. Are you secretly, then, a more dangerous enemy than Cleanthes himself?

And are you so late in perceiving it? replied Cleanthes. Believe me, Demea, your friend Philo, from the beginning has been amusing himself at both our expense; and it must be confessed that the injudicious reasoning of our vulgar theology has given him but too just a handle of ridicule. The total infirmity of human reason, the absolute incomprehensibility of the Divine Nature, the great and universal misery, and still greater wickedness of men—these are strange topics, surely, to be so fondly cherished by orthodox divines and doctors. In ages of stupidity and ignorance, indeed, these principles may safely be espoused; and perhaps no views of things are more proper to promote superstition than such as encourage the blind amazement, the diffidence, and melancholy of mankind. But at present . . .

Blame not so much, interposed Philo, the ignorance of these reverend gentlemen. They know how to change their style with the times. Formerly, it was a most popular theological topic to maintain that human life was vanity and misery and to exaggerate all the ills and pains which are incident to men. But of late years, divines, we find, begin to retract this position and maintain, though still with some hesitation, that there are more goods than evils, more pleasures than pains, even in this life. When religion stood entirely upon temper and education, it was thought proper to encourage melancholy, as, indeed, mankind never have recourse to superior powers so readily as in that disposition. But as men have now learned to form principles and to draw consequences, it is necessary to change the batteries and to make use of such arguments as will endure at least some scrutiny and examination. This variation is the same (and from the same causes)

352

with that which I formerly remarked with regard to skepticism.

Thus Philo continued to the last his spirit of opposition and his censure of established opinions. But I could observe that Demea did not at all relish the latter part of the discourse; and he took occasion soon after, on some pretense or other, to leave the company.

Part XII

After Demea's departure, Cleanthes and Philo continued the conversation in the following manner. Our friend, I am afraid, said Cleanthes, will have little inclination to revive this topic of discourse while you are in company; and to tell the truth, Philo, I should rather wish to reason with either of you apart on a subject so sublime and interesting. Your spirit of controversy, joined to your abhorrence of vulgar superstition, carries you strange lengths when engaged in an argument; and there is nothing so sacred and venerable, even in your own eyes, which you spare on that occasion.

I must confess, replied Philo, that I am less cautious on the subject of Natural Religion than on any other, both because I know that I can never, on that head, corrupt the principles of any man of common sense and because no one, I am confident, in whose eyes I appear a man of common sense will ever mistake my intentions. You, in particular, Cleanthes, with whom I live in unreserved intimacy, you are sensible that, notwithstanding the freedom of my conversation and my love of singular arguments, no one has a deeper sense of religion impressed on his mind or pays more profound adoration to the Divine Being as he discovers himself to reason in the inexplicable contrivance and artifice of nature. A purpose, an intention, a design strikes everywhere the most careless, the most stupid thinker; and no man can be so hardened in absurd systems as at all times to reject it. *That nature does nothing in vain* is a maxim established in all the schools, merely from the contemplation of the works of nature, without any religious purpose; and, from a firm conviction of its truth, an anatomist who had observed a new organ or canal would never be satisfied till he had also discovered its use and intention. One great foundation of the Copernican system is the maxim *that nature acts by the simplest methods and chooses the most proper means to any end;* and astronomers often, without thinking of it, lay this strong foundation of piety and religion. The same thing is observable in other parts of philosophy; and thus all the sciences almost lead us insensibly to acknowledge a first intelligent Author; and their authority is often so much the greater, as they do not directly profess that intention.

It is with pleasure I hear Galen reason concerning the structure of the human body. The anatomy of a man, says he,* discovers above 600 different muscles; and whoever duly considers these will find that, in each of them, nature must have adjusted at least ten different circumstances in order to attain the end which she proposed: proper figure, just magnitude, right disposition of the several ends, upper and lower position of the whole, the due insertion of the several nerves, veins, and arteries, so that, in the muscles alone, above 6,000 several views and intentions must have been formed and executed. The bones he calculates to be 284; the distinct purposes aimed at in the structure of each, above forty. What a prodigious display of artifice, even in these simple and homogeneous parts! But if we consider the skin, ligaments, vessels, glandules, humors, the several limbs and members of the body, how must our astonishment rise upon us in proportion to the number and intricacy of the parts so artificially adjusted! The further we advance in these researches, we discover new scenes of art and wisdom; but descry still, at a distance, further scenes beyond our reach: in the fine internal structure of the parts, in the economy of the brain, in the fabric of the seminal vessels. All these artifices are repeated in every different species of animal, with wonderful variety, and with exact propriety, suited to the different intentions of nature in framing each species. And if the infidelity of Galen, even when these natural sciences were still imperfect, could not withstand such striking appearances, to what pitch of pertinacious obstinacy must a philosopher in this age have attained who can now doubt of a Supreme Intelligence!

Could I meet with one of this species (who, I thank God, are very rare), I would ask him: Supposing there were a God who did not discover himself immediately to our senses, were it possible for him to give stronger proofs of his existence than what appear on the whole face of nature? What indeed could such a Divine Being do but copy the present economy of things, render many of his artifices so plain that no stupidity could mistake them, afford glimpses of still greater artifices which demonstrate his prodigious superiority above our narrow apprehensions, and conceal altogether a great many from such imperfect creatures? Now, according to all rules of just reasoning, every fact must pass for undisputed when it is supported by all the arguments which its nature admits of,

* *De Formatione Fœtus.*

even though these arguments be not, in themselves, very numerous or forcible—how much more in the present case, where no human imagination can compute their number and no understanding estimate their cogency!

I shall further add, said Cleanthes, to what you have so well urged, that one great advantage of the principle of theism is that it is the only system of cosmogony which can be rendered intelligible and complete and yet can throughout preserve a strong analogy to what we every day see and experience in the world. The comparison of the universe to a machine of human contrivance is so obvious and natural, and is justified by so many instances of order and design in nature, that it must immediately strike all unprejudiced apprehensions and procure universal approbation. Whoever attempts to weaken this theory cannot pretend to succeed by establishing in its place any other that is precise and determinate; it is sufficient for him if he start doubts and difficulties and, by remote and abstract views of things, reach that suspense of judgment which is here the utmost boundary of his wishes. But, besides that this state of mind is in itself unsatisfactory, it can never be steadily maintained against such striking appearances as continually engage us into the religious hypothesis. A false, absurd system, human nature, from the force of prejudice, is capable of adhering to with obstinacy and perseverance; but no system at all, in opposition to a theory supported by strong and obvious reason, by natural propensity, and by early education, I think it absolutely impossible to maintain or defend.

So little, replied Philo, do I esteem this suspense of judgment in the present case to be possible that I am apt to suspect there enters somewhat of a dispute of words into this controversy, more than is usually imagined. That the works of nature bear a great analogy to the productions of art is evident, and, according to all the rules of good reasoning, we ought to infer, if we argue at all concerning them, that their causes have a proportional analogy. But as there are also considerable differences, we have reason to suppose a proportional difference in the causes and, in particular, ought to attribute a much higher degree of power and energy to the supreme cause than any we have ever observed in mankind. Here, then, the existence of a *Deity* is plainly ascertained by reason; and if we make it a question whether, on account of these analogies, we can properly call him a *mind* or intelligence, notwithstanding the vast difference which may reasonably be supposed between him and human minds, what is this but a mere verbal controversy? No man can deny the analogies between the effects; to restrain ourselves from inquiring concerning the causes is scarcely possible. From this inquiry, the legitimate conclusion is that the causes have also an analogy; and if we are not contented with calling the first and supreme cause a *God* or *Deity*, but desire to vary the expression, what can we call him but *Mind* or *Thought* to which he is justly supposed to bear a considerable resemblance?

All men of sound reason are disgusted with verbal disputes, which abound so much in philosophical and theological inquiries; and it is found that the only remedy for this abuse must arise from clear definitions, from the precision of those ideas which enter into any argument, and from the strict and uniform use of those terms which are employed. But there is a species of controversy which, from the very nature of language and of human ideas, is involved in perpetual ambiguity, and can never, by any precaution or any definitions, be able to reach a reasonable certainty or precision. These are the controversies concerning the degrees of any quality or circumstance. Men may argue to all eternity whether Hannibal be a great, or a very great, or a superlatively great man, what degree of beauty Cleopatra possessed, what epithet of praise Livy or Thucydides is entitled to, without bringing the controversy to any determination. The disputants may here agree in their sense and differ in the terms, or *vice versa*, yet never be able to define their terms so as to enter into each other's meaning, because the degrees of these qualities are not, like quantity or number, susceptible of any exact mensuration which may be the standard in the controversy. That the dispute concerning theism is of this nature and consequently is merely verbal, or, perhaps, if possible, still more incurably ambiguous, will appear upon the slighest inquiry. I ask the theist if he does not allow that there is a great and immeasurable, because incomprehensible, difference between the *human* and the *divine* mind; the more pious he is, the more readily will he assent to the affirmative, and the more will he be disposed to magnify the difference; he will even assert that the difference is of a nature which cannot be too much magnified. I next turn to the atheist, who, I assert, is only nominally so and can never possibly be in earnest, and I ask him whether, from the coherence and apparent sympathy in all the parts of this world, there be not a certain degree of analogy among all the operations of nature, in every situation and in every age; whether the rotting of a turnip, the generation of an animal, and the structure of human thought be not energies that probably bear some remote analogy to each other. It is impossible he can deny it; he will readily acknowledge it. Having obtained this concession, I

356

push him still further in his retreat, and I ask him if it be not probable that the principle which first arranged and still maintains order in this universe bears not also some remote inconceivable analogy to the other operations of nature and, among the rest, to the economy of human mind and thought. However reluctant, he must give his assent. Where then, cry I to both these antagonists, is the subject of your dispute? The theist allows that the original intelligence is very different from human reason; the atheist allows that the original principle of order bears some remote analogy to it. Will you quarrel, gentlemen, about the degrees and enter into a controversy which admits not of any precise meaning nor consequently of any determination? If you should be so obstinate, I should not be surprised to find you insensibly change sides; while the theist, on the one hand, exaggerates the dissimilarity between the Supreme Being and frail, imperfect, variable, fleeting, and mortal creatures, and the atheist, on the other, magnifies the analogy among all the operations of nature, in every period, every situation, and every position. Consider then where the real point of controversy lies; and if you cannot lay aside your disputes, endeavor, at least, to cure yourselves of your animosity.

And here I must also acknowledge, Cleanthes, that, as the works of nature have a much greater analogy to the effects of *our* art and contrivance than to those of *our* benevolence and justice, we have reason to infer that the natural attributes of the Deity have a greater resemblance to those of men than his moral have to human virtues. But what is the consequence? Nothing but this, that the moral qualities of man are more defective in their kind than his natural abilities. For, as the Supreme Being is allowed to be absolutely and entirely perfect, whatever differs most from him departs the farthest from the supreme standard of rectitude and perfection.*

These, Cleanthes, are my unfeigned sentiments on this subject; and these sentiments, you know, I have ever cherished

---

* It seems evident that the dispute between the skeptics and dogmatists is entirely verbal or, at least, regards only the degrees of doubt and assurance which we ought to indulge with regard to all reasoning; and such disputes are commonly, at the bottom, verbal and admit not of any precise determination. No philosophical dogmatist denies that there are difficulties both with regard to the senses and to all science and that these difficulties are, in a regular, logical method, absolutely insolvable. No skeptic denies that we lie under an absolute necessity, notwithstanding these difficulties, of thinking, and believing, and reasoning, with regard to all kinds of subjects, and even of frequently assenting with confidence and security. The only difference, then, between these sects, if they merit that name, is that the skeptic, from habit, caprice, or inclination, insists most on the difficulties, the dogmatist, for like reasons, on the necessity.

and maintained. But in proportion to my veneration for true religion is my abhorrence of vulgar superstitions; and I indulge a peculiar pleasure, I confess, in pushing such principles sometimes into absurdity, sometimes into impiety. And you are sensible that all bigots, notwithstanding their great aversion to the latter above the former, are commonly equally guilty of both.

My inclination, replied Cleanthes, lies, I own, a contrary way. Religion, however corrupted, is still better than no religion at all. The doctrine of a future state is so strong and necessary a security to morals that we never ought to abandon or neglect it. For if finite and temporary rewards and punishments have so great an effect, as we daily find, how much greater must be expected from such as are infinite and eternal?

How happens it then, said Philo, if vulgar superstition be so salutary to society, that all history abounds so much with accounts of its pernicious consequences on public affairs? Factions, civil wars, persecutions, subversions of government, oppression, slavery—these are the dismal consequences which always attend its prevalence over the minds of men. If the religious spirit be ever mentioned in any historical narration, we are sure to meet afterwards with a detail of the miseries which attend it. And no period of time can be happier or more prosperous than those in which it is never regarded or heard of.

The reason of this observation, replied Cleanthes, is obvious. The proper office of religion is to regulate the heart of men, humanize their conduct, infuse the spirit of temperance, order, and obedience; and, as its operation is silent and only enforces the motives of morality and justice, it is in danger of being overlooked and confounded with these other motives. When it distinguishes itself and acts as a separate principle over men, it has departed from its proper sphere and has become only a cover to faction and ambition.

And so will all religion, said Philo, except the philosophical and rational kind. Your reasonings are more easily eluded than my facts. The inference is not just—because finite and temporary rewards and punishments have so great influence that therefore such as are infinite and eternal must have so much greater. Consider, I beseech you, the attachment which we have to present things and the little concern which we discover for objects so remote and uncertain. When divines are declaiming against the common behavior and conduct of the world, they always represent this principle as the strongest imaginable (which indeed it is) and describe almost all human kind as lying under the influence of it and sunk into

358

the deepest lethargy and unconcern about their religious interests. Yet these same divines, when they refute their speculative antagonists, suppose the motives of religion to be so powerful that without them it were impossible for civil society to subsist, nor are they ashamed of so palpable a contradiction. It is certain, from experience, that the smallest grain of natural honesty and benevolence has more effect on men's conduct than the most pompous views suggested by theological theories and systems. A man's natural inclination works incessantly upon him; it is for ever present to the mind and mingles itself with every view and consideration; whereas religious motives, where they act at all, operate only by starts and bounds, and it is scarcely possible for them to become altogether habitual to the mind. The force of the greatest gravity, say the philosophers, is infinitely small in comparison of that of the least impulse, yet it is certain that the smallest gravity will, in the end, prevail above a great impulse, because no strokes or blows can be repeated with such constancy as attraction and gravitation.

Another advantage of inclination: it engages on its side all the wit and ingenuity of the mind and, when set in opposition to religious principles, seeks every method and art of eluding them, in which it is almost always successful. Who can explain the heart of man or account for those strange salvos and excuses with which people satisfy themselves when they follow their inclinations in opposition to their religious duty? This is well understood in the world; and none but fools ever repose less trust in a man because they fear that, from study and philosophy, he has entertained some speculative doubts with regard to theological subjects. And when we have to do with a man who makes a great profession of religion and devotion, has this any other effect upon several who pass for prudent than to put them on their guard, lest they be cheated and deceived by him?

We must further consider that philosophers, who cultivate reason and reflection, stand less in need of such motives to keep them under the restraint of morals and that the vulgar, who alone may need them, are utterly incapable of so pure a religion as represents the Deity to be pleased with nothing but virtue in human behavior. The recommendations to the Divinity are generally supposed to be either frivolous observances or rapturous ecstasies or a bigoted credulity. We need not run back into antiquity or wander into remote regions to find instances of this degeneracy. Amongst ourselves, some have been guilty of that atrociousness, unknown to the Egyptian and Grecian superstitions, of declaiming, in express terms, against morality and representing it as a sure forfeiture of the Divine favor if the least trust or reliance be laid upon it.

But even though superstition or enthusiasm should not put itself in direct opposition to morality, the very diverting of the attention, the raising up a new and frivolous species of merit, the preposterous distribution which it makes of praise and blame, must have the most pernicious consequences and weaken extremely men's attachment to the natural motives of justice and humanity.

Such a principle of action likewise, not being any of the familiar motives of human conduct, acts only by intervals on the temper and must be roused by continual efforts in order to render the pious zealot satisfied with his own conduct and make him fulfill his devotional task. Many religious exercises are entered into with seeming fervor where the heart, at the time, feels cold and languid. A habit of dissimulation is by degrees contracted, and fraud and falsehood become the predominant principle. Hence the reason of that vulgar observation that the highest zeal in religion and the deepest hypocrisy, so far from being inconsistent, are often or commonly united in the same individual character.

The bad effects of such habits, even in common life, are easily imagined, but, where the interests of religion are concerned, no morality can be forcible enough to bind the enthusiastic zealot. The sacredness of the cause sanctifies every measure which can be made use of to promote it.

The steady attention alone to so important an interest as that of eternal salvation is apt to extinguish the benevolent affections and beget a narrow, contracted selfishness. And when such a temper is encouraged, it easily eludes all the general precepts of charity and benevolence.

Thus, the motives of vulgar superstition have no great influence on general conduct, nor is their operation favorable to morality, in the instances where they predominate.

Is there any maxim in politics more certain and infallible than that both the number and authority of priests should be confined within very narrow limits and that the civil magistrate ought, for ever, to keep his *fasces* and *axes* from such dangerous hands? But if the spirit of popular religion were so salutary to society, a contrary maxim ought to prevail. The greater number of priests and their greater authority and riches will always augment the religious spirit. And though the priests have the guidance of this spirit, why may we not expect a superior sanctity of life and greater benevolence and moderation from persons who are set apart for religion, who are continually inculcating it upon others, and who must themselves imbibe a greater share of it? Whence comes it

360

then that, in fact, the utmost a wise magistrate can propose with regard to popular religions is, as far as possible, to make a saving game of it and to prevent their pernicious consequences with regard to society? Every expedient which he tries for so humble a purpose is surrounded with inconveniences. If he admits only one religion among his subjects, he must sacrifice, to an uncertain prospect of tranquillity, every consideration of public liberty, science, reason, industry, and even his own independence. If he gives indulgence to several sects, which is the wiser maxim, he must preserve every philosophical indifference to all of them and carefully restrain the pretensions of the prevailing sect, otherwise he can expect nothing but endless disputes, quarrels, factions, persecutions, and civil commotions.

True religion, I allow, has no such pernicious consequences; but we must treat of religion as it has commonly been found in the world, nor have I anything to do with that speculative tenet of theism which, as it is a species of philosophy, must partake of the beneficial influence of that principle and, at the same time, must lie under a like inconvenience of being always confined to very few persons.

Oaths are requisite in all courts of judicature, but it is a question whether their authority arises from any popular religion. It is the solemnity and importance of the occasion, the regard to reputation, and the reflecting on the general interests of society which are the chief restraints upon mankind. Customhouse oaths and political oaths are but little regarded, even by some who pretend to principles of honesty and religion; and a Quaker's asseveration is with us justly put upon the same footing with the oath of any other person. I know that Polybius * ascribes the infamy of Greek faith to the prevalence of the Epicurean philosophy; but I know also that Punic faith had as bad a reputation in ancient times as Irish evidence has in modern, though we cannot account for these vulgar observations by the same reason. Not to mention that Greek faith was infamous before the rise of the Epicurean philosophy; and Euripides,† in a passage which I shall point out to you, has glanced a remarkable stroke of satire against his nation with regard to this circumstance.

Take care, Philo, replied Cleanthes, take care; push not matters too far, allow not your zeal against false religion to undermine your veneration for the true. Forfeit not this principle—the chief, the only great comfort in life and our principal support amidst all the attacks of adverse fortune. The

* Lib. vi. cap. 54.
† *Iphigenia in Tauride.*

most agreeable reflection which it is possible for human imagination to suggest is that of genuine theism, which represents us as the workmanship of a Being perfectly good, wise, and powerful; who created us for happiness; and who, having implanted in us immeasurable desires of good, will prolong our existence to all eternity and will transfer us into an infinite variety of scenes, in order to satisfy those desires and render our felicity complete and durable. Next to such a Being himself (if the comparison be allowed), the happiest lot which we can imagine is that of being under his guardianship and protection.

These appearances, said Philo, are most engaging and alluring, and, with regard to the true philosopher, they are more than appearances. But it happens here, as in the former case, that, with regard to the greater part of mankind, the appearances are deceitful and that the terrors of religion commonly prevail above its comforts.

It is allowed that men never have recourse to devotion so readily as when dejected with grief or depressed with sickness. Is not this a proof that the religious spirit is not so nearly allied to joy as to sorrow?

But men, when afflicted, find consolation in religion, replied Cleanthes. Sometimes, said Philo; but it is natural to imagine that they will form a notion of those unknown beings, suitable to the present gloom and melancholy of their temper, when they betake themselves to the contemplation of them. Accordingly, we find the tremendous images to predominate in all religions; and we ourselves, after having employed the most exalted expression in our descriptions of the Deity, fall into the flattest contradiction in affirming that the damned are infinitely superior in number to the elect.

I shall venture to affirm that there never was a popular religion which represented the state of departed souls in such a light as would render it eligible for human kind that there should be such a state. These fine models of religion are the mere product of philosophy. For as death lies between the eye and the prospect of futurity, that event is so shocking to nature that it must throw a gloom on all the regions which lie beyond it and suggest to the generality of mankind the idea of Cerberus and Furies, devils, and torrents of fire and brimstone.

It is true, both fear and hope enter into religion because both these passions, at different times, agitate the human mind, and each of them forms a species of divinity suitable to itself. But when a man is in a cheerful disposition, he is fit for business, or company, or entertainment of any kind; and he naturally applies himself to these and thinks not of religion. When melancholy and dejected, he has nothing to do but brood upon the terrors of the invisible world and to plunge himself still deeper in affliction. It may indeed happen that, after he has, in this manner, engraved the religious opinions deep into his thought and imagination, there may arrive a change of health or circumstances which may restore his good humor and, raising cheerful prospects of futurity, make him run into the other extreme of joy and triumph. But still it must be acknowledged that, as terror is the primary principle of religion, it is the passion which always predominates in it and admits but of short intervals of pleasure.

Not to mention that these fits of excessive, enthusiastic joy, by exhausting the spirits, always prepare the way for equal fits of superstitious terror and dejection, nor is there any state of mind so happy as the calm and equable. But this state it is impossible to support where a man thinks that he lies in such profound darkness and uncertainty between an eternity of happiness and an eternity of misery. No wonder that such an opinion disjoints the ordinary frame of the mind and throws it unto the utmost confusion. And though that opinion is seldom so steady in its operation as to influence all the actions, yet it is apt to make a considerable breach in the temper and to produce that gloom and melancholy so remarkable in all devout people.

It is contrary to common sense to entertain apprehensions or terrors upon account of any opinion whatsoever or to imagine that we run any risk hereafter by the freest use of our reason. Such a sentiment implies both an *absurdity* and an *inconsistency*. It is an absurdity to believe that the Deity has human passions, and one of the lowest of human passions, a restless appetite for applause. It is an inconsistency to believe that, since the Deity has this human passion, he has not others also, and, in particular, a disregard to the opinions of creatures so much inferior.

To know God, says Seneca, *is to worship him.* All other worship is indeed absurd, superstitious, and even impious. It degrades him to the low condition of mankind, who are delighted with entreaty, solicitation, presents, and flattery. Yet is this impiety the smallest of which superstition is guilty. Commonly, it depresses the Deity far below the condition of mankind and represents him as a capricious demon who exercises his power without reason and without humanity! And were that Divine Being disposed to be offended at the vices and follies of silly mortals, who are his own workmanship, ill would it surely fare with the votaries of most popular superstitions. Nor would any of human race merit his *favor* but a very few, the philosophical theists, who entertain or rather indeed endeavor to entertain suitable notions of his Divine perfections. As the only persons entitled to his *compassion* and *indulgence* would be the philosophical skeptics, a sect almost equally rare, who, from a natural diffidence of their own capacity, suspend or endeavor to suspend all judgment with regard to such sublime and such extraordinary subjects.

If the whole of natural theology, as some people seem to maintain, resolves itself into one simple, though somewhat ambiguous, at least undefined, proposition, *that the cause or causes of order in the universe probably bear some remote analogy to human intelligence*—if this proposition be not capable of extension, variation, or more particular explication, if it affords no inference that affects human life or can be the source of any action or forbearance, and if the analogy, imperfect as it is, can be carried no further than to the human intelligence and cannot be transferred, with any appearance of probability, to the other qualities of the mind, if this really be the case, what can the most inquisitive, contemplative, and religious man do more than give a plain, philosophical assent to the proposition, as often as it occurs, and believe that the arguments on which it is established exceed the objections which lie against it? Some astonishment, indeed, will naturally arise from the greatness of the object, some melancholy from its obscurity, some contempt of human reason that it can give no solution more satisfactory with regard to so extraordinary and magnificent a question. But believe me, Cleanthes, the most natural sentiment which a well-disposed mind will feel on this occasion is a longing desire and expectation that Heaven would be pleased to dissipate, at least alleviate, this profound ignorance by affording some more particular revelation to mankind and making discoveries of the nature, attributes, and operations of the Divine object of our faith. A person, seasoned with a just sense of the imperfections of natural reason, will fly to revealed truth with the greatest avidity, while the haughty dogmatist, persuaded that he can erect a complete system of theology by the mere help of philosophy, disdains any further aid and rejects this adventitious instructor. To be a philosophical skeptic is, in a man of letters, the first and most essential step towards being a sound, believing Christian—a proposition which I would willingly recommend to the attention of Pamphilus; and I hope Cleanthes will forgive me for interposing so far in the education and instruction of his pupil.

Cleanthes and Philo pursued not this conversation much further; and as nothing ever made greater impression on me than all the reasonings of that day, so I confess that, upon a serious review of the whole, I cannot but think that Philo's principles are more probable than Demea's, but that those of Cleanthes approach still nearer to the truth.

Of the Standard of Taste

The great variety of taste, as well as of opinion, which prevails in the world is too obvious not to have fallen under everyone's observation. Men of the most confined knowledge are able to remark a difference of taste in the narrow circle of their acquaintance, even where the persons have been educated under the same government and have early imbibed the same prejudices. But those who can enlarge their view to contemplate distant nations and remote ages are still more surprised at the great inconsistency and contrariety. We are apt to call barbarous whatever departs widely from our own taste and apprehension, but soon find the epithet of reproach retorted on us. And the highest arrogance and self-conceit is at last startled on observing an equal assurance on all sides and scruples, amidst such a contest of sentiment, to pronounce positively in its own favor.

As this variety of taste is obvious to the most careless inquirer, so will it be found, on examination, to be still greater in reality than in appearance. The sentiments of men often differ with regard to beauty and deformity of all kinds, even while their general discourse is the same. There are certain terms in every language which import blame, and others praise, and all men who use the same tongue must agree in their application of them. Every voice is united in applauding elegance, propriety, simplicity, spirit in writing and in blaming fustian, affectation, coldness, and a false brilliancy. But when critics come to particulars, this seeming unanimity vanishes, and it is found that they had affixed a very different meaning to their expressions. In all matters of opinion and science, the case is opposite. The difference among men is there oftener found to lie in generals than in particulars and to be less in reality than in appearance. An explanation of the terms commonly ends the controversy, and the disputants are surprised to find that they had been quarreling, while at bottom they agreed in their judgment.

Those who found morality on sentiment more than on reason are inclined to comprehend ethics under the former observation and to maintain that in all questions which regard conduct and manners, the difference among men is really greater than at first sight it appears. It is indeed obvious that writers of all nations and all ages concur in applauding justice, humanity, magnanimity, prudence, veracity, and in blaming the opposite qualities. Even poets and other authors whose compositions are chiefly calculated to please the imagination are yet found, from Homer down to Fénelon, to inculcate the same moral precepts and to bestow their applause and blame on the same virtues and vices. This great unanimity is usually ascribed to the influence of plain reason which, in all these cases, maintains similar sentiments in all men and prevents those controversies to which the abstract sciences are so much exposed. So far as the unanimity is real, this account may be admitted as satisfactory; but we must also allow that some part of the seeming harmony in morals may be accounted for from the very nature of language. The word *virtue*, with its equivalent in every tongue, implies praise, as that of *vice* does blame; and no one, without the most obvious and grossest impropriety, could affix reproach to a term which in general acceptation is understood in a good sense or bestow applause where the idiom requires disapprobation. Homer's general precepts, where he delivers any such, will never be controverted, but it is obvious that when he draws particular pictures of manners and represents heroism in Achilles and prudence in Ulysses, he intermixes a much greater degree of ferocity in the former and of cunning and fraud in the latter than Fénelon would admit of. The sage Ulysses in the Greek poet seems to delight in lies and fictions and often employs them without any necessity or even advantage; but his more scrupulous son, in the French epic writer, exposes himself to the most imminent perils rather than depart from the most exact line of truth and veracity.

The admirers and followers of the *Alcoran* insist on the excellent moral precepts interspersed throughout that wild and absurd performance. But it is to be supposed that the Arabic words which correspond to the English *equity, justice, temperance, meekness, charity* were such as, from the constant use of that tongue, must always be taken in a good sense; and it would have argued the greatest ignorance, not of morals, but of language, to have mentioned them with any epithets besides those of applause and approbation. But would we know whether the pretended prophet had really attained a just sentiment of morals? Let us attend to his narration, and we shall soon find that he bestows praise on such instances of treachery, inhumanity, cruelty, revenge, bigotry, as are utterly incompatible with civilized society. No steady rule of right seems there to be attended to, and every action is blamed or praised so far only as it is beneficial or hurtful to the true believers.

The merit of delivering true general precepts in ethics is indeed very small. Whoever recommends any moral virtues really does no more than is implied in the terms themselves. That people who invented the word *charity* and used it in a good sense inculcated more clearly and much more efficaciously the precept *be charitable* than any pretended legislator or prophet who would insert such a *maxim* in his writings. Of all expressions, those which, together with their other meaning, imply a degree either of blame or approbation are the least liable to be perverted or mistaken.

It is natural for us to seek a *standard of taste,* a rule by which the various sentiments of men may be reconciled, [or] at least a decision afforded, confirming one sentiment and condemning another.

There is a species of philosophy which cuts off all hopes of success in such an attempt and represents the impossibility of ever attaining any standard of taste. The difference, it is said, is very wide between judgment and sentiment. All sentiment is right, because sentiment has a reference to nothing beyond itself and is always real, wherever a man is conscious of it. But all determinations of the understanding are not right, because they have a reference to something beyond themselves, to wit, real matter of fact, and are not always conformable to that standard. Among a thousand different opinions which different men may entertain of the same subject, there is one, and but one, that is just and true, and the only difficulty is to fix and ascertain it. On the contrary, a thousand different sentiments excited by the same object are all right, because no sentiment represents what is really in the object. It only marks a certain conformity of relation, between the object and the organs or faculties of the mind, and if that conformity did not really exist, the sentiment could never possibly have being. Beauty is no quality in things themselves; it exists merely in the mind which contemplates them, and each mind perceives a different beauty. One person may even perceive deformity where another is sensible of beauty, and every individual ought to acquiesce in his own sentiment without pretending to regulate those of others. To seek the real beauty or real deformity is as fruitless an inquiry as to pretend to ascertain the real sweet or real bitter. According to the disposition of the organs, the same object may be both sweet and bitter, and the proverb has justly determined it to be fruitless to dispute concerning tastes. It is very natural, and even quite necessary, to extend this axiom to mental as well as bodily taste;

and thus common sense, which is so often at variance with philosophy, especially with the skeptical kind, is found, in one instance at least, to agree in pronouncing the same decision.

But though this axiom, by passing into a proverb, seems to have attained the sanction of common sense, there is certainly a species of common sense which opposes it, [or] at least serves to modify and restrain it. Whoever would assert an equality of genius and elegance between Ogilby and Milton, or Bunyan and Addison, would be thought to defend no less an extravagance than if he had maintained a molehill to be as high as Teneriffe or a pond as extensive as the ocean. Though there may be found persons who give the preference to the former authors, no one pays attention to such a taste, and we pronounce without scruple the sentiment of these pretended critics to be absurd and ridiculous. The principle of the natural equality of tastes is then totally forgotten, and while we admit it on some occasions, where the objects seem near an equality, it appears an extravagant paradox, or rather a palpable absurdity, where objects so disproportionate are compared together.

It is evident that none of the rules of composition are fixed by reasonings *a priori* or can be esteemed abstract conclusions of the understanding from comparing those habitudes and relations of ideas which are eternal and immutable. Their foundation is the same with that of all the practical sciences, experience; nor are they anything but general observations concerning what has been universally found to please in all countries and in all ages. Many of the beauties of poetry and even of eloquence are founded on falsehood and fiction, on hyperboles, metaphors, and an abuse or perversion of terms from their natural meaning. To check the sallies of the imagination and to reduce every expression to geometrical truth and exactness would be the most contrary to the laws of criticism, because it would produce a work which, by universal experience, has been found the most insipid and disagreeable. But though poetry can never submit to exact truth, it must be confined by rules of art, discovered to the author either by genius or observation. If some negligent or irregular writers have pleased, they have not pleased by their transgressions of rule or order, but in spite of these transgressions; they have possessed other beauties which were conformable to just criticism, and the force of these beauties has been able to overpower censure and give the mind a satisfaction superior to the disgust arising from the blemishes. Ariosto pleases, but not by his monstrous and improbable fictions, by his bizarre mixture of the serious and comic styles, by the want of coherence in his stories, or by the continual interruptions of his narration. He charms by the force and clearness of his expression, by the readiness and variety of his inventions, and by his natural pictures of the passions, especially those of the gay and amorous kind; and however his faults may diminish our satisfaction, they are not able entirely to destroy it. Did our pleasure really arise from those parts of his poem which we denominate faults, this would be no objection to criticism in general; it would only be an objection to those particular rules of criticism which would establish such circumstances to be faults and would represent them as universally blamable. If they are found to please, they cannot be faults, let the pleasure which they produce be ever so unexpected and unaccountable.

But though all the general rules of art are founded only on experience and on the observation of the common sentiments of human nature, we must not imagine that, on every occasion, the feelings of men will be comfortable to these rules. Those finer emotions of the mind are of a very tender and delicate nature and require the concurrence of many favorable circumstances to make them play with facility and exactness, according to their general and established principles. The least exterior hindrance to such small springs, or the least internal disorder, disturbs their motion and confounds the operation of the whole machine. When we would make an experiment of this nature and would try the force of any beauty or deformity, we must choose with care a proper time and place and bring the fancy to a suitable situation and disposition. A perfect serenity of mind, a recollection of thought, a due attention to the object; if any of these circumstances be wanting, our experiment will be fallacious, and we shall be unable to judge of the catholic and universal beauty. The relation which nature has placed between the form and the sentiment will at least be more obscure, and it will require greater accuracy to trace and discern it. We shall be able to ascertain its influence not so much from the operation of each particular beauty as from the durable admiration which attends those works that have survived all the caprices of mode and fashion, all the mistakes of ignorance and envy.

The same Homer who pleased at Athens and Rome two thousand years ago is still admired at Paris and at London. All the changes of climate, government, religion, and language have not been able to obscure his glory. Authority or prejudice may give a temporary vogue to a bad poet or orator, but his reputation will never be durable or general. When his compositions are examined by posterity or by foreigners, the enchantment is dissipated, and his faults appear in their

371

true colors. On the contrary, a real genius, the longer his works endure and the more wide they are spread, the more sincere is the admiration which he meets with. Envy and jealousy have too much place in a narrow circle, and even familiar acquaintance with his person may diminish the applause due to his performances. But when these obstructions are removed, the beauties which are naturally fitted to excite agreeable sentiments immediately display their energy, and while the world endures, they maintain their authority over the minds of men.

It appears, then, that amidst all the variety and caprice of taste, there are certain general principles of approbation or blame whose influence a careful eye may trace in all operations of the mind. Some particular forms or qualities, from the original structure of the internal fabric, are calculated to please, and others to displease; and if they fail of their effect in any particular instance, it is from some apparent defect or imperfection in the organ. A man in a fever would not insist on his palate as able to decide concerning flavors; nor would one affected with the jaundice pretend to give a verdict with regard to colors. In each creature, there is a sound and a defective state, and the former alone can be supposed to afford us a true standard of taste and sentiment. If in the sound state of the organ there be an entire or a considerable uniformity of sentiment among men, we may thence derive an idea of the perfect beauty, in like manner as the appearance of objects in daylight, to the eye of a man in health, is denominated their true and real color, even while color is allowed to be merely a phantasm of the senses.

Many and frequent are the defects in the internal organs which prevent or weaken the influence of those general principles on which depends our sentiment of beauty or deformity. Though some objects, by the structure of the mind, be naturally calculated to give pleasure, it is not to be expected that in every individual the pleasure will be equally felt. Particular incidents and situations occur which either throw a false light on the objects or hinder the true from conveying to the imagination the proper sentiment and perception.

One obvious cause why many feel not the proper sentiment of beauty is the want of that *delicacy* of imagination which is requisite to convey a sensibility of those finer emotions. This delicacy everyone pretends to; everyone talks of it and would reduce every kind of taste or sentiment to its standard. But as our intention in this essay is to mingle some light of the understanding with the feelings of sentiment, it will be proper to give a more accurate definition of delicacy than has hitherto been attempted. And not to draw our philosophy from too profound a source, we shall have recourse to a noted story in *Don Quixote*.

It is with good reason, says Sancho to the squire with the great nose, that I pretend to have a judgment in wine; this is a quality hereditary in our family. Two of my kinsmen were once called to give their opinion of a hogshead which was supposed to be excellent, being old and of a good vintage. One of them tastes it, considers it, and, after mature reflection, pronounces the wine to be good, were it not for a small taste of leather which he perceived in it. The other, after using the same precautions, gives also his verdict in favor of the wine, but with the reserve of a taste of iron, which he could easily distinguish. You cannot imagine how much they were both ridiculed for their judgment. But who laughed in the end? On emptying the hogshead, there was found at the bottom an old key with a leathern thong tied to it.

The great resemblance between mental and bodily taste will easily teach us to apply this story. Though it be certain that beauty and deformity, [no] more than sweet and bitter, are not qualities in objects, but belong entirely to the sentiment, internal or external, it must be allowed that there are certain qualities in objects which are fitted by nature to produce those particular feelings. Now, as these qualities may be found in a small degree, or may be mixed and confounded with each other, it often happens that the taste is not affected with such minute qualities, or is not able to distinguish all the particular flavors, amidst the disorder in which they are presented. Where the organs are so fine as to allow nothing to escape them, and at the same time so exact as to perceive every ingredient in the composition, this we call delicacy of taste, whether we employ these terms in the literal or metaphorical sense. Here, then, the general rules of beauty are of use, being drawn from established models and from the observation of what pleases or displeases when presented singly and in a high degree. And if the same qualities, in a continued composition and in a smaller degree, affect not the organs with a sensible delight or uneasiness, we exclude the person from all pretensions to this delicacy. To produce these general rules or avowed patterns of composition is like finding the key with the leathern thong which justified the verdict of Sancho's kinsmen and confounded those pretended judges who had condemned them. Though the hogshead had never been emptied, the taste of the one was still equally delicate, and that of the other equally dull and languid, but it would have been more difficult to have proved the superiority of the former to the conviction of every bystander. In like manner, though the beauties of writing had never been methodized or reduced to general principles, though no excellent models had ever been acknowledged, the different degrees of taste would still have subsisted and the judgment of one man been preferable to that of another; but it would not have been so easy to silence the bad critic, who might always insist upon his particular sentiment and refuse to submit to his antagonist. But when we show him an avowed principle of art, when we illustrate this principle by examples whose operation, from his own particular taste, he acknowledges to be conformable to the principle, when we prove that the same principle may be applied to the present case, where he did not perceive or feel its influence, he must conclude, upon the whole, that the fault lies in himself and that he wants the delicacy which is requisite to make him sensible of every beauty and every blemish in any composition or discourse.

It is acknowledged to be the perfection of every sense or faculty to perceive with exactness its most minute objects and allow nothing to escape its notice and observation. The smaller the objects are which become sensible to the eye, the finer is that organ and the more elaborate its make and composition. A good palate is not tried by strong flavors but by a mixture of small ingredients, where we are still sensible of each part, notwithstanding its minuteness and its confusion with the rest. In like manner, a quick and acute perception of beauty and deformity must be the perfection of our mental taste; nor can a man be satisfied with himself while he suspects that any excellence or blemish in a discourse has passed him unobserved. In this case, the perfection of the man and the perfection of the sense or feeling are found to be united. A very delicate palate, on many occasions, may be a great inconvenience both to a man himself and to his friends, but a delicate taste of wit or beauty must always be a desirable quality, because it is the source of all the finest and most innocent enjoyments of which human nature is susceptible. In this decision, the sentiments of all mankind are agreed. Wherever you can ascertain a delicacy of taste, it is sure to meet with approbation, and the best way of ascertaining it is to appeal to those models and principles which have been established by the uniform consent and experience of nations and ages.

But though there be naturally a wide difference in point of delicacy between one person and another, nothing tends further to increase and improve this talent than *practice* in a particular art and the frequent survey or contemplation of a particular species of beauty. When objects of any kind are first presented to the eye or imagination, the sentiment which attends them is obscure and confused, and the mind is, in a great measure, incapable of pronouncing concerning their merits or defects. The taste cannot perceive the several excellencies of the performance, much less distinguish the particular character of each excellency and ascertain its quality and degree. If it pronounces the whole in general to be beautiful or deformed, it is the utmost that can be expected, and even this judgment a person so unpracticed will be apt to deliver with great hesitation and reserve. But allow him to acquire experience in those objects, his feeling becomes more exact and nice; he not only perceives the beauties and defects of each part, but marks the distinguishing species of each quality and assigns it suitable praise or blame. A clear and distinct sentiment attends him through the whole survey of the objects, and he discerns that very degree and kind of approbation or displeasure which each part is naturally fitted to produce. The mist dissipates which seemed formerly to hang over the object; the organ acquires greater perfection in its operations and can pronounce, without danger of mistake, concerning the merits of every performance. In a word, the same address and dexterity which practice gives to the execution of any work is also acquired by the same means in the judging of it.

So advantageous is practice to the discernment of beauty that, before we can give judgment on any work of importance, it will even be requisite that that very individual performance be more than once perused by us and be surveyed in different lights with attention and deliberation. There is a flutter or hurry of thought which attends the first perusal of any piece and which confounds the genuine sentiment of beauty. The relation of the parts is not discerned; the true characters of style are little distinguished; the several perfections and defects seem wrapped up in a species of confusion and present themselves indistinctly to the imagination. Not to mention that there is a species of beauty which, as it is florid and superficial, pleases at first, but being found incompatible with a just expression either of reason or passion, soon palls upon the taste and is then rejected with disdain, [or] at least rated at a much lower value.

It is impossible to continue in the practice of contemplating any order of beauty without being frequently obliged to form *comparisons* between the several species and degrees of excellence and estimating their proportion to each other. A man who has had no opportunity of comparing the different kinds of beauty is indeed totally unqualified to pronounce an opinion with regard to any object presented him. By comparison alone we fix the epithets of praise or blame and learn how to assign the due degree of each. The coarsest daubing

375

contains a certain luster of colors and exactness of imitation which are so far beauties and would affect the mind of a peasant or Indian with the highest admiration. The most vulgar ballads are not entirely destitute of harmony or nature, and none but a person familiarized to superior beauties would pronounce their numbers harsh or narration uninteresting. A great inferiority of beauty gives pain to a person conversant in the highest excellence of the kind and is for that reason pronounced a deformity, as the most finished object with which we are acquainted is naturally supposed to have reached the pinnacle of perfection and to be entitled to the highest applause. One accustomed to see and examine and weigh the several performances admired in different ages and nations can alone rate the merits of a work exhibited to his view and assign its proper rank among the productions of genius.

But to enable a critic the more fully to execute this undertaking, he must preserve his mind free from all *prejudice* and allow nothing to enter into his consideration but the very object which is submitted to his examination. We may observe that every work of art, in order to produce its due effect on the mind, must be surveyed in a certain point of view and cannot be fully relished by persons whose situation, real or imaginary, is not conformable to that which is required by the performance. An orator addresses himself to a particular audience and must have a regard to their particular genius, interests, opinions, passions, and prejudices; otherwise he hopes in vain to govern their resolutions and inflame their affections. Should they even have entertained some prepossessions against him, however unreasonable, he must not overlook this disadvantage, but, before he enters upon the subject, must endeavor to conciliate their affection and acquire their good graces. A critic of a different age or nation who should peruse this discourse must have all these circumstances in his eye and must place himself in the same situation as the audience in order to form a true judgment of the oration. In like manner, when any work is addressed to the public, though I should have a friendship or enmity with the author, I must depart from this situation, and considering myself as a man in general, forget, if possible, my individual being and my peculiar circumstances. A person influenced by prejudice complies not with this condition, but obstinately maintains his natural position without placing himself in that point of view which the performance supposes. If the work be addressed to persons of a different age or nation, he makes no allowance for their peculiar views and prejudices, but, full of the manners of his own age and country, rashly condemns what seemed admirable in the eyes of those for whom alone the discourse was calculated. If the work be executed for the public, he never sufficiently enlarges his comprehension or forgets his interest as a friend or enemy, as a rival or commentator. By this means, his sentiments are perverted; nor have the same beauties and blemishes the same influence upon him as if he had imposed a proper violence on his imagination and had forgotten himself for a moment. So far his taste evidently departs from the true standard and of consequence loses all credit and authority.

It is well known that in all questions submitted to the understanding, prejudice is destructive of sound judgment and perverts all operations of the intellectual faculties. It is no less contrary to good taste, nor has it less influence to corrupt our sentiment of beauty. It belongs to *good sense* to check its influence in both cases, and in this respect, as well as in many others, reason, if not an essential part of taste, is at least requisite to the operations of this latter faculty. In all the nobler productions of genius, there is a mutual relation and correspondence of parts; nor can either the beauties or blemishes be perceived by him whose thought is not capacious enough to comprehend all those parts and compare them with each other in order to perceive the consistency and uniformity of the whole. Every work of art has also a certain end or purpose for which it is calculated and is to be deemed more or less perfect as it is more or less fitted to attain this end. The object of eloquence is to persuade, of history to instruct, of poetry to please by means of the passions and the imagination. These ends we must carry constantly in our view when we peruse any performance, and we must be able to judge how far the means employed are adapted to their respective purposes. Besides, every kind of composition, even the most poetical, is nothing but a chain of propositions and reasonings, not always, indeed, the justest and most exact, but still plausible and specious, however disguised by the coloring of the imagination. The persons introduced in tragedy and epic poetry must be represented as reasoning and thinking and concluding and acting suitably to their character and circumstances, and without judgment, as well as taste and invention, a poet can never hope to succeed in so delicate an undertaking. Not to mention that the same excellence of faculties which contributes to the improvement of reason, the same clearness of conception, the same exactness of distinction, the same vivacity of apprehension, are essential to the operations of true taste and are its infallible concomitants. It seldom or never happens that a man of sense who has experience in any art cannot judge of its beauty, and it is no less rare to meet with a man who has a just taste without a sound understanding.

Thus, though the principles of taste be universal and nearly, if not entirely, the same in all men, yet few are qualified to give judgment on any work of art or establish their own sentiment as the standard of beauty. The organs of internal sensation are seldom so perfect as to allow the general principles their full play and produce a feeling correspondent to those principles. They either labor under some defect or are vitiated by some disorder and by that means excite a sentiment which may be pronounced erroneous. When the critic has no delicacy, he judges without any distinction and is only affected by the grosser and more palpable qualities of the object; the finer touches pass unnoticed and disregarded. Where he is not aided by practice, his verdict is attended with confusion and hesitation. Where no comparison has been employed, the most frivolous beauties, such as rather merit the name of defects, are the object of his admiration. Where he lies under the influence of prejudice, all his natural sentiments are perverted. Where good sense is wanting, he is not qualified to discern the beauties of design and reasoning, which are the highest and most excellent. Under some or other of these imperfections, the generality of men labor, and hence a true judge in the finer arts is observed, even during the most polished ages, to be so rare a character. Strong sense, united to delicate sentiment, improved by practice, perfected by comparison, and cleared of all prejudice, can alone entitle critics to this valuable character, and the joint verdict of such, wherever they are to be found, is the true standard of taste and of beauty.

But where are such critics to be found? By what marks are they to be known? How distinguish them from pretenders? These questions are embarrassing and seem to throw us back into the same uncertainty from which, during the course of this essay, we have endeavored to extricate ourselves.

But if we consider the matter aright, these are questions of fact, not of sentiment. Whether any particular person be endowed with good sense and a delicate imagination, free from prejudice, may often be the subject of dispute and be liable to great discussion and inquiry, but that such a character is valuable and estimable will be agreed in by all mankind. Where these doubts occur, men can do no more than in other disputable questions which are submitted to the understanding: they must produce the best arguments that their invention suggests to them; they must acknowledge a true and decisive standard to exist somewhere, to wit, real existence and matter of fact; and they must have indulgence to such as differ from them in their appeals to this standard. It is sufficient for our present purpose if we have proved that the taste of all individuals is not upon an equal footing and that some men in general, however difficult to be particularly pitched upon, will be acknowledged by universal sentiment to have a preference above others.

But in reality, the difficulty of finding, even in particulars, the standard of taste is not so great as it is represented. Though in speculation we may readily avow a certain criterion in science and deny it in sentiment, the matter is found in practice to be much more hard to ascertain in the former case than in the latter. Theories of abstract philosophy, systems of profound theology have prevailed during one age; in a successive period, these have been universally exploded, their absurdity has been detected, other theories and systems have supplied their place, which again gave place to their successors, and nothing has been experienced more liable to the revolutions of chance and fashion than these pretended decisions of science. The case is not the same with the beauties of eloquence and poetry. Just expressions of passion and nature are sure, after a little time, to gain public applause, which they maintain forever. Aristotle and Plato and Epicurus and Descartes may successively yield to each other, but Terence and Virgil maintain a universal, undisputed empire over the minds of men. The abstract philosophy of Cicero has lost its credit; the vehemence of his oratory is still the object of our admiration.

Though men of delicate taste be rare, they are easily to be distinguished in society by the soundness of their understanding and the superiority of their faculties above the rest of mankind. The ascendant which they acquire gives a prevalence to that lively approbation with which they receive any productions of genius and renders it generally predominant. Many men, when left to themselves, have but a faint and dubious perception of beauty who yet are capable of relishing any fine stroke which is pointed out to them. Every convert to the admiration of the real poet or orator is the cause of some new conversion. And though prejudices may prevail for a time, they never unite in celebrating any rival to the true genius, but yield at last to the force of nature and just sentiment. Thus, though a civilized nation may easily be mistaken in the choice of their admired philosopher, they never have been found long to err in their affection for a favorite epic or tragic author.

But notwithstanding all our endeavors to fix a standard of taste and reconcile the discordant apprehensions of men, there still remain two sources of variation which are not sufficient indeed to confound all the boundaries of beauty and deformity, but will often serve to produce a difference in the degrees of our approbation or blame. The one is the different humors of particular men; the other, the particular manners and opinions of our age and country. The general principles of taste are uniform in human nature; where men vary in their judgments, some defect or perversion in the faculties may commonly be remarked, proceeding either from prejudice, from want of practice, or from want of delicacy, and there is just reason for approving one taste and condemning another. But where there is such a diversity in the internal frame or external situation as is entirely blameless on both sides and leaves no room to give one the preference above the other, in that case a certain degree of diversity in judgment is unavoidable, and we seek in vain for a standard by which we can reconcile the contrary sentiments.

A young man whose passions are warm will be more sensibly touched with amorous and tender images than a man more advanced in years who takes pleasure in wise, philosophical reflections concerning the conduct of life and moderation of the passions. At twenty, Ovid may be the favorite author, Horace at forty, and perhaps Tacitus at fifty. Vainly would we, in such cases, endeavor to enter into the sentiments of others and divest ourselves of those propensities which are natural to us. We choose our favorite author, as we do our friend, from a conformity of humor and disposition. Mirth or passion, sentiment or reflection, whichever of these most predominates in our temper, it gives us a peculiar sympathy with the writer who resembles us.

One person is more pleased with the sublime, another with the tender, a third with raillery. One has a strong sensibility to blemishes and is extremely studious of correctness; another has a more lively feeling of beauties and pardons twenty absurdities and defects for one elevated or pathetic stroke. The ear of this man is entirely turned toward conciseness and energy; that man is delighted with a copious, rich, and harmonious expression. Simplicity is affected by one, ornament by another. Comedy, tragedy, satire, odes have each its partisans who prefer that particular species of writing to all others. It is plainly an error in a critic to confine his approbation to one species or style of writing and condemn all the rest. But it is almost impossible not to feel a predilection for that which suits our particular turn and disposition. Such preferences are innocent and unavoidable and can never reasonably be the object of dispute because there is no standard by which they can be decided.

For a like reason, we are more pleased, in the course of

our reading, with pictures and characters that resemble objects which are found in our own age or country than with those which describe a different set of customs. It is not without some effort that we reconcile ourselves to the simplicity of ancient manners and behold princesses carrying water from the spring and kings and heroes dressing their own victuals. We may allow in general that the representation of such manners is no fault in the author nor deformity in the piece, but we are not so sensibly touched with them. For this reason, comedy is not easily transferred from one age or nation to another. A Frenchman or Englishman is not pleased with the *Andria* of Terence, or *Clitia* of Machiavelli, where the fine lady upon whom all the play turns never once appears to the spectators, but is always kept behind the scenes, suitably to the reserved humor of the ancient Greeks and modern Italians. A man of learning and reflection can make allowance for these peculiarities of manners, but a common audience can never divest themselves so far of their usual ideas and sentiments as to relish pictures which nowise resemble them.

But here there occurs a reflection which may, perhaps, be useful in examining the celebrated controversy concerning ancient and modern learning, where we often find the one side excusing any seeming absurdity in the ancients from the manners of the age, and the other refusing to admit this excuse, or at least admitting it only as an apology for the author, not for the performance. In my opinion, the proper boundaries in this subject have seldom been fixed between the contending parties. Where any innocent peculiarities of manners are represented, such as those abovementioned, they ought certainly to be admitted, and a man who is shocked with them gives an evident proof of false delicacy and refinement. The poet's *monument more durable than brass* must fall to the ground like common brick or clay were men to make no allowance for the continual revolutions of manners and customs and would admit of nothing but what was suitable to the prevailing fashion. Must we throw aside the pictures of our ancestors because of their ruffs and fardingales? But where the ideas of morality and decency alter from one age to another and where vicious manners are described without being marked with the proper characters of blame and disapprobation, this must be allowed to disfigure the poem and to be a real deformity. I cannot, nor is it proper I should, enter into such sentiments, and however I may excuse the poet on account of the manners of his age, I never can relish the composition. The want of humanity and of decency so conspicuous in the characters drawn by several of the ancient poets, even sometimes by Homer and the Greek tragedians, diminishes considerably the merit of their noble performances and gives modern authors an advantage over them. We are not interested in the fortunes and sentiments of such rough heroes; we are displeased to find the limits of vice and virtue so much confounded; and whatever indulgence we may give to the writer on account of his prejudices, we cannot prevail on ourselves to enter into his sentiments or bear an affection to characters which we plainly discover to be blamable.

The case is not the same with moral principles as with speculative opinions of any kind. These are in continual flux and revolution. The son embraces a different system from the father. Nay, there scarcely is any man who can boast of great constancy and uniformity in this particular. Whatever speculative errors may be found in the polite writings of any age or country, they detract but little from the value of those compositions. There needs but a certain turn of thought or imagination to make us enter into all the opinions which then prevailed and relish the sentiments or conclusions derived from them. But a very violent effort is requisite to change our judgment of manners and excite sentiments of approbation or blame, love or hatred, different from those to which the mind from long custom has been familiarized. And where a man is confident of the rectitude of that moral standard by which he judges, he is justly jealous of it and will not pervert the sentiments of his heart for a moment in complaisance to any writer whatsoever.

Of all speculative errors, those which regard religion are the most excusable in compositions of genius; nor is it ever permitted to judge of the civility or wisdom of any people, or even of single persons, by the grossness or refinement of their theological principles. The same good sense that directs men in the ordinary occurrences of life is not hearkened to in religious matters, which are supposed to be placed altogether above the cognizance of human reason. On this account, all the absurdities of the pagan system of theology must be overlooked by every critic who would pretend to form a just notion of ancient poetry, and our posterity, in their turn, must have the same indulgence to their forefathers. No religious principles can ever be imputed as a fault to any poet while they remain merely principles and take not such strong possession of his heart as to lay him under the imputation of *bigotry* and *superstition*. Where that happens, they confound the sentiments of morality and alter the natural boundaries of vice and virtue. They are therefore eternal blemishes, according to the principle above mentioned; nor are the prejudices and false opinions of the age sufficient to justify them.

It is essential to the Roman Catholic religion to inspire a violent hatred of every other worship and to represent all pagans, Muhammadans, and heretics as the objects of divine wrath and vengeance. Such sentiments, though they are in reality very blamable, are considered as virtues by the zealots of that communion and are represented in their tragedies and epic poems as a kind of divine heroism. This bigotry has disfigured two very fine tragedies of the French theater, *Polieucte* and *Athalia,* where an intemperate zeal for particular modes of worship is set off with all the pomp imaginable and forms the predominant character of the heroes. "What is this?" says the sublime Joad to Josabet, finding her in discourse with Mathan the priest of Baal. "Does the daughter of David speak to this traitor? Are you not afraid lest the earth should open and pour forth flames to devour you both? Or lest these holy walls should fall and crush you together? What is his purpose? Why comes that enemy of God hither to poison the air which we breathe with his horrid presence?" Such sentiments are received with great applause in the theater of Paris, but at London the spectators would be full as much pleased to hear Achilles tell Agamemnon that he was a dog in his forehead and a deer in his heart or Jupiter threaten Juno with a sound drubbing if she will not be quiet.

Religious principles are also a blemish in any polite composition when they rise up to superstition and intrude themselves into every sentiment, however remote from any connection with religion. It is no excuse for the poet that the customs of his country had burdened life with so many religious ceremonies and observances that no part of it was exempt from that yoke. It must forever be ridiculous in Petrarch to compare his mistress Laura to Jesus Christ. Nor is it less ridiculous in that agreeable libertine, Boccaccio, very seriously to give thanks to God Almighty and the ladies for their assistance in defending him against his enemies.

SIGNETS and MENTORS of Essential Interest